BEARING SIN AS CHURCH COMMUNITY

T&T Clark New Studies in Bonhoeffer's Theology and Ethics

Series editors
Jennifer McBride
Michael Mawson
Philip G. Ziegler

BEARING SIN AS CHURCH COMMUNITY

Bonhoeffer's Hamartiology

Hyun Joo Kim

LONDON • NEW YORK • OXFORD • NEW DELHI • SYDNEY

T&T CLARK

Bloomsbury Publishing Plc

50 Bedford Square, London, WC1B 3DP, UK
1385 Broadway, New York, NY 10018, USA
29 Earlsfort Terrace, Dublin 2, Ireland

BLOOMSBURY, T&T CLARK and the T&T Clark logo are trademarks of Bloomsbury Publishing Plc

First published in Great Britain 2022
Paperback edition published 2024

Copyright © Hyun Joo Kim, 2022

Hyun Joo Kim has asserted her right under the Copyright, Designs and Patents Act, 1988, to be identified as Author of this work.

For legal purposes the Acknowledgments on pp. ix–x constitute an extension of this copyright page.

All rights reserved. No part of this publication may be reproduced or transmitted in any form or by any means, electronic or mechanical, including photocopying, recording, or any information storage or retrieval system, without prior permission in writing from the publishers.

Bloomsbury Publishing Plc does not have any control over, or responsibility for, any third-party websites referred to or in this book. All internet addresses given in this book were correct at the time of going to press. The author and publisher regret any inconvenience caused if addresses have changed or sites have ceased to exist, but can accept no responsibility for any such changes.

A catalogue record for this book is available from the British Library.

Library of Congress Cataloging-in-Publication Data
Names: Kim, Hyun Joo, 1978-author.
Title: Bearing sin as church community: Bonhoeffer's hamartiology / Hyun Joo Kim.
Description: London; New York: T&T Clark, 2022. |
Series: T&T Clark new studies in Bonhoeffer's theology and ethics |
Includes bibliographical references and index. | Identifiers: LCCN 2022004139 (print) |
LCCN 2022004140 (ebook) | ISBN 9780567706584 (hb) |
ISBN 9780567706621 (paperback) | ISBN 9780567706591 (epdf) | ISBN 9780567706614 (ebook)
Subjects: LCSH: Bonhoeffer, Dietrich, 1906-1945. | Augustine, of Hippo, Saint, 354-430. |
Sin, Original–History of doctrines. | Sin–Christianity–History of doctrines.
Classification: LCC BX4827.B57 K55 2022 (print) |
LCC BX4827.B57 (ebook) | DDC 233/.14–dc23/eng/20220512
LC record available at https://lccn.loc.gov/2022004139
LC ebook record available at https://lccn.loc.gov/2022004140

ISBN: HB: 978-0-5677-0658-4
PB: 978-0-5677-0662-1
ePDF: 978-0-5677-0659-1
eBook: 978-0-5677-0661-4

Series: T&T Clark New Studies in Bonhoeffer's Theology and Ethics

Typeset by Integra Software Services Pvt. Ltd.

To find out more about our authors and books visit www.bloomsbury.com and sign up for our newsletters.

for my husband
Young Sung Min

CONTENTS

Acknowledgments	ix
List of Abbreviations	xi
Introduction	1
Thesis of the Book	2
Chapter Summaries	3
Contribution to Knowledge	8
Limitations and Challenges	11

Chapter 1
AUGUSTINE OF HIPPO'S DOCTRINE OF ORIGINAL SIN	13
Introduction	13
Early Hamartiology: The Premise of the Doctrine of Original Sin	14
Later Hamartiology: The Doctrine of Original Sin	25
Conclusion	30

Chapter 2
MARTIN LUTHER'S CHRISTOCENTRIC HAMARTIOLOGY	33
Introduction	33
Early Anthropological Turn	34
The Trajectory of Sin	40
The Bound Will and Freedom in Christ	43
Conclusion	50

Chapter 3
DIETRICH BONHOEFFER'S ECCLESIOCENTRIC HAMARTIOLOGY IN *SANCTORUM COMMUNIO*	53
Introduction	53
Bonhoeffer's Assessment of the Doctrine of Original Sin	54
Christian Personalism	58
The Primal State of Humanity	64
The Dual Structure of Sin	67
Reformulation of the Doctrine of Original Sin	71
Conclusion	75

Chapter 4
BONHOEFFER'S EXEGESIS OF THE CREATION AND THE FALL   77
   Introduction   77
   Theological Turning Point   78
   The Beginning   86
   The Creation   95
   The Fall   100
   Conclusion   110

Chapter 5
BONHOEFFER'S LATER HAMARTIOLOGY AND ETHICS   115
   Introduction   115
   The Twofold Structure of Sin   116
   God's Humanization in Christ   122
   Christian Freedom   127
   Stellvertretung   131
   Conclusion   140

Chapter 6
CONCLUSION: BONHOEFFER'S HAMARTIOLOGICAL LEGACY   143
   Introduction   143
   Communal Sin   145
   The Twofold Structure of Sin: Pride and Submission   147
   Sin and Responsibility: *Stellvertretung*   150
   Conclusion   151
   Areas for Further Study and Implications   153

Notes   154
Bibliography   197
Index   206

ACKNOWLEDGMENTS

This monograph is a revised version of my doctoral dissertation on Dietrich Bonhoeffer's hamartiology (University of Aberdeen, Scotland, 2020). I would like to give my thanks to faculty members in the divinity department of the University of Aberdeen. First of all is my doctoral advisor, Tom Greggs, who has been my primary dialogue partner and mentor from the beginning to the end of my PhD. I am also thankful to the other faculty members of divinity: Paul T. Nimmo, Philip G. Ziegler, Brian Brock, Michael Mawson, Donald Wood, and Katherine Hockey whose theological perspectives have helped me to consider a wider theological spectrum. I also give special thanks to Philip G. Ziegler and Rachel Muers (University of Leeds), who read thoroughly my thesis and gave me invaluable comments.

During the course of my PhD, I received support in July 2018 from the German-American Dietrich Bonhoeffer Network sponsored by the German federal government. This allowed me not only to discuss the theology of Bonhoeffer with Clifford J. Green, Christiane Tietz, and Michael P. DeJonge and with German and American members of the network but also to look for original manuscripts of Bonhoeffer as well as to visit places related to Bonhoeffer in Berlin, including Bonhoeffer's house. The network's seminars expanded my knowledge and perspective on Bonhoeffer's theology, and the experience of visiting places associated with Bonhoeffer helped me get closer to his life and person. I am thankful to the members of the network, especially for our passionate discussions and debates during and after the seminars. I give thanks to Derek W. Taylor, Florian Hoehne, Matthew Ryan Robinson, Jonathan Frommann-Breckner, Joshua Mauldin, Christopher King, Brandin Francabandera, and Kevin O'Farrell.

Before undertaking my doctoral dissertation, I studied at Princeton Theological Seminary. I am indebted to Ellen T. Charry, who gave me the opportunity to read Augustine's foundational works with her independently; Nancy J. Duff, who taught me how to read and write a theological piece, especially on Bonhoeffer's works; Bruce L. McCormack, whose theological insight led me to study systematic theology; and Elsie A. McKee, whose Reformation seminar enriched my knowledge of the theologies of Luther and Calvin.

My gratitude also extends to the faculty of Torch Trinity Graduate University in Seoul, Korea. I appreciate Jung-Sook Lee's continuous theological and pastoral support; Michael J. Choi, who encouraged me to continue my study in theology; and Hyung Jin Park, whose generosity supports me always. I also give special thanks to JinHyok Kim, who has given me much valuable advice and support. I am indebted to Ji-Ae Kim and Sun-A Hong for their loving kindness and sincere prayers.

Seminars and discussions with postgraduate students at the University of Aberdeen clarified my ideas; these students include Kevin O'Farrell, Nam Vo, Jin Kim, Emily Hill, Kait Dugan, and Angelica Bocchetti. I also appreciate Kathryn McKay, whose copyediting helped me to finish my book.

I give thanks to the members of the Korean church community in Aberdeen, including Jiseung Choi, Sungbin Lim, Pungryong Kim, Juheon Kim, Su Young Lee, and Kyongmo Kim, Soon Young Kwon, and especially the Juan Cruz family. I remain indebted to church members of the Church of the Lord in Korea and also of the Chodae Community Church in New Jersey for their prayers and to Jang-Ki Lim of Alliance Theological Seminary in Nyack, New York, for his continuing fellowship with me.

This book would not have been possible without the support and sacrifice of my family. I appreciate the prayers of my parents, Hee Young and Jong Hee Kim, and my brother, Han Joo Kim. I give special gratitude to my sister, Hyun Ae Kim, who has supported my parents and my own family for a long time with her generosity and sincerity. I am also thankful for the constant encouragement of the Min family, especially my sisters- and brothers-in-law. My daughter, Sewon Lillian Min, has frequently read my papers from the beginning of my study of theology, and I am thankful that my son, Sung Woo Min, grew up well during my years of study. Finally, my husband, Young Sung Min, has supported me enormously, covering my long and frequent absences with his sincere and loving kindness. Without his sacrifice and love, this book could not have been completed. I give thanks to the Lord who gave him to me as a blessing.

Finally, I would like to express special thanks to Jennifer M. McBride, Philip G. Ziegler, Michael Mawson, and the other editorial members of T&T Clark for their patience, suggestions, and encouragement.

ABBREVIATIONS

Bonhoeffer's Works

This book draws extensively on the critical edition of the *Dietrich Bonhoeffer Werke*, 16 Bände und Registerbund, ed. Eberhard Bethge et al. (Gütersloh: Chr. Kaiser Verlag/Gütersloher Verlagshaus, 1986–99) (hereafter *DBW*), and its English translation, *Dietrich Bonhoeffer Works*, 17 vols., ed. Wayne Whitson Floyd Jr. et al. (Minneapolis: Fortress Press, 1996–2014) (hereafter *DBWE*). Bibliographic details of the volumes of *DBW* and *DBWE* and other works by Bonhoeffer cited in this book are as follows:

DBW 1	*Sanctorum Communio: Eine dogmatische Untersuchung zur Soziologie der Kirche*, ed. Joachim von Soosten.
DBW 2	*Akt und Sein: Transzendentalphilosophie und Ontologie in der systematischen Theologie*, ed. Hans-Richard Reuter.
DBW 3	*Schöpfung und Fall: Theologische Auslegung von Genesis 1–3*, ed. Martin Rüter and Ilse Tödt.
DBWE 1	*Sanctorum Communio: A Theological Study of the Sociology of the Church*, ed. Clifford J. Green, trans. Reinhard Krauss and Nancy Lukens.
DBWE 2	*Act and Being: Transcendental Philosophy and Ontology in Systematic Theology*, ed. Wayne Whitson Floyd, Jr., trans. H. Martin Rumscheidt.
DBWE 3	*Creation and Fall: A Theological Exposition of Genesis 1–3*, ed. John W. de Gruchy, trans. Douglas Stephen Bax.
DBWE 4	*Discipleship*, ed. Geffrey B. Kelly and John D. Godsey, trans. Barbara Green and Reinhard Krauss.
DBWE 6	*Ethics*, ed. Clifford J. Green, trans. Reinhard Krauss, Charles C. West, and Douglas W. Stott.
DBWE 8	*Letters and Papers from Prison*, ed. John W. de Gruchy, trans. Isabel Best, Lisa E. Dahill, Reinhard Krauss, Nancy Lukens, Barbara and Martin Rumscheidt, and Douglas W. Stott.
DBWE 10	*Barcelona, Berlin, New York: 1928–1931*, ed. Clifford J. Green, trans. Douglas W. Stott.
DBWE 11	*Ecumenical, Academic, and Pastoral Work: 1931–1932*, ed. Victoria J. Barnett, Mark S. Brocker, and Michael B. Lukens, trans. Anne Schmidt-Lange, Isabel Best, Nicolas Humphrey, Marion Pauck, and Douglas W. Stott.
DBWE 12	*Berlin: 1932–1933*, ed. Larry L. Rasmussen, trans. Isabel Best, David Higgins, and Douglas W. Stott.

DBWE 14	*Theological Education at Finkenwalde: 1935–1937*, ed. H. Gaylon Barker and Mark S. Brocker, trans. Douglas W. Stott.
DBWE 15	*Theological Education Underground: 1937–1940*, ed. Victoria J. Barnett, trans. Victoria J. Barnett, Claudia D. Bergmann, Peter Frick, Scott A. Moore, and Douglas W. Stott.
DBWE 16	*Conspiracy and Imprisonment: 1940–1945*, ed. Mark S. Brocker, trans. Lisa E. Dahill and Douglas W. Stott.
n. 1, etc.	In a footnote, this refers to a note by Bonhoeffer himself note in *DBW* or *DBWE*.
n. [1], etc.	In a footnote, this refers to an editor's note in *DBW* or *DBWE*.
SC-A	This refers to material in the original version of Bonhoeffer's 1927 dissertation that Bonhoeffer removed before the dissertation's publication in 1930. This material was not included in German or English editions of *Sanctorum Communio* until the 1986 edition of *DBW* 1 (where it is included in the endnotes) and the 1988 edition of *DBWE* 1 (where it is included in the footnotes).

Other Works

All biblical quotations are taken from the New Revised Standard Version. All Greek quotations are taken from the BibleWorks combined Nestle-Aland Greek New Testament/Septuagint (BGT).

ANF	Ante-Nicene Fathers
CChr	Corpus Christianorum
CH	Church History
FemTh	Feminist Theology
JRE	Journal of Religious Ethics
JTS	Journal of Theological Studies
LCC	Library of Christian Classics
LQ	Lutheran Quarterly
LW	Martin Luther, *Luther's Works*, 55 vols., ed. and trans. Jaroslav Pelikan and Helmut Lehman et al. (Minneapolis: Fortress Press, 1900–86).
NPNF	Nicene and Post-Nicene Fathers
NRSV	New Revised Standard Version
SJT	Scottish Journal of Theology
TS	Theological Studies
TTod	Theology Today

INTRODUCTION

Bonhoeffer is well known as a heroic Christian who challenged the power of Nazism. This means that not only Christians but also people outside Christianity recognize Bonhoeffer as a symbol against sin or communal sin. Despite Bonhoeffer's influence on the world inside and outside of Christianity, which is primarily due to his resistance against sinful acts by communities or individuals in power, his keen analyses and insights on the problem of sin are not well known. Bonhoeffer's observations on the sinful acts of humans and his solution through the power of Christian community have not been fully presented to the world. Importantly, his treatment of sin is not isolated within the doctrine of sin itself but is closely related to his understanding of the church community and its vicarious representative action in Christ. In our contemporary world, regardless of place, race, gender, or class, Bonhoeffer's insights on sin, especially communal sin, provide a guide for Christian attitudes and for a life of loving God and our neighbors and those who seek to live in justice and love as he did.

Although Dietrich Bonhoeffer (1906–45) was a modern theologian whose theology has attracted much attention during the past several decades, he has primarily been known as a symbol of resistance against the sins of humanity and the evil of the world, especially against Nazism. Many scholars of Bonhoeffer and contemporary people consider Bonhoeffer's theology relevant today, not only because Bonhoeffer's theological insights were formed during his struggles against the radical evilness and blind participation of people in concrete social and political circumstances, but also because his insights were based on a solid theological foundation. The theme of sin and evil is everywhere in Bonhoeffer's writings, from the beginning to the end of his theological career. The central hamartiological concern of Bonhoeffer's doctoral dissertation, *Sanctorum Communio*, is closely associated with the Augustinian doctrine of original sin; his first biblical exegesis, *Creation and Fall*, is about the account of the creation and the fall; and his conclusion or reformulation of the Augustinian hamartiology of the West is clearly articulated in his later writings such as *Ethics* and "After Ten Years." Bonhoeffer developed his hamartiology against the backdrop not only of resistance to the Nazi state but also of post-Christendom, in which the power of the secular state as well as the voice of autonomous individualism had been augmented.[1] The modern era was a time in which Western Christianity responded in various ways to the challenges of "the intellectual and social revolutions of the seventeenth and eighteenth centuries."[2] Bonhoeffer's theological reaction to the challenges of the secular world is clearly reflected in his doctrinal descriptions, especially in his hamartiological thought. He constructively fills a theological lacuna in classical Augustinian hamartiology, which failed to demonstrate comprehensively the nature of evil and sin as well as Christian responsibility toward the world. To do this, Bonhoeffer drew upon his Lutheran as well as modern resources. However, it is surprising that Bonhoeffer's hamartiology has not been thoroughly examined previously, especially in relation to the Western hamartiological tradition, despite its significant place in his theology. It is time to retrieve the theme of evil and sin through the perspective of Bonhoeffer and situate it in the historical trajectory of Western hamartiology.

Thesis of the Book

This book offers a holistic investigation of Dietrich Bonhoeffer's hamartiology by engaging with the hamartiological doctrines of Augustine of Hippo as well as those of Martin Luther. It argues that Bonhoeffer's hamartiology transforms and reconstructs Augustinian hamartiology, represented as the doctrine of original sin, by shifting the starting point from the doctrine of God to the doctrine of the church and approaching the concept of humanity from a more Lutheran appropriation of Augustinianism.[3] As a post-Enlightenment or a post-Kantian theologian, Bonhoeffer's hamartiological revision reflects his modern as well as Lutheran perspective that is concerned not only with the relation between God's transcendence and God's immanence but also with the compatibility of God's providence with the terrible reality of evil in the world. This book contends that although Augustine's doctrine of original sin offers a philosophical framework in which the universality of sin and the solidarity of the human race are proposed to counter the heretical teachings of his time, it creates an opening for a certain pessimism in Western Christianity in which the reconciling work of God in Christ toward humanity as well as the responsibility of the Christian person is obscured.[4]

By contrast, Bonhoeffer's hamartiology pays attention to this neglected side of Augustinian hamartiology and corrects it by drawing on Lutheran theological tools. Bonhoeffer uses two major theological axes of his hamartiology in his attempt to fill a gap in Augustine's doctrine of original sin: *Christocentrism* and *communitarian personalism*.[5] These two concepts appear to be merged in Bonhoeffer's ecclesiocentric hamartiology. Bonhoeffer clearly perceives that the doctrine of the church is the appropriate theological locus to begin reconstructing the traditional hamartiology.[6] This is because, as Bonhoeffer sees it, the church community is the place where these two theological axes interconnect and, furthermore, is also where the less emphasized teachings of the Augustinian doctrine of original sin such as human responsibility and Christian freedom can be more fully discovered in accordance with the testimonies of Scripture. More specifically, Bonhoeffer's relocation of the hamartiological locus from the classical doctrine of God to the Christocentric doctrine of the church signifies that he intensifies Luther's existential and relational approach to engage the account of God's being in eternity with the account of God's presence and reconciling action in Christ in temporality.

In this way, a prototypal Augustinian definition of evil as "non-being" or "privation of good" can be properly connected to the existential realities of evil in temporality. In other words, for Bonhoeffer, Christ's calling of the *sanctorum communio* (community of saints) to love the other, both divine and human, has to be fulfilled through the experiential or visible church in which God in Christ not only exists as the community but also reconciles the sin of humanity through the *Stellvertretung* (vicarious representative action) of the Christian person. As a result, this book argues that Bonhoeffer "horizontalizes" or "secularizes" the Augustinian otherworldly concept of *civitate Dei* (the city of God), primarily in the experiential church community in this world in which God in Christ exists as community. By means of this relocation of the heavenly city of God in the *sanctorum communio* to the temporal world, Bonhoeffer opens a way to correct the discrepancy or fill the gap between theory and reality embedded in Augustinian hamartiology in order to deal with issues of his time.

Clearly, despite Bonhoeffer's disassociation from some aspects of Augustine's doctrine of original sin, Bonhoeffer's hamartiology is nevertheless a reformulation of Augustine's doctrine of original sin rather than a refutation of it. This is because Bonhoeffer's hamartiology confirms the foundational hamartiological teachings of the West, such as the universality of sin and the solidarity of the human race, and develops the Augustinian doctrine by emphasizing Christian responsibility and ethics. In the process, Bonhoeffer critically embraces some of the chief but controversial characteristics of Augustinian hamartiology, such as involuntary alien guilt or culpability, the biological transmission of original sin, and limited human freedom and responsibility, converting these concepts in a voluntary and ethical way using his Lutheran resources. Accordingly, Bonhoeffer's doctrine of sin is a modern response to the theological and sociopolitical challenges of the time, one that reforms the traditional hamartiology of the West to make it more legitimate and reasonable to people in the modern era, especially in his German context. Scripture suggests not only human powerlessness but also Christian responsibility with respect to sin and evil.[7] Bonhoeffer argues that Augustinian hamartiology does not closely engage the former with the latter. To correct this theological deficiency, Bonhoeffer addresses the two inseparable aspects of human powerlessness and Christian responsibility within the boundary of Western hamartiology.

Chapter Summaries

This book is composed of six chapters, one on Augustine, one on Luther, and four on Bonhoeffer. Chapter 1, "Augustine of Hippo's Doctrine of Original Sin," outlines Augustine's doctrine of original sin that supplies the resources for the Lutheran hamartiology that is one of the major strands of the Augustinian tradition. It concludes that Augustine's doctrine of original sin is a synthesis of his early hamartiology derived from his Christianized Neoplatonic cosmology and his own interpretation of Paul's writings. The chapter investigates Augustine's early philosophically defined notion of God, which was the prerequisite for Augustine's later doctrine of original sin. It analyzes how Augustine's notion of God along with his Christianized hierarchical Platonic cosmology became the ultimate rule that governed his doctrine of original sin. In the process, it describes Augustine's early focus on fallen humanity's *inward turn of the self* or the *homo incurvatus in se* (man turned in upon himself) as the central Augustinian account of hamartiology that has continued in the West, especially in the Lutheran tradition. The chapter then relates the theological premise in the classical doctrine of God to Augustine's later doctrine of original sin, which is complicated by his earlier philosophically derived notion of sin and evil and his own interpretation of Pauline hamartiology. In so doing, the chapter assesses some foundational confirmations and insights of the doctrine of original sin and further discusses theological questions raised by both contemporaries of Augustine and later critics. The chapter demonstrates that the major issues discussed in the time of Augustine and even in the pre-Augustinian era reappeared in later times in slightly different forms and engaged with issues of concern to Luther and Bonhoeffer. This chapter is the basis for the themes of the chapters that follow. The purpose of this chapter is not simply to repeat or summarize the thought of Augustine but to engage closely with the themes of the rest of the chapters by assessing Augustine's doctrine of original sin and raising critical questions related to the doctrines of Luther as well as of Bonhoeffer, identifying contexts beyond the Lutheran or the Western tradition.

Chapter 2, "Martin Luther's Christocentric Hamartiology," investigates Luther's reformulation of the Augustinian hamartiology. This chapter is critical for the book because Luther's thinking was the most important theological lens through which Bonhoeffer read and then reformulated Augustinian hamartiology. Although Bonhoeffer was strongly influenced by his contemporary Lutheran teachers, he continuously claimed that Luther was the primary reference of his theological considerations. Luther's interpretation of Augustine is pivotal for Bonhoeffer's hamartiology because Luther laid the cornerstone for Bonhoeffer's theology, especially his Christocentrism and existentialism. The chapter contends that Luther's hamartiology is a reinterpretation of Augustine's doctrine of original sin by shifting the starting point from Augustine's Platonically defined notion of God to Luther's relational concept of God in Christ. Luther's Christocentric hamartiology is based on his holistic and relational anthropology, which becomes the presupposition of his doctrine of sin and evil. Luther clearly disassociated from Augustine's hamartiological foundation in classical theism, which was mainly derived from his Christianized Platonic cosmology. Instead, the Christocentric standpoint was the theological premise of Luther's hamartiology. Needless to say, this became the springboard for Bonhoeffer's existential and relational hamartiology. The chapter demonstrates that Luther's new anthropological concepts, such as *totus homo* (the whole person) and the relational *imago Dei* (image of God), became the theological foundation of his doctrine of sin. The later part of the chapter sketches Luther's hamartiological trajectory and examines his appropriation as well as refutation of the Augustinian tradition. On the one hand, as some critics of the Augustinian notion of sin as pride or egocentricity argue, Luther explicitly follows the Western tradition of focusing on this inwardness or, in Luther's phrase, *cor curvum in se* (the heart curved in upon itself). On the other hand, Luther detaches from the philosophically oriented notion of sin and instead focuses on existential and relational sin and the sinfulness of the human as it relates to his relational *imago Dei*. Although Luther seems to follow Augustine's hamartiological framework and content, it is significant that Luther replaces Augustine's theological orientation on the heavenly city of God with the kingdom of God in Christ on the earth.

Chapter 3, "Dietrich Bonhoeffer's Ecclesiocentric Hamartiology in *Sanctorum Communio*," investigates Bonhoeffer's early and foundational hamartiology in his *Sanctorum Communio*. This chapter argues that Bonhoeffer's ecclesiocentric hamartiology critically expands and develops the Augustinian doctrine of original sin by shifting the starting point from the doctrine of God to the doctrine of the church and approaching the concept of humanity from a socio-ethical perspective based on Bonhoeffer's Lutheran tradition. This chapter is central to the book because Bonhoeffer laid the foundation of his hamartiology in his first doctoral dissertation, which was titled *Sanctorum Communio: Eine dogmatische Untersuchung*.[8] Despite Bonhoeffer's inheriting Luther's Christocentrism as the basis of his theology, Bonhoeffer also claims that he appropriated Augustine's ecclesiastical notion that "the Church is joined [to that flesh], and so there is made the whole Christ, Head and body" for his communitarian or communal concept of the church: *die Kirche ist Christus als Gemeinde existierend* ("the church is Christ existing as community").[9] The most important aspect of Bonhoeffer's hamartiology in *Sanctorum Communio* is his reformulation of Augustine's doctrinal loci for his development of hamartiology. In other words, Bonhoeffer does not take Augustine's hamartiological basis in classical theism or the doctrine of God as his hamartiological premise but instead takes Augustine's ecclesiology as the starting point of his doctrine of sin and evil based on Luther's Christocentrism. This methodological turn signifies that Bonhoeffer did not simply repeat the Augustinian tradition but reformulated it. The significance of this revision is related to Bonhoeffer's sociologically derived methodology by which he points out the importance of the communitarian sense of the postlapsarian sinful human nature and the symbiotic relationality between individual and communal persons. Clearly, Bonhoeffer's concept of the church as a collective person is not simply a development of the Augustinian doctrine of original sin, in which the communal concept of sinful solidarity is primitively established, but is also the recovery of the communal aspect of human unity in *sanctorum communio* simultaneously as *peccatorum communio* (community of sinners), which is less emphasized in Luther's theology. In this way, differing from Augustine's transcendental concept of *civitate Dei*, Bonhoeffer suggests that the experiential church community in this world is the place of reconciliation as well as the ultimate destination in which genuine humanity can be discovered in the person and work of Christ.

This is Bonhoeffer's significant hamartiological turn from Augustine's prototypal searching for true humanity in the prelapsarian self or in the heavenly city of God to the ultimate reality revealed in the church community in which Christ not only exists but also bears the sins of the saints. Accordingly, this chapter functions not only as a foundation for the subsequent chapters on Bonhoeffer but also as the central chapter of the entire book.

Chapter 4, "Bonhoeffer's Exegesis of the Creation and the Fall," further investigates Bonhoeffer's intermediate hamartiology found in *Act and Being* and *Creation and Fall*. First, this chapter demonstrates that Bonhoeffer's habilitation thesis (*Act and Being*) supplies the philosophical foundation for the hamartiology of *Creation and Fall* based on the hamartiological theme of Chapter 3. The chapter then discusses how Bonhoeffer integrates the Augustinian doctrine of original sin into his earlier ethical and relational hamartiology through the perspective of Luther's Christocentrism along with his own Christian communitarian personalism. Bonhoeffer's communal interpretation expands the scope of the creation and the fall so that he includes both Adam and Eve as the first community of God as well as the subjects of the fall. Bonhoeffer follows Western hamartiology by his upholding of the sinful solidarity of the human being and of atomistic egocentrism as *cor curvum in se*, which he draws from Augustine's hamartiology. In *Creation and Fall* Bonhoeffer reveals both his residual Augustinian understandings and his modern reaction to the post-Enlightenment era. He reveals his modern reception of the creation account by not viewing scientific knowledge as opposed to the account of Scripture because he conceives of Scripture as a theological description that contains truth beyond the knowledge of humans. Similar to Augustine as well as Luther, Bonhoeffer's renewed attention to Scripture becomes an impetus for his new hamartiological perspective. This is clearly different from his somewhat negative assessment of the Augustinian doctrine of original sin in *Sanctorum Communio*. It is noteworthy that Bonhoeffer integrates Augustine's corporeal aspect of human solidarity, which he criticized in *Sanctorum Communio*, into his earlier ethical view. This occurs because, through his exegesis of the creation account, Bonhoeffer recognizes the importance of human corporeality, which he interprets as the *Grenze* (limit) between I and the other, given as a blessing, in addition to his ethical or spiritual sense of the human being. This holistic perspective on the fall and on the human being leads him to investigate the relation between the fall and human sexuality. At this point, Bonhoeffer's doctrine of sin is more closely associated with Augustine's doctrine of original sin or *concupiscentia* (concupiscence) in which Augustine opens a way to interpret original sin in both the physical and spiritual senses. Despite Bonhoeffer's more holistic interpretation of the human being than his earlier view, his ethical focus remains central to his hamartiology. Clearly, Bonhoeffer's theological concern with the ethical sense of alien culpability is continued in *Creation and Fall* and developed in his later works. Even though Bonhoeffer's *Creation and Fall* is a complicated work in his hamartiology in regard to its relation to the Augustinian tradition, a more important aspect of his hamartiology is established in his continued emphasis on the responsibility of the Christian person. *Creation and Fall* is another turning point for Bonhoeffer in that his hamartiology, which had been discussed within the boundary of the church community in *Sanctorum Communio*, begins to connect to the world outside of the church community in its symbiotic as well as vulnerable relationality with the world, where the power of social and radical evil is more active.

Chapter 5, "Bonhoeffer's Later Hamartiology and Ethics," presents Bonhoeffer's later hamartiology and ethics in which his concern with the sin and evil of the saints as well as of the world is more closely investigated. Although Bonhoeffer's later works are fragmentary and unfinished due to his early death, his later thought clearly shows his thought in regard to sin and evil as well as Christian responsibility. Evidently, his political context accelerated the evolution of his hamartiology. The extreme circumstances under National Socialism compelled him to identify the passive dimension of sin of the postlapsarian self, which had been shadowed by the Augustinian emphasis on the active dimension of sin as pride or egocentricity, as the other side (or the equally important sin) of the self. Despite Augustine's mentioning this passive side of sin in his later doctrine, it is Bonhoeffer who emphasizes the passive side of sin as submission to evil or self-deception and treats this passive sin as equally sinful to the active dimension of sin. Although Bonhoeffer may not have fully recognized that this twofold nature of sin of humanity needed to be connected to the experiences of all human beings regardless of their gender, class, or race, his awareness of or emphasis on this passive dimension of sin in his later thought has theological significance.

Bonhoeffer's recognition of the passive dimension of sin suggests a future way in which the Christian hamartiology of the West can be corrected by embracing the critiques of thinkers such as feminist and liberation theologians. Furthermore, his later ethics expresses his theological characteristics that are explicitly disassociated from the thinking of Augustine as well as of the mature Luther. The major reason for this distinctiveness is related to Bonhoeffer's relational and corporeal interpretation of God's humanization in Christ. He takes the humanization of God in Christ as the ultimate basis of his ethics. His ethical foundation rooted in the person and life of Christ was intensified by his theological lens of the *Stellvertretung*, "vicarious representative action," of the Christian person, as both an individual and a communal person. Moreover, the doctrine of *Stellvertretung* became the apex of Bonhoeffer's hamartiological resolution in his ethics. This radical resolution of Bonhoeffer's ethics demonstrates his modern concerns with God's nature and God's relationality to the world. The doctrine of *Stellvertretung* is closely interconnected with the boundaries of freedom and the ethical responsibility of the saint and the church as well as the problem of alien culpability. On one level, Bonhoeffer's conclusions concerning the issues of freedom and responsibility surpass the Augustinian tradition, including Luther's mature thought. On another level, however, Bonhoeffer builds on the Augustinian legacy not only by confirming the doctrines of the universality of sin and the solidarity of the human race but also by transforming the biological transmission of alien culpability into voluntary and participatory concepts.

Chapter 6, "Conclusion: Bonhoeffer's Hamartiological Legacy," presents the conclusion of the book. The chapter suggests major hamartiological contributions and clarifies the insufficient aspects of Bonhoeffer's doctrine of sin and ethics. Bonhoeffer's hamartiology contains a significant theological legacy that can be applied to the social concerns of contemporary communities concerning the issues of sin and evil and the responsibility of the Christian community. The chapter identifies Bonhoeffer's major hamartiological contributions as his emphases on communal sin, the twofold structure of sin, and close engagement between the doctrine of sin and Christian ethics. Despite these contributions, Bonhoeffer's doctrine of sin and his ethics have some theological inconsistency throughout his corpus. The chapter argues that the imbalance between Bonhoeffer's hamartiological structure and the application to real life is mainly due to his theological premise of Augustinian androcentrism. In the process, the chapter deals with the theological issues raised by feminist and liberation theologians to evaluate the theological insufficiencies and potentials embedded in Bonhoeffer's hamartiology. The chapter concludes with some implications of Bonhoeffer's hamartiology.

Bonhoeffer's reinterpretation of the classical Augustinian hamartiology was grounded in his theological premises such as his Christocentric notion of God and God's voluntary relationality to humanity. In his later ethics, Bonhoeffer reaches quite different ethical conclusions from the Augustinian tradition, as seen in the case of the doctrine of *Stellvertretung*. As Bonhoeffer claims, Luther is his primary dialogue partner, but the book argues that it is the young Luther rather than the mature Luther whom Bonhoeffer follows in his ethics. Furthermore, Bonhoeffer's reading of Luther was tremendously influenced by the perspectives of his Lutheran teachers such as Karl Holl, who appropriated Luther's early theology and ethics as genuine teachings of Luther because Luther's early thinking contained more revolutionary ideas than his mature period since it reflected Luther's ideas and life against the perceived power of the Roman Catholic Church. In Bonhoeffer's case, it is the evil power of the state against which *sanctorum communio* has to exercise self-sacrifice or self-giving for the sake of the neighbor or the other.

Contribution to Knowledge

This book contributes to knowledge in three different categorical levels of theological scholarship. The first and primary purpose of the book is to *contribute to the scholarship on Bonhoeffer*. Notwithstanding the depth of Bonhoeffer's theology on evil and sin, his hamartiology has not received much attention by scholars because it has been shadowed by research on his other theological *foci*, such as on ethics, sociology, and (more recently) ecclesiology. He was an extraordinary theologian who has been known first for his life, especially his Christian resistance to National Socialism of Germany, and then for his theological works. Looking back on the studies on Bonhoeffer, it is not surprising that most of the themes of these scholarly studies are inevitably related to the theme of sin and evil. However, it is surprising that Bonhoeffer's hamartiology, one of the central themes of his theology, has not been treated as a central subject in the scholarship on Bonhoeffer, especially in the English-speaking world.

Some scholars of Bonhoeffer may think that hamartiology is not the main concern of Bonhoeffer, as is the case for Eva Harasta, who comments that "a closer look at Bonhoeffer's writings reveals some reluctance on his part to discuss 'sin' and 'evil' as themes of their own."[10] However, the most crucial reason for the lack of scholarship on this topic is explicitly related to Bonhoeffer's editing of a portion of the original manuscript of his first dissertation, *Sanctorum Communio: Eine dogmatische Untersuchung*, for the publication of *Sanctorum Communio: Eine dogmatische Untersuchung zur Soziologie der Kirche* in 1930.[11] This is significant because in the portion of the original manuscript that was not included in the published version, Bonhoeffer gives detailed descriptions of his hamartiological outline in relation to Augustine's doctrine of original sin along with his transformative reformulation of the doctrine of original sin based on his Lutheran tradition. The book argues that this is why scholars did not notice the importance of Bonhoeffer's hamartiological concerns for a long time. It was not until 1986 that all of the redacted portions of the original manuscript were included in the German edition of *Sanctorum Communio* in the endnotes of *DBW* 1. Then, in 1998, the redacted sections were included in the English edition in the footnotes of *DBWE* 1.[12] However, when one carefully analyzes Bonhoeffer's entire body of work, from the first original full version of *Sanctorum Communio* to his prison writings, one can clearly see that his hamartiology is the foundation of his entire theology. Yet, the full landscape of Bonhoeffer's hamartiology has been hidden or undiscovered by scholars for the above reason. It is time to offer a full trajectory of Bonhoeffer's thinking on hamartiology, especially to the English-speaking world.

Admittedly, three major German works discuss the hamartiology of Bonhoeffer. In *Der verzweifelte Zugriff auf das Leben: Dietrich Bonhoeffers Sündenverständnis in "Schöpfung und Fall"* [Desperate access to life: Bonhoeffer's understanding of sin in *Creation and Fall*], Gottfried Class primarily discusses Bonhoeffer's early and intermediate writings, focusing especially on *Creation and Fall*.[13] Then, Gunter M. Prüller-Jagenteufel published *Befreit zur Verantwortung: Sünde und Versöhnung in der Ethik Dietrich Bonhoeffers* [Released to responsibility: sin and reconciliation in the ethics of Dietrich Bonhoeffer].[14] Recently, Kirsten Busch Nielsen published *Die Gebrochene Macht Der Sünde: Der Beitrag Dietrich Bonhoeffers Zur Hamartiologie* [The broken power of sin: Dietrich Bonhoeffer's contribution to hamartiology].[15] Nielsen discusses sin through the lens of broken power, covering the full range of Bonhoeffer's works. Nielsen's work is probably the only full discussion of Bonhoeffer's hamartiology in German. However, Nielson's focus differs from this book's approach to Bonhoeffer's hamartiology, which engages with the doctrines of Augustine and Luther. It is clear that the *foci* and theological approaches of these German works are quite different from the scope and focus of this book, which investigates how Bonhoeffer appropriated and reformulated his own Lutheran tradition on sin as well as the Augustinian hamartiological tradition.

In the English-speaking world, no extant scholarly work has fully engaged with Bonhoeffer's hamartiology in a full-length study. There are a few articles, such as Tom Greggs's "Bearing Sin in the Church: The Ecclesial Hamartiology of Bonhoeffer," which succinctly sketches the contours of Bonhoeffer's doctrine of sin in relation to Bonhoeffer's ecclesiology and supplies the archetypal framework for this book, and Eva Harasta's "Adam in Christ? The Place of Sin in Christ-Reality," which briefly deals with Bonhoeffer's hamartiology, mainly through *Ethics* but also in a fragmented or indirect way in many monographs as well as in some articles.[16] Although Bonhoeffer explicitly stated that his hamartiological concern or basis was rooted in the Augustinian tradition in *Sanctorum Communio* and in his subsequent works, no work in either German or English deals with Bonhoeffer's hamartiology in relation to the Augustinian tradition and covers major works of Bonhoeffer.[17] It is clear that, at this point, a deeper and more thorough study of Bonhoeffer's hamartiology that engages with the Augustinian tradition is *obligatoire* for Bonhoeffer scholarship and could enrich the theological investigations of adjacent doctrinal loci and encourage scholarship on other topics related to Bonhoeffer as well.

Second, this book contributes to *the scholarship of historical theology* by offering a deeper level of discussion of Bonhoeffer's hamartiology in light of the Western hamartiological tradition. The most significant reason for the lack of studies of Bonhoeffer's hamartiology is closely related to Bonhoeffer's treatment of the doctrine of sin within the Augustinian tradition of the West. As Bonhoeffer articulates in the original manuscript of his first dissertation, *Sanctorum Communio*, his hamartiology was developed on the basis of his Lutheran tradition, which was deeply rooted in the Augustinian tradition, namely, the doctrine of original sin. Thus, Bonhoeffer appropriated and transformed the chief characteristics of the doctrine of original sin. The complicated nature of Bonhoeffer's hamartiology may have prevented scholars from investigating the theme of sin and evil at a deeper level because the study of Bonhoeffer's hamartiology essentially requires a deep knowledge of Augustinian theology as well as that of Martin Luther. Without engaging the hamartiologies of these two figures, a study of Bonhoeffer's hamartiology would only scratch the surface of his thought, which eventually encompassed or surpassed the Lutheran as well as Augustinian traditions. The book, therefore, contributes to the scholarship of historical theology by placing and assessing Bonhoeffer's hamartiology in the lineage of the Augustinian tradition.

Third, the contribution of this book is not limited to the scholarship on Bonhoeffer or the understanding of the Western church but also addresses *the scholarship on hamartiology of the West*, in which the concerns of hamartiology are more actively discussed in relation to issues of gender, class, and race. An example of an issue that needs to be dealt with beyond the category of the Augustinian tradition of hamartiology is feminist and liberation theologians' critiques of the Augustinian understanding of the sin of humanity as pride or egocentricity. Until recently, the tradition of Western hamartiology has not explicitly included the perspectives of *all* people who are outside of the category of elite Western males.

Each of the chapters of this book reflects the claims of those who are outside of the Augustinian tradition. In particular, the chapter on Bonhoeffer's later hamartiology and ethics engages closely with the critiques of feminist and liberation theologians and Bonhoeffer's later doctrine of sin and evil, in which he clearly identifies the unseen or passive side of sin, such as blind submission and selflessness, as well as the symbiotic sinful relationality between the individual and the communal persons. In the process, the chapter identifies and evaluates the theological significance as well as the limitations of Bonhoeffer's later hamartiology. In his later doctrine, Bonhoeffer shifted from the Augustinian hamartiological tradition by describing the dual dimension of sin and evil and the inseparable sinful relationality between individual and communal persons, but he still continued to adhere to the male-centered perspective of the Augustinian hamartiological tradition represented by patriarchy. Thus, the book contributes to the hamartiology of the West by proposing that aspects of the later hamartiological schema of Bonhoeffer, such as the dual dimension of sin and the communal aspect of evil, can be utilized and developed in a new way in which not only the perspective of the Augustinian hamartiological tradition but also the claims of those who are outside of the Augustinian tradition, represented by feminist as well as liberation thinkers, can be integrated in a more holistic way in which the perspectives of *all* people are included.

Limitations and Challenges

Because of the vast scope of this book, which encompasses the voluminous works of three theologians, as well as the limit on the length of the book, there are inevitably limits on the chapters' discussion. In the case of Augustine's hamartiology, the author had planned to deal with the doctrine of original sin as well as with anthropology and ecclesiology because Bonhoeffer more actively appropriated Augustine's ecclesiastical notion of the church, *totus Christus* (the whole Christ), in his rephrasing of it as "the church is Christ existing as community"[18] in his hamartiology. However, the chapter on Augustine mainly focuses on the essential claims of Augustine's hamartiology and addresses the related sections on anthropology and ecclesiology in the chapters on Luther and Bonhoeffer. In a similar way, the chapter on Luther presents Luther's hamartiology in a succinct way in relation to the hamartiology of Augustine in order to sketch the whole trajectory of Luther's hamartiological shifts. In the case of the chapters on Bonhoeffer, the author had to eliminate almost one entire chapter on Bonhoeffer's evaluation of Augustine's doctrine of original sin in *Sanctorum Communio*. Instead, the essential portion of that section has been summarized in Chapter 3 or relocated to other chapters to keep the book within its length limit as well as to avoid unnecessary repetitions of similar arguments in regard to Bonhoeffer's evaluation of Augustine's doctrine of original sin. Moreover, the chapters titled "Bonhoeffer's Exegesis of the Creation and the Fall" and "Bonhoeffer's Later Hamartiology and Ethics" have been shortened, sometimes limiting the discussion of the issues but still addressing their significance.

Finally, it is necessary to acknowledge that throughout this book has referred to the original versions, in Latin or in German, of the works of each of the three theologians whenever it was needed to clarify the original sense of the theologian's thought or to clarify terms or nuances that cannot be conveyed in the translated versions in English. However, because of the limit on length as well as the intention not to distract from the focus of the book, the author has minimized the quotation of the original texts in Latin or in German. In the case of Augustine's corpus, the book has used various English translations in an effort to choose the version that most effectively renders the thought of Augustine in relation to the theme in the chapter as well as the overall argument of the book.[19]

Chapter 1

AUGUSTINE OF HIPPO'S DOCTRINE OF ORIGINAL SIN

Introduction

This chapter argues that Augustine's doctrine of original sin is a synthesis between his own Pauline exegesis and his early hamartiology, which is derived from his notion of a God who is defined as the Supreme Being in Augustine's Christianized Platonism. It investigates Augustine's early doctrine of evil and sin, in which his philosophically defined notion of God is an absolute rule in his hamartiological considerations. It, then, examines his later doctrine of original sin, which incorporates his exegesis of Scripture into his cosmology. To do this, the chapter provides an outline of Augustinian hamartiology that is necessary for the later dialogue with Lutheran hamartiology, in particular with Bonhoeffer's hamartiology, which transforms and reformulates the Augustinian doctrine of original sin by shifting the starting point from the doctrine of God to the doctrine of the church, based on the perspectives of Luther as well as of later Lutherans.

Augustine's hamartiology cannot be understood without examining the interaction between his perception of God and Neoplatonic cosmology, in which God is understood as the one supreme, transcendent being. Despite Augustine's active appropriation of Neoplatonic cosmology as the framework for his hamartiology, the interaction marks a philosophical as well as theological break with Manichaeism as well as Neoplatonism itself in the process of Augustine's search for the monotheistic God. Augustine was convinced that the one supreme being of Neoplatonism was very close to the God of Christianity; accordingly, his understanding of God became the premise for his doctrine of evil and sin. In this way, in his early thought the doctrine of evil and sin functions as a subcategory of his doctrine of God as it gives direction to all of his theological concerns. In his later hamartiology, however, he introduced biblical exegesis into his hamartiological system and formulated the doctrine of original sin that has since governed Western hamartiology as well as anthropology.

Of the many theological doctrines of Augustine, the doctrine of original sin has been one of the most debated and ongoing controversies in Western theology, mainly due to the theological fusion between his hierarchical cosmology and his exegesis of biblical accounts, in which he placed his own Pauline interpretation at the center of the discussion. Augustine basically attempts to justify his doctrine of original sin within his philosophical system in connection with Scripture; however, it is undeniable that his logic and descriptions are strongly bounded by his theological presuppositions, such as his concept of God, his cosmology, and the doctrine of predestination, all of which lead him to an unbalanced view of hamartiology. More importantly, even though Augustine's doctrine of original sin lays a solid foundation for the universality of sin and the sinful solidarity of the human race, it does not fully encompass the doctrine of Christ nor the doctrine of the new created human being in it, focusing more on the qualitative difference between the supreme God and fallen humanity. Accordingly, there is a considerable lack of correspondence between Augustinian doctrine of original sin and the sinful experience of people as well as the testimonies of Scripture, especially in the relationships between the universality of sin and human responsibility, sin as "non-being" and the presence of radical evil in the world, and the sinful experiences of males and females.

This chapter begins with an examination of Augustine's philosophical discussion of theodicy in which his notion of God along with his Christianized Neoplatonic cosmology becomes the foundation of his hamartiology. Second, it describes Augustine's early focus on fallen humanity's inward turn of the self as the central Augustinian account of hamartiology. In the process, the chapter investigates the function of his Christianized Neoplatonic system in his search for human sinfulness. Then, it examines Augustine's later hamartiological shift, which combines his biblical exegesis with his Christianized Neoplatonic cosmology. It discusses the theological meaning and significance of the doctrine of original sin as well as the controversies that are the basis of later chapters dealing with the doctrines of Luther and Bonhoeffer. Finally, it concludes by mentioning the theological implications that are discussed in later chapters.

Early Hamartiology: The Premise of the Doctrine of Original Sin

The problem of evil

The conflict between the presence of evil and the attributes of God is one of the fundamental questions raised by many Christians as well as non-Christians.[1] Addressing this old but resurgent trilemma is essential in understanding not only Augustine's conception of God but also the existence of evil.[2] This is because, as this section explicates, Augustine's hamartiology is interconnected with his Christianized Neoplatonic cosmology. Accordingly, it is necessary to begin by sketching Augustine's theodicy as the prerequisite for his hamartiology.

The problem of evil was one of the key issues with which Augustine struggled before his conversion to Christianity.[3] Augustine's questions related to the problem of evil and the essence of God remained with him on his spiritual journey through the most influential religious and philosophical systems of his time, which were primarily Manichaeism, Neoplatonism, and finally Christianity. When he was a teenager, Augustine had been deeply engaged in the Manichaean religion.[4]

Manichees were deeply concerned with the relation between God and the existence of Evil. According to Manichaeism, there are two opposite primordial beings—one good God and one Evil, light and darkness—and these two opposite forces are continuously wrestling in the universe. Manichees understood the world as a battlefield between two opposite powers. The advantage of this dualistic understanding of God and Evil is the fact that its explanation of the compatibility between the existence of God and the reality of evil in the world caused by the existence of Evil appears more reasonable and simpler than the monotheistic understanding of God.

Thus, it is not surprising that the Manichaean understanding of the universe attracted Augustine, who had been searching for an answer to this dilemma since his youth.[5] This issue had been not only one of the main obstacles for Augustine before his conversion to Christianity but was also a continuous philosophical as well as theological concern in the process of his theological development, especially in his hamartiology. After spending more than nine years as a "hearer" of Manichaeism, however, Augustine found himself unsatisfied with the metaphysics of Manichaeism, which held a materialistic and corporeal conception of God as non-omnipotent. Augustine's dissatisfaction with Manichaeism's concept of evil was primarily due to its understanding of the characteristics of God.[6] He found that a materialistic and corporeal God is contradictory to the presence of evil in the world because if God is filled with the creation physically and materialistically, then there is no place without God, and therefore there is no place for evil.[7] Augustine's concept of God at this point combined the idea of a materialistic and infinite God with that of a monotheistic God. Augustine could not accept the dualistic Manichaean understanding of God and Evil because it made God non-omnipotent and non-omnibenevolent.

Then, Augustine turned to ideas of Neoplatonism. In *Confessions*, he vividly describes his search for an answer to the question of the problem of evil and God. He points out that his reading of "certain books of Platonists" made him understand God *spiritually* for the first time.[8] He began to understand the Christian notion of God and God's creation through a Neoplatonic lens, especially through Plotinus' *Enneads*.[9] He found several important clues to solving the dilemma from his reading of Plotinus. Most importantly, Augustine discovered a hierarchical and ontological cosmology in which one Supreme Being, who is God, is placed at the top. As Lewis Ayres comments, Augustine became convinced that the hierarchical order in creation is "a vehicle of God's self-manifestation."[10] Augustine believed that if one traces up to the top of the hierarchical order of being by the power of reason, then one can discover God, who is eternal and unchangeable.[11] Augustine clearly defines God as *quo nullus est superior*, "to whom none is superior," in the system of the hierarchy of being in which evil can be understood as "privation of good" and as "non-being" rather than an ontological being or substance.[12] Augustine perceived that here he had finally found the explanation for the problem of evil against the idea of Manichaeism.

Certainly, Augustine combines his Christianized, Neoplatonic, hierarchical cosmology with the Christian concept of God. Against Manichaean dualism,

Augustine attempts to refine his doctrine of evil. In the process, Augustine's active appropriation of Plotinus is evident.[13] He reforms Plotinus' cosmology into the Christian way, applying his hermeneutical method that converts pagan intellectual assets to Christian use.[14] As Gerald Bonner properly points out, although Augustine borrows Neoplatonic ideas for his cosmological system, he attempts to reformulate them in a Christian way.[15] Accordingly, Augustine is very careful not to reduce the sovereignty or attributes of God in his description, especially in his appropriation of Neoplatonism. Augustine's revision of Plotinus' cosmology functions in two ways. First, he draws on the order of creation as a means to refute the dualism of Manichaeism. Second, he tries to eliminate the Neoplatonic dualism between matter and soul in which evil is included in the materialistic universe as a necessary result of its emanation from the Supreme Being. This is because the notion of pre-existing matter of Neoplatonism per se inevitably contains the evil nature. Plotinus explains that although the cosmos comes from the Supreme Being by emanation, it is made out of matter that already existed before creation, and it contains evil because it has not yet been brought to order.[16] In other words, the cosmos has two different origins: God and matter. Plotinus understands the cosmos as a mixture of good and evil, soul and matter.[17] The logic of Plotinus does not perfectly eliminate the possibility of dualism because he does not deny possibility of corruption of matter, which Augustine directly relates with evil. Bonner clearly notes this point, writing that "Plotinus, while firmly relegating Evil to the realm of Non-Being, never arrives at the Augustinian position of Evil as simply a privation of Good."[18]

In Neoplatonism, creation has two origins: the one Supreme Being and matter. Thus, this can be considered a kind of dualism in which not only the source of human corruptibility but also the non-omnipotence of God is implied. For this reason, Augustine reformulates Plotinus' system in a Christian way. The conclusion is evident. If God is omnipotent and omnibenevolent and the good God created the universe, God's creation is also "good"; therefore, there should be no place for evil in God's created world.[19] He rejects not only Plotinus' concept of *emanation* but also the concept of the *pre-existence of matter* that prevailed in ancient Greek philosophy.[20] His final choice has to do with denying the existence of evil within his Christianized Neoplatonic cosmology by placing evil at the bottom of the *order of creation* as *non-being* or simply *privation of good*, which undergirds the attributes of God, especially omnipotence and omnibenevolence, in the trilemma.[21] For Augustine, this Christianized Neoplatonic cosmology is the starting point for perceiving the relation between God and evil as well as between God and humanity.[22]

In short, Augustine borrows the ontological frame of Plotinus to uphold God's benevolence and omnipotence and to properly situate evil. Accordingly, evil can be treated as non-being but not as substance. Augustine explicitly finds the Neoplatonic cosmology the most proper lens for approaching the problem of evil as well as the notion of God. However, the difficulty of Neoplatonism in regard to the problem of evil is that Neoplatonism does not perfectly eliminate the risk of dualism between matter and God because of its attribution of evil in matter. To discard the problem of matter, Augustine turns to the doctrine of *creatio ex nihilo* (creation out of nothing) that he received from the Christian tradition.

Creatio ex nihilo

The philosophically derived notion of sin as "non-being," which Augustine viewed as total separation from God, led him to focus on the doctrine of *creatio ex nihilo*, which seemed to give him a way to articulate the problem of evil more logically and plausibly against the dualism of the Manichees between God and Evil as well as that of Plotinus between God and matter. The doctrine of creation out of nothing can be traced back to Irenaeus of Lyons of the second century.[23] At first glance, however, the notion of *creatio ex nihilo* seems to be ambivalent. On the one hand, it means the creation is good because it is created by the benevolent God; on the other hand, however, it contains a negative implication because it is created out of "nothing," which is related to the concept of evil in Neoplatonic metaphysics in which *nihil* (nothing) is derived from matter.

Furthermore, Augustine notices that when one turns to humanity, the problem of evil becomes more complicated because humanity is composed of two components: soul and body. Apparently, these two contradictory aspects have been in humanity since the creation. For his refutation of the dualism of the Neoplatonists, Augustine once again follows his philosophical principle applied in his previous refutation of Manichaeism in which his concept of God functions as the ultimate proposition for his theological consideration. He argues in *The Nature of the Good*:

> The highest good, than which there is none higher, is God, and for this reason he is the immutable good and therefore truly eternal and truly immortal. All other goods are *made only by him but are not made of* him. ... And for this reason he alone is immutable, while all the things are that he has made are mutable because *he has made them from nothing*.[24]

Augustine argues that both the soul and the body are created out of nothing and both are mutable and good. The focus of Augustine's argument here is on defending the attributes of God, who is defined in a philosophical and abstract manner. Although he theoretically has eliminated the possibility of the existence of evil in creation by defining evil as nothing, the issue here is that the concept of *creatio ex nihilo* also implies the possibility of the entrance of evil into creation due to creation's origin in nothingness. The theory of *creatio ex nihilo* explains both the original goodness of humanity, embedded in body and soul, and its natural tendency to go back to its condition before creation, which was nothingness. For Augustine, all created things are mutable because God alone is immutable, unchangeable, good, and a sovereign being.

Therefore, at this point he concludes that all created beings are potentially changeable in two directions: ascension to the higher being or descension to non-being.[25] Augustine clearly differentiates these two aspects of humanity, goodness and mutability, because he perceives that all creation is made *by* God but is not *of* God. There are two levels of hierarchy in Augustine's thought. First, there is the qualitatively different hierarchy between Creator and creation that the creature cannot go beyond; second, there is the degree of being among created beings, which the creature might go up or down. Thus, rational beings are in between the upper and lower levels of being. Augustine's synthesis between the Neoplatonic hierarchy and the theory of *creatio ex nihilo* allows him to avoid the logical conflict between the benevolent God and God's good creation as a basic framework. However, he has to explain further the relation between the theoretical absence of evil and the experiential or physical evil in creation.[26] To explain this, he uses the concept of hierarchy. He explains the discrepancy by saying that the created world itself has had the possibility of change from the beginning of creation.[27] One should notice that, for Augustine, the mutability of creation itself is not evil but a lesser goodness in his cosmological system of hierarchy. The immutable and good God created the heaven and the earth as good, but the quality of the goodness of creation is not the same as that of God because perfect goodness is only found in God, who is the highest goodness or existence. Thus, all created beings have a corruptible nature, and this is the reason we experience evil.[28]

In this new synthesis of the *order of creation* and *creatio ex nihilo*, Augustine explains that principally evil does not belong to creation but exists only as the possibility of evil activity rather than as a substance in the universe as the lesser good. It is noteworthy that Augustine does not see corruptibility itself as evil but only as a potentiality, reformulating the tradition of Irenaeus, who simply suggests that matter itself is good. There is a subtle but crucial gap in Augustine's new synthesis of his appropriation of the Neoplatonically derived concept of evil and of *creatio ex nihilo*, which is derived chiefly from the doctrine of Irenaeus. The conflict is between the concept of matter held by the Neoplatonists and that held by Irenaeus. Irenaeus understands matter as good, and his concept of matter does not imply the negative sense of the potential to be corrupted. As Matthew Craig Steenberg explains, for Irenaeus all things in creation include the substance itself, which is fundamentally good.[29] However, Augustine views the nature of matter as having the potential of changing the human being in both body and soul, although he denies the origin of evil in matter. This ambivalence or amalgamation becomes one of the sources of theological discrepancies in Augustine's hamartiology.

This synthesis is directly applied to conceptualize the notion of "non-being" or "privation of good" in a more systematic way within the framework of Augustine's previous Christianized hierarchy of being. For Augustine, the concept of good is always twofold, coupled with evil. Goodness is the fundamental nature of all created beings, but it is always defective to a certain degree. When good is increased in a being, evil is decreased; therefore, there is no perfect good in a created being. By the same logic, there is no absolute evil in creation because declension to the lowest evil means absence of being. Augustine's thought is probably far from a discussion of nothingness itself as the form of an entity, but it is a form of rhetoric through which he describes evil.[30] Although his approach to the notion of God as

Being is an important step in resolving his ongoing struggle with the problem of evil, the issue is that his hierarchical cosmology becomes the standard of ethics beyond the discussion of theodicy and creation.

Decisively, in Augustine's framework, the notion of "being" is value-judgmental. The "being" or existence itself becomes the rule for evaluating the value of all beings. From the hierarchical ontological perspective, Augustine speculates, on one level, that evil is worthless and futile and thus the lowest being, nothing; on another level, one experiences evil due to the evil that is a manifestation of lacking goodness. As Catherine Conybeare indicates, this shows Augustine's Christian optimism against the dualism of Manichaeism.[31] However, this is Augustine's early optimism, chiefly seen from the perspective of protology or eschatology.[32] In other words, it is explained by the perspective of the good creation or the final perfection rather than the reality of this world. The definition of evil as "non-being" or "privation of good" is related not only to the philosophical and eschatological conclusion of evil but also to the nature of evil described from the perspective of value-judgment based on Augustine's ultimate soteriological criterion, existence.[33] Regarding the nature of good and evil, he states in *Enchiridion*:

> A good that wholly lacks an evil aspect is entirely good. Where there is some evil in a thing, its good is *defective* or *defectible*. Thus there can be no evil where there is no good. This leads us to a surprising conclusion: that ... every being, in so far as it is a being, is good ... *every actual entity is good* [*omnis natura bonum est*].[34]

It is worth noting how Augustine describes evil. When Augustine speaks of evil, it is always in relation to good. In Augustine's theory, there is no perfect goodness in creation because creation is not God. In the same way, there is no absolute evil but only comparative evil in creation because the benevolent God created the universe. There are only degrees of good and evil, just like degrees of creation. Augustine's schema of degrees of being supplies a theoretical justification for his doctrine of evil.

In reality, however, humanity suffers from the power of evil in the inner self as well as in the world. In other words, Augustine needs to relate the temporal reality of evil to the eschatological or protological absence of evil. This means that Augustine has to explain the mechanism by which evil works as a non-entity in this temporal world. Precisely how can evil, which does not have substance, have power over the world or over a human being? The reason for the existence of evil in the world lies in its parasitic nature.[35] It is convincing that evil does not have power in and of itself but only has power in association with an entity. Rational beings, humanity and fallen angels, are the place where evil works. Human beings rather than evil itself deceive other humans because a non-being could not itself deceive human beings independently—only in association with them. Therefore, Augustine can say that "nothing evil exists in itself, but only as an evil aspect of some actual entity."[36] Evil is not the true or final reality but is temporal, and it works in a parasitic way through rational beings. This conclusion that evil is the privation of goodness opens a way for Augustine to search for the origin of evil in the will of humanity.

Free will: The source of evil

The philosophically derived definition of evil as non-entity leads Augustine to turn to the inside of the self as the source of evil. This is a significant theological moment in his hamartiology. As Augustine concludes that there is no evil in God's good creation, the extrinsic origin of evil beyond God's creation is impossible and the good God cannot be the origin of evil.[37] Thus, evil's origin must be found somewhere inside of creation. Augustine focuses on the nature of creation, especially its mutability, as the cause of evil. Evil is non-being ontologically, and thus the reason for our experience of evil ought to be found internally; especially in the case of moral evil, it should be found inside rational beings.[38]

For Augustine, free will is the reason human beings commit sin and experience suffering. He explains, "Free will is the cause of our doing evil and ... thy [God's] just judgment is the cause of our having to suffer from its consequences."[39] Augustine also insists that the nature of the human is the place where evil could have first arisen: "From a human nature, which is good in itself, there can spring forth either a good or an evil will. There was no other place from whence evil could have arisen."[40] This conviction that the mutability of free will is the cause of evil in humanity is clearly a synthesis between his Christianized Neoplatonic cosmology and the doctrine of *creatio ex nihilo*. Augustine argues that as all created things are good, the free will that God bestowed is also good. However, a choice made through free will can be used in a good way or a bad way in the primordial state. Ultimately, there is no moral evil in the world but only evil choices that have arisen from the corrupted will of the human being. Augustine internalizes the source of evil within the human being's will. Following the logic of Augustine, there is no absolutely evil choice but only corrupted or less good choices. He clarifies that having the possibility of sin by exercising free will is better than not having free will.[41] Once again, Augustine's notion of the evil or good choice is always considered in his overarching rule of judgment, the order of creation, in the degrees of goodness such as good and less good.

On one level, Augustine's early responses to the question of the existence of evil and sin in the world are strongly apologetic against the idea of Manichaeism. His conclusion that evil began in the will of humans opens a way for the Western tradition to internalize evil. Augustine's refutation of the system of Manichaeism as well as his refutation of the dualism of Neoplatonism seems foreign to modern people. However, as Bonner comments, Augustine's philosophical discussion is still relevant to those who inquire about the issues that Augustine and his contemporary critics were exploring.[42] On another level, however, some theological considerations are required in regard to the discrepancies that arise through an examination of Augustine's early theodicy as well as his doctrine of free will. It is clear that Augustine's solution to theodicy is based on the attributes of God within the hierarchical framework of a Christianized Neoplatonic cosmology; however, the issue here is that he does not fully associate this with the Trinitarian God in his discussion at this point.

In this regard, Irenaeus' comment is noteworthy. Irenaeus points out that it is hard to trace the problem of evil protologically because Scripture does not directly testify to the origin of evil or it may not be the focus of the biblical testimonies.[43] Furthermore, although Augustine's doctrine of evil and free will is derived from his philosophical epistemology, it seems to require accordance with the notion of God in the Scripture. Certainly, as Stephen N. Williams argues, God is described mainly in an existential and concrete way in the Old Testament as well as the New Testament, and furthermore "[in both Testaments] the sovereignty of the one God is shared with one who is other than the Father."[44] This point may be one of the important questions raised by Augustine's theological successors such as Luther and the Lutherans in regard to their methodological turn to Christocentrism.

Despite these critiques, it is evident that Augustine's observations and insights on the doctrine of evil and its origin in human free will not only became the foundation for his further investigations but also gave inspiration to many modern thinkers. Among many analyses of his early hamartiology, the interiority of evil in the will is one of the most distinctive prerequisites of Augustine's hamartiology. From this, he developed related doctrinal concepts such as those of humanity, the nature of sin, and ethics. The following sections discuss these concerns.

Sin: Free will's downward movement

Augustine's concept of evil, which is derived from philosophical and ontological concerns, is closely connected to his understanding of moral evil manifested in the form of sin. This section explores Augustine's internalized doctrine of evil and sin, which is manifested in three related sequences: free will's turning toward the inside of the self, free will's downward direction between two objects, and the manifestation of the will in the self in pride. From his early thought, Augustine attempts to explain the origin of sin in will's downward movement in two opposite directions.[45] Basically, for Augustine free will is a human faculty and is part of the good creation. However, it has the possibility of being used in two opposite ways, positively as well as negatively.[46] Notwithstanding this ambivalence of free will, Augustine asserts in *On Free Will* that sin is free will's turning away from the immutable Good and turning toward the mutable good.[47] The direction of the will is one of the key elements for perceiving Augustine's hamartiological thought concerning the downward movement. It is noteworthy that as Augustine explores God from the "inside-up" direction, he discovers the evil will's movement in a similar but opposite pattern, an "inside-down" direction.[48] Clearly, the first movement of this current arises in the human being who, in its free will, turns away from God and toward the creation.[49] Augustine considers that the turning of the orientation of the will from God toward other than God is the beginning and the quintessential aspect of moral evil, or sin. In other words, sin is the soul's turning away from God.

The second movement is the will's distorted "downward" orientation toward the lesser good. The will continues to move to the next erring step to find the object of its distorted love or desire. To love something more than God is sin itself and sin's orientation.[50] Sin, for Augustine, is to love something changeable and temporal rather than something stable and eternal.[51] He explains sin mainly from the language of philosophy. Sin is no less than the misoriented "downward" love of humanity; this orientation loses its proper "upward" direction but changes its route to downward to seek the lesser good and, strikingly, enjoys the sin itself.[52] In *Confessions*, Augustine repeatedly describes this downward sinful orientation of the human being toward something other than God. He states: "I found that it is no substance, but a perversion of the will bent aside from thee, O God, the supreme substance, toward these lower things."[53] Perversion of the will is exactly opposite to conversion to God in its direction. Augustine articulates sin using directional terms such as *perversio* (perversion) and *conversio* (conversion) in his hierarchical frame.[54] This orientation is toward other futile things, including other human beings as well as the self.

Finally, the self is the final destination of the distorted will. The *incurvatus in se*, "inward turn of the self," which alienates the human from God and toward the self, is itself Augustine's hamartiological concern. In his *Teaching Christianity*, Augustine's concept of sinful orientation is well summarized by his two notions of *frui* and *uti*, by which Augustine suggests the will's two opposite directions as upward and downward. He argues that only God is the object of *frui* (to enjoy) and that other than God is merely the object of *uti* (to use).[55] Sin is humanity's enjoyment of the object of *uti*, other than God, rather than the object of *frui*, God. Accordingly, Augustine defines sin as nothing less than the will's *conversio ad* (turning toward) something that is a trivial and inferior good.[56] His comparison between these two opposite orientations of the will explicitly shows that his hamartiological foundation or rule of judgment lies in his Christianized Neoplatonic hierarchy in which God is in the top place as the supreme good and the other than God is placed in a lower place as the lesser good. Augustine's vertical gradation of being made him think of the downward direction as the ethical evil, or sin. Cary comments on this, pointing out that, for Augustine, "Moral evil is best described with an adverb rather than a noun: it means choosing evilly rather than choosing an evil."[57] Augustine asserts again that there is no pure evil because evil means "privation of good" or "defection."

In *Teaching Christianity*, Augustine raises an important theological question, which is whether human beings are the object of *frui* or *uti* or of both.[58] Augustine answers as follows:

> We have been commanded, after all, to love one another; but the question is whether people are to be loved by others for their own sake, or for the sake of something else. If it is for their own sake, then they are things for us to enjoy; if for the sake of something else, they are for us to use. ... *Cursed, however, is the one who places his hopes in man* (Jer 17:5).[59]

Scholars of Augustine are not univocal as to whether Augustine is treating humans as the object of *uti* or *frui*.[60] Nevertheless, diverse interpretations of Augustinian thought note that whether he is referring to *uti* or *frui* or both, he explicitly gives primacy to God as *frui*. Clearly, neighbors or other humans are considered as *frui* only in the way that the neighbor is to be treated to promote their love toward God. He states, "If we enjoy things to be used, we are hindering our way to happiness, and sometimes we are deflected from our own track."[61] Similar to the free will's ability to turn in either direction, toward the Supreme Being or non-being, love for the neighbor, for Augustine, fundamentally cannot be equated with love for God. Once again, it is clear that Augustine defines sin based on his understanding of God. The will's downward movement to lesser goodness is the second step of the misdirected will. Then, finally, the will's orientation toward something other than God is manifested in diverse forms of sin such as lust, pride, and egocentricity. However, Augustine observes that the diverse sinful manifestations of the will converge in one distinctive final destination, *the self*. He describes that the nature of this orientation takes a downward turn to something that is a lesser good, using the terms *uti et frui*. Then, among the lesser goods, Augustine designates the final destination of the will in *amor sui* (love of self).[62] The place of God has been replaced by the self: *sicut Deus*, "as God," but curved toward the self. Love of God has been changed into love of the self in pride and egocentricity. Augustine identifies the self's will as the origin of evil.

As Oliver O'Donovan comments, Augustine was the first Latin father who took seriously the notion of *amor sui* in the biblical phrase "as yourself."[63] The doctrine of self-love has been a significant theological theme in several ways. First, the notion of *amor sui* became the tradition of the self *incurvatus in se* of the Western church, followed and transformed by many theologians who have dealt with this concept in the works of Martin Luther and Dietrich Bonhoeffer.[64] Furthermore, the Augustinian doctrine of the self in egocentricity or pride has been controversial during the past several decades, especially among many feminist thinkers as well as liberation theologians as discussed in Chapters 5 and 6. The feminist thinkers' claim marks a decisive theological juncture in the history of the Western church because it is a starting point of the claim against the current of the Western theology or hamartiology that has been continuous for more than a thousand years and that mainly reflects the males' angle. In a similar vein, Migliore properly points out that "feminist and other liberation theologians have rightly exposed the gross one-sidedness of traditional theology."[65] Augustine observed that the sinful downward turn of the will that arrives at the self in egocentricity is the chief manifestation of sin. However, careful attention must be paid to the critique that Augustine's turn to the self's obsessive egocentricity neglects the self's passive side of sin, such as self-denigration and self-denial, which are equally as sinful as obsessive self-love, as feminist thinkers as well as Bonhoeffer have claimed.

For Augustine, the self contains the *imago Dei* (image of God), which is primarily a vestige of the immanent Trinity in the human soul composed of "memory, intellect and will."[66] The route of the erring will goes from the self to the self per se in a circular way. As Cary argues, Augustine was explicitly influenced by the Platonic notion of inwardness based on his reading of Plotinus.[67] Cary as well as many other Augustine scholars agrees that Augustine's turn to God follows the sequence of "in then up" in searching for God in the soul of the human through "memory, intellect and will," which Augustine identifies as the trace of *imago Dei*.[68] Following the tradition of Irenaeus, Augustine argues that the *imago Dei* was not totally destroyed even after the fall.[69] Augustine's doctrine of *imago Dei* is primarily a search for the vestige of the immanent Trinity in the human soul composed of "memory, intellect and will," which is the highest faculty of the human being.[70] This tripartite faculty of the rational soul of the human being reflects the residue of the *imago Dei* even after the fall.

The understanding of the image of God is an important theological premise of Augustine's anthropology upon which he builds the system of his hamartiology as well as his Christian ethics. Furthermore, this is one of the points in which Luther's as well as Bonhoeffer's anthropology diverges the most from Augustine's and arrives at different conclusions in their theological loci, especially in Christian ethics.[71] Augustine considers this vestige of God in the human soul the basis for situating the human being in a higher position in the order of creation. Thus, he conceives that through the possibility left in the *imago Dei* as *analogia entis* (analogy of being), the soul has to ascend toward the Supreme Being as the final destination of the soul's pilgrimage.[72] Augustine's hamartiological thought in his earlier stage can be outlined more coherently in the will's downward fall to the self, which is clearly opposite to the soul's soteriological journey to the heavenly city of God. The downward movement of the will manifests in diverse features. For young Augustine, this self-love or self-obsession is chiefly expressed in the form of "pride."[73] Confessing that "by my swelling pride I was separated from thee," Augustine identifies "pride," which is related to *intellectual pride*, as the chief sin among many sinful manifestations.[74] Although Augustine introduces other concepts of sin in his later period, pride is a *cantus firmus* even in his later works, along with his new vocabulary of sin.

In summary, Augustine's description of sin as the will's downward movement needs to be read in his context. He was surrounded by the heretical teachings of Manichaeism as well as the influence of Neoplatonic resources. Augustine's treatment of sin as self-love at this point describes a trajectory that is exactly opposite to the path of the will's ascension to God, who is understood as having a supreme way of existence over all other created things. However, some critics of Augustine have raised several theological problems. First, it is questionable whether Augustine fully investigated the relation between soul and body in his early theology, especially in his description of the movement of the will.[75] Second, the young Augustine does not proportionally or equally explain the theme of evil and sin from a Trinitarian perspective of relations.[76] Augustine follows the main tenets of the Nicene Trinity, at least in its concern over how the divinity maintains the unity of the triune God. However, it is necessary to consider that "every act of God is the act of the one triune God" in regard to Augustine's early treatment of evil and sin.[77] In his early period, it is undeniable that Augustine described the nature of sin and evil primarily from the perspective of the attributes of the first person of Trinity, neglecting the Trinitarian relations. More fundamentally, this issue is closely related to the theological methodology of Augustine in regard to the doctrine of God. Bruce L. McCormack's note is helpful. McCormack points out:

> [Classical theism has] the belief that the 'order of knowing' runs in the opposite direction to the 'order of being.' That is to say, though the being of God is above and prior to the being of all else that exists (and therefore first in the

'order of being'), our knowledge of God proceeds from a prior knowledge of some aspect or aspects of creaturely reality (and therefore the knowledge of God follows knowledge of the self or the world in the 'order of knowing'). The consequence of this methodological decision is that the way taken to knowledge of God controls and determines the kind of God-concept one is able to generate; thus, epistemology controls and determines divine ontology.[78]

Clearly, Augustine's concept of God, which is derived from his epistemology, determines not only the concept of God but also the concept of sin and evil in the early stage of his hamartiology. Accordingly, this observation implies that Augustine's early doctrine of sin and evil was conceived without consideration of Christology. Third, it is also debatable whether the concept of pride as a representative concept of sin can fully embrace humanity's sinful experience.[79] It is significant that some of these questions were addressed and revised by Augustine himself in his later doctrines as well as by later theologians throughout the history of the Western church.[80]

Later Hamartiology: The Doctrine of Original Sin

Original sin as concupiscence

Augustine's early hamartiology was dominated by the principle of the qualitative difference between Creator and creature in their way of existence, by which God is defined as an eternal and immutable Being and the creature as a temporal and mutable being. His later doctrine, however, shows a shift from his earlier thought under the influence of several factors, such as his experience of priesthood, his reading of Paul, and his polemics against Pelagianism.[81] The central factor was his integration of his biblical reflection into his ongoing philosophical framework. As many scholars agree, there were several crucial transitional points in Augustine's intellectual history.[82] The first decisive turning point was his reading of certain books by Plotinus, and the second was his reading of the Pauline writings.[83] In fact, his interpretation of the Pauline passages strongly influenced his later hamartiology as encapsulated in his doctrine of original sin. Although Augustine maintained his early Christianized Neoplatonic framework as the firm theological basis of his later works, it is clear that he relied greatly on the Pauline writings in his later works, starting around 396 after his letter to Simplicianus.[84] Accordingly, one trait of his later hamartiology is his recognition of the sinful *incurvatus in se* expressed in diverse forms of sin, especially the notion of *concupiscence*, in addition to his continuing focus on *pride*.[85] He incorporates the message in the Pauline writings into his previous conception of the will's downward movement. His hamartiology thus begins to synthesize his previous philosophical contemplation and his Pauline hermeneutics, and in this way he formulates the doctrine of original sin.

Although Augustine never abandons his theodical concern in his early hamartiology, his mature hamartiology contains considerable theological shifts from his previous thought in its both structure and content.[86] In its structure, he distinguishes two different levels of sin: original sin and actual sin. This means that while Adam is responsible for his first sin, which is his own actual sin, his posterity is responsible not only for their own sin but also for Adam's sin, namely, the original sin. The concept of the original sin thus clearly emerges. The posterity of Adam inherits the sinful nature of the postlapsarian Adam as well as the original sin, along with its penalty. It is noteworthy that this logic is closely associated with Augustine's later introduction of the hamartiological concept of *concupiscentia* (concupiscence) as original sin, which is derived from his reading of the Pauline epistles and can be interpreted in both biological and spiritual senses. This signifies that the origin of evil and sin, which has been predominantly discussed within the spiritual category, stretches to the dimension of corporeality. Augustine's new focus on the body as an essential aspect of the human being seems to explicitly surpass his earlier emphasis on the soul as the essence of the human being. Augustine's hamartiological structure in this period is inseparably intertwined with his exegesis of Pauline passages, especially Rom. 5:12.[87] Augustine interprets this as follows:

> By the evil will of that one man all sinned *in him*, since all were that one man, from whom, therefore, they individually derived *original sin*. ... I plainly aver that it is by reason of transgression that they are in the devil's power, and that their participation, moreover, of this transgression is due to the circumstance that they are born of the said *union of the sexes*, which cannot even accomplish its own honourable function without the incident of shameful *lust*.[88]

Although Augustine finds proof texts in several places besides Rom. 5:12, his incorrect interpretation of Rom. 5:12 is pivotal for the formation of the doctrine of original sin. Augustine firmly believes that all human beings literally sinned when Adam sinned, based on his interpretation of this text. Some Augustine scholars point out that one of the chief reasons for the complicated logic of the Augustinian doctrine of original sin is mainly due to his false rendering of Rom. 5:12.[89] This is because Augustine interprets the Greek ἐφ' ᾧ as meaning "in him" rather than "because of." He interprets the verse to mean that all posterity sinned and participated at the moment of the fall because all of future humanity resided in Adam's loins, although he does not clearly explain the manner of its presence. Certainly, as J. N. D. Kelly and Pier Franco Beatrice point out, his exegesis of Rom. 5:12 is foundational for his doctrine of original sin.[90] His new understanding of corporeality makes him synthesize his earlier view with the Pauline message.[91] Through this reading, the physical or material aspect of the human being reappears on the surface of his hamartiological consideration in his exegesis. It is at this point that the notion of original sin is complicated by the new notion of *concupiscentia*, which implies both the spiritual and corporeal senses along with his ongoing notion of pride.

Augustine's articulation of original sin in regard to the relationality between soul and body is controversial among Augustine scholars, and it does seem ambiguous.⁹² As Jeff Nicoll and most other scholars point out, Augustine's theory of original sin creates an inseparable relationship between the will and the concupiscence of a person—in other words, the relationship between body and soul.⁹³ The free will of rational beings has been identified as the locus of the first evil and sin in his early works, but the problem is that Augustine is not clear about the seat of concupiscence, whether it is in the soul or the body, in his doctrine of original sin. On the one hand, Eugene TeSelle argues that "it might be accurate to make original sin equivalent with concupiscence, but only if it is seen as something within the soul... or rather it is the two of them together, for without the body there could be not carnal delight, yet it is the soul that takes delight."⁹⁴ On the other hand, Bonner argues that "there is abundant evidence for the interchangeability of *libido* and *concupiscentia* in their sexual significance."⁹⁵ In spite of these diverse interpretations, one clear fact is that Augustine opens the possibility for the concept of concupiscence to be interpreted as spiritual, physical, or both spiritual and physical. Generally, however, Augustine is not decisive on the mechanism of concupiscence in the body and/or the soul.⁹⁶

Solidarity of the human race

Augustine's new emphasis on *concupiscentia* leads him to another hamartiological conclusion, which is that human beings are inevitably related to the ancestral sin chiefly by the biological transmission of the sinful nature as well as the penalty. Based on his interpretation of Rom. 5:12, Augustine conceives that in Adam the whole of humankind is in unity through the biological inheritance of culpability along with a distorted nature, and in this way sin becomes universal to all.⁹⁷ The problem is that although Augustine distinguishes the *penalty* of the first human's sin from the *condition* of his posterity, he insists that not only the corrupted human condition but also the sin itself, including culpability or guilt, is inherited by his posterity, especially through the sexual union.⁹⁸ In arguing thus, Augustine distinguishes himself from his Latin teachers such as Ambrose and Ambrosiaster, who only agreed with the transmission of the corrupted human nature, not with the punishment for Adam's sin.⁹⁹ The most distinctive point of the Augustinian doctrine of original sin is the transmission of the penalty of Adam's sin in addition to that of the fallen propensity or sinful solidarity of the race. This is the logic of original sin by which Augustine's thinking is explicitly differentiated from the tradition.

Augustine was convinced that there is a strong bond between the first humans, represented by Adam, and their posterity. However, the problem is that Augustine understands this bond mostly in the biological solidarity transmitted by procreation through sexual union.¹⁰⁰ Moreover, in the process of biological transmission, sinful lust or the physical sense of concupiscence is involved.¹⁰¹ Augustine's early designation of the essence of original sin as pride, which connotates spiritual sin, is complicated by concupiscence, which strongly implies both the spirituality and materiality of humans. In his later works, Augustine simultaneously upholds these two aspects of sin, pride and concupiscence. As some later Lutheran thinkers, such as Luther and Bonhoeffer, argue, the concept of original sin can hardly be distinguished from the chief sin in Augustine's theory itself, because Augustine's later induction of *concupiscentia*, which clearly includes physical as well as spiritual senses of sin, opens the way for the binary concept of concupiscence to be conceived as the original sin. Furthermore, despite the doctrine's intention of upholding the biblical message of "both *human responsibility* for and *human powerlessness* with respect to sin,"[102] it is evident that it greatly broadens the biological sense of concupiscence from the binary aspects of concupiscence by its insistence on the biological transmission of sin, neglecting the other aspects of human unity—as Bonhoeffer emphasizes, the social unity of humanity (see Chapter 4).

The doctrine of original sin clearly suggests that *involuntary alien guilt* or *culpability* is transmitted.[103] Following the logic of Augustine, although the original sin and the sin of Adam's descendants are distinguished, the descendants are responsible for Adam's sin because they already *participate* in it in Adam's *seed*.[104] This interpretation strongly implies that the original sin of Adam was itself related to physical concupiscence along with spiritual rebellion. It is true that all humans inherit a sinful nature and become sinners without exception; however, the issue here is that the doctrine suggests that one should be responsible for others' sin in addition to one's own sin. In making this suggestion, it automatically presupposes not only the transmission of the sinful nature but also the penalty for the first sin, even to people such as infants who have not committed an actual sin, which is one of the main claims raised by Pelagians.[105] Furthermore, this is also related to sin after baptism or conversion. Augustine's polyphonic descriptions of original sin after the Pauline exegesis are quite evident. If one eliminates Augustine's biological transmission of culpability from his doctrine of original sin, the description of original sin is closer to the doctrine of the universal sinful state of humanity rather than the original sin of Adam that is transmitted to his posterity. The universality of sin, however, is itself an important anthropological point by which Augustine diverges from the opinion of the Pelagians, who were major critics of his thinking.

To a certain degree, the challenge of the Pelagians made Augustine refine his hamartiology to defend the sovereignty of God as well as the solidarity of the human race.[106] In facing the Pelagian claim, the issue for Augustine was that he had to reconcile God's omnipotence with the free choice of the will. The problem was that the Pelagians' argument was apparently similar to Augustine's early understanding of the compatibility between the benevolence of God and the free choice of humanity. In order to avoid this conflict, Augustine revised his earlier view so that his perspective became different from the Pelagians' claim in two points: humanity's incapacity to overcome sin and the limited extent of the will.[107] Augustine recognized that the idea of the Pelagians did not fully preserve the attributes of God. The high view of the capacity of the human will of Pelagianism was blasphemous and definitely resulted in the restriction of God's omnipotence. Accordingly, Augustine distinguished the primal state of humanity from the state of humanity after the fall in all aspects of human faculties. This implies that the nature of the human being was considerably changed after the fall and that all that resulted came from the moment of the first sin in the fall. The system of original sin was thus further consolidated. However, the doctrine of alien culpability is not persuasive for many people, nor is the biological transmission of sin. However, the doctrine of original sin's apparently illegitimate claim of "taking the culpability of others" is not easy to simply ignore because the biblical message suggests that the notion of alien culpability is related to Christian responsibility as expressed by Christ's vicarious representative action on the cross for the sins of human beings as well as in the teaching of "love your neighbor as yourself."[108] The problem of alien culpability, which seems to surpass the capacity of humans, should probably be addressed in a different theological locus than the doctrine of creation or sin in light of God's action in Christ toward humanity.

Ignorance and difficulty

Furthermore, Augustine's later amalgamation between his Platonizing cosmology and his Pauline exegesis permitted him to add other hamartiological concepts, such as *ignorance* and *difficulty*, as additional primary sinful manifestations.[109] Augustine argues that the state of the primal humans was superior to that of their posterity; therefore, humanity's postlapsarian state is inferior to the first humanity and is described in terms of its ignorance and difficulty.[110]

Augustine asserts that humanity lost its capacity to do right under the state of ignorance and difficulty after the fall. First, humanity became "intellectually inferior" (ignorance) to its ancestors and thus could not properly discern whether to choose to "do something right" (difficulty). As a result of the first sin, the posterity of the first humans as well as the postlapsarian Adam and Eve lost their capacity of the will to choose goodness. Then, the posterity is ethically inferior because, under the power of the difficulty of even knowing what to do and willing to do right, it is not capable of doing right. Although Augustine describes the prelapsarian state of humanity as possessing superior physical and mental ability to its posterity, it is notable that, in his later understanding, the capacity of the human will even before the fall was not independent of the grace of God.[111] The first humans were not incapable of sinning (*non posse peccare*); instead, they had only the capability not to sin (*posse non peccare*).[112] However, from the modern perspective, Augustine's etiological assumption about the state of the first humans is questionable.[113] Moreover, it is necessary to distinguish the original righteousness from the superiority of the first human beings. The fall presupposes their original righteousness; however, the biblical account of creation does not suggest the superiority of the first human beings over their posterity.

The prototypal orientation is evident in Augustine's anthropology.[114] Nevertheless, he barely traces back through the biblical accounts, instead focusing on the prelapsarian humans as the prototype of human beings. As Migliore points out, the notion of the superiority of the first humanity is mainly based on a view that fantasizes that the biblical accounts of the prelapsarian human condition are an archetype to be restored.[115] In this regard, Irenaeus of Lyons's comment is notable. Irenaeus argues that the prototypal search that attempts to identify genuine humanity with the prelapsarian Adam is far from the intention of the biblical accounts; rather, they testify to the fact that true humanity can be found only in Christ, who is the end of humanity's perfection.[116] This issue has been an ongoing point of discussion throughout the history of hamartiology in the West. The meaning of the human being is inseparably related to the doctrine of sin. Furthermore, this is a question that not only Augustine but also his theological posterity has asked, even though they take different theological premises and come to different conclusions.

In summary, in his later works, Augustine juxtaposed a new hamartiological concept, namely, concupiscence, which was derived from his biblical exegesis along with his earlier emphasis on pride. In this context, the theological challenge of Pelagianism compels him to refine his hamartiological system that resulted in the doctrine of original sin. Augustine's doctrine of original sin is distinguished in two ways. On the one hand, Augustine developed the previous Western church tradition by adding the notion of the transmission of Adam's culpability to his posterity. On the other hand, against Pelagianism, he affirmed two important theological convictions: humanity's inability to overcome sin and the limitation of the free will within the scope of predestination. The doctrine of original sin is a result of Augustine's attempt to bind the limitedness of human nature with the biological solidarity of the human race in light of his doctrine of God, in which God is understood as the supreme and highest existence. However, many later thinkers have felt it necessary to refute or reformulate this doctrine.

Conclusion

Augustine's doctrine of sin is a partial description of sin. On one level, it offers a philosophical framework in which the universality of sin and the solidarity of the human race are demonstrated against the heretical teachings of his time as well as of the present time; however, on another level it creates an opening for Western Christian pessimism in which the reconciling work of God in Christ toward humanity in this world is shadowed, chiefly by his mistaken expansion of the result of the fall and its transmission to the first human's posterity. Augustine certainly affirms the ongoing power of the Trinitarian work of God in other doctrinal loci, as in his doctrine of the church as well as of the saints; however, it is clear that the God who is defined in his essence as being, in his philosophical framework founded upon his Christianized Platonism, overwhelms the God who is testified to in Scripture as the Lord and Christ. In this perspective, Augustine's doctrine of sin and evil needs to relate more to the doctrine of Christ or find an equilibrium by adding the Christological or Trinitarian angle. To do this, his hamartiology should further emphasize the calling to ethical responsibility of the saints who already have been reconciled in Christ. This point is the focus of Augustine's theological successors, especially Luther and Bonhoeffer.

Augustine's early hamartiological thought is complicated by his search for the true God. He surely considers the God that he perceives in a Christianized Neoplatonic hierarchy as the rule for all values. In this way, his early theodicy as well as the doctrine of sin developed in close interaction with his understanding of God. His later hamartiology, represented by the doctrine of original sin, however, shows a shift from his early thought due to his integration of his biblical exegesis. However, his concept of original sin contains some theological difficulties as well as insights. There are several theological implications, which this book discusses mainly through the lenses of Lutheran thinkers, especially Luther and Bonhoeffer, in the following four chapters.

First, the Augustinian hamartiology carefully investigates humanity's hopelessness and absolute dependence on the grace of God, chiefly based on Augustine's hierarchical cosmology in relation to the transcendent God. This predominantly one-sided description seems to run the risk of theological determinism, as Augustine's critics claimed. This is primarily due to his approach to hamartiology based on his Platonized notion of the first person of the Trinity, who is explained as in God's essence rather than God's person and work in Christ. Second, Augustine's ontological and philosophical explanation of evil and sin explicates an individual soul's inner struggle on its journey to its final destination in the heavenly city of God. The doctrine teaches unfathomable difference and awe, contrasting the transcendent God and the triviality of human life in eternity; however, it does not fully emphasize the importance of the temporal life as well as the responsibility of the saints in the midst of the threat of cooperative and collective evil and sin in this world, in which Christ commands the saints to be his disciples—not in the other world in eternity but in this world. Finally, the doctrine of original sin is basically a demonstration of the universality of sin and the solidarity of humankind. It effectively affirms the universal nature of the sinfulness of humanity against theories such as those of Pelagianism, which overestimate human capacity. However, Augustine's theory needs to be discussed in regard to the power of the newly created will of the saints in which the Holy Spirit continuously creates new beings. This is especially needed in the church community, in which it is possible that Augustine's notion of alien culpability can be embraced. These issues as well as the implications of Augustine's hamartiology are the central issues that Luther and Bonhoeffer struggled with in their own circumstances and contexts, and these questions are dealt with in depth in the following chapters on Luther and Bonhoeffer.

Chapter 2

MARTIN LUTHER'S CHRISTOCENTRIC HAMARTIOLOGY

Introduction

This chapter argues that Martin Luther's hamartiology is a reinterpretation of Augustine's doctrine of original sin by shifting the starting point from Augustine's Platonically defined notion of God to his relational concept of God in Christ. It investigates Luther's Christocentric hamartiology based on his holistic and relational anthropology, which becomes the presupposition of his doctrine of sin and evil. It then examines his doctrine of sin, which contains distinctive hamartiological characteristics. This chapter functions as a pivotal juncture between the chapter on Augustine and the chapters on Dietrich Bonhoeffer. It provides an outline of Luther's hamartiology that is essential for later Lutherans' understanding of sin and evil, especially Bonhoeffer's hamartiology, which radically transforms and reformulates the Augustinian doctrine of original sin by shifting the starting point from the doctrine of God to the doctrine of the church, chiefly based on Bonhoeffer's Lutheran perspective.

As a magisterial Reformer, Luther offers a new theological angle on the understanding of sin and evil in the sixteenth century. Despite his transformative interpretation of the Augustinian doctrine of original sin, the scholarship on Luther has focused less on his hamartiology compared with other theological loci, such as his soteriology and his Christology.[1] Luther's hamartiology, however, contains important theological resources that guide the doctrinal direction of Lutherans' ethical and relational doctrine of sin. To investigate this theological connection, this chapter provides the framework as well as the details of Luther's hamartiology. His hamartiology cannot be understood properly without examining the interaction between his relational understanding of God in Christ and humanity. Accordingly, Luther's Christocentric notion of God is the premise of Luther's doctrine of sin and evil. In his early thought, aspects of Luther's hamartiology are not distinctive from Augustine's understanding, but Luther's holistic and relational anthropological reform of Augustinianism gives direction to his relational and ethical hamartiology in his theological career. In this way, characteristics of Luther's doctrine of sin and evil are primarily embedded in his anthropological emphasis, such as his focus on *totus homo* (the whole person; a holistic notion of the human being) and his relational understanding of *imago Dei* (image of God). Accordingly, Luther's anthropological reformulation leads him to rearticulate the Augustinian doctrine of original sin by actively applying his anthropological apparatus and eventually shifting the starting point of his doctrine of sin from Augustinian epistemology to existential Christocentrism.

Even though Augustine laid a solid theological basis for Western hamartiology by confirming the universality of sin and the sinful solidarity of the human race, he did not fully connect the doctrine of Christ nor the doctrine of the newly created human being to his doctrine of original sin, resulting in a contrast between the transcendental notion of God and fallen humanity. While Augustine tries to justify his doctrine of original sin within his philosophical system in connection with Scripture, Luther attempts to understand the issue of sin and evil through the relationship between the relational God in Christ and humanity, avoiding the philosophical methodology. However, in his early thought, despite the emergence of his new understanding of the human being in a holistic way, Luther's doctrine of sin was strongly bonded with the Augustinian doctrine of original sin in its logic and content. In his mature thought, however, Luther reformulates the logic as well as the content of the doctrine of original sin by applying his anthropological notion of the holistic human being and the relational image of God, who created the universe and came to the world to save humanity, to his hamartiology. Luther's mature hamartiology thus not only significantly horizontalizes or secularizes the Augustinian notion of the supreme God by focusing on the notion of God in Christ but also shifts the notion of sin from the philosophically defined notion of sin in Augustinianism to a more relational and ethical notion. Accordingly, Luther attempts to relate the doctrine of sin to the doctrines of Christ and the newly created human being, which Augustine does not fully engage in his doctrine of original sin.

This chapter starts with an examination of Luther's hermeneutical turn to Christocentrism based on which he reformulated Augustine's anthropology. In the process, the chapter investigates the significance of Luther's anthropological emphasis on the holistic understanding of the human being and the relational image of God. The second section outlines the development of Luther's doctrine of sin. It demonstrates how his anthropological apparatus was interconnected to the trajectory of Luther's doctrine of sin. Then, the chapter further investigates Christian freedom in regard to the relation between the kingdom of God and the kingdom of the world in which Luther's Christocentrism as well as his contextual exegesis is clearly reflected. The final section deals with some of the wider implications of Luther's doctrine of sin, especially as they connect to the chapters that follow.

Early Anthropological Turn

Christocentrism

It is well known that, as a pioneer of the magisterial Reformation, Luther valued the authority of Scripture more than the speculative tradition. Although Luther highly valued Augustine's theological understanding and its tradition, he preferred and appropriated Augustine's later theological understanding in which Scripture is treated as the central authority of Augustine's theological concerns. One of the distinctive traits of Luther's hermeneutics is his Christocentric exegesis. Luther does not follow Augustine's theological presupposition of the notion of God as understood in Augustine's Christianized Platonic cosmological system. Luther presupposes, as the basis of his hermeneutics, the God in Christ revealed in Scripture rather than the God who is philosophically defined. Early in 1517, in his article entitled "Disputation against Scholastic Theology," Luther heavily criticizes the medieval scholastics' philosophical dependence on theology.[2] Luther's emphasis on the Reformation axiom *sola Scriptura* (by Scripture alone) manifests not only his theological foundation but also his theological orientation from that time forward. Luther clearly rejects the speculative methodology of late medieval scholasticism, and this implies that he does not agree with the contemplative aspect of Augustine's theological approach. Even though Luther upholds the authority of Augustine in general, he does not accept the theology of Augustine in total. Luther is selective when he uses Augustine's work to support his arguments. Furthermore, he actively transforms Augustine's theological characteristics in his own way. At the center of Luther's theological attitude is his Christocentric hermeneutics. Luther's reformulation of Augustine's theology is clearly reflected in his anthropology, which ultimately leads him to construct his own doctrine of sin.

Holistic anthropology

Although Augustine's anthropological basis is inseparably related to his concept of the image of God, who is considered the highest Being, in the human soul,[3] Luther's anthropological foundation is more the relational image of God in Christ, who created the universe and was incarnated as a human being. Admittedly, Luther's approach is more existential than that of Augustine, who was heavily dependent on philosophical methodology. Luther conceives that the human person should be understood in a holistic way without separating soul from body.[4] Luther's notion of the whole person is a distinctive starting point of his anthropology that is clearly distinguished from the dichotomic anthropology of scholasticism and ultimately from Augustinianism.[5] Luther uses the term *totus homo* primarily to indicate how the biblical teaching differs from the scholastic anthropology.[6] Luther's theological point is his conviction that the power of the soul per se cannot be considered a genuine human being; in other words, the soul itself cannot be considered a whole person. Luther's holistic anthropology is a radical shift from scholasticism as well as early Augustinianism.[7] Luther seems to rely more on Augustine's later doctrine of sin in which body and soul are more closely discussed. Furthermore, this indicates a significant shift from the early Augustine as well as the later Augustine in Luther's anthropology. As discussed in Chapter 1, this is because Augustine was not explicit about the essence of the human being but opened a way to interpret it in diverse ways. Based on this theological context, Luther proceeds to formulate his anthropology in a holistic or whole way.

Although he relies heavily on the anthropology of Augustine, Luther transforms the Augustinian anthropology, chiefly in light of his Christocentric hermeneutics of Scripture, to repudiate the anthropology of scholasticism. Luther's holistic doctrine of the human being emerges in his early thought. Passages in Luther's lectures on Romans written in 1515/1516 demonstrate the emergence of the hermeneutical lens of "the whole person," referred to as *totus homo*. Luther writes:

> For he is at the same time both a sinner and a righteous man; a sinner in fact, but a righteous man by the sure imputation and promise of God that He will continue to deliver him from sin until He has completely cured him. And thus he is *entirely* healthy in hope, but in fact he is still a sinner; but he has the beginning of righteousness, so that he continues more and more always to seek it, yet he realizes that he is *always* unrighteous.[8]

Here, Luther clearly identifies the human being in a holistic way in which soul and body are not separated. The distinctive point is that Luther's references to the whole person are coupled with the notion of *simul iustus et peccator* (simultaneously righteous and a sinner). It is noteworthy that although Luther appropriated Augustine's ecclesial concept of "the whole Christ"[9] for his totalistic notion of the human being, Augustine did not closely relate his anthropology to Christology nor to ecclesiology.

For Luther, a person who is *simul iustus et peccator* is righteous before God by "the sure imputation and promise of God." Here, Luther introduces the concept of imputation to his anthropological notion of the "whole person." This indicates that Luther relates Augustine's ecclesial notion of *totus Christus* (the whole Christ) to his understanding of human person, especially one who is a member of the church.[10] Luther reformulates Augustine's ecclesial concept of the whole Christ to connect the righteousness of Christ to the righteousness of the members of the church. In his lectures on Romans 7, Luther deals with the dual status of a person as *coram Deo* (before God) and *coram hominibus* (before human beings).[11] He asserts that "they are sinners in fact, but righteous in hope."[12] It is evident that the notion of the "whole person" is closely related to his new understanding of the imputation of Christ's righteousness and that the formula of *simul iustus et peccator* corresponds to the reality of sin in a saint even after their baptism or conversion.[13]

After his treatise *Two Kinds of Righteousness* (1518/1519), Luther actively modifies Augustine's notion of *totus Christus* in accordance with the shift in his Reformational soteriology.[14] As Erik Hermann points out, the starting point of the divergence from the anthropology of Augustine as well as that of the scholastics is Luther's own reading of Scripture.[15] One of the crucial exegeses in regard to his anthropological transition is his distinction between *spiritus* (spirit) and *caro* (flesh), which reformulates the dichotomic distinction between soul and body. Unlike Augustine, who attempted to find the human essence in the human soul in the frame of soul and body rooted in Platonic cosmology, Luther approaches to human identity primarily through the Pauline distinction between *spiritus* and *caro*.¹⁶ Luther interprets both *spiritus* and *caro* as referring to the whole person. Paul Althaus summarizes this by noting that "it is not as though he [the human being] were partially righteous and partially a sinner but rather he is completely a sinner and completely righteous."¹⁷ It is significant that Luther interprets the terms *spiritus* and *caro* in two ways, first as a whole person and second as aspects of human faculties. For example, he explains the two different anthropological categories of *caro* in *The Bondage of the Will* written in 1525:

> Wherever flesh is treated as in opposition to spirit, you can generally take flesh to mean everything that is contrary to the Spirit, as [in Jn. 6:63]: 'The flesh is of no avail.' But where flesh is treated on its own, you may take it that it signifies the bodily constitution and nature, as for example: 'They shall be two in one flesh' [Matt. 19:5]; 'My flesh is food indeed' [Jn. 6:55]; or 'The Word became flesh' [Jn. 1:14].¹⁸

Luther argues that *flesh* signifies two different meanings in the Scripture. First, it means the opposite of the sense of spirit as Luther uses the term in his anthropological category of *spiritus* and *caro* as the whole person. As Alister McGrath points out, Luther's distinction between *spiritus* and *caro* does not apply to any lower or higher human faculty but to the whole person.¹⁹ Luther's distinction between *spiritus* and *caro* implies that the human person cannot be considered partially body and partially soul before God. Thus, it is evident that Luther's anthropological notion of *spiritus* and *caro* is strongly connected to his doctrine of justification. Luther's concern regarding the human identity is primarily based on his perspective of justification. Second, Luther argues that the two terms *spiritus* and *caro* are also used to mean spirit and body, indicating the faculties of the whole person.²⁰ In this two-tiered anthropology, Luther argues that the faculties of the human being should be discussed under the dimension of the whole person as either the person of *spiritus* in Christ or the person of *caro* outside of Christ. Luther argues that only the person of *spiritus* who has the Holy Spirit undergoes the struggle as *simul iustus et peccator*.²¹ As Notger Slenczka notes, Luther disassociates himself from the schema of the inner and outer beings of scholasticism that understands a person, in his view, from partial angles.²² Luther explains that neither the inner being nor the outer being can be treated as a whole person by itself. Whereas both scholasticism and Augustinianism designate the human identity as residing in the human soul, Luther treats the category of flesh and spirit as under the category of the whole person represented by *spiritus* and *caro*; the person of *spiritus* undergoes a struggle between the two poles as *simul iustus et peccator*. For Luther, the concept of *totus homo* with the *simul* formula more effectively explains the human identity *coram Deo* as well as *coram hominibus*.²³

Luther views *totus homo* as a consistent and thorough interpretation of the human being on the basis of Scripture, but he seeks to solve the problem of sin that is found even in a person of *spiritus*. Although Luther radically defines the human being in his new Christocentric way in which he distinguishes *spiritus* and *caro* as each a whole person, he does not miss the point that a person of *spiritus* is also a sinner in reality. In a similar vein, Luther's doctrine of *simul* is related to the human sinful reality even after baptism or conversion.[24] Although Luther does not agree with the scholastic concept of the sacrament as *ex opere operato* (from the work performed), similar to Augustine, he believes that baptism is connected to the remission of original sin.[25] Both Augustine and Luther believe that the original sin is cleansed by baptism but that the sin represented as concupiscence is not removed. At this stage, Luther's understanding of *simul* is oriented in a new way in which Luther relates the empirical reality of sin with *simul iustus et peccator* as the sub-status of the whole person in Christ. Althaus describes this tension in the whole person of *spiritus* as follows: "[The] contradiction involved in being a righteous man and a sinner 'at one and the same time' does not cease in this life but continues until death."[26] It is clear that Luther's holistic anthropology eliminates the possibility of infusion that scholasticism and Augustinianism had supported. More precisely, Luther's *simul* formula after *Two Kinds of Righteousness* does not signify the progressive development of the human being toward perfection, such as in Platonism, but focuses on the inability of the human being to be righteous. L'ubomir Batka summarizes this point—that for Luther "the passivity of being born into sin is equal to the passivity of becoming righteous."[27]

In short, Luther's early turn to Christocentric exegesis leads him to reformulate Augustine's later anthropology in a holistic way. Unlike Augustine's dichotomic understanding of the human being, Luther interprets the Pauline notion of a person—as *spiritus* and *caro*—through two different anthropological categories: as both whole persons on one level and two kinds of human faculties on the other level. Subsequently, this anthropological shift of Luther away from scholasticism as well as Augustinianism becomes interconnected with the development of his understanding of sin and evil in his mature thought.

Relational imago Dei

Luther's transformative holistic anthropology leads him to interpret the traditional understanding of *imago Dei* in a new way. His anthropological insight related to the concept of *totus homo* rooted in his Reformation discovery of the imputation of *iustitia Christi* (the righteousness of Christ) leads him to approach the *imago Dei* from a different angle. For Augustine, the rational soul of the human being reflects the triadic residue of *imago Dei*—memory, intellect, and will—even after the fall.[28] Furthermore, among the triadic residual substances in the human soul, the intellect or reason has not been totally extinguished.[29] This vestige is the basis for placing the human being in a higher position in the order of creation and, more importantly, for the possibility that the human being has to go up toward the supreme God. However, Luther's interpretation of the Genesis account is far from Augustine's standpoint. Luther is pessimistic about *analogia entis* (analogy of being) as the explanation of *imago Dei*. In his lectures on Genesis in 1535, Luther says:

> Therefore that image of God was something most excellent, in which were included eternal life, everlasting *freedom from fear*, and everything that is good.

However, through sin this image was so obscured and corrupted that *we cannot grasp it* even with our *intellect*.[30]

Luther interprets the Genesis account as signifying that the human intellect is also under the devastating power of the fall.[31] As Bayer points out, Luther's description of *imago Dei* is substantially based on his soteriological perspective,[32] using the vocabulary of justification such as "eternal life" and "freedom from fear." Admittedly, Luther's understanding of the image of God is more relational and directional. Luther explains:

> Therefore my understanding of the image of God is this: that Adam had it in his being and that he not only knew God and believed that He was good, but that *he also lived in a life that was wholly godly*; that is, he was without the fear of death or of any other danger, and was content with God's favor.[33]

Luther does not endeavor to find ontological similarities between God and humanity;[34] rather, he conceives of the *righteous relationality* per se between God in Christ and humanity and among human beings as *imago Dei*. Luther explains the meaning of a godly person relationally from his soteriological perspective.

Luther does not mention any aspect of *analogia entis* except for relational righteousness as the content of *imago Dei* rooted in the concept of *iustitia Dei* (righteousness of God).[35] For Luther, the creation is not only the act *ad extra* (toward the outside) of God but also the act of God's freedom to relate. In other words, although God is self-sufficient, God created the universe with God's free choice.[36] In this way, for Luther, the capacity to relate to others is a chief aspect of the divine image of the human being as revealed in the life and work of God in Christ.[37] Luther perceives that this "relational act" of God in creation reveals the meaning of the *imago Dei*. God's willingness to relate to that which is not God is evident in the creation, and only the human being bears this aspect of the *imago Dei*. For Luther, the relation between God and human is the first and the most fundamental aspect of the *imago Dei*. Furthermore, this relational aspect of the *imago Dei* is not isolated from the other relation of the *imago Dei*, namely that between oneself and one's neighbor.[38] He argues that "in Adam there was an enlightened reason, a true knowledge of God, and a most sincere desire to love *God* and *his neighbor*."[39] It is significant that the relational *imago Dei* is not only vertical but also horizontal.

Iustitia (righteousness) is one of the central images of God for Luther,[40] and this image of righteousness is extended to the relational role of the human being toward God and other human beings and, furthermore, toward the rest of creation. In this way, the *imago Dei* is the *capacity*[41] of the human being to reach out and relate properly to God, neighbors, and other creatures, but this is lost after the fall. In fact, it is Augustine who already defines the first sin as Adam's "turning away" from God as the original relationality; however, Augustine does not directly consider this human relationality per se as the *imago Dei*. The relational and ethical concept of *imago Dei* is abundant in Luther's work, and his doctrine of *imago Dei* supplies the logic and theological language for the Lutherans' later development of anthropology as well as hamartiology.

In short, Luther's anthropological reformulation of *totus homo* and the relational *imago Dei* shows his detachment from scholasticism as well as the early philosophically oriented notion of Augustine in favor of the later Augustinian doctrine in which the human is understood in a more holistic way as body and soul; however, Luther's Christocentrism clearly distinguishes his theological standpoint from Augustine's starting point in epistemology. Furthermore, his relational concept of the *imago Dei* as rooted in God's relationality to humanity revealed in Christ clearly paves to the way for the later Lutherans and Bonhoeffer's ethical and relational anthropology as well as hamartiology.

The Trajectory of Sin

Luther's doctrine of sin can only be understood in close interaction with the development of Luther's anthropology. As mentioned in the preceding section, Luther appropriated Augustine mainly to refute scholasticism, but Luther's transformative reworking of Augustinian anthropology ultimately resulted in new theological conclusions in Luther's hamartiology, in its both form and content.

Pride

Luther's early hamartiology has affinities with Augustine's hamartiology. Luther's reading of Psalm 51 and Romans becomes the central lens by which he assesses not only the teachings of scholasticism but also the Augustinian doctrine of original sin.[42] As early as his lectures on Psalm 51 in 1513–15, Luther considers "pride" the essence of the original sin, similar to Augustine's thought.[43] Luther interprets Psalm 51 as meaning that the most prominent sin is hubris, from which all other sins branch out. This pride evidently comes from Augustine's notion of *homo incurvatus in se* (man turned in upon himself).[44] This egocentric self-love is in opposition to love of God and neighbor, and this self-love is no other than the original sin.[45] The curving of the human nature toward the self is a fundamental characteristic of the postlapsarian person. Luther's early understanding of original sin as pride is changed by his new interpretation of law and the gospel.[46] Despite his emphasis on pride in his early work, Luther soon abandons pride as the overarching concept of sin but considers it one of the distinctive aspects of sin because of his anthropological reworking. This egocentricity, however, becomes *cantus firmus* throughout his work as one of the main aspects of sin after the fall.

Concupiscence

Then, in his lectures on Romans in 1515/1516, Luther's understanding of sin begins to be closely related to his anthropological claims of *simul iustus et peccator* together with the holistic notion of *totus homo*. Luther's holistic anthropology is interconnected with the early form of *simul iustus et peccator*, which contains the trait of progressiveness found in Augustinian soteriology. However, this anthropological transition signifies that Luther is reflecting his Christocentric hermeneutics by relating the imputation of *iustitia Christi* to his anthropological notion of *totus homo*. This holistic anthropology leads him to focus on a more holistic concept of original sin over Augustine's emphasis on pride or concupiscence that contains overtones of a faculty-based anthropology.[47] The theological meaning of this turn is not minor. One of the most important changes involved in this turn lies in Luther's holistic interpretation of "concupiscence."

Luther receives Augustine's doctrine of concupiscence chiefly as a theological alternative to the scholastic understanding of sin as *peccata actualia* (sinful deeds), which treats sin externally in close connection with the sacraments as *ex opere operato*.[48] Luther's reception of concupiscence proceeds in his own way against scholasticism by appropriating the later Augustine, who considers concupiscence per se as the original sin.[49] One of Luther's disagreements with the medieval scholastics in regard to the doctrine of sin is the issue of sin after baptism. Luther perceives the guilt of original sin as forgiven in baptism but remaining in reality, in a similar fashion to Augustine. However, Luther perceives the remission of original sin in baptism through his new Christocentric understanding of "the alien righteousness of Christ." In fact, Luther's newly emerged two-tiered anthropology of *totus homo* as *simul iustus et peccator* effectively explains the issue of sin remaining in a justified person even after baptism. At this stage, Luther equates concupiscence as the original sin, but he interprets concupiscence as the act of a whole person, thus embracing both the spiritual and physical aspects of concupiscence in a similar way to Augustine's late hamartiology.[50]

Thus, in Luther's holistic perspective, concupiscence affects the human being both spiritually and physically. For Luther, the original sin is forgiven by God's imputation, but in reality the power of concupiscence remains. Luther argues:

> This concupiscence toward evil remains, and no one is ever cleansed of it, not even the one-day-old infant. But the mercy of God is that this does remain and yet is not imputed as sin to those who call upon Him and cry out for His deliverance. ... Thus in ourselves we are sinners, and yet through faith we are righteous by God's imputation.[51]

Luther's description of concupiscence resonates with the Augustinian concept of concupiscence, but it is decisively within the boundary of *totus homo* and the *simul* formula. Luther recognizes "concupiscence toward evil" as the human condition that cannot be overcome until death. Luther interprets concupiscence not only as the universality of sin but also as the original sin. At this point, he argues that the inherited inclination of the human being after the fall "does remain and yet is not imputed as sin to those who called upon Him."[52] Luther understands the postlapsarian sinful inclination based on the *simul* formula. It is important to read Luther's understanding of concupiscence in the context of his two-tiered anthropological lens:

> As the ancient holy fathers so correctly said, this original sin is the very tinder of sin, the law of the flesh, the original sickness. ... Thus this is Hydra, a many-headed and most tenacious monster, with which we struggle in the Lernean Swamp of this life till the very day of our death.[53]

Here, Luther's concept of concupiscence is both spiritual and physical, in other words, both original sin and actual sin. For Luther, concupiscence is the total person's sin and sinfulness. As Batka points out, as Luther's Reformation theology deepens, his use of the term *original sin* expresses the notion of the universal sinfulness of the human being in a general sense.[54] Although Luther uses the term *original sin*, his description signifies both original sin and the universality of sin. Furthermore, Luther does not separate the first sin of Adam and the universal sinfulness of all human beings. It is notable that Luther's description of original sin encompasses the past and the present. In his *Against Latomus* in 1521, Luther summarizes his position more clearly:

> Paul calls that which remains after baptism sin; the fathers call it a weakness and imperfection, rather than sin. Here we stand at the parting of the ways. I follow Paul, and you the fathers—with the exception of Augustine, who generally calls it by the blunt names of fault and iniquity.[55]

Although it is debated whether Luther was mistaken in claiming that Augustine was on his side,[56] Luther clearly refused to interpret concupiscence as just a neutral factor, such as "a weakness and imperfection," but instead viewed it as the original sin and the universal sinfulness of the human being. At this transitional stage, his terminology related to concupiscence reflects his anthropological formula of *totus homo* as *simul iustus et peccator*, merging the original sin and the universal sinfulness of the total human being. This tendency to integrate the original sin of Adam and the universality of sin is found in all his theological writings.

Unbelief

In Luther's mature theological stage, his understanding of sin is more closely connected to his other important anthropological tool, the relational image of God. Luther's own understanding of *imago Dei* appears in his mature theological career as a main hermeneutical lens for reading Scripture. In his mature work, as in the lectures on Genesis given in 1535, the relational *imago Dei* becomes Luther's main hermeneutical apparatus for the doctrine of sin along with the *totus homo*. Luther focuses very strongly on the relational concept of sin as original sin, paraphrased as *peccatum radicale* (radical sin). He considers *peccatum radicale* the broken relationality between God and humanity and, in this line of thought, for

Luther the chief sin is *unbelief*. In his exegesis of Genesis in 1535, Luther argues that the original sin is unbelief. He explains:

> [Satan] does not immediately try to allure Eve by means of the loveliness of the fruit. He first attacks man's greatest strength, faith in the Word. Therefore the root and source of sin is unbelief and turning away from God, just as, on the other hand, the source and root of righteousness is faith. Satan first draws away from faith to unbelief.[57]

On the one hand, unbelief is definitely the most quintessential counter notion in Luther's concept of faith. On the other hand, as righteous relationality is the primary foundation of the *imago Dei* over any ontological qualities of the human being, Luther's mature doctrine of *peccatum radicale* is encapsulated in a more theological and relational concept of sin, which is unbelief. In this way, unbelief represents his mature hamartiological concern related to the human standing *coram Deo* in Christ as well as *coram hominibus*. Thus, the greatest sin is unbelief, which is the source of broken relationality. Luther views righteous relationality per se as the original righteousness, which can be restored in the person of *spiritus* as part of the body of Christ. Luther emphasizes that the righteous relationality can be restored in a saint in this life through the gospel.[58] Despite this restoration, however, the saint undergoes a struggle between the righteous person and the sinner.

In summary, Luther develops his interpretation of the doctrine of original sin in parallel with his revision of Augustinian anthropology. In this process, Luther identifies the original sin as pride, concupiscence, and finally unbelief, reflecting his major anthropological angles of the *totus homo* and the relational *imago Dei*. Apparently, Luther's doctrine of original sin does not go beyond the Augustinian logic in its structure. This is because Luther basically follows Augustine's interpretation of Adam and Eve's first sin as the original sin and the transmission of the culpability of the first sin to their posterity. On the one hand, however, Luther's hermeneutical center in Christ, as in his anthropology, implies a crucial theological meaning because he talks about the doctrine of sin from a Christocentric standpoint. On the other hand, Luther is beginning to collapse the distinction between the original sin and the universal sinfulness of the human being in his mature thought. Furthermore, Luther's identification of the original sin as the broken relationality between God and humanity as well as between human beings opens a way for his theological posterity to develop a social and communal as well as ethical hamartiology.

The Bound Will and Freedom in Christ

Having sketched the trajectory of Luther's concept of sin, it is now necessary to extend the scope of this chapter to the issue of freedom of the will because it is essential to the discussion in later chapters of the boundary between human freedom and responsibility developed by later Lutherans, especially Bonhoeffer.

Luther's turn to Augustinianism signifies that his primary theological focus was on his advocacy of humanity's absolute dependence on the grace of God and this became the premise of his theological considerations. Accordingly, it is necessary to engage with Luther's way of thinking in which he distinguishes two dimensions of the freedom of the will. In a similar fashion to Luther's two-tiered anthropology, Luther's understanding of this freedom can be grasped clearly when one sees it through the frame of the two different categorical angles of the *totus homo* and the relational *imago Dei*. On the primary level, Luther discusses the free choice of the will in the perspective of soteriology as in a case of the treatise against Erasmus through his anthropological angle of *totus homo* and *simul iustus et peccator*. On the secondary level, Luther discusses the responsibility of the will in the other anthropological category of the relational *imago Dei*. This section illustrates these two different categorical discussions of Luther as follows.

First, from the early theological stage, Luther deals with the issue of the free choice of the will as a dialectic tension in a justified person. In this period, Luther's point of discussion is focused on the freedom of a justified person rather than on the freedom of all human beings in general. As discussed above, Luther's concept of *totus homo* already emerges with his subcategorical formula of *simul*. Although his doctrine of the free will is discussed in detail in his treatise entitled *The Bondage of the Will* written in 1525, Luther's understanding of the will is firmly joined with his anthropology of *totus homo*, especially after his treatise *Two Kinds of Righteousness* published in 1519. Luther conceives that the freedom of the justified person can be explained with the formula of *simul iustus et peccator*. In his treatise *The Freedom of a Christian* written in 1520, Luther's dual perspective on the freedom of the will is clearly demonstrated:

> I shall set down the following two propositions concerning the freedom and the bondage of the spirit: A Christian is a perfectly free lord of all, subject to none. A Christian is a perfectly dutiful servant of all, subject to all. These two theses seem to contradict each other. If, however, they should be found to fit together they would serve our purpose beautifully.[59]

In the above quote, Luther distinguishes two different kinds of categories of the will: *freedom* and *bondage*. According to this dialectic perspective of Luther, a Christian person is not only free before God but also bound before human beings. Clearly, Luther's understanding of the freedom of the will is linked with his anthropological logic of the whole human being and with the *simul* formula. One of the distinctive aspects of Luther's approach from Augustinianism to the freedom of the will is found in his emphasis on the newly produced *freedom* and *servitude* of the justified person. Once more, Luther's foundation for the freedom and servitude of the will is firmly linked with his anthropological concept of imputation rooted in "the alien righteousness of Christ." This *extrinsic* feature of Luther's concept of the freedom and servitude of the will distinguishes his view from the Augustinian perspective on the internal nature of freedom of the will.

For Luther, the will of a Christian is simultaneously free and bound due to the relationality between *totus homo* and *simul iustus et peccator*. Distinctively, these qualities of freedom and servitude are controlled by the individual's relation to Christ as either *in Christo* (in Christ) or *de Christo* (away from Christ). Clearly, Luther's concept of *simul* is explained in this dialectic connection between the two aspects of the will of the Christian. Although the person of *spiritus* has freedom by the imputation of the righteousness of God in Christ, Luther considers that this freedom functions properly only when the person is in the Spirit of Christ. This implies that the justified person always has the possibility to abuse the freedom when the person is outside of the spiritual boundary of Christ. In this way, the freedom of the person is dependent on the relationality between the person and Christ. Luther continues by demonstrating this point. He says, "Because of this diversity of nature the Scriptures assert contradictory things concerning the same man, since these two men in the same man contradict each other."[60] Even though Luther's focus on the freedom of the will is concerned with both the soteriological freedom before God and ethical responsibility or servitude before other human beings, the former aspect has been highlighted as a symbol of Luther's theology in general. Thus, it is necessary to focus on this less emphasized aspect of the doctrine of the will that becomes the fountain of later Lutherans' ethical and relational interpretation of Luther's theology. This ethical interpretation of the freedom of the will is more closely discussed in the later part of this section dealing with Luther's mature doctrine of the freedom of the will, which is transformed by his relational doctrine of *imago Dei*.

Luther's understanding of the freedom of the will contains clear traits of Reformation soteriology. In his treatise *The Bondage of the Will* written in 1525, Luther definitely articulates his theological position on the freedom of the will. At the first glance, Luther's logic in the treatise is similar to Augustine's later thoughts on the free will, especially in its frame of the doctrines of predestination and grace. In his mature theology, Augustine places the will of the human being under the category of grace and the predestination of God. In a shift from his earlier thinking, Augustine contends that the will was not absolutely free even before the fall. In a similar way to Augustine against Pelagianism, Luther refutes Erasmus's suggestion of the role of the human being's will in salvation. As David M. Whitford points out, the issue between Luther and Erasmus was "the degree to which the human will played a role in that process of salvation."[61] It is evident that the point of controversy between Luther and Erasmus was on the role of the will in salvation rather than the function of the will in everyday life. As Augustine articulates that the will is totally bound by sin after the fall, Luther conceives that the will of the human being is bound by sin. Furthermore, he argues that by definition there is no free will.[62] Luther radicalizes Augustine's position on the will by appropriating Augustine's later doctrine of the freedom of the human will, arguing that "[a] lost liberty... is not liberty at all."[63] At this point, similar to Augustine, Luther defines the freedom of the will in a deterministic way.[64]

In this polemical thesis, Luther insists that there is no true free will of the human being but only "mutable-will."[65] For Luther, the mutable will of the human being is incompatible with the will of God. As Gerhard Müller points out, "Luther's concern was simple: 'It is impossible by any means to fulfill the law without the grace of God.'"[66] Evidently, Luther's point here concerns the role of the will in regard to justification before God. While Erasmus does not exclude the function of the will in salvation even as a secondary cause, Luther rejects any function of the work of the human will in salvation.[67] It is clear that Luther's intention is to maximize the grace of God in salvation, preventing any notion of synergism. Similar to the later Augustine, Luther firmly advocates the total incapability of the will regarding salvation. Indeed, at the conclusion of *The Bondage of the Will*, he attributes this point again to Augustine.[68] Luther's contention is based on Augustine's later doctrine of the total depravity of the human being; however, a transformative anthropological change from Augustinianism is also evident in his new way of understanding in which the human being is explained in the formula of *totus homo* as *simul iustus et peccator*. Luther defines the will of the human being as the "mutable-will" because the will of the human being is incapable of attaining salvation. However, one should notice that this radical definition of the will reflects merely one aspect of the two-tiered human will: that of *totus homo* as *simul iustus et peccator*. The servitude or responsibility of the human will, which is the other aspect of *totus homo* as *simul iustus et peccator*, needs to be explicated.

In Luther's mature theology, the early dual understanding of the will expressed in the tension of *simul iustus et peccator* continues and intensifies with his relational understanding of *imago Dei*. Although Luther's deterministic definition of the will is to maximize the grace of God, as in his treatise *The Bondage of the Will*, the less highlighted emphasis on the servitude of the will needs to be discussed more precisely. For Luther, the bondage or servitude of the will can be translated in two ways according to the context. First, it means the will's orientation toward sin and evil.[69] Second, it signifies free servitude or responsibility toward others in a case of the person of *spiritus*. As discussed above, for Luther, the image of God is primarily relational rather than substantial. In short, on the one hand, Luther's radical denial of the freedom of the will functions as the safeguard of the totality of sin.[70] On the other hand, Luther explains the capacity of the will not only in the tension of the *simul* formula but also in the horizontal relationality of the justified toward others as *imago Dei*.

For Luther, the bondage of the will signifies the human being's inborn orientation toward evil and sin. Luther argues that this sinful orientation is not removed by the imputation of the righteousness of God. He explains the circumstances of the justified person:

> For if God be in us, Satan is from us, and it is present with us to will nothing but good. But if God be not in us, Satan is in us, and it is present with us to will evil only. Neither God nor Satan admit of a mere abstracted willing in us; but, as you yourself rightly said, when our liberty is lost we are compelled to serve sin: that is we will sin and evil, we speak sin and evil, we do sin and evil.[71]

There are two realms of the justified. The justified person is always between two lords—Christ and Satan.[72] One of the distinctive points of Luther's thought in relation to human responsibility is his firm understanding of Christ's real presence with the believer and the resulting capacity of the human will to exercise its freedom. Luther argues that "if God be in us, Satan is from us, and it is present with us to will nothing but good." Even in the state of the simultaneity of being righteous and sinner, Luther allows room for the free choice of the will of the justified.[73] Luther states that "[a] Christian is a perfectly free lord of all, subject to none. A Christian is a perfectly dutiful servant of all, subject to all."[74] When a believer is with Christ, the servitude of the will toward sin becomes servitude to others. The freedom of the will activates when the believer is with Christ. This theme of the freedom of the will becomes clearer when it is seen in connection with Luther's anthropological lens of the relational *imago Dei*.

As in the theology of Augustine, Luther has theological difficulty explaining the relationality between the external and passive nature of justification and the human responsibility toward the world. Wolfhart Pannenberg properly points out this theological complexity embedded in the issue of free will. He argues:

> Two such reasons are to be mentioned above all: the interest in upholding the responsibility of man for his actions and the closely related question of explaining the origin of evil in God's good creation. Every rejection of the free will on theological grounds must do justice to both of these problems.[75]

As Pannenberg notes, Luther needs to address the relation between justification by faith alone and the ethical responsibility of the human being. The solution to this dilemma is found in Luther's relational understanding of *imago Dei*. In his Genesis interpretation, in a similar vein to his necessitarian logic, Luther considers freedom itself as the divine image of God.[76] Creation itself is the free act of God, and the origin of the freedom of the human will is in God. As in his two-tiered anthropological schema, Luther interprets freedom in two ways. First and primarily, freedom means soteriological or juridical freedom or, in other words, freedom from the fear of eternal death.[77] Second, freedom means voluntary relationality with others.[78] Again, this freedom of the human being for Luther is given from outside.[79] This external orientation of the human will contrasts with the human sinful nature of *cor incurvatum in se* (heart curved in upon itself), which designates one of the chief characteristics of sin as egoism or pride.

Luther perceives this directional understanding of freedom of the will from Augustine's doctrine of free will in which the will of the human being is oriented after the fall to something other than God. While for Augustine sin is the human will's turning away from God who is the supreme Good and turning to the inferior good, for Luther sin is the will of the whole human being's turning inward upon the self, breaking the relationality with others.[80] Augustine's downward orientation of the sinful will has been interpreted as Luther's inward turning of the will of the sinful *totus homo*. This focus on the outward orientation of a Christian person was intensified by Luther's successors. For Luther, the core image of God is God's relationality to something other than God revealed in God's work of creation. This concept of *creatio ad extra* (creation toward the outside) is the essence of *imago Dei* for Luther. Bayer insightfully points out a distinctive aspect of Luther's understanding of *imago Dei*. For Luther, "[T]he image of God for the human being consists in the fact that the individual is the representative (vicarious) of God and is the one responsible for carrying out his mandates on earth."[81] Luther perceives that the newly created capacity of the will of the believer is detected in its outward orientation both eschatologically and existentially. It is clear that the free and *voluntary outwardness of the freedom* of the human being becomes the source of later Lutherans' ethical and relational interpretation of Luther's theology.

Luther distinguishes between two different spheres of the will—*freedom* and *bondage*—and thus the Christian person is not only free before God but is also bound before human beings. Luther's coupled concept of freedom and bondage extends to the church's relation to the world. The relation between church and state, namely the idea of two kingdoms or two governments, emerges here.[82] Luther's idea of two kingdoms is definitely rooted in Augustine's distinction between *civitas Dei* (the city of God) and *civitas terrena* (the earthly city). For Augustine, the *civitas Dei* in the world means the spiritual realm in which God rules over the genuine members of the earthly church even though the ultimate destination of this church is heaven.[83] This comparison or opposition between the city of God and the earthly city is none other than the relation between *amor sui* (love of self) and *amor Dei* (love of God). The *civitas terrena* is bound by self-love in original sin and is opposed to the *civitas Dei* in which the saints of the experiential church make the pilgrimage toward the heavenly city. Luther uses the idea of Augustine's two cities in his own way to explicate the relation between church and government or saints and government in this world.[84]

Although Augustine's concept of "city" was definitely formed to defend Christianity in the context of the sacking of Rome against charges that Christians were responsible for the fall of the city, the distinction was used to clarify Christianity's relationship to the temporal order or as a means for the emperor and the pope to gain legitimacy over another power, especially in the medieval era.[85] However, Luther's interpretation of the two kingdoms reveals theologically important revisions to the doctrine of Augustine as well as of the medieval theory, chiefly in two directions: the horizontalization or secularization of both kingdoms and the Christocentric interpretation. Whereas Augustine posited spiritual and temporal cities vertically in a hierarchical cosmology, as in earth and in heaven, Luther placed both kingdoms in this world.[86]

In this regard, Eric Leland Saak's analysis of Luther's understanding of the church is noteworthy. Saak argues that Luther "equated the City of God with the Church."[87] As Saak points out, for Luther the city of God primarily means the church in this world.[88] In a shift from Augustine's distinction between *civitas dei* and *civitas terrena*, Luther distinguishes the internal church from the external church.[89] Saak summarizes the relationship between the internal church and the external church as follows: "[For Luther, t]he spiritual, internal Church is hidden, whereas the visible Church according to the body (*caro*) is manifest."[90] Cleary, Luther's two churches are related to each other in hidden and manifest ways. The focal point of Luther's shift from Augustine's ecclesial notion is that the two churches are related in this world. As Lohse notes, this is Luther's existential turn from Augustine's ontological and ascetic perspective to this world. Luther's positing of two churches in this world clearly shows Luther's disassociation with Augustine's as well as scholastics' theological starting point in epistemology. Furthermore, Luther explicitly makes Christ the theological focal point of his two-kingdom discussion by replacing Augustine's heavenly city of God with the earthly church in which Christ is placed at the center of the church community. Clearly, this methodological revision was the theological premise of Bonhoeffer's hamartiology as a Lutheran, which is dealt with in detail in subsequent chapters.

Luther's idea in regard to the relation between church and state is well articulated in his 1523 treatise *Temporal Authority: To What Extent It Should Be Obeyed*.[91] The primary purpose of the article was to demarcate the limits of power between the civil authority and the church. Luther distinguishes two kingdoms, similar to Augustine's distinction between the kingdom of God and the kingdom of the world, but the boundary between the two kingdoms of Luther is quite different from Augustine's theory.[92] A distinctive trait of Luther's description of the two kingdoms compared to the position of Augustine is that Luther more explicitly articulates that both kingdoms are under the ordination of God. Luther clarifies that the two kingdoms function in different ways: through love in the kingdom of God and through the sword in the kingdom of the world. Luther advocates the natural law of God as the basis of civil authority and even of heathen rulers.[93] As Michael P. DeJonge points out, Luther maintains the middle position between two biblical alternatives—between Romans 13 and the Sermon on the Mount.[94] This means that love is the rule for the spiritual kingdom and that the sword is the means by which the worldly kingdom governs its citizens. On the one hand, Luther supplies theological legitimacy for the civil authority's use of the sword; on the other hand, he suggests that Christians should limit their freedom under the civil power. Luther argues:

> Because the sword is most beneficial and necessary for the whole world in order to preserve peace, punish sin, and restrain the wicked, the Christian submits most willingly to the rule of the sword, pays his taxes, honors those in authority, serves, helps, and does all he can to assist the governing authority, that it may continue to function and be held in honor and fear.[95]

Luther's functional separation of the two kingdoms is applied clearly in the case of the peasants' revolt. In Luther's perspective, the peasants were "acting against this [two-kingdoms] law" and were "worse than heathen or Turks."[96] However, this position of Luther is a radical change from his earlier advocacy of the right of the saints to resist the fallen Roman Catholic Church. This point is crucial for Luther as well as the peasants because the peasants were claiming Luther's early Reformation logic of resistance as their theological basis for opposing existing social and ecclesiastical institutions.⁹⁷ In the face of the Peasants' War, however, Luther insisted that the peasants should limit their freedom under the civil authority, arguing that the authority of the civil state was bestowed by God through the natural law.⁹⁸ In part, Luther's description of the two kingdoms seems to function in his context against the peasants' claim of Christian freedom, but the issue becomes more complicated when it is applied to Christians or people who are in different political and social circumstances, as in the case of those who are under unjust governments or authorities. The boundary between the two kingdoms seems to be clear for Luther at this point; however, it needs to be re-addressed in other circumstances, such as in the case of Nazism. This issue is more closely discussed in Chapter 5, which deals with Bonhoeffer's later ethics that actively reformulates the Western understanding of the relation between church and state.

In summary, Luther's notion of free will also follows his anthropological twofold notion of *totus homo* as *simul iustus et peccator* and the relational *imago Dei*. The will of the saint is simultaneously free before God but bound before human beings. The imputation or covering of Christ's righteousness makes the saint completely righteous before God. Luther perceives that even though the saint undergoes the struggle of *simul* in this world, the relational *imago Dei* makes the saint relate with God as well as with others through its freedom, which is simultaneously free and bound. However, Luther's soteriologically described freedom is complicated when he explains the relation between the church and the civil authority, especially after the Peasants' War. Luther argues that the freedom of Christians should be bound not only by the law of love in the church but also by the law of the sword in the world. However, Luther's demarcation between the two is not absolute because the history of Germany proved that blind repetitions of Luther's conclusion become problematic and sometimes harmful in different political or social situations.

Conclusion

This chapter has illustrated the ways in which Luther reworked the Augustinian doctrine of original sin through a dialectic process between anthropology and hamartiology. The primary goal of this chapter was to show that Luther's revisions of Augustinianism function as the theological premise of Bonhoeffer's hamartiology, especially in regard to Bonhoeffer's ecclesiocentrism as well as his relational and ethical interpretation of the human being and sin. The chapter described, first, the process of Luther's reformulation of anthropology in which Luther conceived of the human being from two main anthropological perspectives, *totus homo* and the relational *imago Dei*, transforming the two doctrines from scholasticism and ultimately from Augustinianism. In the process, Luther radicalized the content as well as the frame of the doctrine of original sin. On the one hand, at the level of the two-tiered dialectic of *totus homo* as *simul iustus et peccator*, Luther worked out the extent of justification before God and before human beings. In this way, Luther shifted his emphasis regarding the original sin or radical sin from pride to concupiscence and finally to unbelief, offering his own theological interpretations of these concepts. On the other hand, at the level of the relational *imago Dei*, Luther firmly established the relational and ethical concept of the human being by which later Lutherans, especially those in the nineteenth and twentieth centuries, expanded and intensified the concept using the doctrine of *analogia relationis* (analogy of relation) and the ethical and relational concept of hamartiology, as in the doctrines of Reinhold Seeberg, Karl Holl, and Dietrich Bonhoeffer.

There are several implications of Luther's transformation of the doctrine of sin that will be addressed further in the chapters on Bonhoeffer. First, although Luther transformed the hamartiology of Augustine, his notion of sin as pride, concupiscence, or unbelief is clearly in line with the Augustinian tradition of *homo incurvatus in se*. As in Augustinian hamartiology, the same question of whether this active dimension of sin can fully engage with the experience of all human beings remains. Second, Luther partly reforms Augustine's logic of the doctrine of original sin in its transmission of sin as well as of culpability by his treatment of original sin and radical sin as interchangeable. However, Luther is not deeply concerned with the issues related to the transmission of alien culpability nor with the logic of original sin. Third, although Luther's understanding of sin is primarily from his soteriocentric perspective on *totus homo*, he opens the way for a Christian ethics in which Christian responsibility functions in the existential categories of *simul iustus et peccator* as well as of the relational *imago Dei*. Fourth, although Luther's Reformation idea itself implies the possibility of civil disobedience, he firmly applies Christian freedom as bound to the civil authority, as addressed in his two-kingdom idea. However, the difficulty with Luther's understanding of the relation between church and state is its poor applicability to certain social or political circumstances, such as the case of Germany under the reign of National Socialism. All of these implications of Luther's hamartiology were the central issues that Bonhoeffer struggled with in his own context, and these questions are dealt with in depth in the following chapters on Bonhoeffer.

Chapter 3

DIETRICH BONHOEFFER'S ECCLESIOCENTRIC HAMARTIOLOGY IN *SANCTORUM COMMUNIO*

Introduction

This chapter argues that Bonhoeffer's hamartiology transforms and reconstructs the Augustinian doctrine of original sin by shifting the starting point from the doctrine of God to the doctrine of the church and approaching the concept of humanity from a socio-ethical perspective based on Bonhoeffer's Lutheran tradition. This chapter is central to this book. This is because Bonhoeffer laid a theological foundation for his hamartiology in his first dissertation, *Sanctorum Communio*, in which he places the Augustinian ecclesial notion of *totus Christus* at the center of his hamartiology, using Lutheran resources such as the Christocentric standpoint and ethical and relational anthropology. Based on the argument of this chapter, this book continues to explicate Bonhoeffer's hamartiological development in connection with the doctrines of Augustine and Luther and with those of Bonhoeffer's contemporary Lutherans.

As a post-Enlightenment Lutheran theologian, Bonhoeffer offers a new angle for understanding the problem of sin and evil in the twentieth-century world. Despite Bonhoeffer's strong engagement with the doctrine of sin and evil throughout his works, his hamartiology is one of the least studied theological areas in Bonhoeffer scholarship. Furthermore, the relationship between Bonhoeffer's account of sin and the Augustinian doctrine of original sin has never been examined, despite Bonhoeffer's long and detailed discussion of Augustinian hamartiology in his original doctoral dissertation and his continued concern with the doctrine of sin and evil in his subsequent works. However, this detailed discussion had not been well known to scholars and other readers of Bonhoeffer's work until its recovery in 1986 (German version) and in 1998 (English version) due to his deletion of this portion when it was first published.[1] In *Sanctorum Communio*, Bonhoeffer's focus on hamartiology is strongly bonded with his Christocentric ecclesiology, and this ecclesiocentric hamartiology continues to be *cantus firmus* in his subsequent works, in which his hamartiology serves as the foundation of his entire theology.[2]

As discussed in Chapters 1 and 2, Bonhoeffer points out the theological insufficiencies of the Augustinian doctrine of original sin, especially its one-sided description of sin and evil that does not engage with the reality of sin that is reconciled by the atoning work of God in Christ who is present in the church community as a total person. Bonhoeffer focuses on the relational dynamics of the church community, rooted in Augustine's concept of the *corpus Christi* (the body of Christ) in which individuals participate in the reconciling work of Christ, not only for their own sins as individuals but also for the sins of the broken community, through the continuous *vicarious representative action* of the church community as *totus Christus* (the whole Christ).[3] Based on Luther's Christocentrism, Bonhoeffer takes Augustine's ecclesiastical axiom of *Christus als Gemeinde existierend* (Christ existing as church-community) as the basis of his hamartiology.[4]

Certainly, the most important aspect of Bonhoeffer's hamartiology in *Sanctorum Communio* is his reformulation of Augustine's doctrinal loci to reconstruct the Augustinian hamartiology per se through his sociologically as well as ecclesiestically derived Christian personalism. Bonhoeffer's concept of the church community as a collective person permits him to relate individuals and community in terms of their inseparable sinful solidarity as well as ethical and relational responsibility toward others. Bonhoeffer, therefore, locates the Augustinian ecclesiology at the center of his hamartiology and closely integrates it with the Augustinian doctrine of original sin by converting the biological and involuntary notion of transmission of the original sin as culpability into the ethical and voluntaristic concept of "bearing the sin of others" through his Lutheran standpoint of Christ who exists as the church community. Bonhoeffer's basic confidence in *Sanctorum Communio* is more deeply expressed in his subsequent theological works, such as in *Act and Being* and *Creation and Fall*; Chapter 4 engages these more thoroughly with the major issues addressed in this chapter.

This chapter begins by investigating Bonhoeffer's analysis of the Augustinian doctrine of original sin and the way in which he criticizes the structure and the content of the doctrine of original sin. Second, the chapter deals with Bonhoeffer's Christian concept of personalism that is derived from both the sociology of his time and Augustine's ecclesial concept of the church. The section discusses the importance of Bonhoeffer's Christian concept of the person by which he paves the way for his ecclesiocentric hamartiology. Third, the chapter explores Bonhoeffer's notion of the dual structure of sin, which more clearly reveals the mechanism of sin detected in the synchronic relation between individual and corporate persons as well as in the diachronic continuity of the human race through his versatile notion of the person. The chapter, then, discusses Bonhoeffer's reinterpretation of Augustinian hamartiology, in which he emphasizes co-responsibility for sin based on his socio-ethical concept of the human race and the concept of *vicarious representative action* and participation in Christ existing as the church community. Finally, the chapter concludes with some implications of these theological concepts.

Bonhoeffer's Assessment of the Doctrine of Original Sin

In his doctoral dissertation, which was originally entitled *Sanctorum Communio: Ein dogmatische Untersuchung*, Bonhoeffer assesses the Augustinian doctrine of original sin in detail. However, this analysis has been neglected by scholars of Bonhoeffer. Thus, it is necessary to deal with Bonhoeffer's evaluation of

Augustine's doctrine of original sin as the groundwork of Bonhoeffer's doctrine of sin in *Sanctorum Communio* as well as his entire hamartiology. After this, the next section discusses Bonhoeffer's Christian personalism by which he integrates the doctrine of sin with the doctrine of the church community, in which Bonhoeffer takes the Augustinian ecclesial notion of *totus Christus* as the theological premise of his hamartiology.

In the original manuscript of *Sanctorum Communio*, Bonhoeffer not only points out the deficient aspects of the Augustinian doctrine but also suggests how to compensate for them. Bonhoeffer's main points of critique of the traditional doctrine of original sin are analogous to the theological controversies that are discussed in detail in Chapter 1. Bonhoeffer identifies two crucial problems in Augustine's doctrine of original sin: *the distinction between original sin and actual sin* and *the biological concept of the transmission of original sin and culpability*. First, in regard to the distinction between original sin and actual sin, Bonhoeffer argues that the concept of original sin itself is not appropriate but should be merged into the concept of universality of sin, arguing that "ideas intended to prove the universality of sin in the first place were mixed into the inquiry about the proliferation of sin."[5] Bonhoeffer's analysis suggests that the concept of original sin presupposes that Adam's sin is qualitatively different from the sin of his posterity and implies the superiority of the prelapsarian human. Bonhoeffer insists that "[n]o one will act differently from Adam; that is, there is in principle a universality of sin."[6] Clearly, following Luther's hamartiological logic, Bonhoeffer does not distinguish between original sin and actual sin in *Sanctorum Communio*.[7] As discussed in Chapter 1, in regard to Augustine's distinction between original sin and actual sin, Bonhoeffer's theological opinion is similar to certain Latin theological predecessors of Augustine such as Ambrose and Ambrosiaster who only agreed with the transmission of the corrupted human nature, namely, the universality of sin, but did not agree with the biological transmission of original sin and culpability. Similar to interpreters of Augustine such as J. N. D. Kelly, Pier Franco Beatrice, and Gerald Bonner, Bonhoeffer considers that not only Augustine's demarcation between original sin and the universality of sin but also the biological transmission of original sin as culpability resulted from Augustine's incorrect interpretation of Rom. 5:12, which is the main biblical passage to which Augustine refers.[8] Bonhoeffer points out that Augustine's "incorrect translation of Romans 5:12 ἐφ' ᾧ as in quo [in whom] has had disastrous effects in the history of doctrine."[9] He argues that the verse originally meant the universality of sin, not the original sin, and that this resulted in the concept of the biological inheritance of culpability. This is because the sin of Adam and the sin of his posterity are not different sins but "the experience of common sinfulness."[10] He states, "We connect consciousness of our deepest personal culpability with that of the universality of our deed."[11] Cleary, Bonhoeffer takes a different theological standpoint from that of Augustine in articulating the sin of the human being.

In his analysis of Augustine's hamartiological system, Bonhoeffer's hermeneutical principle of Christocentrism is pivotal. Bonhoeffer distinguishes Paul's view from Augustine's. He understands that Augustine's parallel analogy between Adam and Christ is a false analogy that overlooks the qualitative difference between Adam and Christ.[12] At the bottom of this contention, there is a difference between Augustine and Bonhoeffer in their approaches to the doctrine of sin. As discussed in Chapter 1, Augustine's theological foundation for hamartiology lies firmly in his notion of God, which is derived from his Christianized Platonic cosmology. As a result, Augustine's understanding of Adam after the fall is described solely in opposition to the attributes of God, which are very much described as part of a transcendental and heavenly concept of the first person of God, and therefore the human being's hopelessness and absolute dependence on God's grace are maximized. However, for Bonhoeffer, the doctrine of sin cannot be separated from the reconciling work of God in Christ, especially in connection with the church community. He is convinced that "in order to establish clarity about the inner logic of theological construction, it would be good for once if a presentation of doctrinal theology were to start not with the doctrine of God but with the doctrine of the church."[13] This theological premise in ecclesiology is applied to his entire theology, but it is more crucial for his hamartiology. The doctrine of sin becomes partial and incomplete if it is described without connecting it with the work of "Christ existing as church-community."[14]

Bonhoeffer's turn away from Augustine's doctrine of God to the doctrine of church as the basis of his hamartiology is a significant relocation of theological loci to correct the classical doctrine of sin of the West. In the analysis of Western hamartiology, Bonhoeffer clearly reflects Luther's Christocentrism, not in the same way as Luther but in a way in which Luther's Christocentrism is extended to the concept of the church community. He argues that "the world of sin is the world of 'Adam'. ... But the world of Adam is the world Christ reconciled and made into a new humanity, Christ's church."[15] The hamartiological focus has been moved from Augustine's theocentric orientation to Bonhoeffer's Christocentric church community. Explicitly, Bonhoeffer's doctrine of sin in *Sanctorum Communio* starts from the sin of the church community or the world that is already reconciled by Christ. This theological turn implies that Bonhoeffer is more conscious of the issue of sin after baptism or conversion—in other words, the sin of *sanctorum communio*—in his early theological period.

Significantly, Bonhoeffer expands the boundary of sin from the individual level to the communal or communitarian level.[16] He points out that another theological problem with the Augustinian doctrine of original sin is Augustine's focus on personal culpability without considering communal culpability.[17] He argues that Augustine put "the emphasis on personal culpability" and "always strove to define personal culpability as truly and strictly *personal*."[18] In Bonhoeffer's eyes, Augustine's consideration of culpability as belonging only to an individual person limits its ability to penetrate the deep-seated nature of sin and evil that is hidden in the dual structure of community composed of individuals and communal persons. Bonhoeffer recognizes the theological risk in the doctrine of original sin that finally leads to the erroneous hierarchical distinction between the original sin and the actual sin by which Adam's sin and culpability become the primary object of justification of a person and the actual sin of the person is considered only as the secondary object of sanctification.[19] He argues that there should be a more coherent unity between justification and sanctification as well as between original sin and actual sin by insisting that "the individual culpable act and the culpability of the human race must be connected conceptually."[20] In the concept of the original sin as the root sin, there is a strong connotation of one's obligated responsibility for alien culpability without one's actual commitment of sin. For Bonhoeffer, the doctrine of original sin lacks explanation of the voluntary nature of sin and ultimately reduces the ethical responsibility of the person as both an individual and a corporate person. Augustine's theory of the biological imputation of culpability not only shrinks the person's voluntary nature of participation in evil in relation to Adam's representative involvement in evil but also neglects the importance of the Christian person's voluntary action "to bear the sins [of others]."[21] Bonhoeffer rejects the possibility of theological determinism embedded in the doctrine of original sin, which all apologists for early Christianity attempted to avoid.[22]

Bonhoeffer further points out that the doctrine of original sin opens a way of Christian pessimism in which the reconciling work of Christ in this world is overshadowed due to Augustine's overemphasis on humanity's hopelessness and absolute dependence on the grace of God, chiefly in the realm of philosophy in relation to the transcendent God, who is defined as the highest being. In this regard, Bonhoeffer's modern intellectual and theological background, especially the influence of nineteenth-century German liberals and Lutheran theologians, is crucial for his reception of Augustine. It is not at all surprising that one of the influential lenses for Bonhoeffer is Adolf von Harnack, one of his Lutheran teachers, who evaluated Augustine's theology as changing optimism in Christianity into pessimistic darkness.[23] Harnack's assessment of Augustine's theology is explicit in Bonhoeffer's assessment of Augustine's doctrine of original sin. Harnack states:

> He taught men to realise the horror of the depth of sin and guilt which he disclosed, at the same time with the blessed feeling of an ever-comforted misery, and a perennial grace. He first perfected Christian pessimism, whose upholders till then had really reserved for themselves an extremely optimistic view of human nature.[24]

Although Harnack's understanding of Augustine is not totally followed by Bonhoeffer, Bonhoeffer's critique of Augustine's doctrine of original sin shares aspects of Harnack's evaluation of Augustine that the doctrines of original sin and predestination contain a pessimistic and fatalistic tendency.[25] Similar to Harnack, Bonhoeffer's negative assessment of the fatalism in Augustine's doctrine of original sin is considerable.[26] Bonhoeffer argues:

> When Augustine considers humanity as a whole, his initial feeling is that he belongs to a species that has been struck by a terrible and overpowering fate, turned upside down in its very nature and corrupted through every fiber of its being. Terrible punishment has been imposed upon him like a catastrophe. ... This concept of the mass is not the sociological one of a social structure, but gathers a multiplicity of persons under a single viewpoint.[27]

Bonhoeffer here asks about the Christian concept of the human race as a communal person. In his perspective, the individualistic concept of person cannot be the starting point of humanity but primarily should be addressed from the perspective of community. He assesses Augustine's treatment of *the human race in the doctrine of original sin* as one-sided because Augustine deals with human solidarity solely in the biological sense, following his mistaken interpretation of Rom. 5:12.[28] In the above quotation, Bonhoeffer clearly argues that Augustine's concept of the "mass" lacks a sociological and ethical perspective. It is noteworthy that, at a deeper level, Bonhoeffer's critiques are based on his theological premises, which are significantly different from Augustine's in two ways: Bonhoeffer's *relational and ethical anthropology* and his *theological standpoint in Christ*.

To sum up, Bonhoeffer's assessment of Augustine's doctrine of original sin is critical in two ways. On the one hand, he criticizes the doctrine's one-sided view of human sinful nature, chiefly the logic between original sin and actual sin and the biological sense of the transmission of original sin. On the other hand, Bonhoeffer suggests a theological tool to correct Augustine's doctrine of original sin by introducing Christian personalism, which is closely connected to the Augustinian notion of the church as the body of Christ or *totus Christus*.

Christian Personalism

As discussed in the previous section, Bonhoeffer's assessment of Augustine's doctrine of original sin implies an alternative to the doctrine in which he emphasizes the ethical dimension of the human race and places Lutheran Christocentrism at its center. To reformulate the traditional Augustinian hamartiology, Bonhoeffer introduces Christian personalism, in which he combines a concept of the person derived from sociology with the Christian concept of the communal or collective person appropriated from Augustine's ecclesial notion of the church as the body of Christ, in other words, *totus Christus*.[29] For Bonhoeffer, insights from sociology and his Lutheran as well as Augustinian understanding of the person as *totus homo* (the whole person) as well as *totus Christus* offered an effective apparatus for reconstructing the hamartiology of the West. In his personalism, Bonhoeffer explicitly changes the standpoint of hamartiology from the doctrine of the first person of God to "the perspective of the sanctorum communio," in other words, to that of ecclesiology, integrating "philosophical considerations into the theological framework."[30] Significantly, this is Bonhoeffer's dogmatic turn from Augustinian methodology to relate God's transcendence with God's immanence as well as God's providence with the presence of evil in the church community and the world.[31]

Personalism and sociology

In *Sanctorum Communio*, Bonhoeffer approaches hamartiology primarily from the perspective of the human race. He declares that sin is "the deed of the human race and of the individual"; thus, he argues that sin should be conceived as located in two related sociological dimensions—"a supra-individual deed" and "an individual deed."[32] According to Bonhoeffer, *sin as an individual act* had been discussed in great depth throughout the history of church doctrine, but *sin as a supra-individual deed* had been less emphasized despite its importance. Bonhoeffer states that there is no terminology that sufficiently encompasses the individual and corporate subject. It becomes important to Bonhoeffer to articulate a Christian concept of the person that adequately describes the reciprocal relation between the individual and the corporate persons for the doctrine of the church, in which the doctrine of sin is located.

At first glance, Bonhoeffer's notion of the person has affinities with a concept developed by personalist thinkers of the 1920s.[33] As Wayne W. Floyd rightly points out, the personalist philosophy was in the air in Bonhoeffer's time, in contrast to the modern idealistic epistemology that absolutizes the subject of the I.[34] For Bonhoeffer, the Christian concept of the person is not the same as the interpersonal concept of the person found in the thought of Brunner, Gogarten, and others as well as that of Martin Buber, which emphasizes the intimacy between the I and the You.[35] Clifford J. Green properly indicates that the chief distinctive trait of Bonhoeffer's concept of the person is his flexible usage of "person," which "goes beyond" the interpersonal concept of the person of dialogical personalism.[36] It is evident that the influence of personalism is dominant in Bonhoeffer's first dissertation, but the concept of the person of dialogical philosophers and theologians is transformed into a distinctively Christian concept of the person.

At the beginning of *Sanctorum Communio*, Bonhoeffer clearly demonstrates that the Christian concept of the person must be understood in reference to three fundamental characteristics: *reality, relationality,* and *responsibility*. He describes the Christian concept of the person as follows:

> At the moment of being addressed, the person enters a state of *responsibility* or, in other words, of decision. By person I do not mean at this point the idealists' person of mind or reason, but the *person in concrete, living individuality*. This is not the person internally divided, but the one addressed as a *whole person*; not one existing in timeless fullness of value and spirit, but in a state of *responsibility in the midst of time*.[37]

It is clear here that Bonhoeffer's person is far from the idealist or Platonist concept of the person identified with mind, soul, or reason; instead, it signifies *a concrete and ethical whole person living in temporality*.[38] In modern idealism, the concept of the person is only delimited in the subject-object relationship, considering the person as mind or reason rather than the whole person. In classical Platonism, in contrast, the concept of the person is internally separated in the dualistic concept of soul and body, and, furthermore, the reality of the person is sought in the transcendental realm rather than in the existential reality in the midst of time. For Bonhoeffer, not only idealism but also Platonism misses a crucial criterion of the person, which is the existential reality of the person in concrete time.[39]

The significance of concrete time for Bonhoeffer is that the person exists "in a state of responsibility... in the value-related—not value-filled—moment."[40] Thus, the Christian concept of the person is not addressed beyond time and space but in a concrete time and place and, most importantly, in relation to others through *ethical responsibility*. Bonhoeffer defines the *ethical relational person* as the Christian concept of the person. He explains the theme of the ethical and relational person in duality:

> *For Christian philosophy, the human person originates only in relation to the divine; the divine person transcends the human person,* who both resists and is overwhelmed by the divine. ... The Christian person originates only in the absolute duality of God and humanity; only in experiencing the barrier does the awareness of oneself as ethical person arise. The more clearly the barrier is perceived, the more deeply the person enters into the situation of responsibility.[41]

It is significant that Bonhoeffer concludes that the Christian concept of the person "originates only in the absolute *duality of God and humanity*."[42] This dual origin of the Christian person indicates the most distinctive and quintessential foundation of his entire theology from which all his doctrines arise. Distinguishing clearly between idealistic and Augustinian anthropology, Bonhoeffer identifies the human origin in "the absolute duality of God and humanity," which is ultimately found in Christ. Bonhoeffer's Christian concept of the person does not rely on the transcendental barrier of the highest values but is firmly rooted in the existential and ethical barrier of the person of Christ.[43]

To be clear, even though Bonhoeffer appropriated some important theoretical concepts of community from sociology to build up his personalism, he differentiates his Christian concept of the person from similar notions in sociology. He explains at length that the Christian concept of the collective person as the church community [*Gemeinde*] is derived not only from the notions of community [*Gemeinschaft*] and society [*Gesellschaft*] used by Ferdinand Tönnies but also from the concept of *Herrschaftsverband* (association of authentic rule), which was used by Max Scheler.[44] Bonhoeffer differentiates between community and society as follows: "If a community [*Gemeinschaft*] is essentially a life-community, then a society [*Gesellschaft*] is an association of rational action."[45] In the sociological framework of Tönnies, the church community belongs to *Gemeinshcaft* rather than *Gesellschaft*; however, from a theological perspective, the church community belongs to *Gemeinschaft* as well as *Gesellschaft*. This is because *Geminde* is not only a life-community but also a purpose-driven community.[46] However, these two concepts are not enough to explain the unique nature of the *Gemeinde* as a person in which Christ exists as the ultimate authority. Bonhoeffer understands that the church community is a collective person composed of two hierarchical parts: Christ and the saints. This unique notion of the church community requires another sociological concept, *Herrschaftsverband*, which can demonstrate the relationship between Christ and the saints in a theological way. The point is that the church community as a collective or communal person surpasses the category of sociology and requires a theological demarcation. To explain this unique structure of the church community as a person, Bonhoeffer applies all three aspects of the sociological notions of *Gemeinschaft, Gesellschaft,* and *Herrschaftsverband*.[47] Accordingly, *Gemeinde* is more than *Gemeinschaft, Gesellschaft,* or *Herrschaftsverband* as conceived in sociology; it is a community of love [*Liebesgemeinschaft*] that encompasses and surpasses these three sociological categories. Bonhoeffer summarizes, "*[In the empirical church,] community [Gemeinschaft], society [Gesellschaft], and association of authentic rule [Herrschaftverband] are truly most closely intertwined.*"[48] Clearly, Bonhoeffer's personalism incorporates the previous three concepts and goes beyond them due to its dual origination in Christ and humanity.

In short, the most distinctive characteristic of Bonhoeffer's Christian personalism is that it includes a concept of the person that is flexible enough to be extended from the individual person to the collective person [*Kollektivperson*] and ultimately to the collective person of the church community in which Christ exists as the church community. Bonhoeffer applies the concept of the person, which can be used in diverse ways to explain the church community as simultaneously both *sanctorum communio* (community of saints) and *peccatorum communio* (community of sinners). This multifaceted concept of the person is pivotal to grasping the hamartiological content that Bonhoeffer concentrates on in *Sanctorum Communio*. This concept of the person makes Bonhoeffer address more appropriately the dual structure of sin and the responsibility of the person as an ethical agent, which traditional Augustinian hamartiology placed less emphasis on.

Personalism and ecclesiology

Seen from the perspective of the dogmatic tradition of the West, Bonhoeffer's notion of the church as a collective person is derived not only from his study of sociology but also from his Lutheran background as well as the Augustinian tradition. Bonhoeffer's understanding of the church community as a collective person is no other than a re-articulation of the Augustinian *ecclesiastical notion* of *totus Christus* as *die Kirche ist Christus als Gemeinde existierend* expressed in the sociological language of the nineteenth and twentieth centuries in Germany.[49]

The notion of *totus homo* is one of Luther's radicalized anthropological insights derived from Augustine in which Luther incorporates two inseparable realities of the saints expressed in the concept of *simul iustus et simul peccator* (simultaneously righteous and a sinner). The concept of the person as *simul iustus et simul peccator* is closely related to the human reality of being simultaneously *coram Deo et coram hominibus* (before God and human beings).[50] In a similar fashion to Luther, Bonhoeffer argues that "the reality of sin and the communio peccatorum remain even in God's church-community; Adam has really been replaced by Christ only eschatologically, ἐπ' ἐλπίδι (*in spe*) [in hope]."[51] However, he does not merely repeat Luther's theological anthropology but rather synthesizes the two realities of the Christian person in the present moment, using the modern sociological resources of personalism. Although Bonhoeffer argues that the perfect replacement of Adam by Christ is only in eschatological hope, he does not view this eschatological hope as only a future event but sees it as reality in the present moment in the church community.

Bonhoeffer argues that "[u]ntil now we have been pursing two, or rather three, different lines of thought that must now be integrated conceptually—or better, we must reflect upon their union that already exists in the reality of the church."[52] Bonhoeffer recognizes that the different lines of thought based on the reality of the saints should be integrated and united in the church community rather than in the *eschaton* because there is a necessary bond between "the new basic-relations" and the "empirical form of community."[53] This is because this bond between the two realities constitutes the essential structure of the church. Bonhoeffer identifies the eschatological hope of the union of the church and Christ in the present moment, especially in the realm of the church community. Thus, the person as *simul iustus et simul peccator* should be understood in the sense of ecclesiastical unity as *totus homo*. This concept of *totus homo* as the church community is clearly connected to the Augustine's concept of *totus Christus* articulated in his ecclesiology, which this book addresses in Chapter 2.

As Barry Harvey points out, Bonhoeffer's notion of the church community is "a recovery and a restatement of Augustine's contention that in the church we encounter the whole Christ."[54] Considering the fact that Bonhoeffer had studied Augustine's theology through seminars led by Lutheran teachers, Adolf von Harnack and Reinhold Seeberg, it is not surprising to discover Bonhoeffer's deep engagement with Augustine's theology based on his Lutheran perspective.[55] In fact, Bonhoeffer appropriates Augustine's concept of *totus Christus* of ecclesiology in close relation to his hamartiology in *Sanctorum Communio*.[56] Although the scholarship on Bonhoeffer has never seriously focused on Bonhoeffer's appropriation of the Augustinian as well as the Lutheran concept of *totus Christus*, Bonhoeffer explicitly relates his notion of the church community to Augustine's ecclesial concept of *sanctorum communio*.[57] Bonhoeffer argues:

> Luther revived Augustine's idea that it is the sanctorum communio that bears the sins of its members. However, later in the same sentence he adds that it is Christ who bears them. ... The church-community is thus able to bear the sins that none of its members can bear alone; it is able to bear more than all of its members combined. As such it must be a spiritual reality that is more than the sum of all the individuals. Not all the individuals, but the church-community as a whole is in Christ, is the 'body' of Christ; it is 'Christ existing as church-community.'[58]

Augustine's concept of *totus Christus* is found mostly in his pastoral writings in reference to the relationality between Christ and the church rather than in his works that deal with the doctrine of sin. Augustine's doctrine of *totus Christus* originally comes from his ecclesial concept of the two-part body of Christ that explains the nature of the earthly church as composed of saints and sinners on their journey to the heavenly city of God.[59] Augustine's concept of the body of Christ is used primarily to describe the church in the world in relation to the celestial city of God, which is the final destination of the saints. For example, in *Expositions of the Psalms* Augustine clearly demonstrates the concept of *totus Christus* in reference to the doctrine of the church community as one person. Augustine writes:

> The apostle tells us, You are Christ's body, and his members (1 Cor 12:27). If then he is the head and we are the members, *one single individual is speaking*. Whether the head speaks or the members speak, the *one Christ speaks*. Moreover it is perfectly proper for the head to speak on behalf of the members.[60]

In Bonhoeffer's view, there is a close connection between the concept of the human being and the concept of the church because the church community is treated as a corporate person. Bonhoeffer identifies the corporate sense of the person in Augustine's understanding of the church as the collective person of Christ. In this regard, it is not surprising that Bonhoeffer's description of sin is always associated with a series of themes composed of *God, humanity and sin,* and *reconciliation*, and these are eventually and ultimately merged in the doctrine of the church community in which, significantly, he refers to the concept of *totus Christus* found in Augustine's ecclesiology through his Lutheran perspective.[61]

Despite the diverse interpretations of Luther's reception of the Augustinian notion of the church among scholars in Germany in Bonhoeffer's time, Bonhoeffer credits Luther as the one who "revived Augustine's idea" of *sanctorum communio*.[62] For Bonhoeffer, the notion of *Gemeinde* is more than a sociological entity but a unique ecclesial entity that is composed of saints and Christ as an organic entity that is not only a reconciled community but also "an instrument of God's will."[63] Clearly, Bonhoeffer connects Augustine's doctrine of the church as *totus Christus* with the doctrine of sin, arguing:

> It was Augustine who maintained that this is possible only in the community of saints. ... Nobody can forgive sins but the person who takes them upon himself, bears them, and wipes them out. Thus only Christ can do it, which for us means his church as the sanctorum communio. ... The individual Christians can do it only by virtue of membership in the church-community, and in that capacity ought to do it. The Christians takes sin from the others' conscience and bears it; but clearly one can do that only by laying it in turn on Christ.[64]

As described in the section entitled "The Problem of Evil" in Chapter 1, the starting point of Augustine's doctrine of sin is mainly the doctrine of God described in Platonic terminology and cosmology, emphasizing God's transcendence and sovereignty over the creation. It is Augustine's ecclesiology in relation to Christology, however, which Bonhoeffer takes as the starting point of his hamartiology and in which Augustine describes the relationality between Christ and its members more closely than he does in his doctrine of God.[65] Clearly, Bonhoeffer's assertion of ecclesiology as the starting point of theology is intended to focus on the church community as "simultaneously a historical community and one established by God."⁶⁶ The starting point of Bonhoeffer's hamartiology is from this existential world of "Adam," which was "reconciled and made into a new humanity, Christ's church."⁶⁷ Furthermore, Bonhoeffer attributes the socio-ethical concept of the person to Augustine's ecclesial concept of the church but notes that it is also embedded in the concept of the person of the early patristic theologians.⁶⁸ Bonhoeffer evidently is attempting to establish the theological legitimacy of his Christian notion of the person within the church tradition of the West in a Lutheran way. Bonhoeffer's hamartiology begins from the concept of the Christian person "who has been justified, who belongs to God's church community, [and] has 'died to sin.'"⁶⁹ Although Bonhoeffer adopts Augustine's ecclesial notion as the foundation of his doctrine of sin, needless to say, he reads this notion within his Lutheran or Protestant theological framework expressed in the two-tiered notion of the saint as the "justified sinner" or *totus homo* as *simul iustus et peccator*.⁷⁰

In summary, Bonhoeffer's personalism is an important theological tool for reconstructing Augustine's hamartiology. On the one hand, the significance of his personalism is that it reflects not only the language of his own time but also the resources of the church tradition of the West, which is rooted in the testimonies of Scripture. On the other hand, it is also noteworthy that his turn to ecclesiology challenges the landscape of the theological methodology of the West in which the doctrine of God is considered the firm ground of theology. In regard to the doctrine of sin, Bonhoeffer observes that hamartiology cannot be explicated fully without relating the doctrine of sin with the doctrine of the church community, and in the intersection he places his Christian personalism.

The Primal State of Humanity

As discussed in the previous section on Christian personalism, the distinctiveness of Bonhoeffer's doctrine of sin compared to Augustinian and Lutheran hamartiology is found primarily in his prioritizing the communal aspect of person and sin. Bonhoeffer conceived that the classical ontological methodology was no longer effectively persuading people in the modern era, especially related to the issue of the primal state of humanity.⁷¹ His alternative approach was to start in the reality, in other words, "in the context of revelation," rather than in pure speculation. Bonhoeffer states:

> The doctrine of the primal state cannot offer us new theological insights. In the logic of theology as a whole it belongs with *eschatology*. Every aspect helpful to its comprehension is imparted through *revelation*. Nothing about it can be ascertained by *pure speculation*. It cannot speak of the essence of human being, of nature, or of history in general terms, but only *in the context of revelation that has been heard*. The doctrine of the primal state is hope projected backward.⁷²

There is evidently, therefore, a gap between the Augustinian transcendental concept of the person and Bonhoeffer's existential and relational concept of the person. Bonhoeffer points out that the Augustinian doctrine of the primal state does not offer any new theological insights in the post-Enlightenment modern era because the doctrine is based purely on speculation. This is the point where Bonhoeffer criticizes the concept of the person of idealism as well as of Platonic Augustinianism. In Bonhoeffer's perspective, the person in the primal state should be addressed as having an existential and relational foundation in Christ rather than in the transcendental concept of soul or mind. This criticism is closely related to Bonhoeffer's theological premise of the revelation of God in Christ, based on which he discovers the genuine and integral meaning of the primal state in relation to the theme of the fall, sin, and reconciliation. He is convinced that the doctrine of the primal state is relevant only when it is addressed in dialogue with the true knowledge of humanity, nature, and history, which is interpreted through the lens of the revelation of God in Christ.

In regard to Bonhoeffer's understanding of the revelation, it is necessary to take a look at his modern theological context. Bonhoeffer's emphasis on "the context of revelation" reveals his theological basis rooted in the concrete reality of history and in the revelation of God in Christ.[73] Here, one may clearly see the influence of Barth on Bonhoeffer's theological reasoning.[74] As Clifford Green rightly points out, the theology of Bonhoeffer was on the side of Barth, especially the concept of revelation, in Bonhoeffer's early career.[75] As Eberhard Bethge notes, however, Bonhoeffer's understanding of the revelation is distinguished from that of Barth in its emphasis and sequence. Whereas for Barth the revelation is the starting point for moving toward the church, for Bonhoeffer the revelation itself is Christ who exists as the church community.[76] This point may appear subtle, but it is significantly different from Barth in that the theology of Bonhoeffer is heavily based on his prioritization of the church community as the body of Christ. As seen in the previous section, Bonhoeffer's Christian personalism is firmly rooted in the revelation of God in Christ or his Lutheran Christocentrism.

However, for Karl Barth, as he addresses in *The Epistle to Romans*, there is an "'infinite qualitative distinction' between time and eternity," as between God and humanity.[77] In his early period, Barth does not closely relate the revelation and the church.[78] In this regard, Bonhoeffer points out that Barth's understanding of revelation makes the doctrine of salvation "a secondary factor" because the revelation of God in Christ is inseparably related to the doctrine of the church as a total person.[79] Bonhoeffer sees the revelation of God in Christ as simultaneously interconnected with the church community because Christ exists as the church community in temporality. On the one hand, as Charles Marsh identifies, Bonhoeffer's Christocentric approach is significant in reference to Barth's theological framework of "the primary and secondary objectivity of revelation."[80] On the other hand, Andreas Pangritz remarks that it is Luther who had the most influence on Bonhoeffer's understanding of revelation prior to Barth.[81] In this line of reasoning, for Bonhoeffer not only the primal state but also the sinful state of humanity needs to be defined and explicated from the perspective of the revelation in the reality established in the church community. It is clear that, for Bonhoeffer, the revelation of God is not only the revelation of God in Jesus Christ but also the revelation of the church as the body of Christ. Evidently, Bonhoeffer binds the church community to Christ more firmly than Barth.

Accordingly, this Christocentric notion of the church community is reflected in Bonhoeffer's understanding of the primal state. Disassociating from Augustine's interpretation of Adam as an individual person, Bonhoeffer insists that Adam in the primal state must be recognized not only as an individual person but also as a collective person, as the human race.[82] He argues that "Augustine turns most strongly toward the purely personal spirit with the statement 'we all were that Adam.'... This puts emphasis on personal culpability."[83] Exactly at this point, Bonhoeffer applies his Christian personalism to the concept of Adam and expands the notion of Adam from an individual concept of the person to a communal and sociological concept of the person.[84] Bonhoeffer defines the primal state of humanity as "the original community between God and humanity as well as that among human beings."[85]

It is not surprising that Bonhoeffer's communitarian interpretation of the primal state comes from his Lutheran heritage. As Robert Kolb rightly points out, Luther's focus in the doctrine of original sin is not on the inherited culpability of Adam but on the broken relationship between God and humanity.[86] Clearly, Luther's emphasis is on the sinful relational reality of the human being rather than Augustine's focus on biologically transmitted culpability.[87] Luther focuses more on the ethical and relational aspects of the primal state. For Luther, the most important characteristic of the prelapsarian person is the person's original righteousness before God and other creation based on his understanding of the relational *imago Dei* or *analogia relationis*.[88] This Lutheran understanding of the primal state shows a clear divergence from the philosophical Augustinian doctrine of the primal state, which affirms the intermediate state of the human being who has the possibility of going up to an upper being or going down toward a lesser being, partly due to humanity's inborn materiality.[89] Clearly, Luther shifted his focus on the primal state from Augustine's faculty-oriented description of the first human to his ethical and relational righteousness before God. As Kolb remarks with precision, one of the most distinctive characteristics of Luther's understanding of sin is his "perception of reality," by which he substantially altered the framework of hamartiology.[90] Based on this way of thinking, Bonhoeffer follows Luther but interprets Adam as a collective person. Bonhoeffer's communitarian concept of Adam not only changes the subject of the first sin but also opens the door to the shared culpability of the collective person as well as the doctrine of *Stellvertretung*, vicarious representative action, of the church community. Clearly, this divergence between Augustine and Luther or Augustine and Bonhoeffer is not simply a matter of interpretation of biblical passages but an issue of their theological standpoints or theological methodology, as Bonhoeffer argues that "methodologically, all statements are possible only on the basis of our understanding of the church, i.e., from the revelation we have heard."[91] This ecclesiocentric approach is continued in *Creation and Fall*. Thus, for Bonhoeffer, the first sin is the rebellion of the first community against God, which is based on his understanding of the church community.

To sum up, the importance of the doctrine of the primal state for Bonhoeffer is that it supplies "an archetype of the church" that can be actualized in temporality only in the church community.[92] Although Augustine mentions an archetypal church in *De Civitate Dei* (The City of God), in Bonhoeffer's eyes, Augustine's theory is not theologically relevant because it is derived merely through pure speculation. In fact, Bonhoeffer critiques the doctrine of the primal state of Augustine for lacking the perspective based on the revelation of God in Christ. The importance of the notion of the primal community, for Bonhoeffer, is that it suggests God's intention of creating Adam as a community. Bonhoeffer conceives that the primal state can be understood only through the life of the church community in which God in Christ not only exists but also relates with the saints. Bonhoeffer's early hamartiological concerns expand beyond the boundary of the church community in his later period. These issues are dealt with in Chapter 5 in the chapter entitled "Bonhoeffer's Later Hamartiology and Ethics."

The Dual Structure of Sin

As discussed in the section entitled "Christian Personalism" above, the distinctiveness of Bonhoeffer's understanding of sin compared to Augustinian and Lutheran hamartiology is found in his focus on the communal aspect of sin. Bonhoeffer views sin as not only an individual act but also a communal or communitarian act. From his early theological stage, in *Sanctorum Communio*, Bonhoeffer's concept of the person implies this dual structure of sin. There is inseparable relationality between the sin of an individual and a community or society as a corporeal person. Clearly, this observation on the nature of sin makes Bonhoeffer's thinking distinctive in the history of hamartiology in the West.

This section sketches Bonhoeffer's primitive but theologically significant recognition of the dual structure of sin. In this early stage, Bonhoeffer focuses on the relation between individual and communal persons chiefly within the boundary of the church community. A unique point of Bonhoeffer's notion of this relationality is his prioritization of communality or the communal person over the individual person in regard to the experience of sinfulness of the human race. Bonhoeffer clearly identifies the sin of the community as a protype of an individual's sin against the divine person as well as the human person, engaging with the doctrine of the universality of sin. In *Sanctorum Communio*, however, this dual structure of sin is limited to the primitive level and only supplies a framework for his mature understanding of sin. As discussed in Chapter 5, in his later theological stage, his notion of the dual structure of sin is more clearly articulated in relation to the social and political circumstances of Germany.

In *Sanctorum Communio*, Bonhoeffer defines Adam primarily as a communal person rather than an individual person. He declares, "The world of sin is the world of 'Adam,' the old humanity."[93] One must recognize that Adam is a collective person to understand Bonhoeffer's argument of the doctrine of sin properly. Bonhoeffer concludes that the first sin is the sin of the first community in which individuals participate. He points out that there is a symbiotic correlation between individual and communal persons. This is no other than the universal sinful nature of humanity after the fall. However, an unrecognized nature of sin is resident in the dynamics between these persons. He argues that "the new social basic relations between I and You, as well as between I and humanity" are the basic structure of sin.[94] For Bonhoeffer, sin is primarily relational rather than personal.[95] This interpersonal sociality is not only the foundation of human society but also the mechanism of the human and divine relationship, as Luther expressed in the concept of *relational imago Dei*. This dual relationship signifies that God treats a community as an individual person, just as in the case of the community of Israel, in which an individual is not absorbed into the collective person but functions as an independent and vital member who influences and is influenced by the empirical community to which that individual belongs.[96]

Bonhoeffer is convinced that the sin of the church and of the world cannot be fully understood without having a proper knowledge of this dual structure of sin, which is intrinsically embedded in the structure of the person. However, he argues that this has not been logically explained.[97] Bonhoeffer realizes that the reality of corporate sin in the church and beyond it in the world is poignant. He writes:

> The world of sin is the world of 'Adam', the old humanity. But the world of Adam is the world Christ reconciled and made into a new humanity, Christ's church. However, *it is not as if Adam were completely overcome*; rather, the humanity of Adam lives on in the humanity of Christ. This is why the discussion of the problem of sin is indispensable for understanding the sanctorum communio.[98]

In Bonhoeffer's perspective, the world of sin is considered the world of the old collective person as Adam and the church as a new collective person in Christ. And it follows that Christ reconciled with the old person and made a new person, a new species. This new species is *sanctorum communio*. However, the problem is the fact that there is sin even in this new person, as in the case of Luther's *simul iustus et peccator*. As a justified individual struggles as *iustus et peccator*, the church community as a communal person also undergoes this struggle. As Robert Kolb comments, the question of the continuation of sin in a saint and the church community, even after the reconciliation of Christ or after baptism, is an important one for Bonhoeffer as well as for Luther.[99] Despite the reconciliation of Christ, the old humanity of Adam continues to live on in the church community. This theological as well as experiential dilemma is expressed in Luther's doctrines of *totus homo* as *simul iustus et peccator*, which he developed in a critical way from Augustine's ecclesial concept of the saint as "partly saint and partly sinner." Similar to Luther, Bonhoeffer introduces Luther's doctrine of *simul iustus et peccator* to the collective person, expanding the scope of Luther's individual concept of *simul* to a communal concept—from the saint to the church community.[100] Bonhoeffer's intention with this formula is to indicate that the problem of sin after baptism or conversion needs to be discussed not only on an individual level but also on a communal level in order to grasp the mechanism of sin hidden in the dual structure.

3. Dietrich Bonhoeffer's Ecclesiocentric Hamartiology 69

In his early theological stage, Bonhoeffer begins to develop his understanding of the dual structure of sin. Nonetheless, as discussed in Chapter 5, his deeper insight on this sinful relationality is expressed more clearly in his later hamartiology as articulated in his prison writings, especially "After Ten Years."

Primarily, for Bonhoeffer, sin is the collective person's turning away from God and is the will of the community when it changes its direction to go against God.[101] The sin of Adam is the community's rebellion against God along with individual members' participation in this. In this regard, it is notable that although Bonhoeffer criticizes the speculative aspect of the classical doctrine of sin, in his early theological stage his understanding of sin is basically in line with Augustinian hamartiology in terms of its orientation as well as its content. Similar to Augustine, Bonhoeffer argues that sin stepped into the unmediated human community with God, and love of the other turned toward the I in egocentricity, following Augustine's concept of the homo *incurvatus in se* (man turned in upon himself).[102] Bonhoeffer's description of the reality of sin clearly follows the Augustinian description of sin as *pride* or *incurvatus in se* with his sociological communitarian paraphrase drawing on Luther's similar notion of *cor curvum in se* (the heart curved in upon itself).[103] The relationality of love not only between God and humanity but also among human beings turned into atomistic self-love, encapsulated in *cor curvm in se*.[104] Therefore, sin is fundamentally the destruction of the relationship that was originally endowed by God. Sin is the radical alteration of the *primal dual relation* between the I and the You, which is the I and the divine You as well as the I and the human You. Put differently, sin is I's usurpation of the place of the other.

Bonhoeffer explains that the mechanism of sin is simultaneously synchronic and diachronic. On the one hand, the broken reality of humanity has a twofold synchronic structure: individual and supra-individual or individual and corporate. Bonhoeffer directly appropriates the notion of Augustine, asserting that the notion of the sinful collective act [*Gesamtakt*] has already been embedded in doctrinal history:

> How can one conceive of the individual culpable act and the guiltiness of the human race together without making one the reason for the other, that is, excusing one by means of the other? *Augustine evidently thought of the sinful collective act [Gesamtakt] as the basis for every individual act*, and Anselm and Thomas basically get no further than this. ... Everything obviously depends upon *finding the act of the whole in the sinful individual act*, without making the one the reason for the other.[105]

Bonhoeffer attributes to Augustine the concept of "the sinful collective act [Gesamtakt] as the basis for every individual act."[106] The relationality is clearly working in the broken community in a negative way. It is remarkable that, as the editor of *Sanctorum Communio* comments, Bonhoeffer appropriates and develops the sinful collective act from Augustine as proposed by his Lutheran teacher Reinhold Seeberg.[107] It is controversial whether Bonhoeffer took the notion of sociality solely from Seeberg; however, as Martin Rumscheidt points out, Seeberg was one of the primary influences on Bonhoeffer's engagement of social and ethical aspects of the church community in "a dogmatic theological reflection," especially in his early theological period.[108]

On the other hand, Bonhoeffer addresses the dual structure of sin *diachronically*. He redefines the concept of humanity from an ethical and social perspective, distancing his concept from Augustine's biologically defined human solidarity, drawing on his Lutheran resources and reflecting Seeberg's ethical and social interpretation of the human race. He writes:

> An ethical category must be related to the individual as a specific person. Precisely the social element, however, is thereby not excluded, but posited simultaneously. …[T]he individual's very own deed against God… is at the same time the deed of the human race (no longer in the biological sense) in the individual person. … Thus all humanity falls with each sin, and not one of us is in principle different from Adam; that is, every one is also the "first" sinner.[109]

Bonhoeffer says that his definition of person is not associated solely with the biological concept but, more importantly, is also associated with ethical and social concepts. In other words, humanity is the sinful community in which every individual person commits the first sin as Adam. This is a significant claim in that Bonhoeffer clearly states that "one's being guilty" [being culpable] is directly based on one's own sin, not on the alien sin of Adam; however, he adds that one's sin is simultaneously and directly related to the communal sin of all humanity in terms of the universality of sin rather than the inheritance of sin.[110] The universality of sin, for Bonhoeffer, substitutes for Augustine's biological sense of human solidarity as well as his concept of the transmission of original sin that connects the human race with Adam. Bonhoeffer traces back to the sin of the first community from the viewpoint of the present and connects the sin of the individual person to Adam as the first communal person based on "the experience of common sinfulness."[111]

In this regard, as Tom Greggs points out, the notion of original sin is closer to the concept of sinful participation in the first sin rather than the inheritance of the first sin.[112] In this way, "[t]here is a *reciprocity*" between individual and communal persons as well as between the I and the first community.[113] To explicate this duality, Bonhoeffer does not focus on identifying the prototypal or original sin of Adam but takes the present reality of the universal sinful state as the starting point of his consideration. He explains that the sin of the human race is not just an individual act but simultaneously an act of the human race as a communal person because "sociality exists before the experience [of a person] and independently of it."[114] Bonhoeffer perceives that sociality or community is divinely given *in advance to* "the experience of ethical solidarity and awareness of oneself as peccator pessimus [the worst sinner]."[115] The community of God or *Gemeinde*, for Bonhoeffer, is the primary focus of his hamartiological discussion, as Chapter 4 further discusses through Bonhoeffer's interpretation of the account of the creation and the fall. Thus, through this methodological priority in sociality, Bonhoeffer supplies a theological tool to connect the sin of all human beings synchronically as well as diachronically, disengaging from Augustine's biological transmission of sin as culpability.

In summary, Bonhoeffer's communitarian concept of sin expands the traditional hamartiology of the West in which individual sin is emphasized. Furthermore, Bonhoeffer laid a foundation for his dual structure of sin between individual and communal persons that permits him to explain the sinful relationality between individual and corporate persons as well as between the individual and the whole human race regardless of time and space from a social and ethical perspective. This observation is related to the problem of continued sin in the church community as well as responsibility for the culpability of others. Bonhoeffer approaches this issue through an ethical and relational way in which *relational human solidarity* and *ethical co-responsibility* are suggested as an alternative.[116] This methodological turn is reflected in the way he reformulates Augustinian hamartiology.

Reformulation of the Doctrine of Original Sin

As discussed in the preceding section, Bonhoeffer's ethical and relational understanding of the person supplies a theological foundation for his hamartiology. As early as in *Sanctorum Communio*, Bonhoeffer laid his hamartiological framework, reformulating Augustine's doctrine of original sin by relocating the theological basis of his consideration from the biological and involuntary transmission of culpability, encapsulated in the notion of alien culpability, to the relational and ethical bearing of the sin of others. This methodological transition is crucial in Bonhoeffer's doctrine of sin. This is because Bonhoeffer remains in the tradition of the Augustinian hamartiology of the West; however, he does not adopt the biological sense of original sin but applies a voluntary and ethical sense to the Augustinian hamartiology, extending this vicarious representative action of God in Christ to the action of the church community. It is now necessary to show that Bonhoeffer's methodological turn from the doctrine of God to ecclesiology determines the content of the doctrine of sin.

The concept of alien culpability has been considered one of the controversial issues in Augustinian hamartiology, not only between Augustine and Pelagius but also among many thinkers from Bonhoeffer's time until today.[117] In a similar vein to G. C. Berkouwer, who points out that many consider the doctrine of alien culpability a "harsh and entirely arbitrary" logic, for many contemporaries of Bonhoeffer the doctrine of alien culpability was outside of their concern.[118] However, although Bonhoeffer himself confesses that "the doctrine of original sin is one of the most difficult logical problems of all theology,"[119] he does not abandon or set aside the doctrine but puts it at the center of his theology by a creative reworking of the concept of involuntary sin as alien culpability.

One of the most important deficiencies of the doctrine of original sin, for Bonhoeffer, is that there is no room for the responsibility of the Christian person. In fact, the scope of the doctrine of the Augustinian doctrine of original sin itself is strongly bonded with the Augustinian doctrines of God and predestination. The emphasis on the sovereignty and benevolence of God is not compatible with any voluntaristic human action toward the doctrine of original sin. However, Augustine writes profoundly about the reconciliation and atonement of Christ toward sinners in his ecclesiology. In short, on the one hand, Augustine discusses the postlapsarian sinful nature and destiny of the human being within the boundary of the doctrine of original sin; on the other hand, he deals with sin after baptism in the realm of the church without a close interaction with the doctrine of original sin. At this juncture, however, Bonhoeffer places "Christ existing as church-community" at the nexus of the two doctrinal loci by placing hamartiology within the boundary of ecclesiology and connecting it with ecclesiology.[120] One of the most revolutionary transitions away from Augustine's methodology occurs when Bonhoeffer locates the sin of others or alien culpability in the church community.[121] As discussed in the preceding sections, Bonhoeffer offers his theological reformulation of alien culpability in relation to the corporate person of the church community beyond the boundary of the individual and the biological concept of alien culpability.

As Bonhoeffer indicates, the culpability of Adam is not biologically inherited; however, it is inseparably related to all human beings individually and corporately by the universal sinfulness after the fall. For Bonhoeffer, Augustine's notion of human solidarity encapsulated in the term *mass* or *massa pertionis* (lump of perdition) is partial because Augustine does not consider the ethical and voluntary solidarity of human beings.[122] Bonhoeffer is explicitly reinterpreting Augustine through Luther as well as his Lutheran teachers, especially Seeberg. In other words, Bonhoeffer reworks the traditional understanding of the biological imputation of Adam's sin through Luther's two-tiered *totus homo* (the whole person), in which the human is simultaneously *iustus et peccator* (righteous and a sinner) but *iustus* overcomes *peccator*. In this vein, Bonhoeffer distinguishes the new person in Christ and the old person in Adam. The old person in Adam is always under the reign of the new person in Christ, as Luther's soteriology indicated. Bonhoeffer's emphasis on the "new person" is fundamentally derived from Luther's imputed righteousness or passive righteousness, but his emphasis on the "ethical being" comes directly from the nineteenth-century Lutheran interpretation of Luther.[123] In the Lutheran understanding, Bonhoeffer uses the Christian concept of the ethical person as the lens for his reading of Augustinian culpability. The issue of alien culpability is central to Bonhoeffer's hamartiology, although his understanding is incompatible with "a biological concept of the species."[124] He argues that the Christian concept of alien culpability should be discussed using the socio-ethical concept of the human species. Bonhoeffer's statement below clearly shows his anthropological emphasis on the inseparable relationality between the human race and the concept of culpability. He states: "The concept of the species [Gattung] should be based upon the concept of culpability, not vice versa. This would allow us to move on to an ethical collective concept of the human race [Geschlecht], which alone can do full justice to the idea of the sin of the human race."[125] Here, one might observe the transition of the focus from Adam as an individual to Bonhoeffer's collective human race as the subject of culpability as well as the turn to an ethical and voluntaristic concept of culpability. Indeed, the most significant point in Bonhoeffer's thought is that he does not cancel or eliminate the theme of the alien culpability of the human race but instead seeks a fully justified explanation in connection with ecclesiology.[126]

Based on the reciprocal structure of human relationality, Bonhoeffer argues that "the experience of ethical solidarity and awareness of oneself as peccator pessimus [the worst sinner] belong together ... in a sinful way, whose 'overcoming' ['Aufhebung'] is only possible in the concept of the church."[127] He perceives that *peccatorum communio* can be overcome only by *sanctorum communio* as the body of Christ.[128] He further expands the concept of the culpability of the corporate person in an ethical and ecclesial way: "God is concerned not only with the nations, but has a purpose for the church. There is not only the culpability of Germans and individual Christians, but also the culpability of Germany and the church. It is not enough for individuals to repent and be justified; Germany and the church must likewise repent and be justified."[129]

It is clear that Bonhoeffer is replacing the individual and biological sense of culpability with the corporate and ethical aspect of culpability. For Augustine, the church is primarily *corpus Christi* (the body of Christ), which comes from his concept of the two-part body of Christ that explains the nature of the earthly church composed of saints and sinners in its journey to the heavenly city of God.[130] For Augustine, the earthly church is the place where saints stay before arriving in the heavenly *civitate Dei* (city of God); however, for Bonhoeffer the church community is the place where God in Christ exists as *sanctorum communio*. Similar to Luther, who understands a person in Christ, *totus homo*, as *simul iustus et peccator*,[131] Bonhoeffer views the church community as *a justified whole person* who is simultaneously in conflict between life in the old Adam and the new life in Christ.

Thus, the church community as a corporate person should not only repent its own culpability but also participate in the culpability of others. As Stanislaus J. Grobowski properly points out, Augustine's concept of participation is applicable only to *sanctorum communio*,[132] but Bonhoeffer expands Augustine's notion to mean that those who participate in *sanctorum communio* also participate in the culpability of *peccatorum communio*.[133] In communitarian life, an individual person can bear the sins of the other as a part of the body of Christ. Bonhoeffer distinctively redefines the church as the collective person and places an emphasis on the relationship between the collective person and the individual person in its bearing of the sin of the other as a part of this community of Christ. Bonhoeffer argues that "none of its members can bear [the sin of the other] alone."[134] The community of Christ is more than a collection of its members; it is one body and one spirit as *totus homo* or *totus Christus*. Bonhoeffer acknowledges the new identity of the church community, which incorporates individual saints and takes the culpability of the other by the good corporate will of the church community as the body of Christ and as Christ himself against the power [*Macht*] of the sin of *cor curvum in se*.[135] In this way, Bonhoeffer relates the vicarious action of Christ to the voluntary action of the church community regarding the sin of the other members through his transformative interpretation of *sanctorum communio* as *totus Christus*.

As Bonhoeffer comments, Luther created a bridge between Augustine's concept of *sanctorum communio* as the body of Christ and Bonhoeffer's notion of the *vicarious representative action* of the church community. Luther says: "Who could then despair over their sins? Who would not rejoice in their sorrows, since they no longer bear their own sins and punishment, or if they do not bear them alone, but are supported by so many holy children of God, yes, by Christ himself; so great a thing is the community of saints in the church of Christ."[136]

Bonhoeffer's discovery of the relationality between the work of Christ and the action of the church community, as he mentions, comes directly through Luther's interpretation of the *sanctorum communio* of Augustine. Luther argued that an individual saint alone could not bear the sins of its members; however, the "holy children of God" are supported by "Christ himself" and also by "the community of saints in the church of Christ," who bear the sin and punishment of the other.[137] Although both Luther and Augustine see the communal aspect of sin and atonement in the church, it is Bonhoeffer who emphasizes the relationality between the community and sin. Furthermore, as Bonhoeffer understands it, participation in the culpability of the other is voluntary and spontaneous because it is based on both the individual's and the collective person's will, which undergoes a dialectic process to reach an integrated decision only through the unity of the new humanity in Christ.[138] Bonhoeffer perceives that only the community of sinners that recognizes the culpability of Adam through its own consciousness of being guilty can be identified as the new community of Christ.[139] Consequently, Bonhoeffer expands the scope of the Lutheran concept of the person and combines the person of Christ with the church community, emphasizing the ethical and voluntary action of this collective person as the "royal rule in God's realm."[140] In this early theological stage, however, his concept of voluntary action toward others remains within the boundary of the traditional practices of the Western church such as "*self-renouncing, active work for the neighbor; intercessory prayer* ... [and] *the mutual forgiveness of sins* in God's name."[141]

To sum up, Bonhoeffer reformulates Augustinian hamartiology directly in reference to ecclesiology and indirectly but fundamentally in reference to Christology. In this process, he establishes the ethical responsibility of the church community based on the *Stellvertretung* of Christ, which neither Augustine nor Luther had clearly articulated. Furthermore, he embraces alien culpability by making this voluntary representative action an ultimate indicator of the church community as *sanctorum communio*, reflecting his Lutheran theological resources. Evidently, the ethical concept of the church community, in Bonhoeffer's early theological stage, remained chiefly at the traditional level that is focused on ecclesiastical practices. However, in his intermediate and later understanding, his notion of *Stellvertretung* is more closely connected to political social issues beyond the boundary of the church community. These issues are discussed in detail in Chapters 4 and 5.

Conclusion

Bonhoeffer's *Sanctorum Communio* offers an alternative reconstruction of the traditional Augustinian hamartiology, by shifting the standpoint of hamartiology from the doctrine of God to the doctrine of the church and approaching the concept of humanity from a socio-ethical Lutheran angle. As did some of his theological predecessors in the Western church, Bonhoeffer identifies the theological insufficiencies of the doctrine of original sin, especially its biological sense of the transmission of sin and human solidarity, which potentially contains risks of theological fatalism as well as of exoneration of Christian responsibility. Bonhoeffer's theological schema for overcoming these theological problems begins with his Christian personalism, which he appropriated from the language of modern sociology as well as the traditional Augustinian ecclesial notion of *totus Christus*. Bonhoeffer's Christian personalism permits him to relate the individual person with the communal or collective person, by which he can approach the sin of the individual but also of the community. Bonhoeffer is explicit that he makes Augustine's ecclesial concept of the church the theological foundation of his hamartiology in a way in which Christian responsibility toward the sin of others can be established as the golden rule of the new community of Christ.

Clearly, Bonhoeffer shifts the standpoint of his hamartiology from classical theism to ecclesiology based on his Lutheran Christocentrism as well as the concept of sociality. This community-focused methodological change is pivotal to the reform of the Augustinian doctrine of original sin by which he is able to readdress the concept of humanity from a socio-ethical perspective as well as approach the issue of sin in a more integrated way by relating adjacent theological themes such as creation, the fall, and reconciliation. In the process, Bonhoeffer firmly follows Luther's or the Lutherans' theological framework in which the sin of the church community is considered a struggle of *sanctorum communio* as *simul iustus et peccator*. Consequently, Bonhoeffer relates the doctrine of sin to the doctrine of the church community in which individual and communal persons can bear the sin of others as well as freely exercise the *vicarious representative action* of Christ as *sanctorum communio*. It is evident that Bonhoeffer's communitarian framework of hamartiology in *Sanctorum Communio* governs the direction of his entire hamartiology in his writings, from *Sanctorum Communio* to his *Letters and Papers from Prison*.

Bonhoeffer's early hamartiology in *Sanctorum Communio* has several noteworthy characteristics. First, Bonhoeffer disassociates from Augustine's philosophical discussion of sin and evil while more closely associating with the existential and relational aspects of hamartiology. Accordingly, Bonhoeffer's doctrine of sin is more focused on the experiential church community in which Christ is present as the community. Whereas Augustine's doctrine of sin focuses on the heavenly *civitate Dei* (city of God) as the ultimate and final destination of *sanctorum communio*, Bonhoeffer views the *civitate Dei* as already actualized in the experiential church community because God in Christ exists in it. Second, Bonhoeffer's hamartiology does not separate the theme of sin from the themes of creation and reconciliation. This maneuver avoids the danger of a one-sided description of the postlapsarian reality and of God's person and work in Christ. Bonhoeffer is concerned that these themes cannot be discussed individually but must always be connected. This is because the doctrine of sin becomes incomplete if the theme of sin is not related to its beginning, its resolution, and its continuing presence in the church community as well as to the theme of Christ's vicarious representative action.

Finally, Bonhoeffer's hamartiology attempts to fill the gap between the human's inability not to sin and the reconciled person's freedom and ethical responsibility in Christ toward the other. These hamartiological traits are dealt with more closely in subsequent chapters, following Bonhoeffer's theological development. This chapter has sketched the framework of Bonhoeffer's early hamartiology, and the next chapter focuses on the beginning of sin and evil based on Bonhoeffer's exegesis of the creation and the fall in Genesis in connection with the thoughts of Augustine and Luther as well as of Bonhoeffer's contemporary Lutherans.

Chapter 4

BONHOEFFER'S EXEGESIS OF THE CREATION AND THE FALL

Introduction

This book argues that Bonhoeffer's hamartiology reconstructs the Augustinian doctrine of original sin by relocating the hamartiological premise of the West from the doctrine of God to the doctrine of the church. Bonhoeffer's interpretation of the accounts of the creation and the fall in his 1932 work in *Creation and Fall* clearly reflects this methodological shift. In this vein, this chapter claims that Bonhoeffer's exegesis of the account of the creation and the fall integrates the Augustinian doctrine of original sin into his previous ethical and relational hamartiology based on his ongoing *ecclesiocentrism* and *modernized Christian personalism* by embracing both the spiritual and physical dimensions of sexuality or concupiscence as original sin, in a similar vein to Luther's early interpretation of *concupiscentia* (concupiscence).

In the process, his epistemological claim in *Act and Being*, which is rooted in his Lutheran concept of *cor curvum in se* (the heart curved in upon itself), offers a guide to his hermeneutics in *Creation and Fall*. Moreover, Bonhoeffer's renewed attention to Scripture becomes the catalyst for his new hamartiological perspective distinct from his previous assessment of the Augustinian doctrine of original sin in *Sanctorum Communio*, completed in 1927. Strikingly, in *Creation and Fall*, Bonhoeffer pays attention to the corporeal aspect of human solidarity and sin in addition to his previous emphasis on the ethical and relational dimensions of humanity and sin. This is primarily because he recognizes the importance of human corporeality throughout his exegesis; he understands the materiality of the human being originally as the *Grenze* (limit) between "the I and the other" as a given blessing as well as a source of hatred after the fall. Specifically, Bonhoeffer's hamartiology in this stage is complicated with his ethical and relational view that incorporates his new focus on the corporeality of humanity. This shift is pivotal in *Creation and Fall* as well as in his later hamartiology in which he deals with the relationality in the family, the church, the state, and the society as well as between God and humanity, especially in light of his understanding of God's humanization in Christ.[1] However, more importantly, despite Bonhoeffer's focus on the corporeality of humanity, his earlier emphasis on the ethical sense of alien culpability expressed in his notion of *Stellvertretung* (vicarious representative action) is continued in *Creation and Fall* as a central rule of the first community and is further intensified in his later hamartiology and ethics. Consequently, Bonhoeffer's interpretation of the creation and the fall account is associated with and distinguished from the traditional hamartiology of the West. On the one hand, Bonhoeffer follows the claim of Western hamartiology by upholding the sinful solidarity of the first community and emphasizing *cor curvum in se* or the egocentricity of the postlapsarian community as the essence of sin. On the other hand, Bonhoeffer expands the scope of the creation and the fall by including both Adam and Eve as the first humanity of God as well as the primary subject of the fall. Furthermore, he approaches the account from a modern angle by refusing to idealize the story of the creation and the fall and taking a more holistic view of the first community.

First, the chapter sketches Bonhoeffer's epistemological and intellectual context as a prerequisite for his interpretation of the chapters of Genesis. It investigates Bonhoeffer's theological epistemology in *Act and Being*, which supplies the hermeneutical principle for his exegesis in *Creation and Fall*. Based on this epistemology, the chapter examines Bonhoeffer's hermeneutical turn to "theological exegesis" and distinguishes it from the historical-criticism of his time. Second, the chapter explicates Bonhoeffer's approach to the creation account in which he critically embraces the traditional theological presuppositions of the West such as the doctrines of *crede ut intelligas* (believe in order that you may understand), *creatio ex nihilo* (creation out of nothing), and *imago Dei* (image of God) from his Christocentric or Trinitarian standpoint along with his Lutheran relational and ethical perspective. Third, the chapter investigates Bonhoeffer's interpretation of the creation of the human being in which he approaches the beginning of humanity and the concept of good and evil through his ecclesiocentric and communitarian perspective. Fourth, the chapter illustrates Bonhoeffer's hamartiological shift from a relational and ethical interpretation to a more holistic understanding of the fall and of the human being by integrating his new concern for the relationality between the fall and sexuality. Finally, the chapter summarizes the theological meaning and implications of Bonhoeffer's hamartiology in *Creation and Fall*.

Theological Turning Point

In focusing on Bonhoeffer's theological turn to Scripture along with his theological epistemology articulated in *Act and Being* and his hermeneutical turn to "theological exegesis," this section first briefly sketches Bonhoeffer's new recognition of the importance of Scripture. Second, it examines his theological epistemology that offers the basis for his exegesis of the account of the creation and the fall. It, then, explicates Bonhoeffer's turn to "theological exegesis," which is distinguished from historical-criticism due to the influence of Barth and Bonhoeffer's Lutheran background. Finally, it concludes by summarizing Bonhoeffer's own epistemological and hermeneutical perspective in *Creation and Fall* encapsulated in the notions of ecclesiocentrism and communitarian personalism.

Turn to Scripture

Bonhoeffer's lectures on the first three chapters of Genesis at the University of Berlin during the winter semester of 1932/1933 were later published as *Creation and Fall*. *Creation and Fall* is a continuation of his previous works, *Sanctorum Communio* and *Act and Being*, concerning ecclesiocentrism and communitarian personalism; however, it is remarkable that in *Creation and Fall* Scripture itself becomes central for the first time. Bonhoeffer's concern with the exegesis of Scripture is unquestionably due to the influence of Karl Barth's *The Word of God and Theology* and *The Epistle to the Romans*.[2] As Hans Urs von Balthasar commented, the second edition of *The Epistle to the Romans* was a decisive point in Barth's theological transition from liberal theology to a scriptural quest in attempting to overcome the theological and existential impasse of the Western church after the First World War.[3] Barth's transition from liberal theology to Scripture was an impetus for Bonhoeffer to recognize the importance of the Bible, which was still stressed in his own Lutheran tradition. As Eberhard Bethge describes, Bonhoeffer's experience of the word of God in 1932 significantly changed his theological direction thereafter.[4] Bonhoeffer wrote about this experience:

> Something different came, something that has changed and transformed my life to this very day. For the first time, I came to the Bible. … The Bible, especially the Sermon on the Mount, freed me from all this. Since then everything has changed. I have felt this plainly and so have other people around me. That was a great liberation.[5]

Bonhoeffer's choice to lecture on Gen. 1–3 in the winter semester of 1932/1933 is in line with his new awareness of the Bible in that time of "confusion, anxiety, and, for many, false hope."[6] Just as Barth considers Scripture the ultimate source of truth, Bonhoeffer focuses on the word of God in a time of chaos and crisis. Evidently, Bonhoeffer's view of Scripture as "a weapon in the course of the church struggle," especially the Old Testament, was the result of "a sudden and unprecedented revival of the use of scripture" in his theological reflections.[7] Although Barth's exposition of Scripture was the primary factor in Bonhoeffer's new interest in biblical exegesis, Bonhoeffer's Lutheran tradition also should be treated as a more fundamental factor.[8] Furthermore, the doctrine of sin, which is the central theme of *Creation and Fall*, also needs to be understood in terms of Bonhoeffer's active reception of Luther as well as Augustine. This neglected aspect of the Lutheran as well as Augustinian influence on Bonhoeffer's interpretation of the account of the creation and the fall is the focus of this chapter.

The mode of knowing in Christ

Bonhoeffer's lectures on the first three chapters of Genesis demonstrated his theological development and the transitions he had made since writing his doctoral dissertation. Primarily, his close attention to Scripture signifies the transition in his theological direction from the socio-theological method to *theological exegesis*. His first dissertation, *Sanctorum Communio*, shows his heavy reliance on a socio-theological foundation in regard to interpreting the meaning of the church in Christ. Then, in his *Habilitationsschrift*, *Act und Zein* (*Act and Being*), he offers an epistemological frame for his theology in which he points out the problem of the philosophical-transcendental epistemology in which reason becomes the basis of knowing God. His alternative to the philosophical-transcendental epistemology is the revelation of God in Christ. In *Creation and Fall*, the exegesis of the creation and the fall account is where Bonhoeffer actively reinterprets the doctrine of original sin through the epistemological foundation already explicated in his previous work, *Act and Being*.

As briefly noted above, Bonhoeffer's epistemological understanding was influenced by two major theological streams: Barth and the Lutheran tradition. As Michael P. DeJonge comments, Bonhoeffer's Lutheran tradition is an important aspect of his attention to Scripture that has been ignored.[9] The hiddenness of this aspect has been partly due to the attention many scholars have paid to Barth's influence on Bonhoeffer's turn to Scripture. Although two of Barth's books were the direct factor in his turn to Scripture, Bonhoeffer's Lutheran tradition was a pre-existing and fundamental part of his theology in which the church community, word, and sacraments are understood in regard to the revelation of God in Christ.[10] Bonhoeffer's attention to the word of God in *Creation and Fall* is understood more clearly when it is read through the lens of his theological epistemology, which is different from that of most other scholars of his time.

Similar to Luther's Reformation argument, Bonhoeffer does not give credit to human reason in the knowledge of God and the human being. Bonhoeffer construes that the inwardly curved human being's reason no longer functions as the epistemological foundation of theology; it never can attain knowledge of God by itself because God is only known through God's self-revelation in Christ.[11] In line with Luther's assertion, Bonhoeffer claims that "reason turned inward upon itself"—*ratio in se ipsam incurve*—is the starting point of philosophical epistemology as well as of transcendental theology.[12] He rejects reason as the basis of knowing God because reason itself is fundamentally "turned inward upon itself."[13] Just as Luther searches for the source of justification *extra nos* (outside ourselves), Bonhoeffer also looks for the foundation of epistemology outside of the human being. To explain his epistemology, he employs an opposing epistemological pair—*actus reflexus* (consciousness of reflection) and *actus directus* (direct consciousness)[14]—to discover the source of the theological mode of knowing.[15] On the one hand, *actus reflexus* is to know through the reflection of human reason; on the other hand, *actus directus* is to know from the act of God's revelation in Christ. He suggests that the knowing through the mode of *actus reflexus* cannot surpass the boundary of the I that is curved in upon itself and cannot stretch out to the knowledge of God, which is only known through the concrete revelation in Christ through faith.[16] He argues that the epistemology of transcendentalism as well as of idealism is merely a vain "attempt of the

I to understand itself" because the I is closed by its egocentricity, known as *cor curvum in se*, and does not have the power to go beyond the boundary of the sinful self.[17]

Analogous to the critique of the concept of the person in idealism demonstrated in *Sanctorum Communio*, Bonhoeffer asserts that the epistemology that presupposes God as the object of human capacity is neither holistic nor concrete because it remains captured in abstract ideas of the I. The fundamental problem of transcendental epistemology for Bonhoeffer is its reversal of subject-object relationality. As long as the I is in the place of the subject, God is in the place of the object. In other words, when the human being is the subject of divine knowledge, God becomes the object of human knowledge, and this knowledge no longer is the knowledge of God but the knowledge of the human self or the knowledge of "my own divine *Doppelgänger*"—it only exists in abstraction.[18] Accordingly, Bonhoeffer suggests that true knowledge of God may be acquired through the mode of *actus directus* found in the revelation of God in Christ.[19] In *Act and Being*, he attempts to rethink the mode of knowing God in terms of the revelation of God in Christ that is initiated by Godself and fundamentally belongs to the boundary of *extra nos*. Bonhoeffer considers that the epistemology of transcendentalism as well as of idealism is a mode of knowing resulting from *actus reflexus*. One of the most problematic features of the epistemology derived from *actus reflexus* for Bonhoeffer is its lack of concreteness. The epistemological way of abstraction in transcendentalism and idealism results in a totally different conclusion about the knowledge of God as well as about the knowledge of sin and the human being. Bonhoeffer views the abstraction in epistemology as a circular logic within the sinful self that has the crucial, dangerous possibility of ignoring the concrete revelation in Christ.

Bonhoeffer further offers the basis of theological knowing from the standpoint of Christ. He argues that "the concept of revelation must, therefore, yield an epistemology of its own."[20] He talks about the origin of theological knowledge that is not abstract but concrete and is revealed in Christ through the Bible.[21] Contrary to *actus reflexus*, *actus directus* arises from the act of revelation and is directed outward toward the other. In Bonhoeffer's eyes, the risk of *actus reflexus* is evident in the epistemologies of most philosophies as well as of transcendental theologies.[22] The *actus reflexus* arises from the self, orienting inwardly toward "its own self in reflection."[23] In this way, knowing God through human resources is impossible for humans. However, Bonhoeffer continues to argue that this impossibility in Adam as a human can be overcome only by the possibility of God in Christ.[24] The reality of the revelation of God in Christ is thus the actualized possibility of God within the history of impossibility. Thus, knowing God as well as knowing humanity and sin is only through God's possibility out of the impossibility in the human being.

In short, for Bonhoeffer, knowing God means primarily knowing or encountering the person of Christ and secondarily knowing the knowledge of Christ. Bonhoeffer's epistemology illustrated in *Act and Being* is inseparably connected to his hermeneutical foundation in Christ expressed in his exegesis of the account of the creation and the fall. Bonhoeffer declares his epistemological position in *Act and Being*—that it is rooted in concrete reality in the revelation in Christ rather than in speculative abstraction. This is clearly a transition from intellectual current of his time.

Theological exegesis

Bonhoeffer's epistemological posture in *Act and Being* is continued in his exegesis of Genesis in his lectures at the University of Berlin. As John W. de Gruchy points out, Bonhoeffer's "theological exegesis" in *Creation and Fall* was scorned by most of the systematic and biblical scholars of his time. Akin to an attempt by Barth at "theological exegesis" in *The Epistle to the Romans*, Bonhoeffer's theological exegesis was not considered a scientific and systematic approach to Scripture compared to the historical-critical method of liberal theologians of the time such as Adolf von Harnack.[25] This atmosphere is clearly seen in a letter from Harnack to Bonhoeffer.[26] In this letter, Harnack warns Bonhoeffer that "our theological existence is additionally threatened by contempt for academic theology and by unscholarly theologies. Hence all those loyal to genuine scholarship must hold its banner high all the more confidently."[27] But, as Bethge notes, after his reading of Barth's writings in 1925, "A new certainty replaced Bonhoeffer's restless wandering."[28] For Bonhoeffer, "theological exegesis" meant more than just an alternative to other interpretive methods with some new theoretical tools. Bonhoeffer perceived the epistemological foundation in the revelation of God in Christ as beyond any system of theories and abstractions. He understood that the genuine hermeneutics of Scripture could not be derived from human capacity.[29] This came from his conviction that Christ is present in the word as well as in the church community and the sacraments.[30] With this agenda, Bonhoeffer asserted that even the best system of hermeneutics could not replace the theological exegesis that arises from the revelation of Christ through the word.

As this indicates, Bonhoeffer's hermeneutical approach toward the revelation of God in Christ definitely originated not only in the theological impact of Barth's turn to Scripture but also in the revival of studies of Luther's works led by Lutheran scholars.[31] In an early paper on biblical exegesis when he was a student of theology, Bonhoeffer insisted that "even the most ingenious interpreter understands things from the 'I.'"[32] Bonhoeffer's disassociation from the exegesis of liberal theology, especially from the methods of liberal Lutheran theologians such as Harnack and Seeberg, is quite clear in his style of hermeneutics in *Creation and Fall*. Adolf von Harnack, under whom Bonhoeffer took at least three special seminars on the early history of the church,[33] was one of the leading Lutheran liberal scholars in Germany and, needless to say, Harnack's historical-critical method of liberal theology was one of the most provocative theological influences in academia in nineteenth- and twentieth-century Germany. As Martin Rumscheidt explains, the ideal of liberal theology was its "free, critical and independent theological thought."[34]

Rumscheidt succinctly summarizes the characteristics of the methodology of the liberal position:

> The 'liberal position' exhibited confidence in the human spirit, reverence for the dignity, competence and authority of the power of thinking, and trust in the ability of human beings to transcend their subjectivity in the endeavour to reach true objectivity.[35]

The epistemological presupposition of liberal theology is its high view of the ability of the human being in terms of the possibility of human freedom to attain true objectivity. In the midst of this intellectual atmosphere of his time, in Bonhoeffer's eyes, his way of "theological hermeneutics" was clearly distinguished not only from historical-critical methodology but also from any other methodology that resulted in mere abstraction without engaging with the concrete revelation of God. Erich Kapproth's notes on Bonhoeffer's introduction to the lectures on Genesis clearly reflect Bonhoeffer's assessment of historical criticism:

> The word of God [is] neither fiction nor fairy tale nor myth; on the contrary one must read it word for word [*buchstabieren*] like a child and learn to rethink *completely* what the historical critical commentaries teach us. One can never hear it, if one does not at the same time live it—and this involves especially *exercitium* ['practice'].[36]

Bonhoeffer turned to the Barthian way of "theological exegesis," but he also simultaneously turned to Lutheran hermeneutics, especially to Luther's Christocentrism represented by *totus Christus* (the whole Christ). Bonhoeffer's hermeneutical claim is in line with Barth's methodology because Bonhoeffer follows Barth's theological interpretation, which most of the scholars of the time criticized as a nonscientific and nonobjective approach to hermeneutics.[37] As de Gruchy points out, the accounts of the creation and the fall in Genesis were considered "primitive tales" by most scholars in the context of the dominance of historical criticism and the development of the natural sciences in Germany of the 1920s and 1930s.[38] Harnack and most of the scholars in Berlin considered the theological exegesis of Bonhoeffer derived from Barth's approach as lacking a scientific or scholarly basis.[39] Bonhoeffer's theological exegesis was viewed as straying from the standards of the scientific method.

However, Bonhoeffer understood that the word of God should be approached in a theological way rather than in a scientific or speculative way. This was because he was convinced that the Scripture should be understood from the angle of theology, not that of science or philosophy.[40] Clearly, Bonhoeffer's renewed epistemology supplied the foundation for his theological exegesis by which he began to interpret the creation account in Genesis. His "theological exegesis" signals his turn to Barth's methodology; however, it is more appropriate to say that it is a turn to Luther's methodology in his own synthetic way.

Ecclesiocentric hermeneutics

In *Creation and Fall*, Bonhoeffer's theological epistemology in *Act and Being* is closely interconnected with his previous *Christocentrism* and *Christian personalism*. In the beginning of *Creation and Fall*, he clearly illustrates some important hermeneutical themes derived from theological epistemology. Bonhoeffer states:

> The Church of Christ witnesses to the end of all things. It lives from the end, it thinks from the end, it acts from the end, it proclaims its message from the end. 'Do not remember the former things or consider the things of old. I am about to do a new thing' (Isa. 43:18–19). The new is the real end of the old; the new, however, is Christ.[41]

The most distinctive point in Bonhoeffer's hermeneutics is that he considers the church of Christ, as the body of Christ, *the subject of the new world*. He argues that all things should be understood from the eyes of the church of Christ. Just as he argued in *Sanctorum Communio*, Christ exists as the community of saints, and the appropriate interpretation of Scripture is the reading of biblical messages from the end, which is the revelation of God in Christ. It is clear that Bonhoeffer's Christian personalism in the concept of the collective person is the starting point for his hermeneutics of the Genesis account. Bonhoeffer declares that the old should be interpreted in the new, which is Christ existing as church community. He considers Christ the subject of Scripture and argues that both testaments are pointing to and witnessing Christ.[42] The ecclesiocentric hermeneutics in *Creation and Fall* indicates his decisive disengagement from the historical-critical approach of Harnack as well as from Seeberg's "pneumatic" interpretation.[43] One of the important aspects of this theological exegesis is his substantively Christocentric and therefore decidedly ecclesiocentric exegesis, which reads Scripture as the witness of Christ.[44] He argues from the standpoint of Christ that "the new is the real end of the old; the new is, however, Christ."[45]

This perspective of Bonhoeffer from Christ came from Barth's Christocentrism, which was itself rooted in Luther's Christocentrism. Surprisingly, when one traces back to the source of the Christocentrism of Barth and Bonhoeffer, it is Luther. A unique aspect of Bonhoeffer's Christocentrism is its overlapping of Luther's thinking with Barth's as well as with his Lutheran teachers.'[46] As Bethge points out,[47] the most important influence on Bonhoeffer in relation to Christocentrism came directly from Luther and secondarily from the perspectives of Barth and Bonhoeffer's Lutheran teachers.[48] At this point, George Hunsinger's argument is helpful. Hunsinger argues that the original impulse of Barth's Christocentrism was from Luther rather than from Lutheran scholastics in the seventeenth century or from modern Reformed theologians such as Schleiermacher and Polanus.[49] Hunsinger suggests:

> Not least among the many powerful themes that Barth would absorb from Luther is that of 'christocentrism,' perhaps the most basic point in all of Barth's theology. Indeed Barth not only owed this point to Luther but went on to radicalize it. In

this respect he would remain truer in some ways to the spirit than to the letter of Luther's thought.[50]

It is evident that Christocentrism is a quintessential characteristic of Bonhoeffer's theology from his early works forward and that the influence of Luther was ubiquitous in his context. However, as Hunsinger points out, just as Barth's turn to Christocentrism was not toward the work of Lutheran scholastics but to Luther himself, it is notable that Bonhoeffer's attention to Christocentric exegesis also was focused on the works of Luther rather than his Lutheran teachers. If Hunsinger's assertion is correct, it is reasonable to say that Bonhoeffer's turn to the Christocentrism of Barth is at the same time a turn to Luther's Christocentrism and theology. Furthermore, Hunsinger assesses that Barth radicalized Luther— in other words, he appropriated Luther's "spirit" rather than Luther's "letter" in regard to Christocentrism. This point is crucial to discerning Bonhoeffer's Christocentrism, especially in his hermeneutics. Bethge describes Bonhoeffer as wanting to follow the Christocentrism of Luther,[51] but Bonhoeffer's Christocentrism is distinct from that of Barth as well as from that of his Lutheran teachers. As Hunsinger explains, whereas Barth distilled the spirit of Luther's Christocentrism and transformed it in his own Reformed way, Bonhoeffer followed not only the spirit but also the letter of Luther's Christocentrism in his own modern as well as Lutheran way.[52] Bonhoeffer explicitly presented his hermeneutical method as different from historical criticism as well as from any other methods derived from human analysis or reasoning.

As already noted, Bonhoeffer's *ecclesiocentrism* is the primary trait of his hermeneutics. The second distinctive aspect is his emphasis on his *communitarian concept of the person* as the basis of his interpretation of the account of creation and the fall. In the beginning of *Creation and Fall*, the premise of the exegesis is that the church is a person as the witness of Christ. In its continuation of *Sanctorum Communio* and *Act and Being*, the church is interpreted as a collective person existing as the community of saints that is the locus of the presence of Christ. This emphasis on the real presence of Christ in the church community is one of the main characteristics of Luther's theology as well as of Bonhoeffer's lens for interpreting the account of the creation and the fall.[53] Bonhoeffer joins this concept of the ubiquity of Christ or of the presence of Christ in the church with his collective concept of the first community in *Creation and Fall*. Bonhoeffer's application of the collective concept of the person to the first human being is compelling for discovering the relationality between God and the human being as well as among the human beings in the first community. Based on his newly vitalized focus on the Bible, Bonhoeffer conceives of the church as a collective person who lives from the beginning of the creation until the end of history. He interprets the church as living not only synchronically but also diachronically, witnessing to "the end of all things."[54] In this way, Bonhoeffer projects backward the revelation of God in Christ in the church community as the reality of the first community.

For Bonhoeffer, the church as the collective person has lived from the beginning of the creation till the end in Christ.[55] In this way, "The church of Christ witnesses to the end of all things. It lives from the end, it thinks from the end, it acts from the end, it proclaims its message from the end."⁵⁶ For Bonhoeffer, the end means the revelation of God in Christ in the church community. Thus, the life of the church as a collective person begins with the creation, and Christ is the center of the church as well as the creation. This inseparable relationality between Christ and the church as a collective person is the essence of Bonhoeffer's "theological exposition" of Scripture. As his methodological transition from the doctrine of God to the doctrine of the church in *Sanctorum Communio*, Bonhoeffer argues that Scripture should be read from "the viewpoint of the church."⁵⁷ In his introduction to *Creation and Fall*, Bonhoeffer suggests his new way of hermeneutics as an alternative to historical criticism.⁵⁸ This "theological exegesis" is a way of hermeneutics that interprets the Bible through "belief" and "theological science."⁵⁹ His emphasis on *belief* and *theology* in biblical hermeneutics signifies his intention to highlight the difference between the foundations of theology and other academic sciences. In other words, the premise of theological epistemology as well as of hermeneutics must be different from any other areas of study. In short, interpretation of Scripture, for Bonhoeffer, is nothing other than reading the book of the church community from the standpoint of the end, which is Christ.⁶⁰ Accordingly, the first three chapters of Genesis "must be read in a way that begins with Christ and only then moves on toward him as its goal."⁶¹ The presence of Christ in the church community explicitly underlies Bonhoeffer's hamartiological exegesis in *Creation and Fall*. Accordingly, two central hermeneutical lenses, ecclesiocentrism and communitarian personalism, work together hand in hand in *Creation and Fall*.

The Beginning

In *Creation and Fall*, Bonhoeffer reinterprets major theological doctrines of the West, such as the doctrines of *crede ut intelligas*, *creatio ex nihilo*, and *imago Dei*, based on his Christocentric and relational perspective. These concepts are intertwined with his exegesis of the story of the creation and the fall.

Crede ut intelligas

Interestingly, whereas Barth started by applying his Christocentrism to the exegesis of the Epistle to the Romans, Bonhoeffer begins with Genesis, extending his Christocentrism to the concept of the first community. His turn to the Old Testament is a significant theological claim in which he embraces the Old Testament as Christian Scripture. Bonhoeffer expresses his concern for the truth hidden in the circular rationale of the first three chapters of the Bible:

> The place where the Bible begins is one where our own most impassioned waves of thinking break, are thrown back upon themselves, and lose their strength in spray and foam. The first word of the Bible has hardly for a moment surfaced

before us, before the waves frantically rush in upon it again and cover it with wreaths of foam. ... Where the beginning begins, there our thinking stops; there it comes to an end.[62]

In his exegesis of the story of the beginning (Gen. 1:1-2), Bonhoeffer clearly follows not only the Augustinian as well as the Lutheran tradition of *crede ut intelligas* but also the proleptic perspective from the end.[63] As Bonhoeffer demonstrates in his epistemology, the story of the beginning belongs to a realm that our reason cannot penetrate. In line with the Augustinian tradition, Bonhoeffer acknowledges that the story of creation belongs to the area of *sacrificium intellectus* (surrender of thinking) in which our thinking stops.[64] He adds that "I am willing to grant that this or that passage of Scripture cannot yet be understood, though with the certainty that one day this passage will indeed be revealed as God's own word. ... This is divine, while that is human!"[65] More importantly, however, he points out that the Old Testament is interpreted from the perspective of the church—in other words, "in light of the new world."[66] The distinctiveness of Bonhoeffer's hermeneutics is clearly illustrated by his emphasis on the end, Christ. This presuppositional argument of *sacrificium intellectus* resonates with the Augustinian tradition of *crede ut intelligas*, but Bonhoeffer's *sacrificium intellectus* is simultaneously based on the revelation of God in Christ in the church community. Bonhoeffer here affirms the precedence of faith over the account of creation, which is absolutely inconceivable.[67] For Bonhoeffer, it is a realm in which belief alone is the key to entering into the story of the creation.

As Bonhoeffer states, he turns to the Augustinian concept of "faith seeking understanding" because he basically agrees with the inconceivability of the enquiries in regard to the account of creation, as in the old question of the "inconsistent triad."[68] In a similar fashion to Augustine's search for the dilemma in theodicy, Bonhoeffer argues that the search for the beginning is unattainable because it is a search that continuously goes back to the same question due to the question itself being within the frame of a *circulus vitiosus*, "a circular argument." In other words, it is located in the frame of "a faulty or erroneous circle."[69] Here Bonhoeffer, using the same logic as in *Act and Being*, criticizes the limitedness of *ratio* (reason) represented by the logic of historical criticism that has a conceptual structure that continuously goes back to the circular argument of the *incurvatus in se* of the self.

Considering the academic context of his time, Bonhoeffer's turn to the Augustinian perspective of *crede ut intelligas* as the starting point for reading the account of creation is a reversal of the current trend of his time to uphold the *ratio* or *experientia* (experience) of the human being in regard to the exegesis of Scripture.[70] In particular, his application of the *crede ut intelligas* tradition in his exegesis of the creation account, which scholars who favored historical criticism considered an unscientific fairy tale as part of the strong movement of dehistoricization, represents a significant shift in his theological orientation from then on. Bonhoeffer does not consider the story of creation in Genesis historically correct or scientifically provable because he perceives that the story should be received theologically as the word of God, which contains unfathomable truth about the relationality between God and creation that only can be understood from the end, Christ. This is not just a story that can be read through the lens of science or psychology but a story that can be read properly only from the perspective of theology in the relationality of God and humanity. In this way, Bonhoeffer's turn toward the approach of Luther and Augustine is a trait of his theological exegesis through which he retrieves the tradition of the Western church or, more precisely, the hermeneutics of Luther who radicalized Augustine's theology.[71]

Creation out of nothing

As already indicated, closely related to Augustine and Luther, Bonhoeffer argues that the question *why* in the story of creation "only gives expression to a series of questions that could be pushed back endlessly."[72] Based on this understanding, Bonhoeffer interprets *creatio ex nihilo* (creation out of nothing) in accordance with the tradition of the church.[73] He evaluates the event of creation as an "unrepeatable, unique, free event in the beginning" of history, but he does not agree with the traditional date of creation, such as "the number 4800 or any such date."[74] Bonhoeffer's acceptance of the doctrine of *creatio ex nihilo* is extended to the question of theodicy. In a similar fashion to Augustine's refutation of Manicheanism, Bonhoeffer also raises and answers the question of the logical relationality between the problem of evil and the benevolent God. Bonhoeffer argues: "The twofold question arises: Is this beginning God's own beginning, or is it God's beginning with the world?"[75] Indubitably, this question is theologically connected to the question of theodicy. Bonhoeffer states:

> Who can speak of the beginning? There are two possibilities. The speaker may be the one who has been a liar from the beginning, the evil one, for whom the beginning is the lie and the lie is the beginning, whom human beings believe because the evil one deceives them with lies. ... It is either the evil one who speaks or that other who speaks, the one who has been the truth from the beginning, and the way and the life, the one who was in the beginning, the very God, Christ, the Holy Spirit.[76]

This inconceivable question on God and evil is significant for Augustine as well as for Bonhoeffer because it is inseparably related to the beginning of evil and sin in the world. Bonhoeffer emphasizes the inability of human beings to discern the beginning of the human being as well as of God.[77] Referring to Augustine, Bonhoeffer argues that the narrative at the beginning of Genesis is the voice of the very God, Christ, the Holy Spirit, and accordingly this story is read properly only from the perspective of the church that is the witness of Christ. The existence of evil in the world is an issue beyond the human capacity to understand and is only addressable through the perspective of the revelation of God in Christ or as belonging to the area of mystery or the realm of *crede ut intelligas*.

In this understanding, Bonhoeffer interprets the doctrine of *creatio ex nihilo* from his Christocentric angle. The creation from nothingness that Augustine understood from his hierarchical Platonic perspective of being is reinterpreted in Bonhoeffer's Christocentric approach. Bonhoeffer relates the nothingness of creation to the resurrection of Christ. Bonhoeffer writes:

> The world exists in the midst of nothing, which means in the beginning. This means nothing else than that it exists wholly by God's freedom. What has been created belongs to the [free] Creator. ... The world exists from the beginning in the sign of the resurrection of Christ from the dead. ... The dead Jesus Christ of Good Friday and the resurrected κύριος of Easter Sunday—that is creation out of nothing, creation from the beginning.[78]

The Christocentric interpretation is distinctive in Bonhoeffer's understanding of *creatio ex nihilo* in regard to his concept of God's creation in freedom. As Bonhoeffer points out, the meaning of nothingness in the church tradition is closely engaged with Augustine's privative understanding of nothingness as seen in his definition of evil as "privation of good." Bonhoeffer interprets the doctrine of *creatio ex nihilo* of the church as *nihil negativum* (absolute nothingness) rather than *nihil provativum* (privative nothingness), arguing that *nihil provativum* is a "somewhat clumsy description of the nothing" by the people of "a bygone time."[79] At this point, Bonhoeffer's frame of *nihil* is different from Augustine's hierarchical understanding of the universe in which evil is understood as nothing or as the privation of good. Bonhoeffer's reading from the perspective of Christ reads nothingness as *nihil negativum*, the starting point of God's creation out of freedom in close relation to God's relational act of freedom in creation as well as Christ's resurrection from nothing. In this way, "Nothingness as the ground for being is understood as a creative nothingness."[80] Bonhoeffer decisively relates the free act of God in *creatio ex nihilo* to the resurrection of Christ. He states that "the one who is the beginning lives, destroys the nothing, and in his resurrection creates the new creation."[81] This Christocentric interpretation is a turn to Luther's theological methodology in which the creation is interpreted based on God's free action toward creatures, in other words, Christ's freedom for others.

Two trees: Tob *and* ra

Bonhoeffer's transformative interpretation of the creation account is continued in his notion of *tob* and *ra* (good and evil). Whereas Augustine describes the prelapsarian garden of Eden as a somewhat unrealistic heavenly community of Adam distanced from the present world, Bonhoeffer's exegesis of the first community is more realistic and is focused on humankind's genuine freedom and limits in relation to the perspective of *extra nos*.[82] Bonhoeffer describes the characteristics of the first created community with his notion of *Mitte* [center] and *Grenze* [limit].[83] This conceptual pair of "center and limit" leads Bonhoeffer to explain the nature of the first community and the trees of knowledge and life through his relational perspective.[84] Bonhoeffer interprets the *Mitte* as the source of the life of humankind in which the freedom of humanity is activated in relationship with God. He demonstrates this communicative relationship by arguing that "Adam has life in the unity of unbroken obedience to the Creator—has life because Adam lives from the center of life, and is oriented toward the center of life, without placing Adam's own life at the center."[85] The possession of life means the possession of freedom for Bonhoeffer.[86] However, he adds that this freedom exists simultaneously with *Grenze*, arguing that "they possess it [freedom] in their *obedience*, in their *innocence*, in their *ignorance*."[87]

The concept of *Mitte* and *Grenze* is more vividly described with Bonhoeffer's understanding of the trees of knowledge and life. The tree of knowledge symbolizes the *Grenze*, which protects Adam and Eve to live in freedom without knowing *tob* and *ra*. The freedom of humankind is like the freedom exercised by children, beyond the notions of good and evil, who have an intimate relationship with their parents.[88] On the one hand, the *Mitte* is the place of God where the first community is supplied its existential resources. On the other hand, the *Grenze* signifies "the limit of human possibility."[89] In the *Mitte*, two trees stand as the symbols of *tob* and *ra*.[90] As Bonhoeffer interprets it, these two trees are simultaneously at the *Mitte* of the community as *Grenze*. In other words, both are related as the source of life and death, signifying God's presence in the community.

Bonhoeffer points out that humanity's desire to be "like God" (*sicut Deus*) is the beginning of the first sin. Although he clearly follows the Augustinian hamartiological tradition of pride, his description of the desire to be like God is related to his understanding of morality. At this point, Jennifer M. McBride and Thomas Fabisiak argue that for Bonhoeffer "the desire to be like God—to grow beyond our humanity and live out of our own moral resources—is, at its core, a religious one."[91] In other words, the beginning of the first rebellion against God comes from the desire to be pious, by which the serpent stimulates Eve and Adam to misuse their genuine freedom for their vain desire to be pious by eating from the tree of knowledge. They need to eat from the tree of knowledge to be more pious and moral based on their own standard of good and evil. Bonhoeffer observes that evil first appears in a disguised form as a pious question. He says, "[W]ith the first pious question in the world, evil appears on the scene."[92] Bonhoeffer perceives that evil hides its real face behind the seemingly religious and ethical question as the serpent in the garden instigates Eve and Adam's desire to be pious or religious. The pious question of the serpent is evil because it "already contains the wrong answer."[93] The fall begins with humanity's desire to be like God in its own piety and morality.[94]

After the fall, the human race lost the limits or boundaries symbolized by the two trees located at the center of the garden. This means that postlapsarian humanity needs to judge good and evil by their own standards or boundaries. Bonhoeffer determines that the problem of Adam and Eve after eating from the tree of knowledge is not their new capacity to know good and evil per se but the fact that their capacity is no longer related to God, who is the source of true knowledge and life. He states, "Now humankind stands in the middle, with no limit. Standing in the middle means living from its own resources and no longer from the center."[95] They need to live based on their own resources for knowing good and evil. They become like God (*sicut Deus*), self-sufficient, but the issue is that they are not God but they desire to be "like" God.[96] Bonhoeffer explains:

> Humankind is now sicut deus. It now lives out of its own resources, creates its own life, is its own creator; it no longer needs to the Creator, it has itself becomes creator, inasmuch as it creates its own life. Thereby its creatureliness is eliminated, destroyed. … Losing *the limit*[,] Adam has lost *creatureliness*.[97]

There are no trees of knowledge and life at the center of the postlapsarian community. As Bonhoeffer criticizes the presupposition of idealism as well as historical criticism's confidence in human reason, he argues that limited resources bound the freedom of the postlapsarian human beings. Accordingly, for Bonhoeffer, the freedom of human beings is not genuine freedom but limited or bound freedom.

Contrary to the limited freedom of humanity, Bonhoeffer contends that the freedom of God is the freedom for others as expressed in the acts of the creation and the atonement. Bonhoeffer understands the freedom of Adam and Eve before the fall is the freedom for the other, for both the divine and the human other. More importantly, this freedom for the other is maintained by boundaries, the trees of knowledge and life. The two trees simultaneously should be at the center of the community for Eve and Adam to live out as free responsible members of the community. After violating the limit after the fall, however, the freedom for others is freed from its genuine limits and turned to freedom for the self in egocentricity, following one's own standards of *tob* and *ra*.

Accordingly, the first community, after eating from the tree of knowledge, undergoes an inner split (*Zwiespalt*). Bonhoeffer argues:

> It is we who have eaten from the tree of knowledge, not Adam. … Both trees are still untouched and untouchable; both constitute the boundary and their center. Whoever grasps at life must die; 'those who want to save their life will lose it.' Only those who have lost it, however, will grasp at it. And those who have attained the knowledge of good and evil, who live as people who are split apart within themselves [im Zwiespalt], have lost their life.[98]

Bonhoeffer reads the meaning of the two trees in a Christocentric and salvific way. He emphasizes that not only the tree of life but also the tree of knowledge is given by God. Furthermore, he considers that Adam's eating from the tree of knowledge is not only the starting point of death but also the step to attain life. Bonhoeffer describes the result of eating from the tree of knowledge as humans "split apart within themselves."[99] The split between good and evil means a split between the people in the community, and it leads them to death. This death is not immediate physical death but the spiritual or ethical death of Adam as humankind or as community. In this way, people have lost their relational life between the I and the human other as well as between the I and the divine other. Adam as humankind has fallen. In short, Bonhoeffer's exegesis of *tob* and *ra* shows his theological emphasis on Adam as a communal person. His Trinitarian or Christocentric methodology makes him connect the concept of *tob* and *ra* with the community of Christ in which sin and evil is overcome by the reconciling work of Christ. Explicitly, Bonhoeffer's analysis of evil and the ignorant participation of Eve and Adam in the cunning question of the serpent foreshadows the German people's "prideful yet stupid" participation in Hitler's brutal regime (see Chapter 5).[100] Furthermore, the notion of freedom for the other is an essential theological nexus by which Bonhoeffer develops the doctrine of Christian ethics and responsibility in his later theology (see Chapters 5 and 6).

Analogia relationis

Furthermore, in a similar way to Luther, Bonhoeffer understands *imago Dei* chiefly in regard to God's freedom, disassociated from *analogia entis* (analogy of being). Bonhoeffer develops and deepens Luther's interpretation of God's freedom in creation. Whereas for Augustine *imago Dei* is primarily a vestige of the immanent Trinity in the human soul, for Bonhoeffer the image of God in the human being primarily signifies the relation between God and the human being as God's creation in community. Bonhoeffer clearly denies the Augustinian interpretation of *analogia entis* as *imago Dei*, and he further radicalizes Luther's relational understanding of God's freedom as expressed in *analogia relationis* (analogy of relation).[101] He argues that "God needed no link between God and the creation; even the nothing constitutes no such 'between.'"[102] Bonhoeffer's understanding of nothingness provides a transformative interpretation of the image of God from Luther's as well as Augustine's perspectives. As Bonhoeffer states, the nothingness is a *nihil negativum* or *creative nothingness*, and this nothingness prevents relating God and the human being in terms of *analogia entis*. This tendency to disassociate from *analogia entis* is seen in Luther's exegesis of Genesis and is clearly articulated in Bonhoeffer's illustration. Bonhoeffer argues:

> The "image that is like God" is therefore no analogia entis in which human beings, in their existence in-and-of-themselves, in their being, could be said to be like God's being. There can be no such analogy between God and humankind. This is so in the first place because God—who alone has self-sufficient being in aseity, yet at the same time is there for God's creature, binding God's freedom to humankind and so giving God's self to humankind. ... The likeness, the analogia, of humankind to God is not analogia entis but *analogia relationis*. What this means, however, is firstly, that the relation too is not a human potential or possibility or a structure of human existence; instead it is a given relation, a relation in which human beings are set, a justitia passiva![103]

The theological meaning of Bonhoeffer's disengagement with *analogia entis* and favoring of *analogia relationis* is one of the nexuses that indicates his theological direction. Clearly, it is a continuation and development of the soteriological ethos of Luther encapsulated in *justitia passiva* (passive righteousness). Seen from an anthropological perspective, similar to Luther's anthropology Bonhoeffer's denial of the traditional anthropological understanding of *analogia entis* is logically related to his objection to the presupposition of idealism as well as to historical criticism, which he considers "the bold and violent action of enthroning reason in the place of God."[104] Bonhoeffer perceives that *analogia entis* presupposes the likeness of God that fragmentally remains in the human mental capability in postlapsarian human beings. This resonates not only with Barth's notion of "the infinite qualitative distinction" between God and humanity but also with Luther's doctrine of creation in which God created the human being in God's *relational* freedom, which is inseparably interconnected with Luther's soteriological notion of *iustitia passiva*.[105] In a similar way, Bernhard Lohse comments that "the uniqueness of Luther's exposition of the article on creation consists first in its existential reference, then in its inclusion of justification."[106] The concept of *analogia relationis* is clearly from Bonhoeffer's development of Luther's doctrine of creation, in which Luther makes the connection between God and humanity through the lens of God's free and relational action toward humanity.

Furthermore, Bonhoeffer's relational understanding of *imago Dei* is essential for his understanding of the human being in regard to the doctrine of sin and the notion of freedom. For Bonhoeffer, the meaning of the human being determines the action and responsibility of the human being as the foundation and the direction of life. He argues for the importance of the relational understanding of the human being as *imago Dei*.[107] Bonhoeffer's interpretation of the image of God shows his agreement with Luther's relational interpretation of *imago Dei*, which is distinct from the traditional concept of *analogia entis*.[108] In regard to Bonhoeffer's relation to his Lutheran tradition, it is helpful to reference a comment of Holl, one of the figures who influenced Bonhoeffer' theology. As DeJonge points out, Holl understood Luther's Reformation as having two main theological characteristics: *radical character of sin* and divine *monergism in justification*.[109] Considering Holl's summary of Luther's theology, Bonhoeffer's embracing of *analogia relationis* is in line with Luther's soteriocentric anthropology.

At this point, it is valuable to analyze the implications of Bonhoeffer's interpretation of *imago Dei* as *analogia relationis*, which signifies several characteristics of his anthropology. First, Bonhoeffer's anthropology is firmly *based on Reformation anthropology*, especially that of Luther. The refutation of *analogia entis* indicates his refusal to take a substantive view of the image of God, which Augustine as well as Catholic theology had upheld.[110] Robert W. Jenson's distinction between the Catholic and Reformation doctrines on *imago Dei* is helpful. Jenson argues that the distinctive point of *imago Dei* per se lies in the fact that humans are unique among other creatures. If *imago Dei* refers to any unique image of God in human beings among all of creation, what are these distinctive aspects? According to Jenson, these are faculties such as "mind, will, and memory" in Catholic theology and "justice and sanctity" in Reformation theology.[111] In other words, whereas the former characteristics are found in the human being as given qualities, the latter are found only in relation with God. Considered from the latter perspective, Bonhoeffer radically follows the strain of magisterial Reformation theology that relates the image of God not to any human capacity or possibility but to the righteousness of the first humanity found only in relationality with God. As already discussed in the chapter on Luther's hamartiology, although Luther's radical interpretation of God's freedom in creation offers a relational and ethical interpretation of *imago Dei*, it is still archetypal and centered on soteriology. In other words, Luther's relational concept of *imago Dei* is derived from his soteriocentric theology. Also, Bonhoeffer articulates Luther's primitive notion of a relational *imago Dei* more clearly and deepens it with his pivotal understanding of *nihil*. Whereas the function of the doctrine of *creatio ex nihilo* for Luther was to uphold monergism in justification, Bonhoeffer extends the role of the doctrine of creation to other doctrinal loci such as anthropology and ethics, well beyond the doctrine of justification in Bonhoeffer's theology.

Second, Bonhoeffer's emphasis on *analogia relationis* reflects his continuing concern with the meaning of the human being based on his early social and communitarian perspective in regard to the relationality between God and human beings as well as among human beings. This means that Bonhoeffer's question is about how the human being is to be a human being in accordance with God's willingness or freedom, not only in *creation* but also in God's *upholding creation*.[112] Bonhoeffer's interpretation of the human being in creation as an archetype of humankind is paraphrased by his communitarian concept of the human being. His concern about relationality in community is illustrated by his concept of humanity "in the duality of man and woman" in its likeness to God, as Luther noted in his commentary on Genesis; this reflects Bonhoeffer's modern perspective.[113] This communitarian concept of the first community as well as of the community in Christ will be discussed in detail in the following section, which deals with the first sin and evil.

Third, understanding humanity as *analogia relationis* suggests that Bonhoeffer emphasized the communal level of sin and evil even in the beginning, which has been ignored due to the focus on the individual level of sin and evil throughout the history of the doctrine. As demonstrated in the above two analyses, Bonhoeffer does not rely on a substantive view of *imago Dei* but on a more relational view to explain who the human being is in its uniqueness in creation. As many theologians categorize it, *imago Dei* is also related to a functional view, which identifies the image of God with humanity's dominion over the rest of creation.[114] Related to this, Bonhoeffer's relational view of *imago Dei* is in part also combined with the functional view. As Luther argued in his Genesis exegesis, God's relational freedom in creation is not only with humanity but also with other creatures. As the image of God, the human being is relationally and functionally distorted after the fall. This distortion is represented in the community of human beings as a form of power over other humans as well as over other creatures and aspects of creation. This observation is related fundamentally to Luther's emphasis on the relational image of God. Bonhoeffer follows him and then expands this reversed relationality as sin that is vividly expressed in the relationality between male and female and among human beings.¹¹⁵ For Bonhoeffer, the starting point of sin and evil is the first distortion or usurpation of *imago Dei*.

In short, in a broad sense, Bonhoeffer's concept of freedom is in line with the tradition of Augustine and Luther in that the genuine freedom of the human being is denied. However, Bonhoeffer clearly recognizes the necessity to articulate the newly created freedom of saints in the community of Christ through the concept of *analogia relationis*. Following Luther, Bonhoeffer does not consider *imago Dei* substantively but relationally. This *analogia relationis* permits him to describe the first community as a collective person that has co-responsibility for the sins of the others.

The Creation

The previous section explicated Bonhoeffer's modern as well as Lutheran interpretation of traditional doctrines such as *crede ut intelligas, creatio ex nihilo*, and the relational *imago Dei* that supply the theological presuppositions for Bonhoeffer's interpretation of the creation account. Based on this groundwork, it is now possible to deal with Bonhoeffer's exegesis of the account of the creation in *Creation and Fall*. Bonhoeffer's methodological transition from the doctrine of God to the doctrine of the church as well as his communitarian personalism is clearly reflected in his interpretation of the account of the creation. This section investigates Bonhoeffer's interpretation of the creation of humanity, the creation of Eve as the other, and the end of creation as the creation of the community.

Creation of humankind

As seen in the previous sections, Bonhoeffer's exegesis of the three chapters of Genesis represents a decisive turning away from the theological and intellectual atmosphere of his time. Bonhoeffer's two major theological standpoints, ecclesiocentrism and Christian personalism, are clearly reflected in his exegesis of the creation accounts.

First, based on his *communitarian personalism*, Bonhoeffer primarily interprets the creation accounts in Genesis 1 and 2 communally by treating Adam as a collective person, as in the case of his exegesis of Gen. 2:7.¹¹⁶ One distinctive aspect of Bonhoeffer's interpretation of Augustine is his reading of the first human primarily as "humankind" rather than as "a man." Bonhoeffer interprets Adam not only as an individual human being [*Mensch*] but also as humankind [*Menschen*]. Furthermore, he consistently interprets "Adam as *Mensch*, 'human being,' rather than as *Mann*, 'man.'"¹¹⁷ Clearly, Bonhoeffer's reading of Adam as humankind is distinguished from the logic of the biological transmission of Adam's sin through his seed, which Augustine argues for in his doctrine of original sin.¹¹⁸ The reason for the interpretation of Adam as *Mensch* or *Menschen* is clear for Bonhoeffer. He understands that the two creation accounts are not separate but are two sides of one story. He writes, "When one first looks at both creation stories together, it is plain that the first and the second accounts are only representations [Darstellungen] of the same thing from two different sides."[119] He continues: "Humankind created in this way is humankind as the image of God."[120] For Bonhoeffer, the creation of Adam is the creation of humankind—in other words, the creation of the community. Furthermore, in this way all human beings are directly *imago Dei*. Bonhoeffer's exegesis goes beyond the individualistic theological anthropology of Augustine.

Bonhoeffer's integral interpretation of the two creation stories based on a sociological and communitarian understanding of the human being leads Bonhoeffer to read the story of the beginning as a story of community rather than a story of Adam as an individual. However, this sociality in the beginning also signifies simultaneously the community between God and humanity in which individuals participate in the community, as discussed in *Sanctorum Communio*. In this way, the creation of Adam, for Bonhoeffer, represents the creation of a twofold concept of community as composed of God and human beings. He describes this dual nature as follows:

> The world is created for God, for God's honor alone, and humankind is the most precious receptacle, the very mirror of the Creator. It is totally for the sake of God's glory and honor as Creator that everything comes to pass. In spite of the creation of humankind, the world remains the world in the deep, the strange, distant world. The second account by contrast is about the world in its nearness and about the Lord who is near on *earth*, living together with Adam in *Paradise*.[121]

Here, one can see Bonhoeffer's emphasis on the importance of the communitarian concept of the creation of humanity. It is for the glory of God, and the creation of human beings is not only the work of God in freedom but also God's creation of community in which human beings as well as God are included.[122] Bonhoeffer explains the created community from a dual perspective. He expounds that, on the one hand, the created community is "deep," "strange," and "distant" in terms of understanding its reality; on the other hand, it is "near" and "together with" humankind in the garden on earth. Bonhoeffer's description alludes to his dual approach to God's creation, considering both the transcendent and the immanent nature of the beginning of creation.

Second, in Bonhoeffer's exegesis his own ecclesiocentric standpoint is distinctive. He describes this first community as like a society in which Christ is at the center and humanity surrounds him. On the one hand, Bonhoeffer illustrates this community from the perspective of the church tradition in which "in the center of the garden stand two trees with particular names that connect them to human existence in a peculiar way: the tree of life and the tree of the knowledge of good and evil."[123] On the other hand, he perceives the tradition from his modern perspective, saying, "But that is all very uncertain. Our concern is the text as it presents itself to the church of Christ today."[124] The picture of the first community that Bonhoeffer describes in *Creation and Fall* is analogous to the church community in which Christ exists as in the garden. Bonhoeffer is clearly reading the creation account from the perspective of the New Testament rooted in the revelation of Christ.[125]

In the same way as for life in the church community, the source of the first community in paradise is not humanity per se but the tree of divine life, which symbolizes the existence of God.[126] Bonhoeffer understands that Adam as humanity has life "in a particular way."[127] This particular way of possessing life is based on Bonhoeffer's relational concept of community. As in his understanding of *analogia relationis*, Bonhoeffer argues that the life of humanity does not originate from the quality of the human person but from the communal unity of "unbroken obedience to the Creator."[128] He explains this particular way of human existence as follows:

> The life that God gave to humankind is not simply part of the makeup [eine Beschaffenheit], a qualitas, of humankind; instead it is something given to humankind only in terms of its whole human existence. Human beings have life from God and *before* God. They receive it; they receive it, however, not as animals but as human beings. They possess it in their obedience, in their innocence, in their ignorance; that is, they possess it in their freedom.[129]

Bonhoeffer's theological approach to the created community has three steps. First, he disassociates the concept of *analogia entis* from his understanding of the relationship between God and humanity. This means that he rejects the Augustinian concept of *analogia entis* as a qualitative likeness between God and human beings. In this way, Bonhoeffer confirms the source of the life of humankind *extra nos*, following Luther's tradition.[130] Second, he follows and develops Luther's transformative but primitive understanding of *analogia relationis*. As Green points out, the *analogia relationis* is not simply the relationship between the Creator and humankind.[131] It is a particular *relational and ethical* way of life that distinguishes humankind from animals. The point of this particular relationship is humans' way of living "in their freedom." Bonhoeffer's sensitivity to the concept of freedom in humankind is the key to relating his anthropology to his ethics. Clearly, Bonhoeffer's keen awareness of human freedom surpasses Luther's radical soteriocentric freedom as well as the Augustinian framework of predestination. In summary, the most significant advancement in Bonhoeffer's understanding of the creation from the Augustinian and Lutheran tradition is his unified interpretation of the two creation accounts by treating the creation of Adam and Eve as the creation of the humanity as well as considering the relationality of Adam and Eve primarily as the communal relationality between I and other. Bonhoeffer transforms Luther's individualistic notion of *analogia relationis* into his own communal concept of the person in which the freedom of the first community is exercised in its self-giving and self-sacrifice, but only in the sense of *extra nos*.

Eve: The creation of the other

Bonhoeffer's treatment of Adam as humankind continues in his treatment of the human relationality between male and female.[132] In this regard, Bonhoeffer's way of integrating the two creation accounts is noteworthy. He interprets them as an integrated whole, saying, "When one first looks at both creation stories together, it is plain that the first and the second accounts are only representations [Darstellungen] of the same thing from two different sides."[133] Bonhoeffer treats the creation of Adam as the community of humankind [Mensch] as one side of the creation story. The other side of the creation story is demonstrated in the relationality between man and woman. For Bonhoeffer, the creation of Eve has theological connotations. First, the creation of Eve is the creation of the other. Second, it is the completion of the creation as the creation of community. Finally, it is the symbol of the *Grenze* (limit) between 'the I and the other' as a given blessing.

First, one of the most significant claims of Bonhoeffer's exegesis of the creation of Eve is his interpretation of Eve as the other; with this claim, he goes beyond the traditional interpretation. He points out that the introduction of woman in the creation account comes right after the introduction of the tree of knowledge.[134] The creation of the community is completed by the creation of the woman as the other. The creation of Eve or woman signifies the existence of the other in the first community. Primarily, for Bonhoeffer, Eve symbolizes the other. It is noteworthy that he does not associate the creation of woman with the order of creation, saying that "it is superficial reasoning to take this as a basis for speaking about marriage as an order of creation."[135] Hilde Pfeiffer, one of Bonhoeffer's students who attended his 1932-3 lectures, notes that "one may not speak of the institution of marriage here. It is the story of human community as such."[136] Bonhoeffer definitely interprets the two creation stories not only as one story but also as the creation of a community in which all members of the first community can be identified. The primary nature of the creation of Eve is as a member of the prelapsarian community rather than as the wife of Adam. Only secondarily is Eve discussed as the wife for Adam.

Bonhoeffer's communitarian understanding of the creation is significant in related doctrines such as anthropology and ecclesiology. As Luther's relational *imago Dei* is derived from his anthropology based on scholasticism and ultimately on Augustinianism, Bonhoeffer's anthropology also shifts away from Luther's, not only by expanding the concept of Adam from individual to community but also by liberating the creation of Eve from the boundary of the marital relationship.[137] However, it is more appropriate to say that the main focus of Bonhoeffer's doctrinal transition from the tradition of Luther in regard to the interpretation of Eve as the other is not about the equality of the female or Eve to the man or Adam but is instead about the ontological equality of all human beings as *imago Dei*, especially in reference to their ethnic background, such as race.[138] For the modern Bonhoeffer, the communitarian understanding of Eve as the other is effective in grasping the origin of the fall in the primal community. He points to the biblical verse Gen. 2:18, in which God says, "It is not good that the human being should be alone; I will make a helper who is a suitable partner," to indicate the necessity of community [*Gemeinschaft*] in creation.[139] "Alone" for Bonhoeffer is not positive; he views it as similar to the concept of *cor curvum in se*. This is because he perceives this atomic inclination of the human being in a negative way in which "we are alone in evil, in hopelessness."[140] Luther's *cor curvum in se* is explicitly demonstrated in Bonhoeffer's exegesis of God's creation of the other. The existence of the other for the I is identical to God's creation of human beings as the other. In other words, the other is given to the I in God's freedom *ad extra*.[141]

Second, the creation of Eve or the other signifies the *completion of the creation* or the community. Bonhoeffer's interpretation of Eve is in the duality by which the human relationality between Adam and Eve is properly understood. Primarily, Eve represents the other in the unity of community; secondarily, Eve signifies the particular gender of the human being as female in terms of human sexuality.[142] In the primal community, the significance of the other is illustrated in Bonhoeffer's treatment of Eve as the other. He states: "Adam understands the uniqueness of this creature that God has shaped with the contribution Adam has made, out of human flesh, but Adam sees what Adam has done for the other wholly in the light of God's gift. That Eve is derived from Adam is a cause not for pride, but for particular gratitude, with Adam."[143]

Bonhoeffer sees that the unity of humankind is explicitly demonstrated in the bond between the I and the other. Considered from the communitarian personalism of Bonhoeffer, the creation of Eve is simultaneously the starting point of community and the end of creation.[144] In other words, without the creation of Eve or the other, humanity is not complete but partial. The relationality between the I and the other actualizes to "the highest possible degree their belonging to each other."[145] Bonhoeffer understands that the unity between the I and the other shows God's intention in the creation of humankind. The other is not the object of *cor curvum in se* in pride but of gratitude. Bonhoeffer's earlier other-oriented understanding of the church community in *Sanctorum Communio* is continued in his exegesis of Eve as the other. Clearly, the creation of Eve indicates the completion of the first community or the human race. Furthermore, Bonhoeffer's ecclesiocentric exegesis signifies that this first community can exist as a genuine community only when it is related to its Creator, Christ.

Finally, as has been discussed, the tree of knowledge is the symbol of the limit set by the center. In a similar way, Bonhoeffer states that the creation of *the other person is the limit* in a positive sense, just as is the other in the church community as the body of Christ:

> The other person is the limit that God sets for me, the limit that I love and that I will not transgress because of my love. … By the creation of the other person freedom and creatureliness are bound together in love. That is why the other person is once again grace to the first person, just as the prohibition against eating from the tree of knowledge was grace. In this common *bearing of the limit* by the first two persons in community, the character of this community as the church is authenticated.[146]

Here, it is apparent that the reflection of the church community in Christ is the main lens through which to interpret the first community. The bond between the I and the other is found in the concept of co-humanity in its freedom and creatureliness. The other is the limit (*Grenze*) for the I, which ultimately keeps the I living before God. Clearly, the *analogia relationis* is explicit in the concept of the human being.[147] In the same way as in the analogy of the tree of knowledge, the other is simultaneously the boundary but also the source of life. Bonhoeffer argues, "That is why the other person is once again grace to the first person, just as the prohibition against eating from the tree of knowledge was grace."[148] In this way, Eve primarily symbolizes the other as members of the community. Bonhoeffer sees the prototype of the church community in the relationality between the first two persons, in which the *limit* of the other is borne as divine grace.

In summary, Bonhoeffer's exegesis of the creation of the human being is based on his previous claim that *Christ exists as the church-community*—in other words, it is based on his ecclesiocentrism and communitarian personalism in *Sanctorum Communio*. Accordingly, Bonhoeffer's interpretation of the creation of the human being has some distinctive exegetical traits. First, he does not view scientific knowledge as opposite to the account of the creation.[149] This is because he understands the Scripture as a theological description that contains unfathomable truth beyond the boundary of human knowledge and language.[150] The modern Bonhoeffer sees the prelapsarian community not as a pristine paradise but as the prototype of the church community. Second, Bonhoeffer's theological exposition of the creation of humankind synthesizes two theological traditions, as evidenced in his integration of the two different creation accounts. As in his theological emphasis on the relationality between God's act and God's being seen in *Act and Being*, Bonhoeffer's understanding of the human being in the creation account merges the Augustinian emphasis on the inconceivable work of the Creator with the Lutheran emphasis on the work of the Lord who is *near us*.[151] Finally, his communal Christian personalism expands the scope of the creation stories from an individualistic concept of Adam to a communal concept of humankind through his treatment of Adam in both as an individual and a community. His communal expansion of the concept of Adam repairs the Augustinian tradition in which Adam is interpreted as the sole hereditary ancestor of humankind, which contradicts scientific discoveries as well as scriptural passages. These characteristics of Bonhoeffer's hermeneutics are continued in his interpretation of the fall.

The Fall

The previous section examined Bonhoeffer's exegesis of the creation account in which his ecclesiocentrism as well as his community-focused personalism is reflected in his hermeneutical lens for the creation and the fall. This section further explicates Bonhoeffer's understanding of the fall. Similar to his interpretation of the creation, Bonhoeffer understands the fall as an act of the first community. As is typical for him, he treats the fall from his communitarian and ecclesiocentric perspective. However, in this process, Bonhoeffer's early rejection of the relationality between the biological sense of sexuality or concupiscence and the original sin or the first sin in *Sanctorum Communio* is complicated by his ethical and relational standpoint. This change is mainly due to his new recognition of the importance of human corporeality. This section investigates this change in his Lutheran angle.

The fall of the community

In Bonhoeffer's treatment of the two creation accounts as one, he interprets the story of the fall based on his socio-communal personalism continued from *Sanctorum Communio*. The most distinctive point of Bonhoeffer's interpretation is that his interest in the account is expressed in his Christian collective personalism in which not only Adam but also Eve is encompassed in a communal concept of Adam in which Eve and Adam as the community rebel against God. On the one hand, in the Augustinian exegesis, Adam is treated as the primary subject of the account of the fall and Eve is considered the secondary subject of the event, but Bonhoeffer's personalism binds these two individuals as one and leads him to interpret the event of the fall as the act of a collective person or, in other words, as the act of the first community.[152] On the other hand, the main concern of Bonhoeffer's doctrine of the fall is far from the traditional concerns, as seen in the disputations concerning the capacity of human will such as those between Augustine and Pelagius or between Luther and Erasmus. Augustine's concern regarding the scope of the will in the accounts of the creation and the fall is focused on the human ability not to sin (*posse non peccare*) or ability to sin (*posse peccare*) in the primal state and on the human inability not to sin (*non posse non peccare*) after the fall; this concern inevitably results in his doctrine of predestination.[153] Bonhoeffer argues that this Augustinian theory of *posse et non posse peccare* does not supply the foundation for hamartiology because he considers it a doctrine derived chiefly from speculation and unable "to comprehend the fact that the deed was done."[154] As Bonhoeffer asserts his theology rooted in the reality of the revelation in Christ, his assessment of Augustine's hamartiology is critical of Augustine's doctrine of *posse peccare* and *non posse peccare*. Clearly, the epistemological notion of the incomprehensibility of the postlapsarian self illustrated in *Act and Being* is reflected in his refutation of the Augustinian understanding of the will. Bonhoeffer again takes the standpoint of the present reality in Christ in which "this deed [of the fall] is final and it cannot be abrogated."[155]

Bonhoeffer turns away from speculative concern with the doctrine of original sin in regard to the fall to the given reality in the human community. His community-focused exegesis is clear in its description of the fall:

> Eve falls first. She falls as the weaker one, as the one who is partly taken from man. But there is no excuse for her fall; she is fully her own person. Yet the culmination of the story is Adam's fall. Only when Adam falls does Eve fall wholly, for the two are after all one. Adam falls because of Eve, and Eve falls because of Adam; the two are one. They are two and yet one also in their guilt. *They fall together as one, yet each carries the whole burden of guilt alone.*[156]

Bonhoeffer's main focus regarding the fall is on the wholeness of the sinful act of Adam and Eve. He describes the fall as being completed by the community's fallen act in its sinful participation. However, the result of the fall is that "each carries the whole burden of guilt alone." The result of the fall is atomistic self-love or the state of *cor curvum in se*.[157] There is a lack of co-responsibility; in other words, there is no sense of bearing the culpability of the other. The fall signifies the broken relationality in the bearing of the burden of guilt. As Tom Greggs points out, the characteristics of Bonhoeffer's hamartiology are explicit in his emphasis on the sinful participation of the human being as well as on Adam and Eve's co-responsibility for the original sin in his exegesis of the fall.[158] It is clear that Bonhoeffer's earlier ethical and communal notion of the original sin is strongly reflected in his exegesis of the fall. This communitarian concept of the fall leads to the impossibility of blaming the other because the inseparability of humankind represented in Eve and Adam is firmly established in the first community. Bonhoeffer argues that the story points out that the fall is a "deed done by humanity [der Menschheit]."[159] He again focuses on the reciprocal nature of the deed rather than on each individual's comparative gravity of sin in the given community.

Despite Bonhoeffer's expansion of the scope of Adam from individual to community, his interpretation of the first sin in its essence clearly follows the hamartiological tradition of the West in this theological stage. The beginning of the fall for Bonhoeffer lies in the prideful *cor curvum in se* of the first human community to be *sicut Deus*.[160] In this way, the fall is the prideful denial of the self as *imago Dei*. It is the denial of creatureliness and a rebellious self-denial. Despite Bonhoeffer's reform of the traditional concept of Adam with his personalism, he continues to interpret the essence of the sin of the first community from the traditional lens of pride or power encapsulated in the Lutheran as well as the Augustinian notion of *cor curvum in se* or *incurvatus in se*.[161] This is because, on the one hand, Bonhoeffer affirms the inseparability of the I and the other as humankind; on the other hand, his description of the fall is chiefly based on the perspective of the I or Adam, reaffirming the Augustinian doctrine of the fall as humanity's prideful *aversio ab* (turning away from) the immutable Good without considering the other side of sin such as selflessness or self-denial.[162]

The communal interpretation of Adam culminates in Bonhoeffer's understanding of the fall. Although the concept of the collective person is not sufficiently versatile to eliminate the incomprehensibility of the account of the fall, Bonhoeffer's transformative concept of the collective person offers a way for modern people to interpret the fall and the questions raised by the many critiques of the doctrine of original sin.[163] The assertion of Bonhoeffer's ethical and collective concept of humankind in *Sanctorum Communio* is affirmed again in his interpretation of the fall. He states that "it is a continual fall, a dropping into a bottomless abyss, a state of being let go, a process of moving further and further away, falling deeper and deeper."[164] As is argued in *Sanctorum Communio*, the fall is continued in generation after generation in their participation in the guilt, and the sin can be borne only in the community of Christ.

Bonhoeffer locates the scope of the fall not only in the primal state of humankind but also in the present and future of humankind in its relationality to the creation. Bonhoeffer understands that the fall affects the whole created world on the earth, beyond the limits of time. Although Augustine conceived that the fall of humanity was the beginning of the entire universe's decline, Bonhoeffer's explanation is more realistic than the traditional perception in his concept of a continual fall in creation by destructive acts of human beings within the boundaries of the earthly world. Bonhoeffer understands the fall in two ways, following Luther's interpretation. He states that "it is not merely a moral lapse but the destruction of creation by the creature."[165] Clearly, here Bonhoeffer is understanding the fall and its effects from his modern perspective. Bonhoeffer's evaluation of the fall's effects is based on the relational boundary of the human being and thus is disassociated from Augustine's cosmic level of the fall. For Bonhoeffer, the fall is an ethical lapse of the human being, but it is also humanity's continual destruction of the creation. As Green points out, although Bonhoeffer does not investigate fully the relationality between the fall and the destruction of the rest of creation, this idea of humanity's continual destruction of the rest of creation indicates his awareness of humanity's destructive and ongoing sinful power over other human beings as well as the rest of creation.[166]

In short, as he typically does, Bonhoeffer reformulates the Augustinian doctrine of the fall by applying his ecclesiocentric standpoint and communitarian personalism. In *Creation and Fall*, Bonhoeffer emphasizes that the genuine nature of the fall is the first community's turning away from God in Christ who exists as the community. In this way, for Bonhoeffer, the fall is not an individual's falling away but the entire community's rebellion; he focuses on the co-responsibility of the human race for the first or original sin. His emphasis on the co-responsibility of the first community with all of humanity is a decisively transformative interpretation that is a shift from the hamartiological tradition of the West. Consequently, Bonhoeffer not only expands the subject of the fall from the individual Adam to the first community but also treats the fall as an ethical lapse rather than a cosmic event.

The fall and sexuality

Strikingly, despite his objection to the physical sense of concupiscence in the original manuscript of *Sanctorum Comunnio*, Bonhoeffer's interpretation of concupiscence or sexuality in *Creation and Fall* is complicated. In light of Bonhoeffer's communitarian concept of the fall as well as his earlier objection to the Augustinian material concept of concupiscence, it is appropriate to investigate Bonhoeffer's notion of concupiscence in regard to the account of the fall. The role of the Augustinian concept of concupiscence in the doctrine of original sin has been discussed at great length throughout the history of Western Christianity. In the modern era, Harnack's influence on Bonhoeffer's interpretation of Augustine is evident in *Sanctorum Communio*. Following Harnack's assessment of Augustine's theology, Bonhoeffer criticizes in *Sanctorum Communio* the devastating power of the material sense of concupiscence that is dominant in the Augustinian doctrine of original sin. Bonhoeffer points out that Augustine's obsession with the material sense of concupiscence made him identify the root of original sin in lust grounded in human physicality and convinced him of the biological transmission of the first sin and the culpability of Adam.[167] Although his emphasis on the ethical and relational concept of the human being is one of the distinctive aspects of Bonhoeffer's doctrine of sin in *Sanctorum Communio*, the relationality between the ethical concept of the person and the biological aspect of the person has not been clearly addressed.[168] In *Sanctorum Communio*, on the one hand, he emphasizes the ethical concept of the human being; on the other hand, as Eva Harasta points out, he follows the Lutheran concept of *totus homo* that "typically stresses that 'sin' affects the whole human being."[169] This complexity is more clearly expressed in *Creation and Fall* in regard to his doctrine of human sexuality and the fall. He does offer a more holistic notion of concupiscence in *Creation and Fall* following Luther's early notion of concupiscence, which embraces both the material and ethical senses of concupiscence. However, Bonhoeffer's earlier ethical emphasis on hamartiology and anthropology is continued in *Creation and Fall* as well as in his later theology, along with his new emphasis on corporeality.

To clarify Bonhoeffer's complex doctrine of concupiscence, it is necessary to analyze related issues in his doctrine of concupiscence represented by the term *sexuality* (*Sexualität*) in *Creation and Fall*. First, it is appropriate to investigate Bonhoeffer's use of the term *Sexualität* in relation to *Geschlechtlichkeit* to understand his notion of sexuality in regard to the doctrine of original sin. Second, it is also necessary to investigate whether there is continuity or discontinuity in the content and the role of sexuality (*Sexualität*) in his hamartiological framework between *Sanctorum Communio* and *Creation and Fall*.

The meaning of concupiscence has been interpreted diversely throughout the history of hamartiology associated with Augustine. Augustine's concept of concupiscence was at the center of his doctrine of original sin. However, scholars have interpreted this concept in various ways. A famous example is the perspective of Adolf von Harnack.[170] As discussed in the chapter on *Sanctorum Communio*, Harnack's assessment of Augustine's notion of concupiscence strongly influenced Bonhoeffer's first dissertation. However, in *Creation and Fall* as well as in *Act and Being*, the tone of Bonhoeffer's evaluation of Lutheran teachers' theological methodology, especially of Harnack's historical-criticism, is quite critical. Accordingly, Bonhoeffer's previous understanding of concupiscence and its content as well as its role in original sin changed to a certain degree.

Bonhoeffer's interpretation of Eve is closely related to his doctrine of *human sexuality* in addition to his primary concept of Eve as the other. Bonhoeffer's use of two German terms rendered by the same English term "sexuality" requires careful attention. Bonhoeffer distinguishes the word "sexuality" in two ways in his German work *Schöpfung und Fall*. First, *Geschlechtlichkeit* signifies the relationality of members of a community composed of men and women, and this term is also used to express human relationality before the fall. Second, *Sexualität* indicates human sinful desire approximately represented by the term *concupiscence*, which generally is used for human sinful relationality after the fall. The German editors make a helpful distinction: "In connection with the community of man and woman as creatures of God (Gen. 2:24), Bonhoeffer used the German term *Geschlechtlichkeit* for sexuality. The relationship after the fall, the 'perversion of the relation of one human being to another,' he characterized with a different term for sexuality, *Sexualität*."[171]

As indicated, Bonhoeffer interprets the creation of woman in two ways. Primarily, seen from the perspective of community, the creation of woman means the creation of the other; only secondarily does it mean the relationality between wife and husband. At the primary and communal level, Adam relates to Eve in a relationship of "belonging to one another" as the I and the other and vice versa.[172] Bonhoeffer explains this given relationality by stating that "the community of man and woman is the community derived from God, the community of love glorifying and worshipping God as the Creator."[173] It is like the relationship between saints in the church community. The original German text clearly articulates this point. Bonhoeffer states, "Dies letzte Einandergehoren ist aber ganz unzweifellheft zusammengesehen mit der Geschlechtlichkeit des Menschen" ("This ultimate belonging to one another is, however, unquestionably associated with human sexuality").[174] It is noteworthy that Bonhoeffer uses the German term *Geschlechtlichkeit* here, which does not connote the postlapsarian sense of sexuality, to describe the prelapsarian human relationality. Following Bonhoeffer's logic, this relationality based on *Geschlechtlichkeit* applies to both the communal and the marital levels of human relationality. However, similar to his assertion of the unknowability of why primal evil exists, the prelapsarian relationality is no longer traceable after the fall.[175] It is accessible only by a backward projection of the church community.[176] Clearly, Bonhoeffer interprets the primal human relationality between Adam and Eve from the perspective of the church community that is the witness of Christ.

In *Creation and Fall*, Bonhoeffer begins to focus on the corporeal aspect of the human being. It is natural to expect that Bonhoeffer would turn to the question of bodily life in his exegesis of the account of the creation and the fall. He states that the "bodily existence" of the human being, considered as a gift before the fall, has turned into a problem for the postlapsarian community.[177] At the center of the problem of the community is the changed and distorted perception of the "bodily existence" or "corporeality" of the human being.[178] Corporeality, once considered a limit and a source of blessing, has now become the origin of hatred. In distinguishing between *Geschlechtlichkeit* and *Sexualität*, it is noteworthy that Bonhoeffer uses the term *Sexualität* to describe the problem in the postlapsarian community due to human beings' awareness of their corporeality after eating from the tree of knowledge instead of the term *Geschlechtlichkeit*, which he uses to describe the prelapsarian relational life.

Bonhoeffer argues that the "new knowledge" of *tob* and *ra* (good and evil) is what causes the fundamental problem with sexuality (*das Problem des Geschlechtlichen*) in the postlapsarian community.[179] He argues that "what is correct in all this is that what is essentially at issue here is the problem of sexuality."[180] Here, Bonhoeffer uses the term *Geschlechtlichen* rather than *Geschlechtlichkeit* to describe the postlapsarian communal relationality between the I and the other or Adam and Eve.[181] He explains that the problem of the postlapsarian community is that *Geschlechtlichen* distorted the original human sexuality (*Geschlechtlichkeit*) into the postlapsarian form of sexuality (*Sexualität*).[182] Bonhoeffer clearly contrasts *Geschlechtlichkeit*, represented as a given limit and a symbol of blessing, with *Sexualität*, which signifies dividedness between man and woman as well as between the I and the other.[183] He describes this distortion of sexuality as follows:

> The man claims his share of the woman's body or, more generally, ... one person claims a right to the other, claims to be entitled to possess the other, and thereby denies and destroys the creaturely nature of the other person. This obsessive desire [*Sucht*] of one human being for one another finds its primordial expression in sexuality [*Sexualität*]. The sexuality [*Sexualität*] of the human being who transgresses his or her boundary is a refusal to recognize any limit at all; it is a boundless obsessive desire to be without any limits. Sexuality [*Sexualität*] is a passionate hatred of any limit.[184]

It is clear that Bonhoeffer uses *Sexualität* to describe the distorted, obsessive, sinful desire of the postlapsarian human self over the other. He understands that the result of the first sin affects all kinds of human relationality and that this sinful desire to exercise the egocentricity of the self is encapsulated in the notion of *Sexualität*. Not surprisingly, Bonhoeffer's understanding of *Sexualität* has affinities with Luther's early concept of *concupiscence*, which can be interpreted both physically and spiritually. For Bonhoeffer, obsessive power "denies and destroys the creaturely nature of the other person [as *imago dei*]."[185] He points out that the distorted relationality between man and woman as well as between the I and the other in the postlapsarian state is not the original state but the result of the fall. This is an important claim because he refuses to treat the relationality between man and woman and among human beings in the category of the order of creation (*Schöpfungsordnung*); instead, he treats them within the relationality between the I and the other.[186] Accordingly, the chief characteristic of sin is Adam's or the I's obsessive power over the other after the fall.[187] In other words, in the present fallen world, in general, "one person claims a right to the other" without having any right to the claim.[188]

Bonhoeffer further investigates this sinful distortion of sexuality, noting that "this obsessive desire [*Sucht*] of one human being for another finds its primordial expression in sexuality [*Sexualität*]."[189] Bonhoeffer interprets desire (*Sucht*) and sexuality (*Sexualität*) not only materialistically but also ethically.[190] Bonhoeffer's emphasis on an ethical concept of humanity in *Sanctorum Communio* is associated with his new recognition of the "corporeality" of the human being in *Creation and Fall*. However, as Michael Brain rightly observes, the complexity or ambiguity of the relationships between man and woman and between the I and the other is not resolved completely in *Creation and Fall*.[191] This is because his description of the fall contains the possibility of diverse interpretations in regard to the relationality between concupiscence and original sin. This complexity is not completely clarified, but this new understanding of corporeality directs Bonhoeffer to interpret the doctrine of incarnation in a new way in his later works, especially in *Ethics*.

In regard to the relationality between the material sense of sexuality and original sin, the change in tone from Bonhoeffer's first dissertation, with its emphasis on an ethical concept of humanity and sin, is evident in his treatment of human corporeality throughout *Creation and Fall*. This transition seems sudden because, until the summer semester of 1932, he maintained that "the transmission [of original sin] by procreation is a poor attempt to do justice to the actual condition of sinful existence."[192] The German editors of *Creation and Fall* note that "by the time Bonhoeffer came to expound Genesis 1–3 during the following semester, however, he no longer saw humankind simply within the limits of what was spiritual and ethical."[193] Bonhoeffer's emphasis on "bodily existence" frequently emerges in his lectures on Genesis. He argues:

> It is the image of God not in spite of but precisely in its *bodily nature*. For in their *bodily nature* human beings are related to the earth and to other bodies; they are there for others and are dependent upon others. *In their bodily existence* human beings find their brothers and sisters and find the earth. As such creatures human beings of earth and spirit are 'like' God, their Creator.[194]

Bonhoeffer's new emphasis on corporeality is distinctive. He perceives that the role of "bodily existence" is crucial to investigating the meaning of *analogia relationis* because humans can relate to the other only "in their bodily existence." The emphasis on bodily existence is extended to the way of God's existence in the world as Jesus Christ.[195] Bonhoeffer's understanding of corporeality is far different from Augustine's concept of the body in terms of the doctrine of God as well as of the human being. The body, he argues, "is the form in which the spirit exists, as the spirit is the form in which the body exists [*Leib ist die Existenzform von Geist, wie Geist die Existenzform von Leib ist*]."[196] Along this line, he argues that "the human body differs from all non-human bodies in that it is the form in which the spirit of God exists on earth."[197] Bonhoeffer recognizes and confirms the mutual connection between body and soul, ethical and physical, and ultimately human and divine because corporeality is essential to being a true human being since the human body is the only place in which God's spirt exists in this world. The corporeality of the human being is the place of God's presence in the world. This understanding mirrors the concept of the church community in which Christ exists. In this way, Bonhoeffer confirms again his reading of the creation and the fall accounts based on the foundation of the revelation of God in Christ.

This new emphasis on corporeality in *Creation and Fall* affects Bonhoeffer's view of the doctrine of original sin, especially his concept of sexuality (*Sexualität*). He perceives that the understanding of "bodily existence," considered the boundary or limit [*Grenze*] and a divine gift in the primal community, turns to "a passionate hatred of any limit" after the fall.[198] In part, it is appropriate to say that due to the nature of his exegesis of the creation and the fall accounts, Bonhoeffer's understanding of the human being in *Sanctorum Communio*, which emphasizes the "ethical aspect" of the human being, becomes associated with a corporeal aspect. He states that "[after the fall] it [sexuality] is extreme lack of respect for things-as-they-are [*Unsachlichket*]."[199] He summarizes that "sexuality seeks to destroy the other person as creature, robs the other person of his or her creatureliness."[200] Strikingly, Bonhoeffer argues that Protestants (Harnack's and potentially his own view in *Sanctorum Communio*) criticize the essence of original sin in sexuality [*Sexualität*] "on the basis of a moralistic naturalism."[201] Bonhoeffer states:

> That church dogmatics has sometimes seen the essence of original sin in sexuality [*Sexualität*] is not as absurd as Protestants have often declared on the basis of a moralistic naturalism. Knowing about tob and ra is not to begin with an abstract knowledge of ethical principles; on the contrary it starts out as sexuality [*Sexualität*], that is, as perversion of the relation of one human being to another. And as the essence of sexuality [*Sexualität*] consists of creating in the midst of destroying, so the dark secret of the nature of humankind, essentially conditioned by original sin, is preserved from generation to generation in the course of continuing procreation.[202]

Bonhoeffer referred to Bernhard Bartmann's *Dogmatik* to explain the essence of original sin in sexuality in *Creation and Fall*.[203] According to Bartmann's assessment, the essence of original sin is in the physical concept of sexuality because the original sin along with its penalty has been transmitted by procreation.[204] However, two different kinds of issues are intertwined: *the method of transmission* and *the concept of concupiscence*. As already noted, Bonhoeffer adds the physical sense of sexuality to his previous ethical concept. However, it is uncertain whether his description of sexuality clearly supports his transition from the refutation of the biological transmission of culpability (penalty for sin) because he describes sexuality (*Sexualität*) as only the result of the first sin and the distortion of *Geschlechtlichkeit*. Similar to Luther as well as other Reformers, he considers the original sexuality (*Geschlechtlichkeit*), which includes both the corporeal and the ethical senses of sexuality, as divine and as a blessing given in the creation. Thus, for Bonhoeffer prelapsarian corporeality is considered something good and divinely bestowed. However, he does not clearly mention the biological transmission of the penalty for sin in *Creation and Fall*. However, one important point is that Bonhoeffer understands the first sin as the act of a whole person as *totus homo* (individual as well as communal persons) that ultimately cannot be separated into physical and spiritual. This issue is dealt with in detail in the next section in relation to his concept of freedom and responsibility in light of his Lutheran tradition.

In short, Bonhoeffer's earlier emphasis on the ethical aspect of sin in *Sanctorum Communio* incorporates the biological aspect of sin in *Creation and Fall*. Consequently, he is viewed as approaching the source of sin from a more holistic perspective in which his notion of sexuality is interpreted in both an ethical and biological way. On a superficial level, this seems closer to Luther's early concept of concupiscence in which Luther primarily follows Augustine's doctrine of original sin as *concupiscentia* interpreted in both the physical and ethical senses. However, on a deeper level, it is more appropriate to say that Bonhoeffer's new recognition of corporeality is rooted more in his Christocentric ecclesiology expressed in the concept of "Christ existing as church-community" rather than Augustine's later notion of *concupiscentia*. This is because his emphasis on corporeality in *Creation and Fall* leads him to connect it with his doctrine of God's humanization in Christ in *Ethics*.

Luther or Lutherans

The root of Bonhoeffer's new awareness of the importance of human corporeality is not limited to the theoretical level. Seen from his Lutheran context, Bonhoeffer's incorporation of the material aspect of sexuality into his hamartiology contains some significant theological meanings. The theological turn from his Lutheran teachers in *Creation and Fall* as well as in *Act and Being* continues in his Finkenwalde period (1935–7). According to Erich Kapproth's notes, Bonhoeffer's Finkenwalde lecture is noteworthy. Bonhoeffer explains the original sin as follows: "According to Gen. 3, sexual impurity is considered particularly close to original sin; there is, indeed, something that the Catholic understanding of original sin expresses, a particularly close relation between πορνεία and original sin."[205] This new understanding of sexuality is how Bonhoeffer embraces the Augustinian material concept of sexuality in addition to his previous ethical concept of concupiscence, following Luther's early emphasis on a totalistic interpretation of concupiscence. The new emphasis on the material concept of sexuality is heightened in *Creation and Fall*. Bonhoeffer's turn to the early anthropology of Luther rooted in the later anthropology of Augustine reflects his pessimistic view of the human capacity, in contrast to twentieth-century Lutherans who eagerly believed in the power of reason and intellect, as Harnack's letter to Bonhoeffer vividly indicates.[206] However, this apparently radical turn from the view of *Sanctorum Communio* is not a total denial of the perspective held by his contemporary Lutherans. This is because the ethical concept of anthropology is strongly continued in his entire doctrine of sin as well as in his anthropology, especially through his doctrine of *Stellvertretung* (vicarious representative action).

Then, what made Bonhoeffer include the material sense of sexuality as part of the first sin or the chief sin? There are several possibilities. One of the possibilities is related to his social and political context in Germany at that time. The theological meaning of this turn might reflect Bonhoeffer's new awareness of the evil nature of the human race transmitted from the first humans combined with the beginning of the German church's struggle in 1932–3.[207] It is reasonable to say that Bonhoeffer considered both the ethical view of modern Lutherans and the Nazis' emphasis on the superiority of German race to be disastrous. As seen in his theological epistemology rooted in the notion of *ratio in se ipsam incurve*, Bonhoeffer viewed the high regard of the ethical and intellectual qualities of the postlapsarian human race, which the majority of modern Lutheran theologians upheld, as a dangerous doctrine.[208] Devastatingly, many theologians of his time were assisting the Nazi ideology of "blood and soil."[209] It is clear that some contemporary theologians' doctrines of race were furthering the Nazis' nationalistic racism. He conceived that the National Socialists were abusing the biological concept of the human race or human solidarity, which was given as a blessing and boundary, by discriminating based on blood or race. Contrary to the current of anthropology of his time, Bonhoeffer attempted to approach the notion of the human being as well as of the postlapsarian sinful nature in a more holistic way, embracing both the biological and ethical aspects of humans. Clearly, Bonhoeffer applied this not only to the Nazis' propagation of the biological superiority of the German race but also to the doctrine of the "order of creation" of the contemporary German Lutheran church.

In summary, despite Bonhoeffer's understanding of the biological aspect of the human solidarity as *merely* a basic element of the human being in *Sanctorum Communio*, he treats the biological and the ethical as the two essential components of the human race in *Creation and Fall*. However, despite Bonhoeffer's recognition of the sinful unity of the human being both biologically and ethically, he does not clearly state whether he conceives that the culpability of the first sin was transmitted in addition to humanity's sinful nature as Augustine understood it. There is a seemingly subtle but significant difference between the transmission of the sinful nature or the universality of sin and the biological transmission of Adam's sin and culpability. As is typical of Lutherans, it is more appropriate to understand the position of Bonhoeffer based on the views of Luther as well as of his Lutheran teachers. On the one hand, Bonhoeffer understands the notion of sexuality (*Sexualität*) or concupiscence in the physical and spiritual senses, aligning with Luther's early notion of concupiscence. On the other hand, he continues his previous ethical position on alien culpability associated with contemporary Lutheran theologians' emphasis on the ethical or spiritual sense of *Stellvertretung*. However, Bonhoeffer's new awareness of the importance of corporeality in *Creation and Fall* leads him to relate the concept of *Stellvertretung* more closely to God's humanization in Christ. As DeJonge points out, Bonhoeffer's appropriation of Luther's theology is derived not only from Luther's theology itself but also through the perspectives of his Lutheran teachers.[210]

Conclusion

Bonhoeffer's first biblical exegesis of the accounts of the creation and the fall takes a central and transitional position in his doctrine of sin. His theological perspective of ecclesiocentrism and Christian personalism that he claimed in *Sanctorum Communio* is continued in his doctrine of sin in *Creation and Fall*, reflecting the theological epistemology articulated in *Act and Being*. Bonhoeffer's focus on the exegesis of Scripture, especially of the accounts of the creation and the fall, signals his turn to the spirit of Luther and to Scripture. On the one hand, his Lutheran Christocentrism is reinforced in *Creation and Fall*, in which he interprets the Old Testament accounts from the standpoint of the church rooted in the revelation of God in Christ. In other words, as Christiane Tietz comments, he changes the angle of the creation and the fall accounts from the Hebrew perspective to the Christian perspective.[211] On the other hand, his communitarian personalism is maintained as the other main angle for interpreting the story of the creation and the fall, through which he advances the traditional doctrine of original sin by encompassing all human beings in the first community as the subject of the story. However, some limitations in his exegesis remain because of his strong adherence to the Lutheran and Augustinian androcentric traditions in which the experiences of some minority groups, especially the experiences of females, are poorly integrated. This issue is discussed in detail in Chapters 5 and 6.

One of the remarkable shifts from Bonhoeffer's earlier hamartiological perspective is his inclusion of both the physical and corporeal dimensions of sexuality or concupiscence in his doctrine of sin. This transition signifies that his earlier emphasis on the ethical standpoint proceeds to a more balanced or holistic standpoint in regard to the notions of humanity and sin. In this theological stage, he recognizes the importance of the corporeal aspect of humanity in addition to his ongoing concern with the ethical and relational aspect of the human race, coinciding with his turn to Scripture. Admittedly, he agrees neither with the perspective of historical criticism that upheld "the power of reason and intellect" nor with the idea of "blood and soil" derived from the received doctrine of the "order of creation" that ultimately assisted the Nazis' propagation of the biological superiority of the German race. It is noteworthy that Bonhoeffer embraces the physical dimension of sexuality as a component of original sin and sinful human solidarity in the midst of the extreme political circumstances in Germany. In *Creation and Fall*, as Eva Harasta points out, Bonhoeffer more closely follows Luther's concept of *totus homo*, which "typically stresses that 'sin' affects the whole human being."[212]

However, Bonhoeffer's inclusion of the physical aspect of sexuality or concupiscence as original sin needs to be differentiated from his acceptance of the biological transmission of alien culpability, which is the hallmark of the Augustinian doctrine of original sin. This is because Bonhoeffer no longer sees the human being as merely within the category of an ethical or physical dimension but as within the boundary of the total person. In contrast, Augustine's doctrine of the biological transmission of Adam's culpability to all humanity is based on a partial or biological aspect of the human being rather than on the perspective of *totus homo*. Despite the ambiguity or silence in Bonhoeffer's position on the biological transmission of alien culpability in *Creation and Fall*, it is more appropriate to say that Bonhoeffer has not departed from his earlier objection to the automatic or involuntary transmission of Adam's sin and culpability. As Bonhoeffer makes clear in *Creation and Fall*, the first sin of humanity was not an act of the soul or body but a total person's or a total community's sin simultaneously against the divine other as well as the human other, and the same logic needs to be applied to his understanding of the biological transmission of alien culpability, which is chiefly derived from the physical or biological dimension of the human race. Clearly, Bonhoeffer does not use a prototypal methodology but employs a Christocentric or ecclesiocentric methodology to explicate the meaning of the original or first sin and its nature. He denies the traceability of the origin of sin and evil based on human reason but suggests that the church in which Christ exists as community is the ultimate basis of his hermeneutics. Furthermore, his new recognition of the importance of corporeality leads him to relate it to the significance of the incarnation or humanization of God in Christ. This signifies that his earlier doctrine of *Stellvertretung* which focused more on the ethical and relational aspect of church community has moved toward the person and work of Christ as the origin of Christians' vicarious representative action, by highlighting God's humanization in Christ. In this regard, Bonhoeffer is clear that the proper doctrinal locus of the issue of alien culpability is not the doctrine of original sin but the doctrine of atonement or reconciliation, which should be dealt with in the theological thread of "primal state, sin, and reconciliation," as he suggests in *Sanctorum Communio*.[213] In this vein, the theme of alien culpability does not disappear in Bonhoeffer's theology but is transformed and appears in the doctrine of *Stellvertretung*. Accordingly, the theme of *Stellvertretung* is one of the central issues of the next chapter.

Bonhoeffer' doctrine of sin in *Creation and Fall* has some implications. First, the old and still present question of the sin that remains in the church community, which Luther as well as Augustine had raised, becomes more urgent to Bonhoeffer and the Lutheran church of his time. The question of who is the human being is connected to the question of what is the nature of evil and sin in the church community and, more importantly, beyond the boundary of the church. His previous somewhat positive view of the church community and the human being in *Sanctorum Communio*, where he focuses on the idealistic and ethical aspects of the church community in which the sins of the saints are mediated by Christ, begins to relate to the other, hidden, sinful side of the church community under the pressures of the sinful powers of the world. He starts to observe the church community as well as human being from a more complicated perspective, similar to Luther's dual concept of *totus homo* as *simul iustus et peccator*. As de Gruchy demonstrates, Bonhoeffer's *Creation and Fall* shows some transitional features of his theology.[214] One of the distinctive turning points is seen in his concept of the postlapsarian human sinfulness inside and outside of the church community in its symbiotic and vulnerable relation with the world in which the power of social and radical evil is more active. His critical observation of the human person, both the individual and the community, as *simul iustus et peccator* begins to emerge in *Creation and Fall* and is reinforced in his later writings.

Second, Bonhoeffer's modern perspective is distinctive in his interpretation of human sexuality. He interprets Eve in a two-tiered categorical level, primarily as the other in the first community and secondarily as a female or the wife of Adam. This shift offers the theological room to interpret the creation and the fall account from the perspective of all human beings, especially from the perspectives or experiences of both females and males. However, Bonhoeffer's interpretation of Adam and Eve is not closely engaged with issues of gender, class, or race in regard to the doctrine of sin. These issues are advanced to some extent in his later work, especially in his prison writings. Accordingly, the next chapter explicates these issues in detail along with his ongoing emphasis on Christian freedom and responsibility.

Chapter 5

BONHOEFFER'S LATER HAMARTIOLOGY AND ETHICS

Introduction

The book argues that Bonhoeffer's hamartiology transforms and reconstructs the Augustinian doctrine of original sin by shifting the starting point from the doctrine of God to the doctrine of the church and approaching the concept of humanity from his Lutheran perspective. The previous chapter sketched Bonhoeffer's hermeneutical approach to the hamartiology of *Creation and Fall* in which his new awareness of the physical dimension of concupiscence and human solidarity with respect to sin and evil is associated with his earlier ethical and relational standpoint, based on his ecclesiocentrism and communitarian personalism. It is now necessary to examine Bonhoeffer's later hamartiology and ethics in which he vividly describes his existential recognition of the twofold reality of the postlapsarian human being and the importance of Christian responsibility. Despite the fragmentary and unfinished nature of his later writings, Bonhoeffer's thinking toward the end of his life reveals latent hamartiological elements that had not been evident in his early understanding. For example, Bonhoeffer poignantly observes the passive dimension of sin expressed as self-deception or selflessness, which has affinities with the claim of feminist thinkers and has never fully been emphasized in Western hamartiology.[1] Furthermore, there is a certain degree of advancement from his earlier doctrines in regard to the doctrine of sin and adjacent theological loci such as Christology, human freedom, and the doctrine of "vicarious representative action." Whereas his earlier doctrine of sin was articulated in a way that focused on the reformulation of the traditional Augustinian doctrine of sin through the Lutheran perspective, his later writing expresses Bonhoeffer's own (and still distinctively Lutheran) approach in which he advances and sometimes distances himself from the traditional Augustinian doctrines as well as his own earlier hamartiological concepts that reflected his social and political circumstances at the time.

The purpose of this chapter is to describe Bonhoeffer's later transformative and radical hamartiological approach that led to his contextual Christian ethics firmly anchored in his new recognition of the meaning of God's becoming human. This chapter argues that Bonhoeffer's later hamartiology and ethics contain the most distinctive characteristics of his theology, clearly distinguished from the

Augustinian tradition, in which he treats equally both the active and passive dimensions of the human being's sinful nature and highlights the responsibility of the Christian person through his doctrine of vicarious representative action based on his doctrine of God's "humanization" in Christ.[2] First, the chapter investigates the dual structure of sin, examining the active as well as the passive sides of sin. After discussing the dual nature of the postlapsarian self, it proposes that the doctrine of God's humanization in Christ is the center of Bonhoeffer's later hamartiology in which he expands the scope of Christian responsibility and radically transforms the traditional doctrine of Christian freedom. Then, the chapter examines Bonhoeffer's Christian ethics in which the concept of *Stellvertretung* (vicarious representative action) embraces the concept of the "voluntaristic taking on of guilt" in an extraordinary situation. Finally, the chapter discusses the theological implications of Bonhoeffer's later doctrine of sin in light of the Augustinian and Lutheran traditions as well as his own early doctrine of sin and ethics.

The Twofold Structure of Sin

As a Lutheran theologian, Bonhoeffer's concept of sin is strongly influenced by the Augustinian tradition that emphasizes the egocentricity of the human self as the chief characteristic of sin. However, as classical feminist thinkers argued, the emphasis of Western hamartiology has been on the active side of sin represented by the concept of pride, which is mainly related to the sinful experiences of males.[3] Even though Bonhoeffer does not directly relate this passive side of sin with the experiences of women or with the issues of gender, race, or class, his observation concerning the unemphasized side of sin is significant. Although the passive aspect of sin has been discussed in the Augustinian hamartiological tradition, it has been treated as secondary to original sin represented as pride. Evidently, this hamartiological or anthropological tradition has not reflected the perspectives or experiences of all human beings, especially those of women and the poor.[4]

Bonhoeffer's early works also show traits similar to the Augustinian doctrine of hamartiology, especially in Bonhoeffer's emphasis on the active aspect of sin, such as egocentricity or power, which can replace the traditional concept of pride as the original or hereditary sin. From the perspective of a metonymy that identifies effects with causes, pride as the original sin has been replaced by other similar active aspects of sin such as concupiscence, unbelief, power, egocentricity, and *sicut Deus* (like God) by scholars in the Western hamartiological tradition. In a similar vein, Luther's term *cor curvum in se* (the heart curved in upon itself), which is derived from Augustine's notion of *homo incurvatus in se* (man turned in upon himself), is at the heart of Bonhoeffer's concept of sin chiefly expressed in the concept of egocentricity in his earlier theological period. Accordingly, egocentricity is the chief aspect of sin of the human being after the fall. In Bonhoeffer's prison writings, however, the passive aspect of sin appears as a major aspect of sin, along with his earlier emphasis on the egocentricity of the human being. Bonhoeffer clearly describes the passive side of sin of a person who has been subjected to evil power and authority and is submissive and hopeless; this combined with his earlier emphasis on the active side of sin forms the dual structure of sin. Bonhoeffer explicitly considers the passive side of sin as equally harmful and destructive as the active side of sin. Thus, this section examines Bonhoeffer's investigation of this dual structure of sin, especially through his prison essay "After Ten Years."[5]

Beginning with his first work, *Sanctorum Communio*, Bonhoeffer's understanding of the self is closely connected to his paired concept of "I and You" or "the self and the other."[6] Bonhoeffer's early notion of sin is expressed chiefly from the vantage point of the postlapsarian sinful self in which the self exercises destructive power over the other. As discussed in Chapters 2 and 3, this destructive power of the I is encapsulated in the well-known Lutheran notion of *cor curvum in se*. In *Act and Being*, he describes the self that is curved inwardly toward the self so that there is no possibility of obtaining any true knowledge of God or of humanity. Not surprisingly, as Clifford J. Green argues, in *Creation and Fall* Bonhoeffer contrasts the creator and the creature in a relational and communal power dynamic from the viewpoint of the self of Adam.[7] Bonhoeffer definitely relates the egocentric self to his understanding of the original sin as "pride" or "power," which represents the traditional Western hamartiological perspective. His advance from the traditional interpretation is that he expands the concept of Adam in a communitarian way. Thus, the fall is the rebellion of the corporate self against the divine other. Bonhoeffer frequently identifies sin with humanity's alienation to be *sicut Deus*, which explicitly resonates with the Western tradition rooted in pride. As Green comments, the *cor curvum in se* of the self in Bonhoeffer's early theology is repeatedly described in terms of the active and destructive aspects of the sinful self, using terms such as "the power of the ego, its dominance of others," and "the violation of created sociality."[8]

Similar to the Augustinian as well as the Lutheran concept of the original or chief sin as pride, Bonhoeffer's early theology contained a discrepancy between the active notion of sin as egocentricity, power, and pride and the notion of the total human being (*totus homo*), which is meant to encompass the totality of the sinful experience of the self but neglects the passive side of sin. When the self is described as egocentric and prideful over others, the implication is that the self should be described through counter-notions such as self-denigration or selflessness, reflecting the passive aspect of the self. Bonhoeffer's early doctrine of the heart curved in upon itself, however, does not totally deny the passive aspect of the sinful self because the I or the self is always explained in the relationality between I and you or the self and the other. As already noted, this paired concept of the self and the other presupposes the counter-experience of the other or the self, but Bonhoeffer appears not to acknowledge the passive aspect of the self's or the other's sinful experience fully in his early understanding. The interchangeability between the self and the other should be fundamental in Bonhoeffer's doctrine of the postlapsarian self because he firmly insists on the universality of sin as well as on the collective concept of Adam as the human race as early as in *Sanctorum Communio*.[9] Although Bonhoeffer distinguishes between the I and the other, in his early writings his description of the postlapsarian self is not closely connected to the totality of sin, which should contain both the active and passive aspects.

In *Sanctorum Communio* as well as in *Act and Being* and *Creation and Fall*, the passive aspect of the sinful self is embedded in a primitive way. In *Sanctorum Communio*, Bonhoeffer interprets sin not only through the lens of "power" or "dominion" but also through the lens of "self-isolation" and "atomism."[10] Bonhoeffer further explains that the power-oriented tendency of the sinful self drives the self to an extremely individualistic sinful state. Bonhoeffer's early expressions of "self-isolation" and "atomism" are evidently related to the passive aspect of the self, but he only treats these concepts as results of the self's sinful exercise of power and pride over others. His description of these passive experiences of the self remains simply an additional explanation related to the central issue of the prideful self. In the stage of his thinking between *Sanctorum Communio* and *Creation and Fall*, he does not fully treat the passive sinful aspect as equal in significance to the active egocentricity of the self.

Bonhoeffer's retrospective essay "After Ten Years," however, clearly describes both the active and the passive aspects of the postlapsarian self. In the beginning of this essay, Bonhoeffer argues, "I want to try to give an accounting of some of the shared experience and insight that have been forced upon us in these times, not personal experiences, nothing systematically organized, not arguments and theories, but conclusions about human experience."[11] He continues, "None of this is new; it is something... given to us to experience and understand anew."[12] Bonhoeffer's recognition of the passive side of sin is related to his new awareness of "the masquerade of evil."[13] He states that "evil should appear in the form of light, good deeds, historical necessity, [and] social justice."[14] He points out that evil is working in the hiddenness in a disguised form and that it is therefore hard to detect the evil from the light, the word of Satan from the word of God.[15] Furthermore, he relates the masquerade of evil to the self's passive submission to it due to the self's credulity or stupidity.[16] Bonhoeffer explicitly recognizes the overlooked aspect of the sinful self who naively participates in the power of evil disguised as the light or the word of God. He argues that even "the Christian who lives by the Bible" can be deceived by evil by his or her naive misreading of reality and become an instrument used to "patch up a [sinful] structure."[17] He identifies the sinful experience of the self in the more passive characteristics of sin, contrasting this with his early perspective on sin illustrated by language such as power, pride, and dominion over others. This is Bonhoeffer's observation from the underside of the self, which is articulated in expressions such as "naive misreading of reality" and "withdraw in resignation or helplessly fall victim to the stronger."[18] This is like Adam and Eve facing the serpent in the garden; they were vulnerable and naive when confronting the words of the serpent.[19]

At this point, it is worthwhile to compare Bonhoeffer's early description of Eve in *Creation and Fall* and the passive sinful aspect of the self in "After Ten Years." Similar to how first-generation feminists describe the female self, Bonhoeffer interprets the sin of Adam and the sin of Eve from the perspective of activity and passivity. The sinful experience of Eve, for Bonhoeffer, is simply due to her ignorance.[20] On the one hand, Eve is described as a passive participant in the event in the garden; in her ignorance and stupidity, she fails to notice the gravity of her passive sinful action. On the other hand, similar to Kathryn Greene-McCreight's critique of feminists' emphasis on the female's passivity despite their good intentions, Bonhoeffer's exegesis of Eve that focuses primarily on her passivity runs the risk of consolidating the female self's *imago Dei* as unintelligent and dependent.[21] He states:

> Eve's answer remains on the level of ignorance. She does not know about evil; she does not recognize it. Therefore all she is able to do is to repeat the given commandment and state it correctly. And that is a great deal; she holds fast to the commandment. But in doing this she allows herself to become involved in this clever conversation.[22]

Bonhoeffer's description of Eve in *Creation and Fall* is strikingly analogous to his description of people in "After Ten Years" who, in their stupidity and self-deception, insist on principles without recognizing the true meaning of the word of God due to their lack of wisdom and courage.[23] However, in "After Ten Years" Bonhoeffer clearly shifts his point of view from his earlier position, in which he illustrates the passive aspect of the self chiefly with the female self, to the communal concept of the self in connection with evil power and authority. In this essay, Bonhoeffer goes beyond his earlier individualistic frame of the self, in which he distinguished the experiences of Adam and Eve in a way similar to classical feminist thinkers' claim that the female experience is based on passivity.[24] The self's passivity is seemingly liberated from the frame of gender, such as viewing Adam as in pride and Eve as in ignorance.[25]

Clearly, Bonhoeffer describes the postlapsarian self from the standpoint of the self who is on the outside or underside of power and pride.[26] He can see that sin from the underside of the self is related to a more abysmal, unnoticeable, and disguised evil. He focuses on the disastrous, sinful way of the self's passive participation in and submission to evil hidden in the form of "duty," "principle," and "mediocrity."[27] He writes:

> With their ability to see impaired, they want to do justice on every side, only to be crushed by the colliding forces without having accomplished anything at all. Disappointed that the world is so unreasonable, they see themselves condemned to unproductiveness; they withdraw in resignation or helplessly fall victim to the stronger.[28]

Bonhoeffer illustrates the dual nature of the sinful self by rediscovering the gravity of the self's passive submission to evil power with self-denigrating words such as disappointment, helplessness, resignation, unproductiveness, and victim.[29] Bonhoeffer further argues that the self can be easily deceived by the disguised evil that appears in the form of principles and duty *or* the self deceives the self per se without recognizing the self's submission to the evil power. This is devastating because the self participates in evil "with the purity of a principle."[30] Bonhoeffer's early emphasis on the egoistic and prideful self is simultaneously related to the other, passive side of the self through terms such as "self-satisfied" and "stupidity."[31]

In "After Ten Years," although Bonhoeffer primarily emphasizes the passive dimension of the sinful self's inwardness, the active dimension still functions as the foundational aspect underlying the passive side of the self.[32] He does more clearly demonstrate this dual dimension of the sinful self. He illustrates the interwoven dual nature of the *cor curvum in se*, because of which "the fanatic believes that he can meet the power of evil with the purity of a principle. But like the bull in the arena, he attacks the red cape rather than the person carrying it."[33] Bonhoeffer describes the self in pride as insisting on its capacity to overcome evil by principles but ending up with vain confidence; it is in deep despair and suffering in the trap of evil.[34] This dual aspect of the self's incurvature extends to his distinction between duty and responsibility.[35] Strikingly, Bonhoeffer argues that when the self is bound by principles, the self does its duty—even, in the end, to evil.[36] The self doing its duty is definitely in the passive state of *cor curvum in se*, deceiving the self in "restlessness or turning the self into a hypocritical, self-righteous, [and] small-minded human being."[37] Bonhoeffer is here describing the state of the self as a state of self-denial or self-denigration in a manner similar to many feminist thinkers' descriptions of the experience of women. Bonhoeffer's depiction of the self has clearly expanded and developed from his description of the sinful self's incurvature in egocentricity in his early works.[38] His later use of terminology shows his turn toward the passive aspect of the self as an equally dangerous characteristic of sinful inwardness that he did not clearly articulate in his early works.

The following quotation from Bonhoeffer is crucial in understanding the dual sides of the sinful self as prideful yet stupid:

> There are human beings who are of remarkably agile intellect yet stupid, and others who are intellectually quite dull yet anything but stupid. We discover this to our surprise in particular situations. The impression one gains is not so much that stupidity is a congenital defect but that, under certain circumstances, people are made stupid or ... they allow this to happen to them. ... And so it would seem that stupidity is perhaps less a psychological than a sociological problem.[39]

Bonhoeffer argues that human beings can be simultaneously proud and stupid in certain situations. Furthermore, the stupidity of the self is not just a psychological matter but a sociological problem. Bonhoeffer's concern here is more on the relationality between the submissive self and the broad social and political system or, more precisely, the evil power or corporate person behind the system.[40] Bonhoeffer once again has found that this passive incurvature is equally as grave as active inwardness because it denies the self's dignity as the image of God. As Hannah Arendt observes regarding this submissive aspect of the sinful self in her famous phrase "the banality of evil," in certain situations human beings become stupid, swallowed up by the evil sociopolitical system without noticing its evilness.[41] This is more devastating when the stupidity of the person is interconnected with blind submission to the law and the principles of an evil authority, as in the case of Otto Adolf Eichmann.[42] Strikingly, similar to Bonhoeffer's description of blind submission to the law, Arendt writes, "He did his *duty*, as he told the police and court over again and again; he not only obeyed *orders*, he also obeyed the *law*."[43] Bonhoeffer's analysis of the dual aspect of sin leads him to rethink the importance of human choice or responsibility as a true human being. This is demonstrated in his Christian ethics, especially in the later doctrine of *Stellvertretung*.

One of the difficulties in Bonhoeffer's early thought lies in his treatment of the human other. In his early works, he treats the human other in an extremely positive manner as the boundary or limit that ultimately guards the I or the self; however, he does not sufficiently discuss the human other's or the self's passive side as *simul iustus et peccator* (simultaneously righteous and a sinner).[44] In *Sanctorum Communio*, his focus is primarily on the relationality between the I and the other already reconciled in Christ within the boundary of the church community, even though his doctrine of *Stellvertretung* is not restricted to the community.[45] However, in "After Ten Years" Bonhoeffer's concern for the self and the other, both inside and outside the Christian community, is explicit.[46] When confronted with radical sinful power outside of the church community, the self's incurvature is more clearly demonstrated as a mixture of these two dimensions of the self in self-confusion or self-deception. In his early work, self-giving and self-sacrifice can be smoothly equated with his other-oriented doctrine of the body of Christ who exists as the church community. However, in the extremely distorted society that is the context of his later works, Bonhoeffer recognizes that the self that becomes passive and submissive is similar to that of the other who is the object of self-giving and self-sacrifice. The I who was in pride exists in the position of powerlessness or self-deception in "After Ten Years." The self in despair now needs self-liberation and self-centeredness to be the true self who is mediated by Christ. Accordingly, the discovery of the self's freedom in Christ is the major theme of Bonhoeffer's later hamartiology.

In summary, Bonhoeffer's hamartiological concepts such as "power" and "egocentricity" chiefly express the active side of the sinful characteristics of the postlapsarian human being. However, in his later work, such as "After Ten Years," Bonhoeffer focuses more on the passive side of sin expressed by notions such as "self-deceiving," "self-satisfying," and "stupidity," which had not been highlighted as major characteristics of sin in the history of the Augustinian hamartiological tradition in the modern era.[47] Although Augustine's later doctrine of sin partially discusses the passive side of sin, which he describes as "ignorance" and "difficulties," it is Bonhoeffer who clearly articulates the destructive power of this sinful passivity. In part, Bonhoeffer's dual structure of sin is analogous to the thinking of the majority of classical feminist thinkers who argue that woman's sin is in passivity; however, his anthropological structure seemingly does not distinguish between the sinful experiences of men and women but encompasses the dual aspects of sin as belonging to all human beings. Despite his emphasis on "I and the other" relationality, Bonhoeffer's anthropological structure is inconsistent, especially in the relationality between men and women or wife and husband. His later assertion of the dual nature of sin articulates the human being's passive form of sinfulness that is as destructive as the active form, especially in an extraordinary situation. Bonhoeffer asserts that the self who is caught in this dual chain of sin can only be a responsible Christian person when the self is liberated by encountering Christ's person and life. He identifies Christ as the ultimate source of the Christian person's inner liberation and of vicarious representative free action for the sake of neighbors. The related doctrines of Christ's person and work and *Stellvertretung*, which are intensified from his earlier concepts, are discussed more closely in the following sections.

God's Humanization in Christ

In his early theology, Bonhoeffer's transformative interpretation of the traditional doctrine of original sin culminates in his doctrine of reconciliation and the life of the church community in which he emphasizes the vicarious Christian action of bearing the sin of the other. Then, his new emphasis on corporeality in *Creation and Fall* offers an unshakable foundation for doctrinal loci such as the doctrines of Christ, human freedom, and ethics in his later theology. His new awareness of the importance of the corporeality of Christ leads him to radicalize the doctrine of Christ in a more Lutheran way in the existential and Christocentric sense. Bonhoeffer's focus on corporeality functions in two different directions—in his anthropology and his Christology. In his anthropology, as he addresses in *Creation and Fall*, Bonhoeffer no longer relies on the high ethical anthropology of his contemporary Lutherans, who emphasize a high view of the human. Bonhoeffer's awareness of the importance of human corporeality, as recognized in *Creation and Fall*, clearly reflects German political circumstances such as the Nazi's discriminatory misapplication of concepts of human race and the influence of contemporary Lutheran theology as exemplified by *Ansbacher Ratschlag* (the Ansbach Memorandum) signed by Wermer Elert and Paul Althaus.[48] Bonhoeffer's pessimistic perspective on the human being, however, finds a breakthrough in his new recognition of Christ in regard to Christ's humanity, especially in Christ's being in human form.[49]

The corporeality of Christ becomes an important foundation of Bonhoeffer's later hamartiology. The Nazi regime continued to oppress his theological and existential life after Hitler's appointment as chancellor in 1933.[50] Bonhoeffer's Christology lecture represents the culmination of his early theology and is the cornerstone of his mature theology.[51] His early understanding of the church community as the body of Christ is intensified in his new understanding of the corporeality of the human being and of Christ. As seen in *Creation and Fall*, Bonhoeffer's exegetical methodology is firmly rooted in reality in Christ. Strikingly, in this way of reading the Bible, the corporeality of the human being is based not on any archetypal ancestors but on the reality in the revelation of God in Christ. In other words, the origin of the human being both materially and spiritually is the person of Christ. Bonhoeffer states:

> The figure [Gestalt] of the reconciler, of the God-man Jesus Christ, steps into the middle between God and the world, into the center of all that happens. In this figure is disclosed the mystery of the world, just as the mystery of God is revealed in it. No abyss of the world can remain hidden from him through whom the world is reconciled to God. But the abyss of the love of God embraces even the most abysmal godlessness of the world. In an incomprehensible reversal of all righteous and pious thought, God declares himself as guilty toward the world and thereby extinguishes the guilt of the world.[52]

It seems apparent that Bonhoeffer is affirming Chalcedonian Christology by saying that Christ is the reconciler as mediator between God and the world as the true human being as well as the true God.[53] However, his use of "the figure [Gestalt] of the reconciler" implies that he approaches this from a different side of Christology, in other words, from Christ's humanity. Surprisingly, he focuses on Christ's being human rather than the Nicene as well as Chalcedonian Creeds' focus on Christ's divinity.[54] Bonhoeffer continues, "Ecce homo—behold God become human, the unfathomable mystery of the love of God for the world."[55] It is significant that contrary to the Athanasian declaration that "God became human that we might become divine," Bonhoeffer reverses this: "In an incomprehensible reversal of all righteous and pious thought, God declares himself as guilty toward the world and thereby extinguishes the guilt of the world."[56] Once again, Bonhoeffer places the origin of reconciliation as well as ethics in the "formation of Jesus Christ" rather than the "divinization" of human beings.[57] He argues that "human beings do not become God. They could not and do not accomplish a change in form; God changes God's form into human form in order that human beings can become, not God, but human before God."[58] For Bonhoeffer, Augustine's as well as Athanasius' focus on going up to the higher being or on becoming divine is considered a human-centered understanding of reconciliation or justification, neglecting Christ's becoming a human being.[59] Thus, for Bonhoeffer the genuine way of Christian ethics is found in the way that the human becomes more truly a human being.

Approaching this from a different direction than the Nicene tradition and going beyond the Chalcedonian creed, Bonhoeffer focuses on the full humanity of Christ for humanity's new life in the church community.[60] In a similar vein to many scholars' critique of classical Christology for its formulation "in a language that is obscure, abstract, and far removed from the experience of faith,"[61] Bonhoeffer focuses more on Christ's bodily existence in the world than on Christ's divinity, which had been discussed chiefly in a form of metaphysical speculation.[62] He perceives that the reality of God is revealed in Jesus Christ in Christ's full humanity through Christ's person and work without any separation of the two.

Bonhoeffer's approach to the Nicene tradition from the other direction leads him to conclude that the reason for God's becoming human is "not to despise real human beings."[63] He further argues that God's becoming human is "not because of the real human being's inherent value, but because God has loved and taken on the real human being."[64] God's humanization takes on significant meaning for Bonhoeffer because it is the sole basis of humanity's becoming true human beings in real life. Now, the true meaning of the human being can be connected to God's existence in the world through the humanized God in Christ.[65] Bonhoeffer's preference for the German term *Menschwerdung* rather than *Inkarnation* reveals his emphasis on God's becoming the full human being.[66] As Green properly comments, it is important to note that Bonhoeffer's use of the term *Menschwerdung* is not to point out the enfleshment of God Godself but to indicate that God became the full human being.[67] Precisely speaking, for Bonhoeffer the good news is God's humanization.

God's humanization means a great deal for Bonhoeffer's doctrine of reconciliation. The reconciled community or person does not exist in the realm of speculation or abstraction but in the real world in connection with the Nazareth Jesus Christ in Christ's person and work. This concrete existence of the reconciled person is possible only as the body of Christ. Bonhoeffer's Lutheran existential recognition of Christ is reinforced by his understanding of the reconciled human being. He explains that the human Christ becomes the reconciler by his being subject to the judgment of God. He argues:

> Ecco homo—behold the one whom God has judged! The figure of the mystery and of pain. This is how the reconciler of the world appears, upon whom humanity's guilt has fallen, pushing Christ into shame and death under God's judgment. Reconciliation with the world cost God so dearly. Only by executing God's judgment on God can peace grow between God and the world, between human and human.[68]

God's becoming human is for the purpose of judging humanity's sin and guilt. It is noteworthy that Bonhoeffer's Christological discernment is not limited to a certain point in Christ's life or work but encompasses the entire person and work of Christ in regard to humanity's sin and guilt. As Daniel L. Migliore points out, Bonhoeffer approaches this from a neglected side of Christology that the Western tradition has not fully investigated.[69] Bonhoeffer attempts to draw a connection between the person of Christ and the reconciled human person, in contrast to Augustine's or Athanasius' attempt to elevate the quality of the human being closer to that of the divine Being. It is clear that Bonhoeffer is reinforcing the point that God is in the world in the form of the church community, which he argued in his first dissertation.

God's humanization, for Bonhoeffer, is the sole basis of the human's humanization. For him, the divinization of human beings is only possible in the realm of speculation. He reconciles this through the humanization of humans rather than their divinization. God's humanization signifies the possibility of humans becoming true humans. This possibility of the human's humanization is found in the resurrection of Christ:

> Ecce homo—behold the human being, accepted by God, judged by God, awakened by God to a new life—see the Risen One! God's Yes to this human being has found its goal through judgement and death. God's love for this human being was stronger than death. A new human being, a new life, a new creature has been created by God's miracle. ... What happened to Christ has happened for all, for he was *the* human being. The new human being has been created.[70]

Bonhoeffer relates Christ's resurrection, which overcomes the limits of humanity, with the reconciled person's new identity. The doctrine of the new creation, which Luther as well as Augustine did not fully emphasize as the source of humans' humanization, is concerned with the powerful source of humanity's ethical life. For Bonhoeffer, the term *sanctification*, which signifies "to make holy," seems inappropriate for the reconciled person. Although in *Discipleship* he emphatically argues the inseparability of justification and sanctification, in his later understanding his earlier notion of sanctification has been transformed into the concept of humanization.[71]

Bonhoeffer's attention to the doctrine of the new creation is significant in his later hamartiology in regard to related theological concepts, especially human freedom and its limits. Characteristically, Bonhoeffer appropriates Luther's early ethics through the lens of Karl Holl's moral interpretation of Luther's theology. As in his assertion in *Discipleship*, the notion of inseparability between justification and sanctification allows Bonhoeffer to retrieve Luther's early emphasis on the ethical life that is weakened in Luther's mature theology along with Holl's linking this with "the power of Christ."[72] In this regard, Holl's ethical interpretation of Luther's theology is noteworthy. One of the significant points of Holl's ethics is his appropriation of Luther's early theology. In *The Reconstruction of Morality*, Holl examines Luther's early writings, especially those written from 1513 through 1515.[73] Holl's description of Luther's ethic resonates with Bonhoeffer's concept. He interprets Luther's concept of ethics as follows:

> At the same time Luther forcefully developed the idea that this 'foolish' gospel, of God's turning to the sinner rather than to the righteous, does not destroy morality but actually produces it. Forgiveness provides a most powerful new impulse for gratitude. From it flows that joyful willing of the good in which Luther saw the perfection of morality.[74]

Holl derives Luther's awareness of the close connection between justification and sanctification from Luther's early thought in which Luther does not hesitate to articulate the inseparability of justification and sanctification in which forgiveness of sin functions as the source of morality in the lives of Christians.[75] Holl clearly relates the reconciling power of Christ to the notion of voluntaristic human action toward the good. Similar to Holl, Bonhoeffer considers the humanization of God in Christ as the powerful beginning of the humanization of human beings who are in Christ. The meaning of humanization is nothing other than God's voluntaristic love for humanity revealed in Christ's becoming human as well as Christ's resurrection. The resurrection of Christ symbolizes a new way of human life in which Christians voluntarily live for others with joy.[76] As Holl interprets Luther's early doctrine of morality as the result of the forgiveness of sin, Bonhoeffer argues that "what happened to Christ happened for all, for he was *the* human being."[77] Bonhoeffer's transformative interpretation of sanctification as humanization allows him to intensify the connection between Christ and the saints as the body of the church community, which he already had strongly argued. Although Bonhoeffer emphatically rejects Holl's psychological interpretation of Luther's theology, he embraces Holl's emphasis on Luther's morality, which is demonstrated in Luther's early works.

The doctrine of the new creation is pivotal to Bonhoeffer's later ethics. It is quite clear that the role of sanctification in Luther's early theology has diminished in Luther's mature theology, chiefly due to his focus on faith over obedience or, in other words, alien righteousness over active righteousness. In Luther's mature soteriology, the role of faith is pushed to the extreme, as it were, and the role of obedience is secondary to the role of faith; the mature soteriology of Luther does not explain the relationship between faith and obedience fully. Interestingly, however, in *Discipleship* Bonhoeffer points out the lack of concern for believers' faithful engagement with and for the world, blaming Lutherans rather than Luther.[78] Bonhoeffer argues that Luther's theology per se does not separate justification from sanctification; he claims there is an inseparable unity between the two. It is plausible that Bonhoeffer's attribution to Luther is analogous to Holl's argument regarding Luther's morality derived from Luther's early works such as his lectures on the Psalms between 1513 and 1515 and his lectures on Romans in 1515 and 1516.[79] Bonhoeffer's way of integrating Luther's ethics is noteworthy. On the one hand, Bonhoeffer insists that he is clearly following Luther's Reformation theology by arguing that Luther treats faith and obedience as inseparable, as Bonhoeffer does in *Discipleship*. On the other hand, he takes Luther's morality demonstrated in his early theology as the source of his doctrine of ethics.[80] In line with his equal emphasis on faith and obedience, Bonhoeffer's focus on the new creation leads him to connect the lives of Christians with the concept of "formation," which says that Christian ethics means "to become like Jesus."[81] Because Bonhoeffer uses the term *Gestaltung* (formation) to mean ethics, the given way of life for the saints is "to become like Jesus."[82]

In summary, Bonhoeffer's concept of humanization supplies the theological foundation for his ethics. In *Creation and Fall*, he clearly rejects the "order of creation" that is manipulated by the Nazi ideology of "the blood and soil."[83] He interprets the corporeality of the human being in two ways—as the source of human sinful solidarity and the basis of the reconciliation of humanity. This is because Bonhoeffer understands the humanization of God as demonstrating the existential hope of human beings in regard to God's becoming human and Christ's resurrection as a human. He perceives that God's humanization indicates the way of

Christian persons who are reconciled in Christ. This way of life does not mean that human beings are attempting to be divinized; rather, human beings are becoming true human beings in the form of Jesus Christ. Although Bonhoeffer's doctrine of reconciliation is firmly rooted in traditional Western post-Nicene Christology, his emphasis on Christ's full humanity allows him to focus on Christian ethics as humanization. For Bonhoeffer, the traditional concept of sanctification is transferred by the notion of humanization. One of the distinctive characteristics of Bonhoeffer's concept of humanization is the influence of Luther's early morality, from which Bonhoeffer absorbs the essential traits given in Holl's interpretation of Luther. However, Bonhoeffer's Lutheran way of humanization is not intrinsic but extrinsic, rooted in God's humanization and resurrection. His Christocentric notion of humanization also offers significant theological room for other related concepts such as freedom, *Stellvertretung*, and finally the nature of sin and evil to be interpreted in his particular existential circumstances in his later theology. These related concepts are discussed in the following sections.

Christian Freedom

For Bonhoeffer, the concept of humanization becomes the foundation of related doctrines such as Christian freedom. It is necessary, therefore, to consider his later writings that radically transform the notion of Christian freedom and action to the world through his Lutheran perspective. Christian freedom is one of the doctrinal areas of Bonhoeffer's theology that is distinct from the Augustinian tradition. The starting point of his transformative doctrine of freedom is decisively his existential and Christocentric interpretation of sanctification expressed in the doctrine of humanization. As noted above, the concept of humanization plays a crucial role in several related doctrines. Bonhoeffer defines humanization as the way of sanctification of the Christian person rooted in the concept of *extra nos* (outside ourselves) in Christ. For Bonhoeffer, the concept of humanization is inseparably attached to the presence of Christ in the church community. Without the presence of Christ, there can be no humanization or sanctification. In his lectures on Christology, Bonhoeffer illustrates the form (*Gestalt*) of Christ in three ways: Word, sacrament, and the church community.[84] This emphasis on the presence of Christ in the world is one of the unique traits of Bonhoeffer's Lutheran way of thinking. It is necessary to delve into this concept in relation to Christian freedom.

Of the threefold forms of Christ's presence in the church, the church community has the most central place for human freedom and action in Bonhoeffer's theology.[85] Bonhoeffer's early ecclesiocentric notion of "Christ existing as church-community" is continued in his later theology. As discussed in Chapter 3, the meaning of "Christ as the church community" needs to be interpreted using his collective concept of the person. Bonhoeffer's argument that Christ's presence in the church community is in the form of a collective person is quite significant. This assertion is crucial because it implies the "vicarious representative presence" of the church community as the physical presence of Christ in the world. For Bonhoeffer, whereas the Word and sacrament are engaged in the church community, the church community per se as the collective person exists as Christ vicariously and representatively.[86] This vicarious notion becomes the theological foundation of Bonhoeffer's doctrines of freedom and ethics in *Ethics*. It is necessary to pay careful attention to the vicariousness of Christian freedom because there can be a question of the extent of Christian freedom, especially in regard to Bonhoeffer's engagement in a plot of tyrannicide. Although Bonhoeffer argues that the church community attains Christ's freedom *only* vicariously and representatively, the limits of Christian freedom beyond the boundary of laws such as the Decalogue have not been fully resolved at this point. This issue is potentially controversial in two areas: the human possibility of vicarious representative action itself and the limit of the Christian person's freedom. At this point, it is necessary to take a brief look at the understanding of Christian freedom, especially in regard to the concept of vicariousness and its scope in the Western tradition, mainly in Augustine and Luther.

Augustine's philosophical concept of freedom is closely related to the doctrine of original sin. Because he identified the beginning of the fall as the misused will of the first rational beings, in his doctrine there is no genuine freedom after the fall, not even for the saints. This is because he perceives that the freedom of the Christian person is interlocked with the will, which moves back and forth between the supreme Good and the lesser good. Accordingly, his description of freedom is mainly focused on the individual level of chastity rather than on the social and ecclesial levels of freedom. As Robert Dodaro explains, for Augustine Christ is the model of "civic virtues such as piety (*pietas*) and mercy (*misericordia*)," which could not perfectly be imitated as such by human beings.[87] Augustine clearly distinguishes between the human being's imitation of Christ and Christ himself. There is a qualitative difference between Christ and the Christian person.[88]

For Augustine, the possibility of the vicarious representative action of Christ is not a human possibility but is found only in the virtues of Christ.[89] In this way, nevertheless, Augustine offers Bonhoeffer the quintessential notion that "the church is the body of Christ" as the cornerstone of Bonhoeffer's ecclesiology. The scope of the freedom of the experiential church community for Augustine is far more limited than Bonhoeffer's notion of the freedom of the church community as a collective person. It is noteworthy that despite Bonhoeffer's directly connecting the freedom of Christ with the freedom of the church community, Augustine interprets "the church is the body of Christ" in a more spiritual and symbolic way than Bonhoeffer's existential reception. Despite recognizing the church community as part of the city of God, Augustine views this community as traveling through the temporal world toward its destination in the heavenly city of God. Truly, Augustine's focus in not on the worldly city. Augustine therefore sought the theoretical foundation for the relationality between church and state in Pauline passages, especially Rom. 13:1–7, which primarily support the authority of civil rulers over Christians.[90] In a similar vein, John M. Rist describes Augustine as viewing evil authority as "the tyrant, seeking to be divine, as to a degree are all sinners including Augustine himself."[91] Seen from the perspective of *analogia entis* (analogy of being), for Augustine, Christ's person and life cannot be the direct example of the church community's or the Christian person's freedom because of the fundamental qualitative gap between Christ and the Christian person or the church community. For Augustine, the apostles, especially Paul, and the Christian martyrs would be better existential models for Christian ethics.[92] Augustine's notion and Bonhoeffer's radical Christocentrism diverge at this juncture.

However, Luther's exegesis of the creation accounts supplies the archetypal model of God's freedom in regard to the freedom of the church community as well as of the saints. For Luther, the notion of freedom logically belongs to God, in line with the Augustinian definition of freedom. However, traits of Luther's understanding that are differentiated from Augustine's are in Luther's interpretation, based on his Christocentric exegesis, of God's freedom in God's relationality toward the creation. In other words, he understands freedom not from the lens of *analogia entis* but from that of *analogia relationis* (analogy of relation).[93] Oswald Bayer properly points out a distinctive aspect of Luther's notion of the freedom of the saint: "the image of God for the human being consists in the fact that the individual is the representative (vicarious) of God."[94] Whereas Luther relates his notion of God's freedom to the individual saint's freedom as *imago Dei*, Bonhoeffer in his later understanding applies this freedom to the communal Christian person as well as to an individual saint's free action.[95]

For Bonhoeffer, the bound freedom signifies that the church community's vicarious action is protected by the will of God in Christ. Clearly, Bonhoeffer interprets the will of God not as an obstacle but as a blessing when a person is in Christ. It is noteworthy that in *Ethics*, the boundary of freedom is expanded beyond the realm of the church community.[96] This expansion of Christian freedom beyond the church signifies two theological implications. On the one hand, Bonhoeffer recognizes that Christ's presence in the world, as he articulated in his "Lectures on Christology," led him to expand Christ's presence or freedom to the world.[97] He argues that the church is the hidden center of the world because only the church community can know the reality that is Christ's or the church community's centrality in history.[98] On the other hand, the new political circumstances in Germany inevitably make him think about the relationality between church and state in a new way that differs from the Lutheran doctrine of two kingdoms (*Zwei-Reiche-Lehre*). Bonhoeffer argues that "there has been a *new relation* between state and church since the historical event of the cross. The state has existed in its truest sense only since there has been a church."[99] As the editors of *Ethics* comment, the prevalent dichotomous way of thinking, such as between church and state, gospel and law, and faith and reason, had prevented the church from taking responsible action toward the state when it was necessary.[100] Furthermore, Luther's two kingdoms doctrine begins to be manipulated in an "anachronistic and shorthand" way for political means.[101] Bonhoeffer's argument of the centrality of the church clearly went against the current in Germany and in the West, where the place of Christianity had shrunk to fit within the boundary of the church community. The logic of Christ's centrality in history is the proclamation that allows Bonhoeffer to connect Christ's freedom with the Christian person's freedom in the state and society.[102]

On a superficial level, the nature of freedom is seemingly paradoxical. Freedom, for Bonhoeffer, would be contradicted by the traditional concept of the good deeds of the human being when a Christian person is in an extraordinary situation (*die außerordentliche Situation*) or a borderline case (*der Grenzfall*). He explains this contradictory aspect of the freedom of the Christian person as follows:

> In flight from public controversy this person or that reaches the sanctuary of a *private virtuousness*. Such people neither steal, nor murder, nor commit adultery, but do good according to their abilities. But voluntarily renouncing public life, these people know exactly how to observe the permitted boundaries that shield them from conflict. They must close their eyes and ears to the injustice around them. Only at the cost of self-deception can they keep their private blamelessness clean from the stains of responsible action in the world.[103]

Bonhoeffer clearly recognizes the conflict between the individual level of blamelessness and the communal level of cowardice found in the dual structure of the sinful self and the ethical evil of society, which he prototypically offered in *Sanctorum Communio*. This reflects his awareness of the weakness of principles and laws in the face of social and systematic injustice and evil in connection with the power of the state. The dilemma between "private virtuousness" and the "stains of responsible action" vividly shows Bonhoeffer's recognition of the hiddenness of ethical evil and sin found in the alienated relationship between individual and communal persons, as in the relationality between church and state.[104] This discrepancy becomes greater in extraordinary social and political circumstances, such as those of Bonhoeffer. In his early writings he emphasized the sociality of community, whether it is inside or outside of the church community; there resides the person's egocentricity or *cor curvum in se* as the root of the radical evil of the state or the world. Bonhoeffer clearly sees that "private blamelessness" or "private virtuousness" simply cannot be equated with the good deeds of a person. In many cases, the good deeds of a person at a superficial level would be considered sinful deeds when they are restricted to the sanctuary of an individual level of virtues, renouncing the person's relationality with the realm of public life—in other words, when the person closes her "eyes and ears to the injustice" around her.[105] The good deeds of a Christian person become ultimate good only when the deeds are connected to the ultimate good in Christ. Bonhoeffer contrasts the Christian person's blameless servitude to evil with stained or guilty responsible freedom. Blameless servitude to a private virtuousness is only worthy when it is related to the ultimate will of God. If not, this blamelessness just serves evil and deceives the person through self-deception. For Bonhoeffer, freedom becomes true freedom when the Christian person engages in a responsible action against evil.

In short, Bonhoeffer's break from the traditional Augustinian doctrine of freedom is explicitly his placing freedom's foundation in Christ's freedom and his expansion of its scope beyond the boundary of the church community. Augustine as well as Luther and Bonhoeffer saw that the concept of true freedom per se belongs to the freedom of God; however, the divergent point of Bonhoeffer's understanding is his strong Lutheran conviction of the presence of Christ as the church community and his focus on the newly created Christian freedom through the perspective of *analogia relationis*. Bonhoeffer clearly interprets the church community as the body of Christ who is present in the world; therefore, the church community can exercise its freedom vicariously and responsibly. Augustine, however, argues that Christ could not be an exemplar of Christian ethics, mainly due to the qualitative difference between Christ and the saint seen chiefly through the lens of *analogia entis*. Accordingly, Augustine considers the responsible free action of the saint partial and imperfect. In contrast, Bonhoeffer's Christocentric interpretation of the vicarious freedom of the Christian person permits him to engage with the doctrine of "a vicarious representative action." As already briefly discussed, Bonhoeffer's concept of *Stellvertretung*, however, contains some potential ethical dilemmas caused by his radical interpretation of Christian freedom, such as in the concept of "readiness to take on guilt" (*Schuldübernahme*) that will be dealt with in the next section.[106]

Stellvertretung

As discussed in the section entitled "Christian Freedom" in this chapter, one of the traits that distinguishes Bonhoeffer's later doctrine of freedom from the Augustinian tradition is his radical sense of the imputation of Christ's freedom to the church community or the saints. The responsible action of a Christian person for the other is the way to exercise new freedom in Christ. However, the problem with Bonhoeffer's concept of guilty responsible action is its theological legitimacy and its legitimate exercise. The relationality between "blameless virtues" represented as a law or principles and "stained responsible action" requires a theological rationale. In "History and Good [2]," Bonhoeffer suggests the legitimacy of stained responsible action in an extraordinary situation. He explains:

> There are occasions when, in the course of historical life, the strict observance of the explicit law of a state, a corporation, a family, but also of a scientific discovery, entails a clash with the basic necessities of human life. In such cases, appropriate responsible action departs from the domain governed by laws and principles, from the normal and regular, and instead is confronted with the extraordinary situation of ultimate necessities that are beyond any possible regulation by law. …
> It is equally certain, however, that these necessities, as primordial facts of life itself, cannot be captured by any law and can never become laws themselves.[107]

Bonhoeffer's article explicitly reflects the political circumstances of Germany in the late period of Nazi rule. His discussion of *Stellvertretung* here clearly presupposes the conflict between the "basic necessities of life" and "a law or principles of a state, a corporation, and a family."[108] To assert the necessity of a Christian person's responsible action beyond a law or principles of a state, he compares responsible action in ordinary situations and extraordinary circumstances of history. In his later theology, he uses the doctrine of *Stellvertretung* to place equal emphasis on individual responsible action, which he articulated in "History and Good [2]," and his earlier focus on communal action strongly bounded by his communitarian ecclesiology. In *Sanctorum Communio*, the individual's action is clearly the action of a member or a part of the church community, which ties in with his strong notion of "Christ existing as church-community."[109] His communal sensitivity in *Sanctorum Communio* makes him insist on an individual person's participation in the communal person's *Stellvertretung* rather than on direct individual Christian action. As he expands his doctrine of Christ's presence beyond the boundary of the church community, the hidden presence of Christ in the world as well as the centrality of Christ in history articulated in his "Christology Lectures" becomes the theological backbone of his later doctrine of *Stellvertretung*, which legitimates vicarious representative action toward the world beyond the realm of the church community.[110]

In the process of engaging with the concept of *Stellvertretung*, Bonhoeffer articulates what may be one of the most controversial issues in his theology—the inclusion of guilt in certain extraordinary situations.[111] Bonhoeffer already affirmed the voluntaristic taking on of the sin of the other in *Sanctorum Communio* as a transformative interpretation of the alien culpability of the Augustinian doctrine; however, this does not contain explicit implication of a guilty action but the voluntaristic sharing of the sin of the other. In *Sanctorum Communio* as well as in *Creation and Fall*, Bonhoeffer's attribution of Luther's understanding of bearing the sin of the other is mostly a Christocentric as well as ecclesiocentric imputation without any direct sense of guilt in it. Bonhoeffer credits Luther as the source of the vicarious representative action of the church community.[112] Luther's communitarian sense of bearing the sins of other members of the church community is continued and developed by Bonhoeffer. However, in Bonhoeffer's later understanding, such as in "History and Good [2]," the *Stellvertretung* is accompanied by the guilt of the agent who exercises a free responsible action for the other, especially in an extraordinary situation.[113] One of the crucial points in Bonhoeffer's later concept of *Stellvertretung* is that the Christian person who participates in the vicarious action of Christ is *simul iustus et peccator*. Although the person per se is a *peccator* (sinner), the person who participates in *Stellvertretung* is *iustus* (righteous) in Christ. The qualitative distinction between Christ and the Christian person in *Stellvertretung* is overcome through the relationality of Christ's sinlessness and the Christian person as *iustus*, similar to Luther's soteriological emphasis on imputation. It is quite clear that Bonhoeffer is applying the imputation of Christ's righteousness not only to the doctrine of justification but also to the area of sanctification. This ethical sense of being guilty and bearing the sin or guilt of the other is the chief characteristic of his later understanding of *Stellvertretung*.

The inclusion of guilt in *Stellvertretung* is a radical interpretation of Luther's ethics in relation to the church community because the responsible action of Bonhoeffer allows the possibility of resistance or violence, which Luther's mature understanding does not fully support; however, Bonhoeffer perceived that Luther's Reformation breakthrough is itself a model of resistance.[114] As

Mark U. Edwards Jr. comments, Luther's position after the Peasants' Revolt contains a theological conflict because "he had advocated that mercy and love be shown to friend and enemy alike while he condoned and advocated slaying and killing."[115] However, as already noted, Bonhoeffer appropriated Luther's early doctrine of the church community, written in 1520 before the Peasant's Revolt, in his *Sanctorum Communio* as the prototype of *Stellvertretung*.[116] Here, Luther's ethics in the church community emphasizes the reconciling work of the church community, and Bonhoeffer's doctrine of reconciliation of the church community is maintained throughout his entire theology. In his manuscript "Ethics as Formation," Bonhoeffer's rationale of resistance that contains the possibility of violence appears. Bonhoeffer argues that the reality of radical evil is only dealt with by the reality of Christ, who is the center of history and society.[117] In regard to "readiness to take on guilt" (*Schuldübernahme*), Bonhoeffer distinguishes between the contexts of extreme and extraordinary social and political circumstances and normal circumstances. He argues that in the former case, inappropriate responsible action "is confronted with the extraordinary situation of ultimate necessities that are beyond any possible regulation by law."[118] His earlier doctrine of *Stellvertretung* has expanded to the use of violence based on his rationale regarding the two different types of situations, ordinary and extraordinary.

Consequently, the guilty responsible action in Bonhoeffer's later understanding requires an appropriate criterion as justification. Bonhoeffer argues:

> Today we have villains and saints again, in full public view. … The contours are sharply drawn. Reality is laid bare. Shakespeare's characters are among us. The villain and the saint have little or nothing to do with ethical programs. They arise from primeval depths, and with their appearance tear open the demonic and divine abyss [Abrund] out of which they come, allowing us brief glimpses into their suspected secrets. It is worse to be evil than to do evil. It is worse when a liar tells the truth than when a lover of truth lies, worse when a person who hates humanity practices neighborly love [Bruderliebe] than when a loving person once falls victim to hatred. The lie is better than truth in the mouth of a liar, as hatred is better than acts of neighborly love by a misanthrope. One sin is not like another. They have different weights. There are heavier and lighters sins. Falling away [Abfall] is far more serious than falling down [Fall].[119]

The traditional analogy of good and bad trees used by Augustine and Luther is reflected again in Bonhoeffer's theological foundation for the comparison between villains and saints.[120] Here, Bonhoeffer follows Luther's early Reformation emphasis on the freedom in a Christian person. As is typical in his communal logic, Bonhoeffer transforms and applies the traditional analogy applied to the individual level of the person to the public person. His description of "the villain" or "evil" alludes to the evil regime or the evil state that exercises its own sinful will against the will of God.[121] More importantly, his comparison between the villain and the saint is explicitly related to the state and the church in the struggle in Germany. Bonhoeffer talks about the necessity of the guilt in relation to responsible action of the church community or the saint against the communal evil or the evil state. For Bonhoeffer, it is time to reconsider the relationality between church and state that is firmly anchored in the Lutheran doctrine of the two kingdoms but is anachronistic given the situation of Germany.

Luther's interpretation of the two kingdoms theory, for Bonhoeffer, is no longer appropriate for an extraordinary situation such as Nazi Germany. As Michael P. DeJonge as well as Christiane Tietz points out, however, the fundamental difference between Bonhoeffer and Luther on the issue of resistance lies in Bonhoeffer's treatment of Luther's active and passive righteousness underneath Bonhoeffer's reformulation of the doctrine of the two kingdoms.[122] DeJonge cites Tietz's analysis that "the difference between Bonhoeffer and Luther on the issue of active versus passive righteousness [is] largely one of emphasis, with Bonhoeffer placing more on God's active, punishing righteousness and Luther placing more on God's passive righteousness."[123] However, it is more accurate to say that Bonhoeffer treats active and passive righteousness more equally than does the mature Luther. Accordingly, the difference is not only between Luther and Bonhoeffer but also between the young Luther and the mature Luther. Clearly, Bonhoeffer's equal emphasis on the active and passive righteousness is the key point in his doctrine of *Stellvertretung*. At this point Bonhoeffer is relying on the early thought of Luther in which Luther treats faith and obedience more proportionally and focuses on morality as well as Christian freedom.

Bonhoeffer conceives that in extraordinary circumstances it is not possible to choose between good and evil but only to decide whether one is "to be evil" or "to do evil."[124] In such an extreme situation, doing evil is a lesser sin than being evil itself. "To do evil" for the sake of one's neighbor signifies the guilty vicarious responsible action of the saint when there is no way to exercise *Stellvertretung* for the other without sinning. Similar to the comment of Tietz, Green points out that the *Stellvertretung* in Bonhoeffer's later writings implies an active sense of "readiness to take on guilt" rather than a passive way of "acceptance of guilt."[125] This voluntaristic taking on of guilt is not for the sake of the self but on behalf of the other for the sake of the other. Significantly, Bonhoeffer argues that the voluntaristic taking on of guilt over the law is rooted in Christ's work and person, which is actively expressed in Luther's early theology, especially in its more equal treatment of active and passive righteousness and of justification and sanctification, such as in *Lectures on Romans* written in 1515–16.[126] Bonhoeffer argues:

> The freed conscience aligns itself with the responsibility, which has been established in Christ, to bear guilt for the sake of the neighbor. In contrast to the essential sinlessness of Jesus Christ, human action is never sinless but always contaminated by original sin, which is part of human nature. Nevertheless, as responsible action, in contrast to any self-righteous action justified by a principle, it does participate indirectly in the action of Jesus Christ. Responsible action is thus characterized by something like a relative sinlessness, which is demonstrated precisely by the responsible taking on of another's guilt.[127]

Once again, Bonhoeffer's Christocentric foundation is applied to his rationale to support his notion of a responsible action that takes on guilt. Bonhoeffer equally treats the *freed conscience* (justification or the passive righteousness of God) and Christian *responsibility* (sanctification or the active righteousness of God) in his concept of "bearing guilt for the sake of the neighbor" established in Christ. In this regard, DeJonge's comment on Bonhoeffer's correction of Luther's interpretation is significant:

> Bonhoeffer claims that Luther misunderstands the 'righteousness of God': 'Δικαιοσυνη θεοῦ largely, probably also in [Rom.]1:17, God's righteousness (contra Luther).' In the very verse where Luther is supposed to have made his Reformation discovery, Bonhoeffer suggests that God's righteousness should be understood not passively, as the righteousness God gives us, but as God's own righteousness.[128]

In part, Bonhoeffer's correction of Luther's understanding of God's righteousness is a critique of Luther's soteriology in which God's active righteousness is reduced by the emphasis on God's passive righteousness. Bonhoeffer's Lutheran anthropology as *simul iustus et peccator* as well as his equal emphasis on justification and sanctification or the passive and active righteousness of God is strongly and clearly reflected in the doctrine of *Stellvertretung*. The exclusion of guilt or sinlessness in *Stellvertretung*, for Bonhoeffer, is not only unrealistic but also outside of Christian possibility in an extreme situation. He once again reaffirms Luther's notion of the Christian person as *simul iustus et peccator* when acting as an agent of *Stellvertretung*.

Bonhoeffer's concept of responsible action is firmly founded in his continued notion of "for the sake of the neighbor." He explains the theological tension between an action that takes on guilt and an other-oriented action: "In responsibility both *obedience* and *freedom* become real [realisieren sich]. Responsibility has this inner tension. Any attempt to make one independent of the other would be the end of responsibility. Responsible action is bound and yet creative."[129] In Luther's two kingdoms theory, the responsible action does not contain great tension between "obedience to the state" and "free action for the sake of the other" because the state exercises its ordinary function of protecting its people. However, when the state as a communal person exercises sinful egocentricity over its citizens or other people except for a certain group of people who are in power, the situation produces tension between free responsible action and obedience to the law or principles. Bonhoeffer's rationale for resolving this tension is as follows:

> But now is it not the case that the law of God as revealed in the Decalogue, and the divine mandates of marriage, work, and government, establish an inviolable boundary for any responsible action in one's vocation? Would any transgressing of this boundary not amount to insubordination against the revealed will of God? Here the recurring problem of law and freedom presents itself with ultimate urgency. It now threatens to introduce a contradiction into

the will of God itself. Certainly no responsible activity is possible that does not consider with ultimate seriousness the boundary that God established in the law. Nevertheless, precisely as responsible action it will not separate this law from its giver. ... For the sake of God and neighbor, which means for Christ's sake, one may be freed from keeping the Sabbath holy, honoring one's parents, indeed from the entire divine law.[130]

Going one step further from his discussion of the boundary of the law or principles of the state, Bonhoeffer clearly compares the law or principles such as the Decalogue with the will of God in regard to free responsible action. His paired concept of penultimate (*Vorletztes*) and ultimate (*Letztes*) is parallel to his comparison between the law or principles and the will of God.[131] When the law or principles are not for the sake of the other or the love of neighbors—in other words, when the penultimate no longer functions as the standard of *Stellvertretung*—the obedience of the saints needs to be redirected to the ultimate standard rather than to the penultimate principles that ignore the needs of the other.[132] Bonhoeffer explains this dynamic as follows: "The justifying word of God is also, however, the *temporally* ultimate word. Something penultimate always precedes it, some action, suffering, movement, intention, defeat, recovery, pleading, hoping—in short, quite literally a span of time at whose end it stands."[133] Based on Bonhoeffer's criteria of the freed conscience and the needs of the other, the freedom of the saints possibly risks the guilt of taking responsible action in rare situations. As Bonhoeffer argues in "After Ten Years," in extraordinary circumstances, the law or principles do not function properly because they are bound to a superficial level of meaning of the law without association with the true will of their giver, which only can be known through the eyes of a freed conscience.[134] In this state, even a law such as the Decalogue is misused or manipulated by people for the sake of their own *cor curvum in se*, ignoring the true meaning of the law and detaching the superficial formality from its true content.[135] As Nancy J. Duff argues, "Once you have rules... [d]oing the right thing no longer requires being in right relationship to Christ, it only requires having the right rules."[136]

More importantly, beyond the two criteria of *Stellvertretung*, "the freed conscience" and "the sake of the neighbor," Bonhoeffer finds the final authority of his doctrine of the taking on of guilt due to a free action in the action of Christ. He argues that the ultimate origin of the voluntaristic action that takes on guilt is in Christ's voluntaristic violation of the law of the Sabbath. He writes:

> The origin and goal of my conscience is not a law but the living God and the living human being as I encounter them in Jesus Christ. *For the sake of God and human beings Jesus Christ became a breaker of the law: he broke the law of the Sabbath in order to sanctify it*, out of love for God and human beings; he left his parents in order to be in his Father's house, and thus to purify the obedience owned to one's parents; he ate with sinners and outcasts, and, out of love for humanity, he ended up being forsaken by God in his final hour. As the one who

loved without sin, he became guilty, seeking to stand within the community of human guilt. ... The freed conscience bound aligns itself with the responsibility, which has been established in Christ, to bear guilt for the sake of the neighbor.[137]

It is significant that Bonhoeffer clearly attributes the origin of the guilt arising from taking free action to Jesus Christ's action for the sake of people who were in an extraordinary, urgent situation. In Bonhoeffer's logic, because Christ who is the giver of the law has the authority to be freed from the law to recover the original intention of the law, the church community as the body of Christ as well as the individual saint who has the conscience of Jesus Christ can exercise the guilt-including free responsible action for the sake of neighbors, but only in extreme circumstances. He adds, however, that "in contrast to the essential sinlessness of Jesus Christ, human action is never sinless but always contaminated by original sin."[138] Despite the limitation of human free action due to the human being's innate sinful nature, the responsible action "does participate indirectly in the action of Jesus Christ."[139] He further explains that "responsible action is thus characterized by something like a relative sinlessness, which is demonstrated precisely by the responsible taking on of another's guilt."[140] It is noteworthy that his concept of taking on guilt presupposes that the free but guilt-producing responsible action can be performed by anyone, just like Christ acted on the Sabbath, when the life of the other or the community as a whole is in danger without this free action. As Christ stated, Bonhoeffer agrees that the law is not given as a punishment or judgment but as a gift and protection for the well-being of humanity.[141] He continuously claims this point in *Discipleship*, stating that costly grace "is costly because it was costly to God, because it cost God the life of God's Son."[142] As Christ is the Lord of the Sabbath, the church community is the center of the world and can act in its freedom for its neighbor. Furthermore, he argues that such an act is fully associated with the commandment to love your God and your neighbor, which is superior to the bounded principle or law.

Augustine's doctrine of church and state frequently cites Rom. 13:1–7 to uphold the legitimacy of civil rulers.[143] Furthermore, in some circumstances Augustine does not oppose the use of violence as a means of restoring peace, suggesting New Testament passages as well as Old Testament passages as the foundation of the theory.[144] The distinction between Augustine's use of violence and Bonhoeffer's notion of the voluntaristic taking on of guilt lies in the subject of the action. Augustine's theory clearly presupposes the ruler as the primary subject who takes on the responsibility of a just war as he defends the authority of civil rulers. María Teresa Dávila properly points out:

> In Augustinian tradition it is dependent on privileging a narrative of power and order that Augustine himself inherits from neo-Platonism and the *Pax Romana* which framed his known universe. This narrative of power and order stands in contrast to the particular narrative of everyday life and vulnerability among those directly affected by conflict and violence, wherever they are situated.[145]

Clearly, the Augustinian theory does not deeply address circumstances like Bonhoeffer's in which the civil ruler is not the subject of the responsible action for the sake of the citizens but the object of the *Stellvertretung*. More importantly, even though Augustine considers Christ the founder and ruler of the city of God, he perceives that neither the earthly city nor the experiential church community can be equated to the city of God.[146] For Augustine, the experiential church in the world is a part of the universal church in which the saints participate in a pilgrimage toward the city of God.[147] Accordingly, Augustine's doctrine of responsible action against sin as well as ethical evil is approached from the presupposition that there are irreconcilable qualitative differences between Christ and the church community or the saints and between the church and the state. Augustine does not relate Christ's action to the Christian person's vicarious representative action.

In a similar vein, Luther follows the Augustinian doctrine of church and state, and this is evident in his doctrine of the two kingdoms. However, Luther radically interprets the Augustinian doctrine of the church in a way that emphasizes the experiential church community's avoidance of philosophical and abstract discussions. Luther's concept of the church reflects his Reformation situation in which the dynamics of church and state were intertwined with the political and ecclesiastical situation of his time. The two kingdoms theory of Luther under the authority of Rom. 13:1–7 was mutually beneficial for the church and the state in his context in sixteenth-century Germany. Similar to Augustine's just war theory or the relationality between church and state, Luther's theory did not need to consider an extraordinary situation such as Bonhoeffer's time in which the civil authority was the object of the responsible and guilt-risking action.

In respect to Bonhoeffer's doctrine of a guilt-inducing action, neither Augustine's doctrine of just war nor Luther's two kingdoms theory directly fits the situation of Bonhoeffer nor his conviction concerning God's humanization. This is because he views the foundation of both theories as based on the penultimate or the law rather than the ultimate in Christ's person and life. Bonhoeffer radicalizes Luther's Christocentrism along with his contemporary Lutherans' ethical sensitivity to resolve the dilemma in which the traditional doctrines no longer supply the theological framework for Christian action in the world. Bonhoeffer's theological basis for his concept of guilt resulting from responsible action is derived from Christ's person and life in regard to Christ's breaking the law to save people's lives. The doctrine of the "divine mandate" in respect to marriage, work, and church that he reforms from the order of creation to the order of preservation now serves as the divine authority, which is over the authority of the state. Bonhoeffer argues that the legitimate role of the government is "maintaining good and promoting good."[148] If the government does not do this, the church can ask the state whether its actions are legitimate. In an extraordinary situation, he argues, the church also can go beyond the action of binding "the wounds of victims beneath the wheel … [and] seize the wheel itself."[149] Bonhoeffer's justification of the use of violence against the government, however, is not fully elaborated after his essay "History and Good [2]," mainly due to his early death.

Despite the unfinished nature of his work on the doctrine, Bonhoeffer suggests certain criteria that distinguish a responsible action that results in taking on guilt and engaging in an illegitimate action against the community. He suggests two criteria: "the freed conscience" and "the sake of the neighbor."[150] On the one hand, as seen in Bonhoeffer's "Inaugural Lecture" in 1930, he argues that the conscience per se is not the place where "God encounters humanity and, therefore, the place from which to answer the anthropological question," which is against Holl's psychological approach to justification.[151] Precisely speaking, however, despite Bonhoeffer's criticism of the role of conscience in the justification of sinners who are in Adam, he does not totally abandon the role of conscience but more actively revives the role of the conscience of a justified person in relation to free responsibility. He argues that the conscience of the justified person is renewed and takes on a significant role in a person's free responsible action. It is clear that the conscience appropriately functions in the justified person's way of sanctification rather than the sinner's way of justification. In this way, for Bonhoeffer, the conscience of a justified person is a liberated conscience but the conscience of an unjustified person is bound by the limits of human psychology or only leads to "self-righteous action."[152]

Bonhoeffer's notion of the voluntaristic taking on of guilt in responsible free action is seemingly far from his early and middle period of opposition to violence.[153] Although it is controversial whether his doctrine of peace is maintained or not or, more fundamentally, whether his doctrine of peace itself can be identified as pacifism or not, it is clear that his later doctrine of *Stellvertretung* includes guilt, which was not explicit in his early thought.[154] Furthermore, as his 1942 "History and Good [2]" articulates, the free responsible action and the action bound by law are both culpable in an extraordinary situation. Bonhoeffer says: "For in either case a person becomes culpable and so can live only from God's grace and forgiveness. Each of these people—whether bound by law or acting in free responsibility—must hear and accept the accusation of the other. Neither can become the judge of the other. Judgment remains with God."[155]

His earlier logic of bearing the sin of the other in *Sanctorum Communio* reappears in a slightly different form in the concept of "taking on the guilt of the other." Bonhoeffer treats the free responsible action in extraordinary circumstances as no different from the action bound by law in ordinary circumstances in terms of its ethical culpability. Neither action nor decision can be judged by other people but will instead be judged by the ultimate authority, God. Despite his advocacy of the free responsible action of a person in extraordinary circumstances, Bonhoeffer notes that the decision of a person requires "God's grace and forgiveness" because of its ethical culpability when it transgresses the law. The *Stellvertretung* is not a denial of law and principles; in an extreme situation, however, when the law and principles do not serve the will of God, they need to be redirected to fit the ultimate authority.[156] The responsible action cannot go with penultimate forms such as the misinterpreted law and principles because the law and principles are not related to the ultimate internally; they are only related superficially. In this mismatched condition between ultimate and penultimate, the free responsible action risks ethical culpability for the other's sake.

In summary, similar to Bonhoeffer's early interpretation of the Augustinian doctrine of alien culpability, in his later doctrine of *Stellvertretung* he once again suggests the voluntaristic taking on of another's guilt for the sake of the other. His other-oriented theology is continued in his later doctrine of *Stellvertretung*. At first glance, however, Bonhoeffer's logic contains a radical turn from the Lutheran doctrine of the two kingdoms that strongly advocates the limit (*Grenze*) between church and state. However, Bonhoeffer's later doctrine of *Stellvertretung* presupposes the extraordinary circumstance when the state or the law is no longer functioning properly. In this situation, the law or the principles of the state are manipulated to serve a certain evil group of people or a dictator and are used to dehumanize the people of the state. No longer is the limit (*Grenze*) a gift or blessing of God that protects the lives of people. Rather, it becomes the means of restricting people within its boundaries, depriving people of the freedom and responsibility that God bestowed on God's people. Bonhoeffer finds the true *Grenze* that guards human life and necessities in God's humanization in Christ. He argues that guilt-risking free action is the only responsible answer in such a situation. He further asserts that the origin of this responsible action is the responsible action of Jesus Christ, who broke the Sabbath to save the life of a person. His radical equation of Christ with the church community becomes the central logic that supplies the foundation for the free action that takes on guilt. In other words, the basis of the responsible action is his Lutheran conviction of Christ's presence in the church community. His argument, however, still requires further theological discussion to determine the criteria for exceptions to avoid misuse or overuse of the doctrine. This is mainly because Bonhoeffer's work on this doctrine is fragmentary and unfinished.

Conclusion

Engagement with the current sociopolitical situation is one of the most existential ways to review any doctrine relating to anthropology. In the case of hamartiology, confronting sin and ethical evil in everyday life sometimes gives insight into how to reinterpret a traditional doctrine that has become fossilized in its theories or principles. In this way, the extraordinary circumstances of Nazi Germany's sociopolitics supplied Bonhoeffer with the chance to reconsider the neglected side of traditional hamartiology. Although Augustine in his later theology pointed out the passive aspect of sin expressed by "ignorance" and "difficulties" in addition to his continuous emphasis on the active side of sin such as "pride," his doctrine of sin has been reinterpreted by many thinkers throughout the history of the church chiefly by focusing on the active side of sin. Bonhoeffer follows the Augustinian model in most of his works, but in his later period he newly recognizes the neglected passive side of sin that equally and sometimes more harshly damages the reconciliation of the community of the saints as well as the state.

Bonhoeffer's development away from the traditional understanding of sin and ethical evil is primarily in his reading and appropriation of New Testament teachings, especially those of the life and person of Christ rather than Paul's teachings from which Augustine as well as Luther mainly gleaned their resources for Christian ethics. Bonhoeffer's Christocentrism or ecclesiocentrism in his later period was intensified by his direct relation of God's humanization to the Christian person. This Christocentrism also offers a foundation for his transformative reinterpretation of Christian ethics in regard to the doctrine of church and state. Whereas the Augustinian as well as the Lutheran theories of church and state predominantly relied on Pauline passages such as Rom. 13:1–7, Bonhoeffer explicitly goes to the work and life of Jesus Christ in the Gospels in which Christ is described as breaking and reinterpreting the law in order to save and liberate the lives of human beings who are imprisoned by the ossified law. Bonhoeffer argues that *Stellvertretung* is an action that follows the example of Christ's action toward the world. Furthermore, his notion of the voluntaristic taking on of the guilt of the other clearly reflects a transformative restatement of his earlier interpretation of the Augustinian doctrines of the transmission of alien culpability as well as of original sin. The origin of Bonhoeffer's transformative reformulation of the Augustinian tradition in his later Christian ethics is grounded in his new recognition of God's humanization in Christ that, he argues, defines the true meaning and direction of the Christian life.

Despite the fragmentary nature of Bonhoeffer's later writings, Bonhoeffer's hamartiology offers some significant theological implications. First, his later doctrine shows a certain degree of synthesis of his entire theology, especially in his comprehensive approach to the sinful nature of humans. Bonhoeffer's concept of the double structure of the sinful human self has potential common ground with other groups of thinkers such as feminists, liberation theologians, and ecumenical theologians. This is because he cast light on the neglected side of the human sinful nature in its passivity, which the Western Christian tradition had not focused on but should have been concerned with. Second, despite Bonhoeffer's claim that he followed the Augustinian doctrine of Christian freedom through Luther's theology in its basic structure, his doctrine of freedom reflects his own Lutheran approach in which he not only expands the scope of the Augustinian tradition but also reformulates the content of Christian ethics. Bonhoeffer's discussion of Christian freedom reflects his post-Christendom context in which the freedom of God needed to be expressed in the free responsible action of Christians rather than in the inner life of the Christian person. Third, despite Bonhoeffer's existential awareness of the sinful nature of the postlapsarian Christian person in relation to Christian communal ethics, his hamartiology lacks some essential parts of the Christian doctrine of sin. Bonhoeffer's social and political context may have driven him to focus more on the sociopolitical dimension of sin and evil. However, the question remains as to whether Christian hamartiology can be discussed without also addressing sin and evil on the individual level of morality and chastity, which is one of the major themes of the Bible.

Chapter 6

CONCLUSION: BONHOEFFER'S HAMARTIOLOGICAL LEGACY

Introduction

Bonhoeffer is known as a heroic German Christian who challenged the sinful power of Nazism. Although Bonhoeffer's influence on the world is primarily due to his resistance to sinful acts by communities or individuals in power, his theological insights on the problem of sin and evil are not as well known. As my primary purpose has been to investigate Bonhoeffer's hamartiology as a whole, I have examined his reformulation and reconstruction of Augustine's doctrine of original sin that chiefly draws on Lutheran theological resources. From a bird's-eye perspective, Bonhoeffer's hamartiology contains a significant theological legacy that can be applied inside and outside of Christianity for the safety and well-being of people in communities in response to sinful and evil power. Significantly, Bonhoeffer has been influential because his treatment of sin and evil is not isolated within the theoretical level but is closely related to contemporary social issues in the world. In this context, this concluding chapter describes Bonhoeffer's hamartiological legacy and suggests a way to utilize his insights to address contemporary concerns. The chapter also clarifies the risks embedded in his hamartiology and ethics to avoid misunderstanding or misapplying his theology. Although Bonhoeffer was a modern theologian whose theology was intertwined with his time and circumstances, his doctrine of sin and ethics provides necessary theological resources for constructing the Christian doctrine of sin and adjacent theological concerns. I discuss and evaluate three major theological contributions and some unsatisfactory aspects of Bonhoeffer's hamartiology as the conclusion of this book.

First, while Western Christian hamartiology has been mainly focused on the individual's sin and its solution, Bonhoeffer was one of the first modern theologians who seriously focused on human beings' communal or collective sinful acts and structures. As I have noted, for over a thousand years Western hamartiology, especially Augustinian hamartiology, has chiefly delved into the problem of an individual's sin and its resolution. The primary contribution of Bonhoeffer's hamartiology is his treatment of communal sin as a central theme in his discussion. He shifts the hamartiological concern from the individual level to the communal level of sin, which is crucial but has been ignored for a long time.

The second hamartiological contribution of Bonhoeffer is his concern for the passive dimension of sin, which the Augustinian tradition did not treat seriously. Bonhoeffer examines the significance of the binary—passive and active—nature of sin. His treatment of communal sin led him to identify the passive characteristic of sin as submission to evil or self-deception, an aspect of sin that has been overshadowed by the emphasis on the active dimension of sin in the Augustinian doctrine of original sin. Bonhoeffer's notion is more clearly expressed in his later work, connected with his experience under German National Socialism. His attention to the twofold aspect of sin led him to a transition in his perspective from the traditional angle to the "viewpoint from below."[1] Despite the unfinished and unbalanced nature of his description of the twofold nature of sin, it became the theological repository or catalyst for minority or non-Western theologies.

Bonhoeffer's third contribution is his tight binding of the doctrine of sin to Christian responsibility. One of the insufficiencies of Augustinian hamartiology, for Bonhoeffer, is the lack of a holistic connection between theological loci such as *the doctrines of sin, the church, and the new humanity.*[2] The doctrine of original sin, for Bonhoeffer as well as for many other theologians in his own time and in our contemporary era, is treated as a relic of the theological past.[3] One of the main reasons is its fatalistic tendency and the danger of exoneration of Christian responsibility toward others, neglecting the newly created Christian's responsibility or freedom in Christ. To correct this theological imbalance, Bonhoeffer binds the *church community's Stellvertretung* (vicarious representative action) with the *Stellvertretung* of Christ.

As examined in previous chapters, hamartiology is a central theological area for Bonhoeffer, and his life lived in opposition to the power of evil and sin reflects this. His approach contains crucial theological insights and resources connected to contemporary concerns. This chapter also deals with the theological insufficiencies of his hamartiology and ethics to prevent its theological and anthropological misunderstanding or misapplication and to build up a more balanced hamartiology and anthropology. Although his doctrine of sin and evil advances from the traditional doctrines in some areas, there is a continuous theological imbalance between his theological rationale and some of his arguments. Both the hamartiological contributions and the theological critiques raised by commentators on Bonhoeffer can be utilized well beyond his time and place to develop contemporary issues such as gender, race, and class that are embedded in social and cultural structures in societies around the world. Accordingly, this chapter aims not only to credit Bonhoeffer for his hamartiological insights but also to suggest a more balanced theological perspective through an assessment of Bonhoeffer's doctrine of sin and related ethics.

This chapter starts with Bonhoeffer's communal or collective notion of sin and evil and evaluates the theological significance of the communal approach and how it relates to contemporary social issues. Second, the chapter deals with the significance of the twofold structure of sin and the theological controversy in light of feminist critiques. Third, the chapter investigates Bonhoeffer's notion of sin and Christian responsibility, engaging with the notion of *Stellvertretung*. Finally, the chapter offers some implications of these findings.

Communal Sin

The primary contribution of Bonhoeffer's doctrine of sin is his treatment of communal sin as a major theme in his hamartiology. As humanity experienced First and Second World Wars and the continuing threat of sinful communal acts worldwide, many have realized the danger of communal sin and its devastating results, which Christian theology had not seriously treated. Bonhoeffer's hamartiological concerns are more focused on communal and social sin and evil and its effects than on individual sin. Many in the world have experienced or heard about sinful acts happening in every corner of the world. However, it is also true that evil powers are evasive because they are usually hidden in social and economic structures. Social and communal evil comes to us in the forms of violence, poverty, hatred of the other, and, more fundamentally, in the forms of social, cultural, and economic systems. Whereas Western hamartiology is mainly concerned with the individual level of sin and its solution, Bonhoeffer focuses on the sin of the community and its nature using his versatile notion of the person. Even though Augustine does deal with communal sin in a basic way, as in *Confessions*, his primary concern with the doctrine of original sin is on the individual's sin and how individuals can find a way to be healed from humanity's sinful condition throughout their life.[4] As Bonhoeffer indicates in *Sanctorum Communio*, his primary focus is the socio-ecclesial level of sin in which individuals participate. His analysis of communal sin is primarily about the relationality between the collective sin of the church community and the sins of the saints and about the sins of those in power and the participants in that evil. He investigates communal sin and evil throughout his corpus. This book has examined Bonhoeffer's focus on communal sin and its nature in his major works, *Sanctorum Communio*, *Creation and Fall*, *Ethics*, and *Letters and Papers from Prison*. As noted, Bonhoeffer's hamartiological focus moves from the concern of the church community, the primal state of human beings, and then to society.

It is noteworthy that Bonhoeffer's insights on communal sin have guided the development of public theology in the non-Western world. Even though Bonhoeffer's notion of communal sin was shaped by the German sociopolitical circumstances of his time, similar phenomena have continued to occur globally. Throughout Christian history, the problem of communal sin and participation in evil power is not clearly articulated because it is usually intertwined with sociocultural structures and blurred by the emphasis on the individual level of sin. Western hamartiology was caught within the boundaries of the Augustinian theme of sin for a long time, searching for the root of sin and its effect within the limits of the individual level of sin until confronting the destructive power of communal sin as experienced during the two world wars and the continuing threats of violence and evil structural power that followed in many societies in the world. As a result, the task of hamartiology is both a retrospective analysis of the origin of humanity's sinful deeds and a prophetic warning of future sinful deeds of the human race, especially by communities in power and their participants. In Bonhoeffer's case, we may learn from his poignant experiences under Hitler's

Nazi Party as well as his prophetic vision in his later theology. Humanity's sinful experience under evil power is a particular or local phenomenon, but it is also global and chronic. We may identify the danger and effects of communal sin in many societies globally, but communal sin is sometimes hard to notice because it appears in different or disguised forms in various contexts.

The popularity of Bonhoeffer's work in many places where people have experienced the evil power of communal sin, such as Latin America, South Africa, and Asia, is not surprising. Those living under sinful communal power can identify similar bitter experiences of communal or structural sin in Bonhoeffer's work and life. In this vein, Oscar Romero's definition of social and structural sin is noteworthy. He defines structural sin as "the crystallization of individual egoisms in permanent structures which maintain this sin and exert its power over the great majorities."[5] Although it is controversial whether Latin American liberation theologians have overinterpreted Bonhoeffer's later thought contained in his prison writings, it is proper to say that Bonhoeffer's notion of communal sin was the catalyst for the development of liberation theology.[6] As seen in the theology of de Gruchy, Bonhoeffer's notion of communal sin is also closely related to the development of South African theology, especially regarding apartheid.[7] Bonhoeffer's context for the notion of communal sin contained in his work does not directly match the concerns of the sinful socioeconomic structures in Latin America, the socio-racial issue in South Africa, or the contexts of Asian theologies such as *minjung* theology in Korea. However, one common theological significance of the above theologies is their relation to the notion of communal sin and the evil power of societies, especially when it is connected to Bonhoeffer's later "viewpoint from below."[8]

Furthermore, Bonhoeffer's treatment of communal sin as anterior or essential sin is a radical hamartiological claim in the Augustinian tradition in which the sin of Adam as an individual is considered the first and foremost sin. Significantly, Bonhoeffer treated the first sin as the first community's act rather than as an individual act in *Creation and Fall*. This is related to Bonhoeffer's recovery of the biblical notion of communal sin as the Bible treats the sin of Israel as a collective person's sin, which has not been a focus in the Western tradition for a long time.[9] Western hamartiology has long been immersed in the discussion of the individual level of sin and reconciliation, neglecting social or communal sin and its destructive effect on the human race as well as social reconciliation.

It is noteworthy that Latin American liberation theology approaches structural or communal sin from "the Johannine notion of the sin of the world."[10] José Ignacio González Faus explains the sin of the world in John's gospel as follows: "'the world' means a socio-religious order hostile to God or an oppressive system based on money or power for the few."[11] Faus sees Latin American theology as recovering the biblical notion of communal or structural sin. From a similar but different angle, Asian liberation theologians focus on the oppressed or the *ochlos* (crowd) as a communal person related to the life of Jesus, who was surrounded by the *ochlos* and was compassionate toward them.[12] They view the oppressed as the victims of structural sin.[13] The theological point is that Bonhoeffer and liberation theologians recognize the problem of communal or structural sin, which had never been clearly articulated in the Christian doctrine of sin. In short, Bonhoeffer's recovery of communal sin suggests an important theological turning point for Western hamartiology by confirming that God treats humanity's sins by considering not only the individual but also the communal level of sin. Accordingly, the first major hamartiological contribution of Bonhoeffer was his redirection or recovery of the hamartiological priority from individual to communal, which had been neglected in Western theology.

The Twofold Structure of Sin: Pride and Submission

The other important hamartiological contribution of Bonhoeffer is his concern for the passive dimension of sin, which the Augustinian tradition did not address in any depth. Traditional Western hamartiology maintains that the active dimension of sin represented by pride is the essential and chief sin and thus mainly concentrates on this dimension. Pride (hubris) is indeed one of the sinful manifestations of human beings, but this notion has been treated as the fundamental and essential sin of the human race and is understood as qualitatively different from other sins, mainly based on Augustine. On a larger scale, pride has been considered a representative notion of sin that integrates similar theological concepts articulated by terms such as "egocentricity," "self-love," *sicut Deus* (like God), and "power." A critical aspect of these concepts is that they are theological expressions used by prominent theologians of the West, such as Augustine, Luther, Barth, and Bonhoeffer, under the overarching notion of pride. In *Confessions*, Augustine confesses that his "swollen pride" is the starting point of his turning away from God and turning to himself.[14] It is undeniable that Platonism strongly influenced Augustine's identification of pride as the essential sin, in addition to certain biblical passages.[15] Augustine's description of pride in *Confessions* is closely intertwined with his notion of "swollen pride" based on Platonic thinking.[16] Pride might be the primary sin for Augustine, who is prideful of his intelligence. Although Augustine mentions the other side of the sinful aspect of the self throughout his corpus, Augustine's emphasis on the active dimension of sin, as well as that of his followers, results in negligence of the passive dimension of sin.

As discussed in Chapter 5, Bonhoeffer's experience under Nazism and his theological analysis led him to recognize the passive side of sin and its destructive effect on the church community as well as the world. As Bonhoeffer explicates in *Letters and Papers from Prison*, and especially in "After Ten Years," the passive sin of *sanctorum communio* (the community of saints), such as submission to evil power or self-deception, is as harmful as active sins such as pride, power, and egocentricity, with which Western hamartiology has been preoccupied.[17] He strongly criticizes the passive sinful state of the German church community, saying, "Only at the cost of self-deception can they keep their private blamelessness clean from the stains of responsible action in the world."[18] Bonhoeffer discloses the seriousness of sin's passivity and its result, which had been neglected in the history of hamartiology.

He perceives that the passive sin of saints is closely related to the identity of the Christian person both as an individual and as the church community, which is the *imago Dei* (image of God) and the body of Christ.

Bonhoeffer views the passive side of sin is equally sinful to the active because it is not only the negation of Christian identity as the image of God but also the rejection of Christian freedom or responsibility toward others. In this vein, Daniel L. Migliore properly explains the nature of the passive side of sin: "[The passive] form of sin is no less a turning from God who calls us to freedom, maturity, and responsibility in community."[19] Bonhoeffer examines the significance of the dual—active and passive—nature of sin. The state of pride or power is not static in a person but is flexible in different circumstances. Once they are in an active sinful state, a person may also experience the passive sinful state, and vice versa. Furthermore, it is more accurate to say that most people simultaneously experience both or multiple dimensions of the sinful state throughout their life. People usually demonstrate the dominant side of a sinful state; the other dimension is hidden underneath the dominant sinful manifestation. Bonhoeffer highlights this deficiency in Western hamartiology, in which active aspects of sin such as pride, power, or egocentricity have been at the center of the discussion to the neglect of the passive aspect of sin.

Seen from the history of hamartiology in the West, Bonhoeffer's emphasis on the twofold—active and passive—structure of sin potentially suggests a holistic anthropological structure. One of the problems with the Augustinian hamartiological tradition is its one-sided focus on the active dimension of sin. However, sin is not only active but also passive and sometimes multidimensional. Migliore summarizes this by noting that "sin ... is not only titanic, Luciferian rebellion but also the timid, obsequious refusal to dare to be fully human."[20] The Western hamartiological tradition did not seriously focus on the passive aspect of sin and its destructive effect until the modern era. In his early work, Bonhoeffer's hamartiology focused on active manifestations of sin such as pride, egocentricity, and power. However, in his later work, his focus shifted to the passive dimension of sin and its devastating effects.[21] As discussed in Chapter 5, Bonhoeffer observes that many German Christians under the Nazi reign were involved in the passive side of sin. The theological point here is that this concern with the passive side of sin had not been treated seriously, neither in theological anthropology nor in hamartiology, prior to Bonhoeffer. This new approach is an important hamartiological development from the Augustinian tradition. However, Bonhoeffer's twofold structure of sin contains both problems and potential.

Although Bonhoeffer recognizes the twofold structure of sin, the structure is still vulnerable and imbalanced in some important aspects. The fundamental problem is that the twofold structure is based on androcentrism or an I-centered perspective. Bonhoeffer identifies the twofold structure of sin mainly from the viewpoint of Western males or elites rather than from the perspective of all of humanity. There is a significant imbalance between his theological framework of the "I and the other" relationship, which presupposes interchangeability as the basis of his anthropology, and his treatment of male and female relationships in real-life applications.[22] As feminist scholars such as Rachel Muers, Jennifer M. McBride, Hyun Kyung Chung, Karen V. Guth, and Lisa Dahill point out, Bonhoeffer supports the patriarchal system, as expressed in his wedding sermon and on other occasions.[23] In this vein, Bonhoeffer's hamartiology should be read and applied in light of the criticisms raised by feminist theologians to build up a more balanced Christian anthropology and ethics. There are two potential reasons for Bonhoeffer's inconsistency on the theme of the male and female relationship, especially the wife and husband relationship. One is that Bonhoeffer may not recognize that the incongruity between his communal or anthropological structure of the "I and the other" relationship and his practice in real life is immersed in the patriarchal system of his time; the other is, as Guth argues, that he might understand the male and female relationships as a part of mandate, an exception to his communal structure.[24] Both cases reveal that Bonhoeffer's anthropology as well as the twofold nature of sin has an unbalanced or unfinished nature and our contemporary theology needs to properly assess this aspect to avoid theological misunderstanding and misapplication by readers of Bonhoeffer in the world.

In this regard, one crucial theological concern is that Bonhoeffer's partial treatment of the "I and the other" relationship is continued throughout his corpus. As I discussed in Chapter 4, the unbalanced nature of his anthropological structure appears in his exegetical treatment of Adam and Eve in *Creation and Fall*. Bonhoeffer continuously treats Adam as the subject and Eve as the assistant in the story. Bonhoeffer generalizes Adam and Eve as the I and the other to universalize the relationality of the human being concerning hamartiological issues embedded in the doctrine of original sin. The problem is that Bonhoeffer always uses Adam, which implies a male characteristic, for the I, and thus Eve implies a female characteristic for the other. This has the possibility of alienating women in his theological discussions in which the woman is always identified as the object of the I or as the limit rather than as the subject or the center. Despite Bonhoeffer's later theological perspective of the "viewpoint from below" being crucial to theological development concerning the themes of class and race, as seen in the theologies of Latin America and Asia and South Africa, his hierarchical notion of gender remains an exception to his "viewpoint from below." The influence of Bonhoeffer's theology on nontraditional or non-Western theologies might be mainly due to his endeavor to see the reality from the perspective of people who suffer from communal sin embedded in the social and cultural structures in many societies. Bonhoeffer observes that the doctrine of the order of creation supported the Nazis' racism, but Bonhoeffer's notion of the male and female relationship also contains the risk of consolidating a hierarchical notion of human relationship, especially between male and female and between wife and husband.[25]

Although Bonhoeffer focuses on the passive dimension of sin in his later career, it is undeniable that his twofold understanding of sin is addressed from the viewpoint of I, mainly from that of elite White males.[26] The problem of this I-centered perspective is also related to the theme of race and class because the I-centered perspective potentially excludes the perspectives of those outside of the boundary of the I. This means that the major non-Western theologies, such as

Latin American liberation theology, South African theology, and Asian theology, may repeat Bonhoeffer's perspectival error in which the male is in the position of the I and the female is in the position of the other. Ironically, however, the theoretical or prototypal level of the twofold structure of sin supplies a tool for reassessing Augustinian anthropology and hamartiology as well as Bonhoeffer's theology itself, once his theological framework is properly rectified.

Sin and Responsibility: Stellvertretung

The third hamartiological contribution of Bonhoeffer is his close engagement of the problem of sin with Christian responsibility. As he diagnoses in *Sanctorum Communio*, Augustine's doctrine of original sin mainly focuses on the origin and nature of the sin of an individual, neglecting not only the sin of the church community but also its ethical action for others. Bonhoeffer takes the starting point of the doctrine of sin as the reality of the church community in which Christ reconciled the sin of the saints.[27] At this point, he connects the *Stellvertretung* (vicarious representative action) of Christ to the *Stellvertretung* of the church community as a way to bear the sins of the church community and the world. As seen in *Sanctorum Communio* and *Act and Being*, for Bonhoeffer the *Stellvertretung* primarily means the reciprocal vicarious actions of church members for the sins of others.[28] As articulated in the expression "Christ existing as community," Bonhoeffer's *Stellvertretung* is grounded in the soteriological sense of the *Stellvertretung* of Christ as well as the ecclesial notion of Christ's presence in the church community. Christine Schliesser summarizes this point by writing that, for Bonhoeffer, "[T]he consequence of Christ's *Stellvertretung* for us is our *Stellvertretung* for others."[29] The theological and existential issue of *Stellvertretung* is how to reconcile the inequilibrium between the *Stellvertretung* of Christ and that of the church community. On the one hand, Bonhoeffer's radical Christocentric ecclesiology emphasizes the church community's ethical and sacrificial actions for others. On the other hand, his approximation of the church community with Christ left the theological task of explaining the gap between Christ and the church community in regard to the notion of *Stellvertretung*. The gap between justification and sanctification, or between faith and obedience, for Bonhoeffer, should be eliminated. In this way, he understands that the suffering of Christ for the sins of all humanity is the basis of the saints' vicarious representative actions toward the world. The late focus of *Stellvertretung* is mainly about the relationship between the church community and the sins of the world under the Nazi government.

As observed in the United States and other places in the world, recently many people have used Bonhoeffer's anti-Nazi expression of "taking the wheel of the madman"[30] to claim their political and social convictions or benefits.[31] The controversy embedded in *Stellvertretung* is its inclusion of guilt.[32] Admittedly, the guilt-taking action of Bonhoeffer was a Christian response to the dead-end political situation in Germany; however, the notion risks misuse or misapplication in different social or political circumstances. Accordingly, Bonhoeffer's *Stellvertretung* is a valuable Christian legacy for reconsidering not only the genuine meaning and role of the church community in this world but also the relationship between faith and obedience. Furthermore, he created a theological task for the *sanctorum communio*, which is to discern its subject and limit to avoid confusion or the faulty application of this notion.[33] As in the case of Bonhoeffer's participation in the plot to assassinate Hitler, in extreme circumstances, the responsible action entails taking on guilt by violating the unjust law of an evil government and sometimes the law of God itself. Although Luther and other Magisterial Reformers did not clearly mention the possibility of civil resistance,[34] Bonhoeffer is convinced that the ultimate will of God, to love your God and your neighbors, surpasses the law of the evil authority and sometimes the literal meaning of the law in Scripture, which he addresses in *Ethics* concerning Jesus' breach of the Sabbath.[35] The Lutheran Bonhoeffer is radically reconstructing the mature Luther's emphasis on justification and his negligence of the role of sanctification by identifying Luther's early life during the Reformation as an example of *Stellvertretung*.[36]

Bonhoeffer recognizes the theological imbalance between Luther's justification and sanctification in which the role of sanctification is greatly decreased. His radical equation of Christ's *Stellvertretung* with the church community's *Stellvertretung* is related to the question of the identity and vocation of the church community. For Bonhoeffer, the *sanctorum communio* is the main subject of *Stellvertretung*; however, only in an extraordinary circumstance, such as the Nazi rule, may an individual saint bear the sin of the church community by exercising *Stellvertretung* as a prophet and sinner. Bonhoeffer's hamartiology and ethics are closely engaged with the voluntary concept of taking on the sins of others. Clearly, Bonhoeffer's doctrine of *Stellvertretung* is a radical transition from Augustine's and Luther's ethics. Whereas Augustine and Luther embrace the sin of others in the boundary of the *sanctorum communio*, Bonhoeffer's notion of *Stellvertretung* definitely goes beyond the traditions of Augustine and Luther.[37] Furthermore, he extends the scope of the guilt-taking notion of *Stellvertretung* from the saints to people in the world. In this sense, his guilt-taking concept of *Stellvertung* is his most radical and controversial doctrine in his own time as well as in our contemporary era. His doctrine of *Stellvertretung* left to Christians the theological and existential task of defining its limit and legitimacy.

Conclusion

Bonhoeffer is a transitional theologian who paves the way to the theology of the twenty-first century. One of the aims of this book has been to establish the significance of Bonhoeffer's hamartiology in relation to Augustine's and Luther's traditions, a neglected aspect of scholarship on Bonhoeffer. I have demonstrated that Bonhoeffer's complicated hamartiological arguments are closely related to his major theological concerns. Bonhoeffer's fundamental claim in his hamartiology is summarized by the expression "bearing sin as church community."[38] This voluntary, ethical, and ecclesial conclusion of Bonhoeffer's hamartiology is surely a radical as well as transformative reinterpretation of Augustine's involuntary and biological hamartiology, namely, the doctrine of original sin. Readers may question the discrepancy between aspects of Bonhoeffer's hamartiology that appear to contradict Augustine's doctrine of original sin and the main argument made in this book. However, I claim that Bonhoeffer's hamartiology is a revision, rather than a refutation, of the Augustinian doctrine of original sin through the lens of his Lutheran tradition.

The primary reason for this conclusion is two aspects of Bonhoeffer's hamartiology. First, Bonhoeffer's hamartiology remains in line with Augustinian hamartiology because he reaffirms two important hamartiological presuppositions, the universality of sin and the solidarity of the human race. Second, despite Bonhoeffer's disassociation from Augustine's biological transmission of original sin as well as the involuntary or obligatory transmission of culpability or guilt to the posterity of the first humans, he does not discard these notions but transforms them into a voluntary, ethical, and ecclesial/communitarian approach based on Luther's (or the Lutherans') theological resources as well as Augustine's ecclesiastical foundation in Christ.[39] In this way, Bonhoeffer was able to radically develop his ethics represented by the doctrine of *vicarious representative action*, which is the central theme of his hamartiology, based on his ecclesiocentric notion of "Christ existing as church-community."[40] Accordingly, I conclude that Bonhoeffer relocates the locus of Augustinian hamartiology from the doctrine of God to the doctrine of the church.

Seen from the history of hamartiology, Bonhoeffer's reinterpretation of the classical hamartiology of the West is a modern Lutheran theologian's reply to the doubts of the world. Some aspects of traditional Christian teachings, especially in regard to the Augustinian doctrine of original sin, were considered ossified doctrines of the Christianity of the past. Furthermore, the biblical account of the creation and the fall was being treated as a story of the ancient world or as a myth that was no longer relevant to the hamartiological issues of Bonhoeffer's own time. Bonhoeffer perceived that the problem of sin and evil is an unavoidable, fundamental question for the human being. However, he recognized that simply repeating the traditional hamartiology not only was unsatisfactory for the people of his time but also could be manipulated to support evil. This is because the doctrine of original sin implies the risk of neglecting Christian responsibility, mainly due to the doctrine's fatalistic tendency. In other words, the Augustinian hamartiology does not closely relate the newly created freedom of *sanctorum communio* with the suffering in the world. Certainly, Bonhoeffer offered a way to explicate the teachings of the Scripture in regard to sin and evil, approaching it from the perspective of the church and using his modern Lutheran terminology. He paid attention to the Augustinian hamartiological tradition and continued to transform it throughout his theological career. Consequently, he developed a more holistic perspective on the sinful nature of the postlapsarian human based on his appropriation of Lutheran Augustinianism. Bonhoeffer's perspective offers contemporary hamartiology resources for correcting or reconstructing the classical Augustinian hamartiology as well as Bonhoeffer's own doctrine of sin.

6. Conclusion: Bonhoeffer's Hamartiological Legacy

Areas for Further Study and Implications

This book suggests some areas of further study along with some theological implications. First, even though Bonhoeffer did not fully develop his understanding of the dual dimension of sin with the issues of gender, class, or race, the book suggests that Bonhoeffer's analysis of this twofold nature of the postlapsarian human can be utilized as a tool for developing Christian anthropology as well as hamartiology. It argues that this twofold dimension of sin can offer some useful theological resources for Western hamartiology as well as anthropology in connection with issues of gender, race, and class as expressed by first-generation feminist and liberation thinkers, who chiefly emphasize the passive dimension of sin as the basis of their experiences. It is hoped that Bonhoeffer's holistic but underdeveloped perspective of humanity can offer a new framework by which Western hamartiology can be enriched by new insights.

Second, despite the limited scope of the book due to limits on length, the book argues that it is necessary to extend the discussion of the relationality between Bonhoeffer's ethics and Luther's early ethics. During the discussion of Bonhoeffer's later ethics in Chapter 5, it is noted that Luther's early ethics offered Bonhoeffer a solid ethical basis, mainly due to his reading of Luther as well as the influence of his Lutheran teachers, chiefly Karl Holl. Bonhoeffer expressed that his ultimate theological source other than Scripture was Luther, but this was frequently complicated by the question of which Luther (young or mature) or which of Luther's works Bonhoeffer appropriated. This dissertation views this theological question as important because Luther's mature social ethics are radically divergent from his early ethics mainly because of his experience of the German Peasants' War. Based on the knowledge of the author of this book, this aspect has never been seriously addressed by the scholarship on Bonhoeffer.

Finally, for the wider hamartiological endeavor, this book suggests a further theological discussion regarding the legitimacy or appropriateness of Bonhoeffer's radically *this-worldly* ecclesiocentric methodology that emphasizes the importance of the life and ethics of the saints in the visible church. Scholars need to ask whether this world-oriented or existential hamartiology, which was less emphasized in the Augustinian classical hamartiology, can be or should be related to classical hamartiology's emphasis on the afterlife and the spiritual formation of a saint.[41] This is because the Scripture talks not only about life after death or the heavenly life as the final destination of the saints but also about the inner life of the saints as an essential part of Christianity along with neighborly sacrificial love in this world. Although Bonhoeffer's hamartiology as well as ethics sheds invaluable insights on Christian life and action toward neighbors in this world, he does not fully emphasize the spiritual formation of the inner life solely *coram Deo*. Certainly, his relational and other-oriented ethics and spiritual formation filled the gap in the traditional Christian teachings of the West, but the question remains whether these old teachings should be reformed or discarded. If they should be reformed, the task is to determine how to integrate them into his outward-oriented hamartiology and ethics.

NOTES

Introduction

1   James C. Livingston, *Modern Christian Thought* (Upper Saddle River, NJ: Prentice Hall, 1988), 3.
2   Livingston, *Modern Christian Thought*, 3. See also Bruce L. McCormack, Introduction to *Mapping Modern Theology: A Thematic and Historical Introduction*, ed. Kelly M. Kapic and Bruce L. McCormack (Grand Rapids, MI: Baker Academics, 2012), 4. McCormack further describes the characteristics of the modern period as follows: "Basic decisions were thus made in the areas of creation, the being of God and his relation to the world, and other areas of doctrinal concern." McCormack, Introduction to *Mapping Modern Theology*, 4.
3   Two important theological concerns are involved in the claim of this book. The first is the matter of what is the foundational theological locus of Bonhoeffer's hamartiology. The second is the issue of how to define the term *Augustinianism*. First, Bonhoeffer considers the doctrine of the church as the basis of his hamartiology as he argues in *Sanctorum Communio* (*DBWE* 1:134). Bonhoeffer's dogmatic turn from the doctrine of God to the doctrine of the church is noteworthy. It is because his methodological turn contrasts not only with the opinion of Augustine but also with that of some modern thinkers as seen in the case of John Webster, who considers the doctrine of God as the foundational theological locus. Wester argues: "The temporal economy, including the social reality of the church in time, has its being not *in se* but by virtue of God who alone is *in se*. ... [I]ts account of the church is an extension of the doctrine of God." John Webster, "In the Society of God: Some Principles in Ecclesiology," in *Perspectives on Ecclesiology and Ethnography*, ed. Pete Ward (Grand Rapids, MI: Wm. B. Eerdmans, 2011), 203–4. For a detailed discussion of John Webster's approach to ecclesiology, see Tom Greggs, "Proportion and Topography in Ecclesiology: A Working Paper on the Dogmatic Location of the Doctrine of the Church," in *Theological Theology: Essays in Honour of John Webster*, ed. R. David Nelson, Daren Sarisky, and Justin Stratis (London: T&T Clark Bloomsbury, 2016), 89–106. See also Michael Mawson, *Christ Existing as Community: Bonhoeffer's Ecclesiology* (Oxford: Oxford University Press, 2018), 178–80. Second, this book argues that Bonhoeffer reformulates the Western or Augustinian hamartiology based on Lutheran appropriation of Augustinianism. In this regard, how to define the "Augustinianism" is crucial for the claim of this book. In this regard, Eric Leland Saak's discussion of Augustinianism is noteworthy. Saak contends that the concept of "Augustinianism" is an ambiguous and abstract term. He explains that "[t]here was no medieval term equivalent to our 'Augustinianism', 'Augustinianism', and its variant 'Augustinism', was, as so many '-isms', a creation of the nineteenth century." Eric Leland Saak, *Creating Augustine: Interpreting Augustine and Augustinianism in the Later Middle Ages* (Oxford: Oxford University Press, 2012), 3–4. Among diverse definitions with respect to Augustinianism, the definition of Eugène Portalié that encompasses both "the teachings of the Augustinian School and the historical development of Augustine's

thought" is comprehensive. Saak, *Creating Augustine*, 4. See also Eugène Portalié, "Augustinisme," in *Dictionnaire Théologie Catholique* (Paris: Letouzey et Ané, 1931), 1:2485–561. In this context, this book uses the term *Augustinianism* (including its adjectival form *Augustinian*) in a broader sense as "the teachings of Augustine and the historical and theological development of Augustine's thought."

4   This does not mean that Augustine does not deal with the reconciling work of God in Christ in his entire theology; rather, it means that he does not closely engage the notions of sin and evil with the doctrines of the church as well as Christ *in* his doctrine of original sin.

5   For the precise meaning of Christian personalism, see the section entitled "Christian Personalism" in Chapter 3, especially note 16.

6   *DBWE* 1:134. Bonhoeffer states, "It would be good for once if a presentation of doctrinal theology were to start not with the doctrine of God but with the doctrine of the church."

7   The Scriptures not only proclaim that all human beings are powerless before sin and evil (Isa. 53:6; Rom. 3:23–24) but also teach that Christians are new creations who are responsible for sin and evil (2 Cor. 5:17; 1 Jn. 1:5–10). See also Ian A. McFarland, *In Adam's Fall: A Meditation on the Christian Doctrine of Original Sin* (Chichester, UK: Wiley-Blackwell, 2010), 143.

8   For a detailed history of the text along with an explanation of the lack of scholarly investigation of Bonhoeffer's hamartiology, see the section titled "Contribution to Knowledge" in this introduction.

9   *DBW* 1:127, *DBWE* 1:190, *DBW* 1:100, *DBWE* 1:157. See also Augustine, *Homilies on the First Epistle of John*, 1:1–2:11.

10 Eva Harasta, "Adam in Christ? The Place of Sin in Christ-Reality," in *Christ, Church and World*, ed. Michael Mawson and Philip G. Ziegler (London: T&T Clark, 2016), 61.

11 Bonhoeffer finished the dissertation in July 1927 and edited it during his assistant pastorship in Barcelona in 1930. He cut about 20 to 25 percent of the dissertation for publication. The primary reason for this redaction was to save on the printing cost during the Depression as well as to align the content of the publication with his advisor Reinhold Seeberg's theological direction. See Clifford J. Green, "Editor's Introduction to the English Edition," in Bonhoeffer, *DBWE* 1:9–10.

12 For more detailed information on the history of text, see Green, "Editor's Introduction," in Bonhoeffer, *DBWE* 1:9–13.

13 Gottfried Class, *Der verzweifelte Zugriff auf das Leben: Dietrich Bonhoeffers Sündenverständnis in "Schöpfung und Fall"* [Desperate access to life: Dietrich Bonhoeffer's understanding of sin in *Creation and Fall*] (Neukirchen: Neukirchen-Vluyn, 1994).

14 Gunter M. Prüller-Jagenteufel, *Ethik Im Theologischen Diskurs* [Ethics in theological discourse], vol. 7, *Befreit Zur Verantwortung: Sünde Und Versöhnung in der Ethik Dietrich Bonhoeffers* [Released to responsibility: Sin and reconciliation in the ethics of Dietrich Bonhoeffer] (Münster: LIT, 2004).

15 Kirsten Busch Nielsen, *Die Gebrochene Macht Der Sünde: Der Beitrag Dietrich Bonhoeffers Zur Hamartiologie* [The broken power of sin: Dietrich Bonhoeffer's contribution to hamartiology] (Leipzig: Evangelische Verlagsanstalt, 2011).

16 See Tom Greggs, "Bearing Sin in the Church: The Ecclesial Hamartiology of Bonhoeffer," in *Christ, Church, and World*, ed. Michael Mawson and Philip G. Ziegler (London: T&T Clark, 2016), 77–100; Harasta, "Adam in Christ?" 61. Some examples

of works in English that address Bonhoeffer's doctrine of sin are as follows: Clifford J. Green, *Bonhoeffer: A Theology of Sociality*, rev. ed. (Grand Rapids, MI: Wm. B. Eerdmans, 1999); Mawson, *Christ Existing as Community*, especially ch. 5, "The Fall: The Sinful Collective Person," 101–18; and Christiane Tietz's "The Mystery of Knowledge, Sin, and Shame," in *Mysteries in the Theology of Dietrich Bonhoeffer: A Copenhagen Bonhoeffer Symposium* (Göttingen: Vandenhoeck & Ruprecht, 2007), 27–48.

17 On the relation of Bonhoeffer to Luther and Lutherans, see Michael P. DeJonge, *Bonhoeffer's Reception of Luther* (New York: Oxford University Press, 2017); Michael P. DeJonge, *Bonhoeffer's Theological Formation: Berlin, Barth and Protestant Theology* (Oxford: Oxford University Press, 2012). See also Wolf Kröte, "Dietrich Bonhoeffer and Martin Luther," in *Bonhoeffer's Intellectual Formation: Theology and Philosophy in His Thought*, ed. Peter Frick (Tübingen, Germany: Mohr Siebeck, 2008), 53–82. On the relation of Bonhoeffer to Augustine, see Barry Harvey, "Augustine and Thomas Aquinas in the Theology of Dietrich Bonhoeffer," in *Bonhoeffer's Intellectual Formation: Theology and Philosophy in His Thought*, ed. Peter Frick (Tübingen, Germany: Mohr Siebeck, 2008), 11–30.

18 *DBW* 1:127, *DBWE* 1:190. See also *DBW* 1:100, *DBWE* 1:157.

19 Details on translations are given parenthetically in each chapter.

Chapter 1

1 The problem of evil has been one of the central and recurring philosophical and theological issues from the time of the ancient philosophers to the contemporary period. The concept of the "inconsistent triad" is readdressed by David Hume (1711–76), who bases his notion on the idea of Epicurus in his treatise *Dialogues Concerning Natural Religion* (1779). Hume deals with the relationship between the attributes of God and the existence of evil in the world. He argues that "Epicurus' old questions are yet unanswered." David Hume, *Principal Writings on Religion: Including Dialogues Concerning Natural Religion and the Natural History of Religion*, ed. J. C. A. Gaskin, Oxford World's Classics (Oxford: Oxford University Press, 1998), 100.

2 In brief, three broad strategies have been employed to solve the problem of evil: God is omnipotent; God is omnibenevolent; there is evil. The first is the atheist approach, which solves the dilemma by denying the existence of God, a position that many philosophers and people outside of the church advocate. The second is a dualistic understanding of God, which is how Manichaeism understands the universe, in which two primal forces, one good God and one Evil, continuously battle. The last approach is the theist solution, which upholds a monotheistic cosmology in which the compatibility of the one supreme being and evil is possible by defining evil as *non-being* or a *privation of good* in its cosmological system. See Michael W. Hickson, "A Brief History of the Problems of Evil," in *Blackwell Companion to the Problem of Evil*, ed. Justine P. McBrayer and Daniel Howard-Snyder (Chichester, UK: John Wiley & Sons, 2013), 3–18.

3 Augustine was born in the late Roman Empire and was officially a Catholic, but he did not convert to Christianity until he was in his thirties. See Peter Brown, *Augustine of Hippo: A Biography* (Berkeley: University of California Press, 2000), 7–15.

4 Augustine, *Confessions*, in *Augustine: Confessions and Enchiridion* (Louisville, KY: Westminster John Knox Press, 2006), 5.10.18, 5.10.19.

5   See Augustine, *Confessions* 5.10.18, 5.10.19.
6   Augustine, *Confessions* 7.1.2.
7   Augustine, *Confessions* 7.5.7.
8   Augustine, *Confessions* 7.9.13.
9   Augustine, *Confessions* 7.9.13.
10 Lewis Ayres, *Augustine and the Trinity* (Cambridge: Cambridge University Press, 2010), 192. This book offers a detailed treatment of the relationship between Augustine and all forms of Platonism.
11 Augustine, *On Free Will* (*De Libero Arbitrio*), in *Augustine: Earlier Writings*, LCC (Louisville, KY: Westminster John Knox Press, 2006), 2.6.14.
12 Augustine, *On Free Will* 2.6.14. For Latin text, *Sancti Augustini, De Libero Arbitrio*, in *Opera* CChr, vol. 29, ed. W. M. Green (Turnhoult, Belgium: Brepols, 1970), 2.6.14. Augustine defines evil as a privation of good. See Augustine, *Confessions*, 7.12.18. See also Augustine, *The City of God (De Civitate Dei) XI–XXII*, vol. 7, in *The Works of Saint Augustine: A Translation for the 21st Century* (Brooklyn, NY: New City Press, 2013), 11.9.
13 Augustine, *Confessions* 7.9.13.
14 Augustine prefers to use secular knowledge such as history, science, and even heathen literature to assist him in discovering the meaning of the Scripture. But he rejects extreme superstitions and superfluous elaboration in speech. His analogy of "stealing Egyptian gold" clearly shows Augustine's way of treating pagan intellectual assets. He asks Christians to convert the knowledge of the ancients to Christian use. See Augustine, *Teaching Christianity* (*De Doctrina Christiana*), vol. 11, in *The Works of Saint Augustine: A Translation for the 21st Century*, trans. Maria Boulding (Brooklyn, NY: New City Press, 1996), 2.16.17–2.40.61, 2.41.62–63. Thomas Aquinas famously summarizes Augustine's methodology by writing, "Whenever Augustine, who was imbued with the doctrines of the Platonists, found in their teaching anything consistent with faith, he adopted it; and those things which he found contrary to faith he amended." Thomas Aquinas, *Summa Theologia*, in *Basic Writings of Saint Thomas Aquinas*, vol. 1, ed. Anton Charles Pegis (Indianapolis: Hackett Publishing, 1997), 1.84.5.
15 Gerald Bonner, *St. Augustine of Hippo: Life and Controversies* (Norwich: Canterbury Press Norwich, 2002), 201.
16 The Supreme Being is also called the One or the Good. Plotinus' cosmology begins with the Being and gradates to mind (*nous*), the world's soul (*psyche*), and the lowest level, which is nature. See Plotinus, *The Six Enneads*, abridged ed., trans. Stephen Mackenna and John M. Dillon (London: Penguin, 1991), 1.8.3.
17 Plotinus, *The Six Enneads* 1.8.7.
18 Bonner, *St. Augustine of Hippo*, 201.
19 Augustine, *On Free Will* 2.6.14.
20 For example, Plato argued that the Demiurge used pre-existing matter to form the objects in the universe. See Hickson, "A Brief History of the Problems of Evil," 4–6. See also Plato, *Republic*, ed. and trans. Chris Emlyn-Jones and William Preddy (Cambridge, MA: Harvard University Press, 2013).
21 Augustine, *Confessions* 7.12.18; Augustine, *The City of God* 11.9.
22 TeSelle summarizes Augustine's early appropriation of Platonism as follows: "Many of Augustine's ideas are not as new as they have appeared. But he did think through the problems once more, and then repeatedly, for himself; and even where he merely reaffirmed older insights he transmuted them by bringing them into the different

context of Christian belief and obedience." Eugene TeSelle, *Augustine the Theologian* (Eugene, OR: Wipf and Stock, 2002), 54–5. In regard to Augustine's reception of Platonism, see TeSelle, *Augustine: The Theologian*, 43–55. See also Brown, *Augustine of Hippo*, 79–92.

23 Irenaeus of Lyons's doctrine of *creatio ex nihilo* was primarily against the Gnostics' teaching of creation made out of pre-existent matter. See Irenaeus of Lyons, *Against Heresies* (*Adversus Haereses*), in *The Writings of the Fathers Down to A.D. 325 Volume I—The Apostolic Fathers with Justin Martyr and Irenaeus*, ANF, ed. Alexander Roberts, James Donaldson, and A. Cleveland Coxe (Grand Rapids, MI: Wm. B. Eerdmans, 1989), 2.10.4.

24 Augustine, *The Nature of the Good* (*De Natura Boni*), in *Augustine: Earlier Writings* (Louisville, KY: Westminster John Knox Press, 2006), 1.1, emphasis added.

25 Augustine, *On Free Will* 3.7.21.

26 This implies both natural and physical evils such disease, illness, and death and, potentially, ethical evil.

27 Augustine, *Confessions* 7.13.19.

28 This suggests not the actuality but the potentiality of corruption.

29 Matthew Craig Steenberg, *Irenaeus on Creation: The Cosmic Christ and the Saga of Redemption* (Leiden, the Netherlands: Brill, 2008), 45.

30 It is probable at this point that Augustine's explanation of evil as nothing is drawn more from his philosophical rhetoric against the dualism of Manichees than from his experiential analysis. According to Amy K. Hermanson, "Augustine refashioned rhetoric to remove its pagan associations while, at the same time, appropriated Greco-Roman rhetoric to serve the Christian's ultimate exigency: saving souls for Christ." Amy K. Hermanson, "Saint Augustine and the Creation of a Distinctly Christian Rhetoric," in *The Rhetoric of St. Augustine of Hippo: De Doctrina Christiana and the Search for a Distinctly Christian Rhetoric* (Waco, TX: Baylor University Press, 2008), 7.

31 Catherine Conybeare, "Review of *Creatio ex nihilo and the Theology of St. Augustine: The Anti-Manichaean Polemic and Beyond* by N. Joseph Torchia," *CH* 70, no. 4 (2001): 778.

32 However, this optimism is mixed with pessimism in his later doctrine of original sin. On the one hand, Bonner describes Augustine's optimism as the "long-term view"; see Bonner, *St. Augustine of Hippo*, 207. On the other hand, Irenaeus points out that Scripture does not fully supply the details of *creatio ex nihilo* and that therefore this doctrine cannot purely be perceived protologically. Irenaeus, *Against Heresies* 2.28.7.

33 Augustine identifies the final destination of the soul with the heavenly city of God. See Augustine, *Confessions* 7.10.16.

34 Augustine, *Enchiridion*, in *Augustine: Confessions and Enchiridion*, LCC (Louisville, KY: Westminster John Knox Press, 2006), 4.13, emphasis added.

35 Augustine, *Enchiridion* 4.13.

36 Augustine, *Enchiridion* 4.13.

37 Augustine's concepts of evil and the devil require careful attention. Augustine distinguishes his philosophically defined concept of evil and the existence of the devil (Satan), who was a good angel but fell by its own will in pride. See Augustine, *On Free Will* 3.25. Augustine views the fallen angels as ontologically good as part of creation. See Augustine, *Of True Religion* (*De Vera Religion*), in *Augustine: Earlier Writings*, LCC, ed. and trans. J. H. S. Burleigh (Louisville, KY: Westminster John Knox Press, 2006), 13.26.

38 Augustine, *On Free Will* 1.1.1. For Augustine, sin is both the moral evil and its penalty. See also William E. Mann, "Augustine on Evil and Original Sin," in *The*

     Cambridge Companion to Augustine (Cambridge: Cambridge University Press, 2001), 46.
39 Augustine, *Confessions* 7.3.5.
40 Augustine, *Enchiridion* 4.15. Augustine's conclusion is also based on his exegesis of the Scripture. He cites Matt. 7:18 in his argument that the human heart is the starting place of the bringing forth of both evil and good.
41 Augustine, *On Free Will* 3.5.12; "Therefore, do not be troubled by the blame accorded to sinful souls, and do not say in your heart it would have been better had they never existed."
42 Bonner, *St. Augustine of Hippo*, 193.
43 Irenaeus, *Against Heresies* 2.28.7.
44 Stephen N. Williams, "The Sovereignty of God," in *Engaging the Doctrine of God: Contemporary Protestant Perspectives*, ed. Bruce L. McCormack (Grand Rapids, MI: Baker Academic, 2008), 169–70.
45 According to the degrees of being, the goodness descends eventually down to the empty darkness of non-being, which is evil.
46 As William E. Mann indicates, for Augustine, as God created the universe without any necessity or cause, sin also does not have a cause or origin. Mann, "Augustine on Evil and Original Sin," 46.
47 Augustine, *On Free Will* 1.16.34, 2.19.53.
48 Augustine, *Confessions* 9.10. In regard to the self's movement, see Philip Cary, *Augustine's Invention of the Inner Self: The Legacy of a Christian Platonist* (New York: Oxford University Press, 2000). See also John C. Cavadini, *Visioning Augustine* (Hoboken, NJ: John Wiley & Sons, 2019), 138–55. In this vein, Ellen T. Charry explained the two opposing movements of the will as "inside-up-out" and "inside-down-in" during my independent study of Augustine at Princeton Theological Seminary in fall 2015.
49 Augustine, *Confessions* 7.16.22; Augustine, *On Free Will* 1.16.34. Cf. Augustine, *Confessions* 9.10. See also Philip Cary, "Book Seven: Inner Vision as the Goal of Augustine's Life," in *A Reader's Companion to Augustine's Confessions*, ed. Kim Paffenroth and Robert P. Kennedy (Louisville, KY: Westminster John Knox Press), 107–26.
50 Augustine, *On Free Will* 1.15.31; Augustine, *Teaching Christianity* 1.4; Augustine, *The City of God* 14.28.
51 Augustine, *On Free Will* 1.15.31.
52 Augustine, *Confessions* 2.4.
53 Augustine, *Confessions* 7.16.22
54 Cary, "Book Seven: Inner Vision," 118.
55 Augustine, *Teaching Christianity* 1.5–10. See also Augustine, *On Free Will* 1.16.35, 2.19.51.
56 Augustine, *On Free Will* 2.19.53.
57 Cary, "Book Seven: Inner Vision," 118.
58 Augustine, *Teaching Christianity* 1.22.20.
59 Augustine, *Teaching Christianity* 1.22.20, emphasis in original.
60 See Oliver O'Donovan, "*Usus* and *Fruitio* in Augustine, *De Doctrina Christiana* I," *JTS* 33, no. 2 (1982): 389–90. See also Raymond Canning, "uti/frui," in *Augustine through the Ages: An Encyclopedia*, ed. Fitzgerald (Grand Rapids, MI: Wm. B. Eerdmans, 2009), 860.
61 Augustine, *Teaching Christianity* 1.4.
62 Self-love can be interpreted in diverse ways. Here, self-love is used in a negative sense to mean the will's egocentric love or desire toward the self. The negative sense

of self-love is closer to self-obsession in *cupiditas* (desire) rather than true love for the self. Augustine considers that true self-love is only possible with the love of the human for God. The lexicographical classification of love in Latin includes *caritas*, *dilectio*, and *amor*. O'Donovan explains that "Scripture uses caritas to express the nature of God (1 John 4:8, 16, constantly quoted by Augustine) [which] seems to impart an air of sanctity to the world. Between dilectio and amor, however, Augustine shows no very clear resolve to distinguish. He uses either of them indifferently to express the love of man for God, the love of God for man, and the love of man for lower objects." Oliver O'Donovan, *The Problem of Self-Love in St. Augustine* (Eugene, OR: Wipf and Stock, 2006), 11.

63 O'Donovan, *The Problem of Self-Love*, 2.
64 Augustine, *The City of God* 14:28.
65 Daniel L. Migliore, *Faith Seeking Understanding* (Grand Rapids, MI: Wm. B. Eerdmans, 2004), 151.
66 Augustine, *On the Holy Trinity* (*De Trinitate*), vol. 3, NPNF, ed. Philip Schaff (Grand Rapids, MI: Wm. B. Eerdmans, 1978).
67 Cary, *Augustine's Invention of the Inner Self*, 30–6. See Augustine, *Confessions*, 7.
68 Cary, *Augustine's Invention of the Inner Self*, 37. Cary argues that Augustine's concept of the self's inwardness is problematic for a Christian understanding. Cary insists that "Augustine's problem is how to locate God within the soul, without affirming the divinity of the soul. He wants (like Plotinus) to find the divine within the self, while affirming (as an orthodox Christian) that the divine is wholly other than the self. He solves this problem by locating God not only within the soul but above it. … The concept of private inner space arises in consequence of this modification, for the place in which we find ourselves when we have entered within (and not yet looked up) is our very own space—an inner world of human memory and thought, not identical with the intelligible world of the divine Mind." Cary, *Augustine's Invention of the Inner Self*, 246–7. Ellen T. Charry argues, however, that "for Cary, the crux of the problem with the Augustinian self is that it is private. … For Augustine, this privacy is a moral problem. Cary's problem comes from the modern use of this privacy that sees the inner, private self as essential and necessary, a given, not a problem." Ellen T. Charry, Book Review of "Augustine's Invention of the Inner Self: The Legacy of a Christian Platonist," *TTod* 58, no. 2 (July 2001): 232–4.
69 In the church tradition, *imago Dei* usually is understood in two categories: the image (*eikon*) and the likeness (*homoiosis*) of God. Both Irenaeus and Augustine interpreted *imago Dei* in these two ways. Augustine understood that human beings lost the likeness (*homoiosis*) of God but retained the residual image (*eikon*) of God. See Irenaeus, *Against Heresies* 3.23.1. Augustine, *On the Holy Trinity* 10.11.18. Contra Augustine, Luther sees not only the likeness (*homoiosis*) but also the image (*eikon*) of God as totally under the power of the fall.
70 Augustine, *On the Holy Trinity* 10.11.18.
71 See ch. 5.
72 The capacity of the soul is related to its function of ascending to the highest, to God. In *Confessions*, Augustine says that "by this very soul will I mount up to him." Augustine, *Confessions* 10.7.11.
73 Augustine, *Confessions* 7.7.11, 7.9.13, 9.4.7.
74 Augustine, *Confessions* 7.7.11.
75 For example, Martin Luther radically appropriated Augustine's later anthropology without associating it with Augustine's early philosophical treatment of soul as the essence of human being.

76 Cary argues that "[Young Augustine] wants us to worship and pray to the god of philosophy in the name of Jesus Christ." Cary, *Augustine's Invention of the Inner Self*, 123. It is controversial whether Augustine's concept of the Trinity is identical with the Niceno-Constantinopolitan Trinity.

77 Both the Nicene and Constantinople Creeds affirm that God is one in essence, distinguished in three persons. In this regard, Daniel L. Migliore argues that "to protect the unity of God's being, the governing rule is, 'All of the acts of the triune God in the world are indivisible.'" Migliore, *Faith Seeking Understanding*, 71. See also Ayres, *Augustine and the Trinity*, 42.

78 Bruce L. McCormack, "The Actuality of God: *Karl Barth in Conversation with Open Theism*," in *Engaging the Doctrine of God: Contemporary Protestant Perspectives*, ed. Bruce L. McCormack (Grand Rapids, MI: Baker Academic, 2008), 187.

79 Many feminist thinkers have debated whether the active sinful manifestation, such as pride, can be considered the foundational sin of the human being without considering the passive aspect of sin, such as the selflessness and self-denigration found in the majority of women. In this regard, Bonhoeffer's later anthropology gives emphasis on the passive dimension of sin, chiefly in relation to his political context without considering experiences based on gender.

80 In *On the Holy Trinity*, Augustine clarifies the indivisibility of the divine operation. See Augustine, *On the Holy Trinity* 1.4.7.

81 It may be said that the polemics is also against the Donatists, but this chapter focuses on Pelagianism, which is directly related to the development of the doctrine of original sin. In regard to his ecclesiastical responsibility, Augustine was ordained in 391. Some scholars consider this period a moment of theological transition. See TeSelle, *Augustine the Theologian*, 156–8.

82 Augustine scholars have noted that after his sudden interest in the epistles of Paul around 394, Augustine's anthropological theory of sin and grace shows a change in tone. See TeSelle, *Augustine the Theologian*, 156–8. See also John M. Rist, *Augustine: Ancient Thought Baptized* (Cambridge: Cambridge University Press, 1994), 15–16.

83 Augustine, *Confessions* 7.9.13, 8.10.16. Many commentators agree that Augustine experienced two main conversions—intellectual and religious. The first is his reading of Plotinus' books described in book 7 of *Confessions* and the second is his episode in the courtyard at Milan described in book 8 of *Confessions*. On the other hand, Rist rightly points out that it is thought that when Augustine was ordained, his knowledge of the Scripture was quite limited and unscriptural. See Rist, *Augustine: Ancient Thought Baptized*, 15.

84 The shift in Augustine's thought is seen after his reply to Simplicianus. *Ad Simplicianum* is Augustine's first literary work as a bishop, in which he answers Simplicianus' collection of questions.

85 See Augustine, *On Marriage and Concupiscence* (*De Nuptiis et Concupiscientia*), in *St. Augustine: Anti-Pelagian Writings*, vol. 5, NPNF, ed. Philip Schaff (Grand Rapids, MI: Wm. B. Eerdmans, 1978), 2.15. See also Augustine, *The City of God* 14.13.

86 This was against Pelagianism as well as Donatism. There has been an ongoing controversy over the decisive point of the introduction of the doctrine of original sin between the reply to Simplicianus in 396 and *De Genesi ad litteram* in 406. As Paul Rigby explains, until 1967 *Ad simplicianum* had been considered the place that contains the doctrines of original sin and grace by most scholars, but Sage proposed in 1967 that the mature doctrine of original sin was formulated later against the Pelagian controversy. Paul Rigby, *Original Sin in Augustine's Confessions* (Ottawa: University of Ottawa Press, 1987), 26.

87   In addition to Rom. 5:12, Augustine finds proof passages in Psalm 51, Job, Eph. 2:3, and Jn. 3:3–5, along with the writings of the church fathers. See J. N. D. Kelly, *Early Christian Doctrines*, revised ed. (New York: HarperCollins, 1978), 353.
88   Augustine, *On Marriage and Concupiscence* 2.15, emphasis added.
89   It is debated whether Rom. 5:12 is the most central scriptural verse in the doctrine of original sin. Kelly argues that Augustine followed Ambrosiaster, who mistakenly interpreted Rom. 5:12 based on the Old Latin version of Scripture. Kelly, *Early Christian Doctrines*, 353. In this vein, Pier Franco Beatrice argues that "[w]e may conclude therefore that Augustine, in his conflict with the Pelagians, defends ideas that were broadly shared in his ecclesiastical environment." Pier Franco Beatrice, *The Transmission of Sin: Augustine and the Pre-Augustinian Source* (New York: Oxford University Press, 2013), 111. According to Roland Teske, Augustine cites this verse eleven times in *On the Merits and Remission of Sins* (*De Peccatorum Meritis et Remissione*) alone. Roland Teske, "Scriptural Index to *Answer to the Pelagians*," ed. John Rotelle, vol. 23 in *The Works of St. Augustine: A Translation for the 21st Century* (New York: New City Press, 1997), 565.
90   Kelly, *Early Christian Doctrines*, 353; Beatrice, *The Transmission of Sin*, 110–11.
91   See Augustine, *Revisions* (*Retractationes*), in *The Works of Saint Augustine: A Translation for the 21st Century*, trans. Boniface Ramsey (Hyde Park, NY: New City Press, 2010), 1.17.
92   One famous example is Adolf von Harnack who criticized Augustine's doctrine as "Christian pessimism." See Adolf von Harnack, *History of Dogma*, vol. 5 (Eugene, OR: Wipf & Stock Publishers, 1997), 74–5.
93   Jeff Nicoll, *Augustine's Problem: Impotence and Grace* (Eugene, OR: Wipf and Stock, 2016), 54.
94   TeSelle, *Augustine the Theologian*, 317.
95   Bonner, *St. Augustine of Hippo*, 389. In regard to the Augustinian meaning of *concupiscentia*, see Bonner, *St. Augustine of Hippo*, 398–401.
96   See Augustine, *The Literal Meaning of Genesis* (*De Genesi ad Litteram*), in *Ancient Christian Writers*, trans. John Hammond Taylor (New York: Newman Press, 1982), 10.12.20.
97   Bonhoeffer argues that human beings have sociological unity in addition to biological solidarity.
98   Augustine, *On Marriage and Concupiscence* 2.15.
99   According to Kelly, neither Ambrose nor Ambrosiaster agreed with the transmission of the culpability of Adam to his posterity. See Kelly, *Early Christian Doctrines*, 353. See also Beatrice, *The Transmission of Sin*.
100 Augustine, *On Marriage and Concupiscence* 2.15. Augustine, however, conceives the communal sinful solidarity of human beings in *Confessions* in a primitive manner. See Augustine, *Confessions*, 3.
101 It is quite convincing that Augustine viewed the physicality of humans as a lesser goodness than the spirituality of humans following his hierarchical notion of goodness or perfection, even in his later period.
102 McFarland, *In Adam's Fall*, 19.
103 There have been diverse interpretations of the essence of original sin. Paul Rigby explains, "The first claims that the essence of original sin is Adam's pride insofar as all his descendants participate in it by the death of their soul (the loss of sanctifying grace), because of their solidarity with Adam. The second asserts that the essence of

original sin is the guilt of concupiscence inherited from Adam as a punishment for Adam's pride." Rigby, *Original Sin in Augustine's Confessions*, 85–7.
104 See Augustine, *The City of God* 13.1, 13.20; Augustine, *The Literal Meaning of Genesis* 9.12.20.
105 Potentially, people who are mentally disabled are included. For this theological dilemma, Augustine developed the theory of infant baptism, which functions to remit the original sin of infants.
106 See Bonner, *St. Augustine of Hippo*, 316–18. Beatrice argues that "for Augustine the urgency of the [Pelagian] controversy was the decisive factor, and that he was committed to defending the traditional belief at all costs." Beatrice, *The Transmission of Sin*, 110–11.
107 Augustine, *Revisions* 1.9.3; 1.9.4–5. Augustine states, "There are also things done through necessity that must be reproved, when a person wills to act rightly and is unable to do so. That is the reason for these worlds: For I do not do the good that I will, but the evil that I hate is what I do (Rom. 7:15). And these: To will lies near at hand, but to accomplish the good does not (Rom. 7:18). And these: The flesh lusts against the spirit, and the spirit against the flesh, for they are mutually opposed, so that you do not do the things that you will (Gal. 5:17). But all of these things pertain to human beings who are under the sentence of death." Augustine, *Revisions* 1.9.5.
108 Matt. 22:39; Mk. 23:31.
109 Augustine, *On Free Will*, 3.18.50–51. Augustine addresses the notions of *ignorantia* and *difficultas* mainly based on Pauline passages such as 1 Tim. 1:13; Rom. 7:18–19; Ps. 25:7; Gal. 5:17. The passive dimension of sin resonates with the claims of feminist as well as liberal theologians in a primitive way. Seen from the modern perspective, these newly introduced concepts have not received as much attention as the other previous two concepts (pride, concupiscence) in the history of Western hamartiology, but there is much of theological significance in regard to the issue of the theological subject, as is argued by feminist and liberation theologians.
110 Augustine, *On Free Will* 3.18.50–51. Augustine uses passages from 1 Tim. 1:13, Ps. 24:7, Rom. 7:18–19, and Gal. 5:17 in *On Free Will* 3.18.51. According to Mann, ignorance references not only ignorance of the Scripture but also of Platonism. See Mann, "Augustine on Evil and Original Sin," 46.
111 Augustine, *On Marriage and Concupiscence*, 1.6–8. Augustine, *On the Merits and Remission of Sins, and on the Baptism of Infants* (*De Peccatorum Meritis et Remissione, et de Baptismo Parvulorum*), in *St. Augustine: Anti-Pelagian Writings*, vol. 5, NPNF, ed. Philip Schaff (Grand Rapids, MI: Wm. B. Eerdmans, 1978), 1.65. See also Augustine, *The City of God* 13.20. From the perspective of modern people, the superior intelligence of the human before the fall is probably doubtful. For example, Bonhoeffer does not consider the first humanity as superior to its posterity.
112 Augustine, *On Rebuke and Grace* (*De Correctione et Gratia*), in *St. Augustine: Anti-Pelagian Writings*, vol. 5, NPNF, ed. Philip Schaff (Grand Rapids, MI: Wm. B. Eerdmans, 1978), 33.
113 See McFarland, *In Adam's Fall*, 47–8. See also Migliore, *Faith Seeking Understanding*, 151.
114 Augustine, *On Free Will* 3.24.71.
115 See Migliore, *Faith Seeking Understanding*, 151.
116 For Augustine, there is always a degree of perfection. Human perfection is qualitatively different from the perfection of God. Eric Osborn explains Irenaeus' perspective on perfection, which differs from that of Augustine: "Perfection

Chapter 2

1. Recently, contemporary scholars such as Oswald Bayer have focused on the relational aspect of Luther's hamartiology. See Oswald Bayer, *Martin Luther's Theology: A Contemporary Interpretation* (Grand Rapids, MI: Wm. B. Eerdmans, 2008).
2. Martin Luther, "Disputation against Scholastic Theology," *LW* 31 (1517): 9–16.
3. Augustine, *On the Holy Trinity* 14.2.10.
4. See Bernhard Lohse, *Martin Luther's Theology: Its Historical and Systematic Development*, trans. and ed. Roy Harrisville (Minneapolis: Fortress Press, 1999), 47.
5. As indicated in the introduction to this book, the term *Augustinianism* is an invention of the nineteenth century. There was no medieval term equivalent to Augustinianism. According to Eric Leland Saak, "[T]he adjectival form 'Augustinian' referring to members of the Augustinian Order dates to 1602 and referring to 'the Augustinian spirit' to 1674. Yet 'Augustin(ian)ism' was first used in English in 1830 to designate the theological position of Thomas Aquinas, noting the close connection between 'Augustinianism' and the doctrines of John Calvin." See Saak, *Creating Augustine*, 3–4. In this regard, see also note 3 in the introduction to this book.
6. Martin Luther, *LW* 31:9–6.
7. It is debatable whether Augustine's later understanding is clearly distinct from this standpoint.
8. Martin Luther, *LW* 25:260, emphasis added.
9. Augustine, *Expositions of the Psalms*, 140.3. Augustine interprets this to mean: "If then he is the head and we are the members, one single individual is speaking. Whether the head speaks or the members speak, the one Christ speaks." See also Augustine, *Homilies on the Gospel of John 1–40*, vol. III/12, *The Works of Saint Augustine: A Translation for the 21st Century*, trans. O.P. Edmund Hill (Hyde Park, NY: New City Press, 2009), 21:8. See also Stanislaus J. Grabowski, *The Church: An Introduction to the Theology of St. Augustine* (St. Louis, MO: B. Herder Book Co., 1957), 3–92. See also Joseph Carola for a more detailed discussion of Augustine's *totus homo* and *totus Christus*. Joseph Carola, *Augustine of Hippo: The Role of the Laity in Ecclesial Reconciliation* (Rome: Gregorian Biblical Book Shop, 2005).
10. Luther, *LW* 42:162. It is evident that Luther fully acknowledges the ecclesial concepts of *totus homo* and *totus Christus* in his early work. In the *Fourteen Consolations* written in 1520, he asks, "Who can hurt one part of the body without hurting the whole body? What pain can be suffered by the little toe that is not felt by the whole body. We are one body. Whatever another suffers, I also suffer and endure. ... Thus Christ says that whatever is done unto one of the least of his brethren is done unto him." Luther, *LW* 42:162. Later, the doctrine of *totus Christus* of Augustine became the origin of Dietrich Bonhoeffer's concept of the church as a corporate person existing as the church community. Bonhoeffer attributes both Augustine and Luther as the originators of the doctrine. See Bonhoeffer, *DBWE* 1, 189–90 (*DBW* 1:127).

for Irenaeus lies at the end, not at the beginning, of man's education by God, a process which takes account of the fall from the beginning." Eric Osborn, *Irenaeus* (Cambridge: Cambridge Press, 2001), 218–19.

11 Luther, *LW* 25:260.
12 Luther, *LW* 25:258.
13 Sin after baptism requires a clear explanation doctrinally as well as existentially, for both Luther and Augustine.
14 At this time, Luther begins to distinguish alien righteousness from actual righteousness. Luther, *LW* 31:299.
15 Erik Herrmann, "Luther's Absorption of Medieval Biblical Interpretation," in *The Oxford Handbook of Martin Luther's Theology*, ed. Robert Kolb, Irene Dingel, and L'ubomir Batka (Oxford: Oxford University Press, 2016), 78–9. Luther's notion of the imputation of Christ's righteousness is more clearly connected to his understanding of *totus homo* through his interlineal reading of Romans 7 and Psalm 51. See Clifton C. Black, "Unity and Diversity in Luther's Biblical Exegesis: Psalm 51 as a Test-Case," *SJT* 38, no. 3 (August 1985): 325–45.
16 In the early and even in the late period (e.g., in *De Trinitate*), Augustine mentioned the soul as the essence of the human being.
17 Paul Althaus, *The Theology of Martin Luther* (Philadelphia: Fortress Press, 1996), 243.
18 Luther, *The Bondage of the Will*, *LW* 33:215.
19 Alister E. McGrath, *Luther's Theology of the Cross: Martin Luther's Theological Breakthrough*, 2nd ed. (Oxford: Blackwell Publishing, 1985), 133.
20 Luther, *LW* 25:473.
21 Luther, *LW* 25:68.
22 Notger Slenczka, "Luther's Anthropology," in *The Oxford Handbook of Martin Luther's Theology*, ed. Robert Kolb, Irene Dingel, and L'ubomir Batka (Oxford: Oxford University Press, 2016), 215.
23 According to Matt Jenson, "When considering how the *totus homo* can be simultaneously spirit and flesh, righteous and sinful, Luther draws on the *communicatio idiomatum* ['communication of properties']." See Matt Jenson, *The Gravity of Sin: Augustine, Luther and Barth on "Homo Incurvatus in Se"* (London: Bloomsbury T&T Clark, 2007), 69, n. 121. See also Luther, *LW* 25:332.
24 Luther views baptism as effective for remission of original sin, not in the sense of *ex opere operato* but in relation to faith. See Luther, *LW* 3:274. For Augustine's view of the sin after baptism, see Augustine, *On Nature and Grace* (*De Natura et Gratia, contra Pelagium*), in *St. Augustine: Anti-Pelagian Writings*, vol. 5, NPNF, ed. Philip Schaff (Grand Rapids, MI: Wm. B. Eerdmans, 1978), 45.
25 In his treatise *Two Kinds of Righteousness*, Luther explains that alien righteousness justifies original sin and that actual righteousness deals with actual sins. On the other hand, in *Lectures on Romans*, Luther's primary concern is his turn from scholastic and Aristotelian anthropology to an anthropology that supports his pro-Augustinianism. In *Lectures on Romans*, Luther argues that "Augustine says very clearly that 'sin,' or concupiscence, is forgiven in Baptism, not in the sense that it no longer exists, but in the sense that it is not imputed." Luther, *LW* 31:299.
26 Althaus, *The Theology of Martin Luther*, 243.
27 L'ubomir Batka, "Luther's Teaching on Sin and Evil," in *The Oxford Handbook of Martin Luther's Theology*, ed. Robert Kolb, Irene Dingel, and L'ubomir Batka (Oxford: Oxford University Press, 2016), 245.
28 Augustine, *On the Holy Trinity* 14. 2. 10; 15.1.1.
29 Augustine, *The City of God* 22.24.
30 Luther, *LW* 1:65, emphasis added.

31 Luther does not distinguish the likeness (*homoiosis*) of God from the image (*eikon*) of God used in Gen. 1:26; he considers them synonyms.
32 Bayer, *Martin Luther's Theology*, 96.
33 Luther, *LW* 1:62–3.
34 Emphasis added. See also McGrath, *Luther's Theology of the Cross*, 134. McGrath argues that Luther uses the image of covering to illustrate how God clothes the sinner with *iustitia Christi aliena* (righteousness bestowed from outside the person).
35 Luther, *LW* 1:64. Luther says: "[N]ow the Gospel has brought about the restoration of that image. Intellect and will indeed have remained, but both very much impaired. And so the Gospel brings it about that we are formed once more according to that familiar and indeed better image, because we are born again into eternal life or rather into the hope of eternal life by faith."
36 Luther believes that true freedom belongs only to God. See Luther, *LW* 1:63–5.
37 Luther, *LW* 1:63–5.
38 See Bayer, *Martin Luther's Theology*, 98.
39 Luther, *LW* 1:63–4, emphasis added.
40 See McGrath, *Luther's Theology of the Cross*, 134.
41 For Luther, the relational capacity of the human being is within the framework of God's grace and predestination. See Luther, *The Bondage of the Will*, *LW* 33:49.
42 Batka, "Luther's Teaching on Sin and Evil," 236–7.
43 In his lectures on Psalm 51, Luther states that "only his heart is puffed up and soiled ... their spirit is bent and curved in on themselves (*in se curvatus*) for empty glory and pride." Luther, *LW* 10:241–2. See also Luther, *LW* 10:172.
44 Luther, *LW* 10:235–6. See also Luther, *LW* 10:241; Luther, *LW* 25:345.
45 Luther states that "this curvedness is now natural for us, a natural wickedness and a natural sinfulness. Thus man has no help from his natural powers, but he needs the aid of some power outside of himself." Luther, *LW* 25:345.
46 Batka, "Luther's Teaching on Sin and Evil," 243.
47 From the early stage, Luther uses term *peccatum radicale* (radical sin) interchangeably with the concept of original sin. See Batka, "Luther's Teaching on Sin and Evil," 243.
48 Batka, "Luther's Teaching on Sin and Evil," 238–9.
49 See Batka, "Luther's Teaching on Sin and Evil," 239. Batka argues that "Luther claimed that Augustine was on his side in regard to the concupiscence remaining in a baptized person. The guilt of sin is forgiven in baptism (*in reatu*), but in reality it remains even after baptism (*in actu*). In fact, Augustine's passages relate to concupiscence but not to original sin itself."
50 Luther, *LW* 25:300.
51 Luther, *LW* 25:261.
52 Luther, *LW* 25:261.
53 Luther, *LW* 25:300.
54 Batka, "Luther's Teaching on Sin and Evil," 235–6.
55 Luther, *LW* 32:220.
56 According to Batka, Luther understood Augustine's terminology but misinterpreted it. Batka, "Luther's Teaching on Sin and Evil," 239.
57 Luther, *LW* 1:162.
58 Luther, *LW* 1:65.
59 Luther, *LW* 31:344.
60 Luther, *LW* 31:344. This concept of the two contradictory men is also closely connected to his soteriological notion of two kinds of righteousness. Luther

distinguishes righteousness using the two categories of passive and active. Passive righteousness is concerned with one's salvation, whereas active righteousness is related to the life of a new person. See also Luther, *Two Kinds of Righteousness*, in Luther, *LW* 31:299.
61 David M. Whitford, *Luther: A Guide for the Perplexed* (London: T&T Clark, 2011), 87.
62 Luther, *The Bondage of the Will*, *LW* 33:50–1.
63 Luther, *LW* 33:50.
64 See Harry J. McSorley, *Luther: Right or Wrong? An Ecumenical-Theological Study of Luther's Major Work, The Bondage of the Will, by a Roman Catholic Scholar* (Glen Rock, NJ: Newman Press, 1969), 305.
65 Luther, *LW* 33:51.
66 Gerhard Müller, "Luther's Transformation of Medieval Thought: Discontinuity and Continuity," in *The Oxford Handbook of Martin Luther's Theology*, ed. Robert Kolb, Irene Dingel, and L'ubomir Batka (Oxford: Oxford University Press, 2016), 107.
67 Lohse, *Martin Luther's Theology*, 162.
68 Luther, *LW* 33:167.
69 Luther, *LW* 33:167.
70 See McSorley, *Luther: Right or Wrong?* 305.
71 Luther, *LW* 33:49.
72 According to Heiko A. Oberman, "Christ and the Devil were equally real to him: one was the perpetual intercessor for Christianity, the other a menace to mankind till the end." Heiko A. Oberman, *Luther: Man between God and the Devil*, trans. Eileen Walliser-Schwarzbart (New Haven, CT: Yale University Press, 2006), 104.
73 It is necessary to pay careful attention to Luther's understanding of the will of an unjustified person. Although he does not totally deny the capacity of the free will of an unjustified person to exercise good in reality, in Luther's soteriological perspective, the work of the will of an unjustified person is not sufficient to attain salvation.
74 Luther, *LW* 31:344.
75 Wolfhart Pannenberg, "Christlicher Glaube und menschliche Freiheit," KuD, III (1968), 272, as cited in McSorley, *Luther: Right or Wrong?* 365.
76 Luther, *LW* 1:65.
77 Luther understands the freedom of saints primarily as legal or juridical freedom. This notion is extended to Luther's concept of the church. In this regard, Eric Leland Saak points out that "[for Luther] the Church may have been many things, but it was, perhaps first and foremost, a legal, juridical institution." See Eric Leland Saak, *Luther and the Reformation of the Later Middle Ages* (Cambridge: Cambridge University Press, 2017), 256.
78 Luther, *LW* 1:63.
79 See also Slenczka, "Luther's Anthropology," 216–17.
80 Cf. Augustine, *On Free Will* 1.16.34; 2.19.53.
81 Bayer, *Martin Luther's Theology*, 95.
82 Bernard Lohse argues that Luther distinguishes the two kingdoms from two governments. Citing Heinrich Bornkamm, he explains that "'kingdom' denotes a 'sphere of rule' whereas 'government' denotes a 'type of rule.'" Lohse, *Martin Luther's Theology*, 318, 153–7. The Bornkamm citation is from "Die Frage der Obrigkeit in Reformationzeitalter," in *Das Jahrhudert des Reformation: Gestalten und Kräfte*, 23rd ed. (Göttingen: Vandenhoeck & Reprecht, 1966), 15.
83 See Augustine, *The City of God* 1.35, 20.9.

84 See Lohse, *Martin Luther's Theology*, 316–17.
85 See Lohse, *Martin Luther's Theology*, 316–17.
86 It is also debatable whether Augustine and Luther would agree that the kingdom or city of God is ultimately in heaven.
87 Saak, *Luther and the Reformation of the Later Middle Ages*, 262.
88 According to Saak, Luther primarily interpreted "the City of God" in Ps. 45 (46):5 as "relating to the early Church (*primitive Ecclesia*)." Saak, *Luther and the Reformation of the Later Middle Ages*, 260.
89 Saak, *Luther and the Reformation of the Later Middle Ages*, 260.
90 Saak, *Luther and the Reformation of the Later Middle Ages*, 260.
91 Luther, *Temporal Authority: To What Extent It Should Be Obeyed*, LW 45:75–129.
92 Luther, *Temporal Authority*, LW 45:91. Luther explains the relation as follows: "God has ordained two governments: the spiritual, by which the Holy Spirit produces Christians and righteous people under Christ; and the temporal, which restrains the un-Christian and wicked so that—no thanks to them—they are obliged to keep still and to maintain an outward peace."
93 Luther, *Admonition to Peace: A Reply to the Twelve Articles of the Peasants in Swabia*, LW 46:27.
94 DeJonge, *Bonhoeffer's Reception of Luther*, 84–5. See Luther, LW 45:91–104.
95 Luther, *Temporal Authority*, LW 45:94.
96 Luther, *Admonition to Peace: A Reply to the Twelve Articles of the Peasants in Swabia*, LW 46:27.
97 The opponents of magisterial Reformers such as the peasants or the Anabaptists criticized Luther and his followers. Luther sates: "Nowadays, when the sectarians cannot condemn us overtly, they say instead: 'These Lutherans have a cowardly spirit. They do not dare speak the truth frankly and freely and draw the consequences from it. ... But the beginning, the middle, and the end must be joined together. God has assigned to them the task of accomplishing this; He has left it to us.'" Luther, *LW* 26:50. See also Charles M. Jacobs and Robert C. Schultz, "Introduction to *Admonition to Peace: A Reply to the Twelve Articles of the Peasants in Swabia*," LW 46:5–6.
98 See Jacobs and Schultz, "Introduction to *Admonition to Peace*," LW 46:5–6.

Chapter 3

1 For a detailed history of the text along with an explanation of the lack of scholarly investigation of Bonhoeffer's hamartiology, see the section entitled "Contribution to Knowledge" in the introduction to this book. See also Green, "Editor's Introduction to the English Edition," in Bonhoeffer, *DBWE* 1:9–13.
2 Bonhoeffer states that "in order to establish clarity about the inner logic of theological construction, it would be good for once if a presentation of doctrinal theology were to start not with the doctrine of God but with the doctrine of the church." Bonhoeffer, *DBWE* 1:134. Tom Greggs also argues that ecclesiology is the foundation of Bonhoeffer's theology. Greggs, "Bearing Sin in the Church," 78. Wayne Whitson Floyd states that "Bonhoeffer begins here a lifelong preoccupation with his conviction that the church 'is' its sociality—that community which, as he will later put the matter from prison, radically 'exists for others.'" Wayne Whitson Floyd, "Dietrich Bonhoeffer," in *Modern Theologians: An*

Introduction to Christian Theology since 1918, ed. David F. Ford and Rachel Muers, 3rd ed. (Oxford: Blackwell Publishing, 2005), 49. See also Christiane Tietz, "Bonhoeffer on the Ontological Structure of the Church," in *Ontology and Ethics: Bonhoeffer and Contemporary Scholarship*, ed. Adam C. Clark and Michael Mawson (Eugene, OR: Pickwick Publications, 2013), 32–3. Tietz says, "Ecclesiology and Christology go hand in hand for Bonhoeffer." See also note 3 in the introduction to this book.

3   Bonhoeffer, *DBWE* 1:190–1; 1:157, 214.
4   Bonhoeffer, *DBW* 1:127; Bonhoeffer, *DBWE* 1:157, 190.
5   Bonhoeffer, *DBWE* 1:109, 110.
6   Bonhoeffer, *DBWE* 1:110 (SC-A).
7   See Batka, "Luther's Teaching on Sin and Evil," 245–56.
8   Bonhoeffer, *DBWE* 1:110–11 (SC-A). It is controversial whether Augustine's doctrine of original sin is mainly based on Rom. 5:12. Augustine's old Latin Bible renders the Greek term ἐφ' ᾧ, which means "because," into "in whom." Bonhoeffer, *DBWE* 1:117 (SC-A). According to Eric Plumer, "The version of the Bible that Augustine used in writing his Commentary is one of the Old Latin versions, whose origins antedate those of the Vulgate by more than two hundred years. For the letters of Paul, for example, the existence of a Latin translation in North Africa is attested as far back as the Acts of the Scillitan Martyrs, dated 180." Eric Plumer, "Appendix 2 of Augustine," in *Augustine's Commentary on Galatians*, Oxford Early Christian Studies (Oxford: Oxford University Press, 2003), 240. For a detailed discussion of Augustine's interpretation of Rom. 5:12, see Beatrice, *The Transmission of Sin*, 95–111.
9   Bonhoeffer, *DBWE* 1:110 (SC-A).
10 Bonhoeffer, *DBWE* 1:116.
11 Bonhoeffer, *DBWE* 1:116.
12 Bonhoeffer, *DBWE* 1:110 (SC-A).
13 Bonhoeffer, *DBWE* 1:134.
14 Bonhoeffer, *DBWE* 1:214.
15 Bonhoeffer, *DBWE* 1:107.
16 The term *communitarian* encompasses concepts such as collective, corporate, and communal. This term is primarily based on Bonhoeffer's appropriated sociological term for *community* [*Gemeinschaft*], which is connected to the concept of the church community [*Gemeinde*]. It is used to emphasize the characteristic of Bonhoeffer's hamartiology that always places sin within the concept of the community in which individual persons participate in relationships in community between the I and the divine other as well as between the I and the human other. Thus, the term *communitarian* in this book is interchangeable with the similar terms suggested here.
17 This does not mean that Augustine does not deal with the culpability of the community in his entire theology; rather, it means that he does not closely engage the concept of culpability with the culpability of community *in* his doctrine of original sin.
18 Bonhoeffer, *DBWE* 1, 112 (SC-A), emphasis added.
19 Bonhoeffer follows Luther's merging of the original sin and the universal sinfulness of the total human being.
20 Bonhoeffer, *DBWE* 1:110–11.
21 Bonhoeffer, *DBWE* 1:190–1.
22 Bonhoeffer argues that "this idea [of predestination] has a persistent corrosive effect on the concept of the church, for individual persons perceive themselves as ultimate

in God's sight; every community seems to be fragmented into the components of individual persons." Bonhoeffer, *DBWE* 1:163. See also Paul Rigby, "Original Sin," in *Augustine through the Ages: An Encyclopedia*, ed. A. Fitzgerald (Grand Rapids, MI: Wm. B. Eerdmans, 2009), 607.

23 See Nicoll, *Augustine's Problem*, 22. See also Harnack, *History of Dogma*, 5:74–5.
24 Harnack, *History of Dogma*, 5:75.
25 For a detailed discussion of Bonhoeffer's concept of predestination, see Bonhoeffer, *DBWE* 1:162–5.
26 Bonhoeffer, *DBWE* 1:111 (SC-A).
27 Bonhoeffer, *DBWE* 1:111 (SC-A).
28 However, one should be aware that Bonhoeffer does not see all of Augustine's doctrines as one-sided. Bonhoeffer appropriates Augustine's other doctrinal locus, ecclesiology, for the development of his doctrine of original sin or his hamartiology.
29 Bonhoeffer, *DBWE* 1:190. In Bonhoeffer, *DBW* 1:127, Bonhoeffer says that "Nicht alle Einzelnen, sondern sie als Ganzheit ist in Christus, is der, Leib Christi; sie is, *Christus als Gemeinde existierend*" (Not all individuals, but the church-community as a whole is in Christ, is the 'body of Christ'; it is "Christ existing as church-community").
30 Bonhoeffer, *DBWE* 1:122–3.
31 In this regard, John Webster's approach to ecclesiology contrasts with Bonhoeffer's. For a detailed discussion of John Webster's methodology, see note 3 in the introduction to this book.
32 Bonhoeffer, *DBWE* 1:108.
33 In the 1920s, many thinkers, such as Martin Buber, Hans Ehrenberg, and Ferdinand Tönnies, used the terms *the I* and *the other* to explain relationships in society. Floyd, "Dietrich Bonhoeffer," 49.
34 Floyd, "Dietrich Bonhoeffer," 49.
35 Bonhoeffer, *DBWE* 1:48. See also Clifford J. Green, "Editor's Introduction to the English Edition," in Bonhoeffer, *DBWE* 1:5.
36 Green, *Bonhoeffer*, 29–30.
37 Bonhoeffer, *DBWE* 1:48, emphasis added.
38 According to Sheri Katz, in the classical Augustinian tradition there are two kinds of senses of the person. The primary concept of the person is used in the Trinitarian concept of persons. The secondary concept of the person is related to the concept of the human person by which each individual is distinguished not only from other things but also from other human beings. Katz argues that "Augustine is basically a Platonist—the soul is better than, and hence remains vitally more important than, the body in a person's constitution. The individuation of persons is a matter of having a unique, separate soul (*Trin.* 13.2.2). A person is a soul using or ruling a body. … In more mature works Augustine does come to view the person as more of a unity, but the Platonic position can be found there too. We are not bodies but are intelligible beings (*Trin.* 11.1.1)." Sheri Katz, "Person," in *Augustine through the Ages: An Encyclopedia*, ed. A. Fitzgerald (Grand Rapids, MI: Wm. B. Eerdmans, 2009), 647–9.
39 Bonhoeffer, *DBWE* 1:48.
40 Bonhoeffer, *DBWE* 1:48.
41 Bonhoeffer, *DBWE* 1:49, emphasis in original.
42 Bonhoeffer, *DBWE* 1:49, emphasis added.
43 The concept of barrier is used in both the positive and negative senses in Bonhoeffer's works, especially in *Creation and Fall*.

44 Bonhoeffer, *DBWE* 1:89–90. Bonhoeffer uses Ferdinand Tönnies's sociological division between the two in which the first type signifies "community" and the latter "society." Tönnies, in *Community and Society*, "differentiates between the organic and real culture of the community [*Gemeinschaft*] and the ideal and mechanical culture of the society [*Gesellschaft*]." Ferdinand Tönnies, *Community and Society*, 33ff., 64ff, as cited in Bonhoeffer, *DBWE* 1:89, n. 22. He adds the other concept in regard to "a relation of rule [*Herrschaftsverhaltnis*]," referencing the notion of Max Scheler. See Bonhoeffer, *DBWE* 1:91, n. [106].
45 Bonhoeffer, *DBWE* 1:90.
46 Bonhoeffer, *DBWE* 1, 91–2. Bonhoeffer explains that the church is a purpose driven society [*Gesellschaft*] because "Love is the purpose of this Realm." Bonhoeffer, *DBWE* 1:264.
47 Bonhoeffer, *DBWE* 1:91–2, 263, 266.
48 Bonhoeffer, *DBWE* 1:264, emphasis in original.
49 Bonhoeffer, *DBW* 1:127, Bonhoeffer, *DBWE* 190; Bonhoeffer, *DBW* 1:100, Bonhoeffer, *DBWE* 157. See Augustine, *Homilies on the First Epistle of John*, 1:1–2:11 Augustine here argues: "He has made himself a bridegroom and has made himself a bride, because they aren't two but one flesh, for *the Word was made flesh and dwelled among us*. The Church is joined to that flesh, and Christ becomes the whole, head and body." Emphasis in original.
50 See Luther, *LW* 25:258.
51 Bonhoeffer, *DBWE* 1:124. Here, Bonhoeffer says he cited Luther's *Lectures on Galatians* (*WA* 2:457), but according to an editor's note in *DBWE* 1, it corresponds to Luther's *Lectures on Romans 1515/1516* (*LW* 25:258) in the Ficker edition. See Bonhoeffer, *DBWE* 1:124, n. [8].
52 Bonhoeffer, *DBWE* 1:124.
53 Bonhoeffer, *DBWE* 1:124.
54 See also Harvey, "Augustine and Thomas Aquinas," 12.
55 Eberhard Bethge, *Dietrich Bonhoeffer: A Biography*, ed. Victoria J. Barnett, rev. ed. (Minneapolis: Fortress Press, 2000), 67.
56 Bonhoeffer, *DBWE* 1:189–90.
57 One should be aware that Bonhoeffer's Christianized concept of the person is appropriated not only from the ideas of modern thinkers such as Hegel but also (or more fundamentally) from Augustine's as well as Luther's ecclesial notion of *totus Christus* derived from the Bible (e.g., 1 Cor. 12:27; 12:12). In this regard, the scholarship on Bonhoeffer has emphasized Hegel's influence, neglecting Bonhoeffer's claim that "Luther revived Augustine's idea." According to Green, one of the major influences on Bonhoeffer's Christian concept of the person was Hegel, who used "Geist as a concept applying to both corporate and individual life." See Green, *Bonhoeffer*, 30. For Bonhoeffer's understanding of the New Testament view of the church as a collective person, see Bonhoeffer, *DBWE* 1:135–9 (SC-A).
58 Bonhoeffer, *DBWE* 1:189–90. See also Bonhoeffer, *DBWE* 1:100; Bonhoeffer argues that "it is none other than Christ who 'is' the church."
59 Augustine, *Teaching Christianity* 3.31.44; 3.32.45. See also Stanislaus J. Grabowski, "Sinners and the Mystical Body of Christ according to St. Augustine," *TS* 9, no. 1 (March 1948): 49–50.
60 Augustine, *Expositions of the Psalms* (*Enarrationes in Psalmos*): *121–150*, vol. 6, *The Works of Saint Augustine: A Translation for the 21st Century*, trans. Maria Boulding (Hyde Park, NY: New City Press, 2004), 140.3.

61 Bonhoeffer, *DBWE* 1:189.
62 Bonhoeffer, *DBWE* 1:189–90.
63 Bonhoeffer, *DBWE* 1:188.
64 Bonhoeffer, *DBWE* 1:189.
65 For a detailed discussion of Bonhoeffer's prioritization of ecclesiology, see Mawson, *Christ Existing as Community*, 176–80. See also Greggs, "Proportion and Topography in Ecclesiology," 89–106. See also Webster, "In the Society of God," 203–4.
66 Bonhoeffer, *DBWE* 1:126.
67 Bonhoeffer, *DBWE* 1:107.
68 Bonhoeffer, *DBWE* 1:37, *DBWE* 1:37, n. 3.
69 Bonhoeffer, *DBWE* 1:123.
70 Bonhoeffer, *DBWE* 1:214.
71 Carl Trueman argues that "in the wake of the Enlightenment... the doctrine of original sin had become both distasteful and a matter of ridicule and consequently dropped from theological discourse." See Carl R. Trueman, "Original Sin and Modern Theology," in *Adam, the Fall, and Original Sin: Theological, Biblical, and Scientific Perspectives*, ed. Hans Madueme and Michael Reeves (Grand Rapids, MI: Baker Academic, 2014), 168–9.
72 Bonhoeffer, *DBWE* 1:58–61, emphasis added.
73 Bonhoeffer, *DBWE* 1:126.
74 Although Bonhoeffer is strongly influenced by the Lutheran renaissance theology represented by Karl Holl and Reinhold Seeberg, he rejects Holl's psychological interpretation of revelation. Bonhoeffer views Holl's psychological interpretation of Luther's theology as reducing revelation to a human possibility. Bonhoeffer contends that Holl's reductionism finally ends up in the transcendental concept of God, which does not properly deal with the act and being of God nor with the human being. See Bonhoeffer, *DBWE* 2:103–35. According to Rumscheidt, Holl and Seeberg rediscovered Luther's search for the true church and the Gospel but in a way that synthesized Lutheran and German idealism. Martin Rumscheidt, "The Formation of Bonhoeffer's Theology," in *The Cambridge Companion to Dietrich Bonhoeffer*, ed. John W. de Gruchy (New York: Cambridge University Press, 1999), 59.
75 Green, preface to *DBWE* 1:5.
76 Bonhoeffer's notion of revelation is taken from Barth, but he critiques it. Bethge states that Bonhoeffer "adopted Barth's distinction between religion used as human self-justification and faith; he corrected the use of revelation as the point of departure instead of the church. Bonhoeffer questioned whether the sequence in Barth's thought, in which he moved from revelation toward the church, didn't make the doctrine of salvation too secondary a factor. Bonhoeffer did not want a revelation cut off from its soteriological aspect." Bethge, *Dietrich Bonhoeffer*, 77. Bethge argues that, for Bonhoeffer, "Revelation is contained in Scripture because God speaks in it; that is undemonstrable—not a conclusion but a premise." Bethge, *Dietrich Bonhoeffer*, 80.
77 Karl Barth, *The Epistle to the Romans*, trans. Edwyn C. Hoskyns from the 6th ed. (New York: Oxford University Press, 2015), 10.
78 Barth, *The Epistle to the Romans*, 79.
79 Bethge, *Dietrich Bonhoeffer*, 77. See also Bonhoeffer, *DBWE* 2:90–1.
80 Charles Marsh, *Reclaiming Dietrich Bonhoeffer: The Promise of His Theology* (New York: Oxford University Press, 1994), viii. Tom Greggs adds that "one may ... wish to supplement Marsh's reading of Barth on primary and secondary objectivity by pointing to Barth's active engagement with the relation of God's primary and

secondary objectivity in his consideration of God as the one who 'loves in freedom', and in his work in the first volume of *Church Dogmatics* on revelation. ... Barth is hardly a theologian simply of so-called primary objectivity. This being said, an evolutionary progression does take place in Barth theology, which sees Barth take a more deeply Christocentric approach in his work, and an engagement with *Church Dogmatics* II/2." Tom Greggs, *Theology against Religion: Constructive Dialogues with Bonhoeffer and Barth* (London: Bloomsbury Publishing, 2011), 76. See also Andreas Pangritz, *Karl Barth in the Theology of Dietrich Bonhoeffer* (Grand Rapids, MI: Wm. B. Eerdmans, 2000), 1–2.

81 Pangritz, *Karl Barth in the Theology of Dietrich Bonhoeffer*, 1. For a detailed discussion of Bonhoeffer's Christocentrism, see the section entitled "Theological Exegesis" in Chapter 4. See also Hunsinger, "What Karl Barth Learned from Martin Luther," 129.
82 Bonhoeffer, *DBWE* 1:112 (SC-A). Augustine mainly describes the primal state of Adam only as an individual person and in reference to Adam's intellectual and physical superiority in comparison to postlapsarian humanity. See Augustine, *The City of God* 13.1.1.
83 Bonhoeffer, *DBWE* 1:112 (SC-A).
84 This does not mean that Augustine does not consider the communal level of sin or evil; it means that his primary focus on the doctrine of original sin is on the individual sinful act and then the solidarity of humanity through the biological inheritance of sin.
85 Bonhoeffer, *DBWE* 1:61 (SC-A).
86 Kolb, "The Lutheran Doctrine of Original Sin," 112.
87 Kolb, "The Lutheran Doctrine of Original Sin," 112.
88 Luther, *LW* 1:31. See Lohse, *Martin Luther's Theology*, 251. See also Dietmar Wyrwa, "Augustine and Luther on Evil," in *The Problem of Evil and Its Symbols in Jewish and Christian Tradition*, ed. Henning Graf and Yair Hoffman (London: T&T Clark International, 2004), 136–7.
89 See Augustine, *On Free Will* 3.26.71–74.
90 According to Kolb, Luther's ontological understanding "arose out of his concept that reality rests on God's Word and consists fundamentally in the relationship between each person (thing he created) and the Creator." Robert Kolb, "The Lutheran Doctrine of Original Sin," in *Adam, the Fall, and Original Sin: Theological, Biblical, and Scientific Perspectives*, ed. Hans Madueme and Michael Reeves (Grand Rapids, MI: Baker Academic, 2014), 112. See also Luther, *LW* 1:21–4, and Luther's lectures on Ps. 12:32–33.
91 Bonhoeffer, *DBWE* 1:65. Bonhoeffer cites Augustine's phrase in *De Civitate Dei* 16.2: "[Christ's] church, which is the city of God, proclaimed from the very beginning of human history." However, Bonhoeffer doubts the content of Augustine's knowledge on the primal state in regard to Augustine's methodology. See Bonhoeffer, *DBWE* 1:64, n. 1.
92 Bonhoeffer, *DBWE* 1:65.
93 Bonhoeffer, *DBWE* 1:107, emphasis in original.
94 Bonhoeffer, *DBWE* 1:107.
95 Bonhoeffer, *DBWE* 1:116–17.
96 Bonhoeffer, *DBWE* 1:118.
97 Bonhoeffer, *DBWE* 1:107. See also Reinhold Seeberg, *The History of Doctrine*, vol. 1, trans. Charles E. Hay (Philadelphia: Lutheran Publication Society, 1997), 346.

98 Bonhoeffer, *DBWE* 1:107, emphasis added.
99 Kolb, "The Lutheran Doctrine of Original Sin," 121. This is also a theological issue for Augustine.
100 Bonhoeffer, *DBWE* 1:155, 212–14.
101 Bonhoeffer, *DBWE* 1:107. See also Augustine, *On Free Will* 1.16.34, 2.19.53.
102 Bonhoeffer, *DBWE* 1:117, 146; Bonhoeffer, *DBWE* 2:58, 135; Bonhoeffer, *DBWE* 3:165. Augustine, *The City of God* 14:28. For Luther's notion of *cor curvum in se*, see Luther, *LW* 25:345; 426.
103 Bonhoeffer, *DBWE* 2:46. See also Bonhoeffer, *DBWE* 3:165.
104 Bonhoeffer, *DBWE* 1:108; Bonhoeffer, *DBWE* 2:41, 46; Bonhoeffer, *DBWE* 3:165. In regard to Bonhoeffer's concept of *cor curvum in se* or the egocentricity of the postlapsarian self, Kristen Busch Nielsen explains, "It is a turned-inside-out-representation when the individual sinful person recognizes himself or herself as sinful humanity." Kristen Busch Nielsen, "Community Turned Inside Out," in *Being Human Becoming Human: Dietrich Bonhoeffer and Social Thought*, ed. Jens Zimmermann and Brian Gregor (Eugene, OR: Pickwick Publications, 2010), 98.
105 Bonhoeffer, *DBWE* 1:115, emphasis added.
106 Bonhoeffer, *DBWE* 1:115. See also Bonhoeffer, *DBWE* 1:115, n. [14]. Augustine's description of the relationality between individual and communal acts is described through the event of stealing pears. See Augustine, *Confessions* 2.4.9–2.10.18. It is debatable whether Augustine considers the sinful collective act as the basis for every individual act. Bonhoeffer's crediting Augustine for the concept of the collective act is not clear and unambiguous because Bonhoeffer insists that Augustine's focus is solely on personal culpability in other places in *Sanctorum Communio*. See Bonhoeffer, *DBWE* 1:112 (SC-A).
107 See Reinhold Seeberg, *Dogmengeschichite*, 2:50ff, 518, and *Dogmatik*, 2:4ff, as cited in Bonhoeffer, *DBWE* 1:115, n. [14]. See also Bethge, *Dietrich Bonhoeffer*, 56–68. Clifford Green argues that "[t]he complex set of concepts he uses to explicate sociality was not simply taken over from Seeberg, but hammered out in debate with others." Green, *Bonhoeffer*, 24, n. 8.
108 Martin Rumscheidt, "Harnack, Seeberg and Bonhoeffer," in *Bonhoeffer's Intellectual Formation* (Tübingen: Mohr Siebeck, 2008), 205.
109 Bonhoeffer, *DBWE* 1:115.
110 According to Green, "Since for many people the English noun 'guilt' primarily expresses a subjective feeling, whereas Schuld refers to an objective condition, we avoid the use of the noun 'guilt.' The English adjective is closer to the German—as in the legal verdict 'guilty,' which refers to the objective judgment of a court, not to the subjective emotion of the accused." Bonhoeffer, *DBWE* 1:114, n. [12].
111 Bonhoeffer, *DBWE* 1:116.
112 Greggs, "Bearing Sin in the Church," 81.
113 Greggs, "Bearing Sin in the Church," 81, emphasis in original.
114 Bonhoeffer, *DBWE* 1:117.
115 Bonhoeffer, *DBWE* 1:116.
116 In a similar vein, Greggs argues that "original sin is, for Bonhoeffer, corporate and something for which we are co-responsible." See also Greggs, "Bearing Sin in the Church," 80.
117 G. C. Berkouwer, *Studies in Dogmatics: Sin* (Grand Rapids, MI: Wm. B. Eerdmans, 1971), 424. See also Trueman, "Original Sin and Modern Theology," 167–86. See also Chapter 1. For a detailed discussion of Augustine's doctrine of original sin and the pre-Augustinian development, see Beatrice, *The Transmission of Sin*.

118 Berkouwer, *Studies in Dogmatics: Sin*, 424. Bonhoeffer refers to other thinkers, such as Schleiermacher and Ritschl. Bonhoeffer, *DBWE* 1:114–15. For a detailed discussion of alien culpability, see Beatrice, *The Transmission of Sin*, especially the section entitled "The Essence and Transmission of Original Sin." See also McFarland, *In Adam's Fall*, 143.
119 Bonhoeffer, *DBWE* 1:114.
120 Bonhoeffer, *DBW* 1:127; Bonhoeffer, *DBWE* 1:157, 190.
121 Bonhoeffer, *DBWE* 1:145–57.
122 Bonhoeffer, *DBWE* 1, 112 (SC-A). It is controversial how to interpret Augustine's notion of the universally fallen human race as *massa pertionis*; however, it is clear that Augustine emphasized the biological aspect of human beings in his doctrine of original sin in his later career.
123 See also Bethge, *Dietrich Bonhoeffer*, 67.
124 Bonhoeffer, *DBWE* 1:114.
125 Bonhoeffer, *DBWE* 1:114.
126 However, Bonhoeffer does not ignore the individual identity when he "moves on to an ethical collective concept of the human race." He goes back to Leibniz's concept of the "monadic image" that "represents the whole world." Bonhoeffer, *DBWE* 1:116. In basic social relations, the personhood of every human being is related, even in the state of the monad. The concept of the monad has a twofold structure: closed and open. The monadic I is closed as the individual self but is open as the human race. Bonhoeffer, *DBWE* 1:79–80. In this structure, an individual person is not absorbed into a community but participates in it, keeping the boundary of the self, and the communal person does not exist abstractly but exists in its reality. Bonhoeffer, *DBWE* 1:80.
127 Bonhoeffer, *DBWE* 1:116–17.
128 It is remarkable that Bonhoeffer uses the term *sanctorum communio*, which can be interpreted as either "the communion of saints" or "the community of saints," to mean "the community of saints" following "Augustine who called the church a congregation sanctorum [community of saints]" through Seeberg's own interpretation of Augustine. Bonhoeffer, *DBWE* 1:122–3 (SC-A).
129 Bonhoeffer, *DBWE* 1:121.
130 Augustine, *The City of God* 20.9.
131 Whereas Augustine's concept of "partly righteous and sinner" represents the progressive journey of a saint toward justification, Luther's *simul iustus et peccator* signifies the struggle of a justified person. Cf. Luther, *LW* 25:66.
132 Grabowski, *The Church*, 295.
133 Bonhoeffer, *DBWE* 1:121–3.
134 Bonhoeffer, *DBWE* 1:189–90.
135 The concept of sin as power is more closely discussed in Green, *Bonhoeffer* and Nielsen, *Die Gebrochene Macht Der Sünde*. Nielsen discusses sin through the lens of sin as broken power.
136 Bonhoeffer, *DBWE* 1:189 n. 63; Luther, *LW* 42:162 (translation edited by Bonhoeffer).
137 Bonhoeffer, *DBWE* 1:189, n. 63.
138 Bonhoeffer, *DBWE* 1:120–1.
139 Bonhoeffer, *DBWE* 1:121, emphasis in original.
140 Bonhoeffer, *DBWE* 1:148.
141 Bonhoeffer, *DBWE* 1:178–92, emphasis in original. See also Nicola J. Wilkes, "Life and Health: Bonhoeffer's Normative and Divergent Accounts of Private Confession

of Sin," *TTod* 71, no. 1 (April 2014): 58–68. For a detailed discussion of "public confession of sin and repentance," see Jennifer M. McBride, *The Church for the World* (New York: Oxford University Press, 2012).

Chapter 4

1. The term *humanization* is used by Bonhoeffer instead of *incarnation*.
2. Bethge, *Dietrich Bonhoeffer*, 73.
3. According to von Balthasar, "In Barth we may find two decisive turning points. The first, his turn from liberalism to radical Christianity, occurred during the First World War and found expression in *The Epistle to Romans*. The second was his final emancipation from the shackles of philosophy. … ending in about 1930." Hans Urs von Balthasar, *The Theology of Karl Barth: Exposition and Interpretation*, trans. Edward T. Oakes (San Francisco: Ignatius Press, 1993), 93. See also Bethge, *Dietrich Bonhoeffer*, 568.
4. See also Bethge, *Dietrich Bonhoeffer*, 205.
5. Dietrich Bonhoeffer to Elizabeth Zinn from Finkenwalde, January 27, 1936 Bonhoeffer, *DBWE* 14:134.
6. de Gruchy, "Editor's Introduction to the English Edition," in Bonhoeffer, *DBWE* 3:1.
7. Bethge, *Dietrich Bonhoeffer*, 568.
8. See DeJonge, *Bonhoeffer's Reception of Luther*, 16–17.
9. DeJonge, *Bonhoeffer's Reception of Luther*, 16–17.
10. Bonhoeffer, *DBWE* 2:158.
11. Bonhoeffer, *DBWE* 2:31–2.
12. Bonhoeffer, *DBWE* 2:41.
13. Bonhoeffer, *DBWE* 2:41. See also Luther, *LW* 25:332, 345.
14. Bonhoeffer, *DBWE* 2:28.
15. Bonhoeffer, *DBWE* 2:28–32.
16. Bonhoeffer, *DBWE* 2:31–2, 137. See also Eva Harasta, "Adam in Christ? The Place of Sin in Christ-Reality," in *Christ, Church, and World: New Studies in Bonhoeffer's Theology and Ethics* (London: Bloomsbury T&T Clark, 2016), 61–75.
17. Bonhoeffer, *DBWE* 2:33.
18. Bonhoeffer later summarizes this point in a letter to *Rüdiger Schleicher* on April 8, 1936: "Every other place outside the Bible has become too uncertain for me. There I am always afraid of encountering merely my own divine *Doppelgänger*." Bonhoeffer, *DBWE* 14:169.
19. Bonhoeffer, *DBWE* 2:159.
20. Bonhoeffer, *DBWE* 2:31.
21. Dietrich Bonhoeffer to *Rüdiger Schleicher*, April 8, 1936, in Bonhoeffer, *DBWE* 14:169.
22. Bonhoeffer distinguished *act theology* from *transcendental theology* in *Act and Being*. He designated any philosophical understanding of theology without engaging with the revelation of God in Christ as transcendental theology and act-theology as the reverse.
23. Bonhoeffer, *DBWE* 2:28.
24. Bonhoeffer, *DBWE* 2:144–61.
25. See de Gruchy, "Editor's Introduction to the English Edition," in Bonhoeffer, *DBWE* 3:5–6.

26 Harnack to Bonhoeffer, December 22, 1929 in Bonhoeffer, *DBWE* 10:196–7.
27 See also Martin Rüter and Ilse Tödt, "Editors' Afterword to the German Edition," in Bonhoeffer, *DBWE* 3:152; Bethge, *Dietrich Bonhoeffer*, 62. Bethge describes two theological streams in Germany led by Harnack and Barth in the 1920s. However, even though Bonhoeffer claims to use his own way in his theological exegesis, he does not ignore historical criticism in his interpretation of Scripture.
28 Bethge, *Dietrich Bonhoeffer*, 62.
29 Bonhoeffer, *DBWE* 14:418.
30 Bonhoeffer, *DBWE* 2:158.
31 DeJonge, *Bonhoeffer's Reception of Luther*, 17.
32 Bonhoeffer, *DBWE* 9:291.
33 Bethge, *Dietrich Bonhoeffer*, 67–8. See also Martin Rumscheidt, "Harnack, Seeberg and Bonhoeffer," in Frick, *Bonhoeffer's Intellectual Formation*: 211.
34 Rumscheidt, "Harnack, Seeberg and Bonhoeffer," 211.
35 Rumscheidt, "Harnack, Seeberg and Bonhoeffer," 212.
36 Bonhoeffer, *DBWE* 2:23, n. [11], emphasis in original.
37 See Rüter and Tödt, "Editors' Afterword to the German Edition," in Bonhoeffer, *DBWE* 3:151–3.
38 de Gruchy, "Editor's Introduction," in Bonhoeffer, *DBWE* 3:6–7. See also Bonhoeffer's treatment of the relationship between science and Scripture, Bonhoeffer, *DBWE* 3:50–1; Bonhoeffer says, "The ancient image of the world confronts us in all its scientific naïveté. …. In view of the rapid changes in our own knowledge of nature, a derisive attitude that is too sure of itself is not exactly advisable here; nevertheless in this passage the biblical author is exposed as one whose knowledge is bound by all the limitations of the author's own time."
39 See Rüter and Tödt, "Editors' Afterword to the German Edition," in Bonhoeffer, *DBWE* 3:152.
40 Bonhoeffer, *DBWE* 3:50.
41 Bonhoeffer, *DBWE* 3:21.
42 Bonhoeffer, *DBWE* 3:21–2. Bonhoeffer accepted the Old Testament as Christian Scripture. The most extreme German Christians rejected the Old Testament as the Scripture of Judaism.
43 Bethge, *Dietrich Bonhoeffer*, 568. Bethge states that "in 1925 in Berlin, the stronghold of historical-critical research under Seeberg, he had tackled the problem of historical and 'pneumatic' interpretation, following the direction taken by Karl Barth." However, one should note that Bonhoeffer does not totally refute the historical-critical method. See Bonhoeffer, *DBWE* 9:286, 14:419.
44 Bonhoeffer, *DBWE* 14:421–2.
45 Bonhoeffer, *DBWE* 3:21.
46 DeJonge, *Bonhoeffer's Reception of Luther*, 16–18.
47 Bethge, *Dietrich Bonhoeffer*, 568.
48 As Michael P. DeJonge explains, sometimes it is hard to separate Bonhoeffer's own interpretation of Luther from the thinking of other interpreters. However, an interpretation is considered to be Bonhoeffer's interpretation of Luther whenever Bonhoeffer claims it to be from Luther. See DeJonge, *Bonhoeffer's Reception of Luther*, 18, n.13.
49 Hunsinger, "What Karl Barth Learned from Martin Luther," 128. Hunsinger argues that Barth finally appropriated Luther's rather than Schleiermacher's Christocentrism. He states that "the real christocentrism that Barth absorbed was not finally

Schleiermacher's but Luther's. Schleiermacher's christocentrism can be distinguished from Luther's primarily by its strongly formal tendency. Schleiermacher's theology, we might say, was formally but not substantively Christocentric." See Hunsinger, "What Karl Barth Learned from Martin Luther," 129.
50 Hunsinger, "What Karl Barth Learned from Martin Luther," 128.
51 Bethge, *Dietrich Bonhoeffer*, 568.
52 Bonhoeffer explains that his "theological exegesis" was derived from the viewpoint of Christ. Bonhoeffer, *DBWE* 3:22.
53 Bonhoeffer, *DBWE* 1:222.
54 Bonhoeffer, *DBWE* 3:21.
55 Bonhoeffer, *DBWE* 3:21.
56 Bonhoeffer, *DBWE* 3:21.
57 Bonhoeffer, *DBWE* 3:23.
58 Bonhoeffer wrote the introduction and the preface to *Creation and Fall* for the 1933 edition after his lecture at the University of Berlin. See Bonhoeffer, *DBWE* 3:23, n. [11].
59 Bonhoeffer, *DBWE* 3:23.
60 Bonhoeffer, *DBWE* 3:22.
61 Bonhoeffer, *DBWE* 3:22.
62 Bonhoeffer, *DBWE* 3:25, emphasis in original.
63 In regard to *crede, ut intelligas*, Augustine states, "Do not seek to understand in order to believe, but believe that thou mayest understand; since, 'except ye believe, ye shall not understand.'" Augustine, *Homilies on the Gospel of John 1–40*, 29.6. Anselm of Canterbury later appropriated Augustine's phrase, saying "*credo ut intelligam*" (I believe so that I may understand) in his *Proslogion* 1.
64 Bonhoeffer, *DBWE* 14:169, n. [13].
65 Bonhoeffer, *DBWE* 14:169. This quote is from Bonhoeffer's April 8, 1936, letter to his brother-in-law Rüdiger Schleicher. In this letter, Bonhoeffer explains his way of reading the Bible. See also Rüter and Tödt, "Editors' Afterword to the German Edition," in Bonhoeffer, *DBWE* 3:153–4.
66 Bonhoeffer, *DBWE* 3:21.
67 See Bonhoeffer, *DBWE* 3:25, n. [2].
68 In regard to the "inconsistent triad," see the section entitled "The Problem of Evil" in ch. 1.
69 Bonhoeffer, *DBWE* 3:26–7.
70 Holl considered the experience of Luther the central element of Luther's theology, especially in his doctrine of justification. See DeJonge, *Bonhoeffer's Reception of Luther*, 21–2.
71 Bethge, *Dietrich Bonhoeffer*, 568. See ch. 2. See also Rüter and Tödt, "Editors' Afterword to the German Edition," in Bonhoeffer, *DBWE* 3:154–5.
72 Bonhoeffer, *DBWE* 3:26.
73 See Bonhoeffer, *DBWE* 3:25, n. [1].
74 Bonhoeffer, *DBWE* 3:32. See also de Gruchy, "Editor's Introduction to the English Edition," in Bonhoeffer, *DBWE* 3:32, n. [24].
75 Bonhoeffer, *DBWE* 3:31.
76 Bonhoeffer, *DBWE* 3:28–9.
77 Bonhoeffer, *DBWE* 3:29.
78 Bonhoeffer, *DBWE* 3:34–5.
79 Bonhoeffer, *DBWE* 3:34.

80   Bonhoeffer, *DBWE* 3:33.
81   Bonhoeffer, *DBWE* 3:35.
82   In this regard, Philip G. Ziegler's comment is noteworthy. He states that "Bonhoeffer suggests that in as much as theological ethics aims to be realistic, it must always treat of human being 'in Adam' and 'in Christ' rather than aspiring after an abstract account of human being 'in Eden.'" Philip G. Ziegler "'Completely within God's Doing': Soteriology as Meta-Ethics in the Theology of Dietrich Bonhoeffer," in *Christ, Church, and World: New Studies in Bonhoeffer's Theology and Ethics* (London: Bloomsbury T&T Clark, 2016), 107.
83   According to the editor's note, *Grenze* and its cognates are also translated as "'limit or boundedness,' 'limit or constraint,' 'limitedness and unlimitedness.'" See Bonhoeffer, *DBWE* 3:845, n. [15].
84   In regard to "conceptual pairs," see Ernst Feil, *The Theology of Dietrich Bonhoeffer*, trans. Martin Rumscheidt (Minneapolis: Fortress Press, 1985), 30.
85   Bonhoeffer, *DBWE* 3:84.
86   Bonhoeffer, *DBWE* 3:84.
87   Bonhoeffer, *DBWE* 3:84, emphasis added.
88   Similar to Bonhoeffer's treatment of Adam and Eve or the first humanity, Irenaeus treats Adam and Eve as infants or youths. Irenaeus, *Epideixis*, in *On the Apostolic Preaching*, trans. John Behr (Crestwood, NY: St. Vladimirs Seminary Press, 1997), 12.
89   Bonhoeffer, *DBWE* 3:83.
90   See Bonhoeffer, *DBWE* 3:88, n. 23. The note says, "*tob* and *ra* are Hebrew words, each having a range of meanings. *Tob* means 'good, pleasing, pleasant, delightful, delicious, happy, glad, joyful,' while *ra* means 'bad, evil, disagreeable, displeasing, unpleasant, harmful.'"
91   Jennifer M. McBride and Thomas Fabisiak, "Bonhoeffer's Critique of Morality: A Theological Resource for Dismantling Mass Incarceration," in *Deitrich Bonhoeffer, Theology, and Political Resistance*, ed. Lori Brandt Hale and W. David Hall (Lanham, MD: Lexington Books, 2020), 95.
92   Bonhoeffer, *DBWE* 3:107.
93   Bonhoeffer, *DBWE* 3:107.
94   In regard to Bonhoeffer's notion of morality, see McBride and Fabisiak, "Bonhoeffer's Critique of Morality," 89–109.
95   Bonhoeffer, *DBWE* 3:117.
96   Bonhoeffer, *DBWE* 3:117.
97   Bonhoeffer, *DBWE* 3:117, emphasis in original.
98   Bonhoeffer, *DBWE* 3:89.
99   Bonhoeffer, *DBWE* 3:89.
100 Bonhoeffer, *DBWE* 8:37–52.
101 Bonhoeffer, *DBWE* 3:65.
102 Bonhoeffer, *DBWE* 3:34.
103 Bonhoeffer, *DBWE* 3:64–5, emphasis in original.
104 Bonhoeffer, *DBWE* 3:27.
105 Barth, *The Epistle to the Romans*, 12.
106 Lohse, *Martin Luther's Theology*, 241.
107 Bonhoeffer, *DBWE* 3:65.
108 According to an editor's note, "Karl Barth in his doctrine of creation, which he began to set forth in the summer semester of 1942, took over from Bonhoeffer the idea of the *analogia relationis* as the key to understanding the image of God." Bonhoeffer,

DBWE 3:65, n. [22]. Clifford Green also points out that "*Schöpfung und Fall* was the first of Bonhoeffer's books which Karl Barth read. Although Barth had reservations about some of the exposition, he appropriated Bonhoeffer's concept of the *analogia relationis*; cf. *Church Dogmatics* (Edinburgh: T&T Clark) III/1 especially pp. 194ff., III/2, III/3. Barth used the *analogia relationis* to develop his formulation of the *analogia fidei* with which he had replaced the *analogia entis* of natural theology." Green, *Bonhoeffer*, 192–3, n. 19.

109 DeJonge, *Bonhoeffer's Reception of Luther*, 30, emphasis added.
110 See Robert W. Jenson, *Systematic Theology*, vol. 2 (New York: Oxford University Press, 2001), 55.
111 Jenson, *Systematic Theology*, 2:54–5. Jenson also discusses whether other rational creatures, including angels or Satan as well as other animals, retain the image of God.
112 Bonhoeffer distinguishes between *creatio continua* and the *upholding of creation*. He argues that the concept of *creatio continua* "deprives God's creatorship of its utter freedom and uniqueness." Bonhoeffer, *DBWE* 3:46–7, emphasis in original.
113 Bonhoeffer, *DBWE* 3:66.
114 See David H. Kelsey, *Eccentric Existence: A Theological Anthropology* (Louisville, KY: John Knox Press, 2009). See also Ian A. McFarland, *Difference and Identity: A Theological Anthropology* (Cleveland: Pilgrim, 2001).
115 Bonhoeffer, *DBWE* 3:66.
116 Bonhoeffer, *DBWE* 3:74, Bonhoeffer interprets Gen. 2:7: "Then Yahweh God fashioned *humankind* out of dust from the ground, and blew into its nose the breath of life; so the human being became a living being" (emphasis added). Cf. "Then the LORD God formed *man* of dust from the ground, and breathed into his nostrils the breath of life; and the man became a living being" (Gen. 2:7, emphasis added).
117 See Hilde Pfeiffer and Ferenc Lehel's notes on Bonhoeffer's 1932–3 lectures in Bonhoeffer, *DBWE* 3:79, n. [21].
118 For Augustine, Adam signifies simultaneously a man and a representative of the human race. In this regard, see the section entitled "Later Hamartiology" in Chapter 1, especially pp. 51–2. See Augustine, *The City of God* 13.1, 13.20; Augustine, *The Literal Meaning of Genesis* 9.12.20.
119 Bonhoeffer, *DBWE* 3:71.
120 Bonhoeffer, *DBWE* 3:79.
121 Bonhoeffer, *DBWE* 3:72, emphasis in original.
122 Bonhoeffer's Christocentric or ecclesiocentric hermeneutics is expressed in his inclusion of Christ in paradise.
123 Bonhoeffer, *DBWE* 3:83.
124 Bonhoeffer, *DBWE* 3:83.
125 Bonhoeffer's approach to hermeneutics requires careful attention. In Bonhoeffer's 1936 article "Contemporizing New Testament Texts," he warns against contemporizing biblical texts from the standpoint of the present situation. One example of this, Bonhoeffer suggests, is the case of Adolf von Harnack's distinction between the eternal kernel and the temporal husk. He argues that the whole Bible is the witness of Christ. For Bonhoeffer, the standpoint of the present means that it is the standpoint of the revelation of Christ by which the present circumstances should be interpreted and not vice versa. Bonhoeffer, *DBWE* 14:413–33. See also Bonhoeffer, *DBWE* 9:285–300 for his criticism of historical-critical exegesis. On the other hand, Bonhoeffer rejects Rudolf Bultmann's concept of the New Testament

as the mythologization of a universal truth by arguing that it is a way of "reducing Christianity to its 'essence.'" See Bonhoeffer, *DBWE* 8:430.
126 Bonhoeffer, *DBWE* 3:84.
127 Bonhoeffer, *DBWE* 3:84.
128 Bonhoeffer, *DBWE* 3:84.
129 Bonhoeffer, *DBWE* 3:84, emphasis in original.
130 Bonhoeffer views his Lutheran tradition as ultimately the perspective of Luther. As DeJonge argues, however, there always has been the possibility that Bonhoeffer's reception of Luther's theology is not identical to Luther's own theology. Bonhoeffer's reading of Luther is influenced by his theological education under his Lutheran teachers. See DeJonge, *Bonhoeffer's Reception of Luther*, 6–8.
131 Green, *Bonhoeffer*, 192.
132 See Bonhoeffer, *DBWE* 3:79, n. [21].
133 Bonhoeffer, *DBWE* 3:71.
134 Bonhoeffer, *DBWE* 3:95. Bonhoeffer says, "After the tree of knowledge comes the creation of the woman, and finally it is the serpent that leads to the act of grasping at the tree of knowledge and of life."
135 Bonhoeffer, *DBWE* 3:95, n. [5]. According to Ferenc Lehel's notes, Bonhoeffer says, "'It is superficial reasoning to take this as a basis for speaking about marriage as an order of creation.'" However, it is controversial whether Bonhoeffer's rejection of marriage and family as the order of creation signifies that he treated the female as an equal partner in marital relations. In his wedding sermon for Eberhard and Renate Bethge, he supported the man's headship of the family. Bonhoeffer, *DBWE* 8:83.
136 Bonhoeffer, *DBWE* 3:95, n. [5].
137 For example, despite Luther's affirmation of the ontological equality of Eve as *imago Dei* in his Genesis exegesis, he consistently interprets the female's role within the boundary of her marital status, neglecting the female's calling in Christ beyond her marital status. Luther, *LW* 1:115. According to the editor's note, "Luther had maintained that marriage or the family (like the state) is a natural order of creation that confronts us with ethical obligations[;] some German Protestants used the concept to justify nationalist and even National Socialist ideas about the demands of the nation or even the race." Bonhoeffer, *DBWE* 3:95, n. [5].
138 This theme reflects Bonhoeffer's critique of the German Evangelical Church constitution's exclusion of Jews from theological study under the influence of the Aryan paragraph. See Bonhoeffer, "The Jewish-Christian Question as *Status Confessionis*," in Bonhoeffer, *DBWE* 12:371–3.
139 Bonhoeffer, *DBWE* 3:96.
140 Bonhoeffer, *DBWE* 3:96.
141 It is controversial whether Bonhoeffer always sees Adam as the I and Eve as the other. However, here it is appropriate to perceive that in Bonhoeffer's intention, Adam represents the I and Eve the other and that these representations are supposed to be interchangeable at the level of human relationality. The problem of interchangeability between the I and the other in Bonhoeffer's theology is discussed in Chapters 5 and 6.
142 Bonhoeffer, *DBWE* 3:122–3. Bonhoeffer differentiated sexuality in two ways in German, as either *Geschlechtlichkeit* and *Sexualität*, designating the former as prelapsarian human relationality and the latter as postlapsarian relationality. This theme is dealt with in detail in the following section.

143 Bonhoeffer, *DBWE* 3:97.
144 However, Bonhoeffer does not intend that the communal personalism continued from *Sanctorum Communio* should reject the identity of individuals. Bonhoeffer, *DBWE* 3:98.
145 Bonhoeffer, *DBWE* 3:98.
146 Bonhoeffer, *DBWE* 3:99, emphasis added.
147 See Green, *Bonhoeffer*, 196.
148 Bonhoeffer, *DBWE* 3:99.
149 See Bonhoeffer, *DBWE* 3:23, n. [11]; Erich Klapproth notes that Bonhoeffer states, "one must read it word for word [*buchstabieren*] like a child and learn to rethink completely what the historical critical commentaries teach us. .... For *us* the word of God always lies hidden like a treasure in a field [Matt. 13:44]." Emphasis in original.
150 Bonhoeffer states, "Yet both [the first and the second accounts of the creation] are only human works, childlike but humble words, about the same God and the same humankind." Bonhoeffer, *DBWE* 3:72.
151 One may argue that this also reflects the influence of Barth's emphasis on the transcendent work of God.
152 However, cautious attention must be paid to the primary intention of his exegesis. It is clear that Bonhoeffer's collective personalism is not meant to argue for the equality of male and female but to treat humankind as a community in order to understand humankind in its sinful universality and co-responsibility in the relationality of the I and the other.
153 Bonhoeffer, *DBWE* 3:119. See Harnack, *History of Dogma*, 5:215–16. Bonhoeffer refuted the Augustinian doctrine of predestination. Bonhoeffer, *DBWE* 1:163. Harvey states that "he [Bonhoeffer] claims that Augustine's doctrine of election, and in particular the concept of the *numerus praedestinatorum*, the number of the predestined, acts as a solvent that tends to dissolve the church-community into the set number of predestined individuals." Harvey, "Augustine and Aquinas," in *Intellectual Formation of Bonhoeffer's Theology*, 13.
154 Bonhoeffer, *DBWE* 3:119.
155 Bonhoeffer, *DBWE* 3:119.
156 Bonhoeffer, *DBWE* 3:119, emphasis added.
157 Bonhoeffer, *DBWE* 1:108; Bonhoeffer, *DBWE* 2:41, 46; Bonhoeffer, *DBWE* 3:165.
158 Greggs, "Bearing Sin in the Church," 80–1.
159 Bonhoeffer, *DBWE* 3:119.
160 Bonhoeffer, *DBWE* 3:117. "They themselves stand in the center. This is disobedience in the semblance of obedience, the desire to rule in the semblance of service, the will to be creator in the semblance of being a creature." It is controversial whether prideful self-assertion is the essence of the first or primary sin. Many feminist thinkers have identified pride or power as the male's sinful experience rather than the female's sinful experience.
161 Bonhoeffer, *DBWE* 3:103–10. In similar way to Augustine and Luther, Bonhoeffer interprets the role of the devil or the serpent in Eden as a deceiver or a tempter rather than a main influence on humanity's first sin. Until this theological stage, Bonhoeffer's discussion of the role of Satan or the devil with respect to the sin of humanity in real life is not conspicuous. In this regard, Philip G. Ziegler's comment is noteworthy. Ziegler argues, "Downstream from Schleiermacher's pronouncement, contemporary treatments of the doctrine of sin by leading Reformed theologians

very rarely afford the devil any real role in relation to their theme." Philip G. Ziegler, "'Bound Over to Satan's Tyranny': Sin and Satan in Contemporary Reformed Hamartiology," *TTod* 75, no. 1 (2018): 91. Although Ziegler's argument is closely related to that of the Reformed theologians, this hamartiological view is no different from that of many modern Lutheran theologians (e.g., Karl Holl, Reinhold Seeberg, Adolf von Harnack), including early Bonhoeffer, who focuses more on the social relationality of postlapsarian persons (as demonstrated in *Sanctorum Communio* and *Act and Being*). Clearly, Bonhoeffer's description of the devil and Satan in his early works is not closely associated with real-life situations; however, the theme of the devil or radical evil is strongly evident in his later and prison works in both direct and indirect ways.

162 David G. Hunter, "Augustine on the Body," in *A Companion to Augustine*, ed. Mark Vessey and Shelley Reid, Blackwell Companions to the Ancient World (Chichester, UK: Wiley-Blackwell, 2012), 357.
163 Bonhoeffer, *DBWE* 1:114. See McFarland, *In Adam's Fall*, 143. See also Berkouwer, *Studies in Dogmatics: Sin*, 424.
164 Bonhoeffer, *DBWE* 3:120.
165 Bonhoeffer, *DBWE* 3:120, emphasis added.
166 Green, *Bonhoeffer*, 232. Green interprets Bonhoeffer as follows: "Unlike humanity, it [nature] is not under guilt, and therefore does not need reconciliation; but it does need to be delivered from its bondage so that it is 'freed to a new freedom' for God and for humanity."
167 Bonhoeffer, *DBWE* 1:111 (SC-A). See Harnack, *History of Dogma*, 5:75.
168 See Bonhoeffer, *DBWE* 1:112 (SC-A). Bonhoeffer briefly comments that "one must acknowledge that, besides the mass, another concept has been added here that could be called that of the realm of ethical persons." It seems that Bonhoeffer's comment on "mass" is expressing only the basic biological aspect of the human species rather than its sinful solidarity.
169 Harasta, "Adam in Christ?" 62.
170 Harnack interprets Augustine's concept of concupiscence as physical desire alone rather than as both spiritual and physical. However, Harnack's assessment of Augustine's understanding of concupiscence (not even considering Augustine's own identification with concupiscence) is one of many interpretations of Augustine.
171 Rüter and Tödt, "Editors' Afterword to the German Edition," in Bonhoeffer, *DBWE* 3: 125.
172 Bonhoeffer, *DBWE* 3:100.
173 Bonhoeffer, *DBWE* 3:100 (*DBW* 3:94).
174 Bonhoeffer, *DBW* 3:94 (*DBWE* 3:100).
175 See Michael Brain, "Sexuality and Community in the Theology of Dietrich Bonhoeffer," *SJT* 71, no. 1 (2018): 77–8.
176 Bonhoeffer, *DBWE* 1:64.
177 Bonhoeffer, *DBWE* 3:121. "The end of God's way is bodily existence." A similar expression is found in Friedrich Christoph Oetinger: "the end of God's ways/works." See *DBWE* 3:121, n. [3].
178 See Bonhoeffer, *DBWE* 3:121, n. [3]. A similar expression appears in "Elizabeth Zinn's doctoral dissertation that appeared in 1932, *Die Theologie des Friedrich Christoph Oetinger*: 'Bodily existence [corporeality] is the end of God's ways.'"
179 Bonhoeffer, *DBWE* 3:122 (*DBW* 3:114–15).
180 Bonhoeffer, *DBWE* 3:122 (*DBW* 3:114–15).

181 It is important to carefully distinguish the term *Geschlechtlichen* from *Geschlechtlichkeit*. Bonhoeffer uses the latter to describe the prelapsarian human relationality between Adam and Eve as well as the I and the other. The German term *Geschlechtlichen* is the neuter, second declension noun form of the adjective *geschlechtlich*, which means "sexual." The term *Geschlechtlichen* is more closely associated with the term *Sexualität* in Bonhoeffer's usage in *Creation and Fall*.
182 Bonhoeffer, *DBWE* 3:122. See Rüter and Tödt, "Editors' Afterword to the German Edition," in Bonhoeffer, *DBWE* 3: 171.
183 Bonhoeffer, *DBWE* 3:122.
184 Bonhoeffer, *DBWE* 3:123 (*DBW* 3:115–16).
185 Bonhoeffer, *DBWE* 3:123.
186 However, many feminist thinkers criticize Bonhoeffer for continuing to interpret women from a patriarchal and androcentric framework.
187 Bonhoeffer generalizes Adam and Eve as "the I and the other" to universalize the relationality of the human being in regard to hamartiological issues embedded in the doctrine of original sin. This still contains a controversial aspect, however, because Bonhoeffer always uses Adam, which implies a male characteristic for the I, and thus Eve implies a female characteristic for the other. This has the possibility of alienating women in his theological discussions in which the woman is always identified the object of the I or the limit rather than the subject or the center.
188 Bonhoeffer, *DBWE* 3:121.
189 Bonhoeffer, *DBWE* 3:123.
190 Bonhoeffer's understanding of the concupiscence of Augustine in *Sanctorum Communio* is biological, following Adolf von Harnack's interpretation.
191 Michael Brain, "Sexuality and Community in the Theology of Dietrich Bonhoeffer," *SJT* 71, no. 1 (2018): 67–84.
192 Rüter and Tödt, "Editors' Afterword to the German Edition," in Bonhoeffer, *DBWE* 3:150–1, and n. [11].
193 See Rüter and Tödt, "Editors' Afterword to the German Edition," in Bonhoeffer, *DBWE* 3: 151.
194 Bonhoeffer, *DBWE* 3:79, emphasis added.
195 See Bonhoeffer, "Lectures on Christology," in Bonhoeffer, *DBWE* 12:299–360.
196 Bonhoeffer, *DBWE* 3:78 (*DBW* 3:73).
197 Bonhoeffer, *DBWE* 3:79.
198 Bonhoeffer, *DBWE* 3:123.
199 Bonhoeffer, *DBWE* 3:123.
200 Bonhoeffer, *DBWE* 3:123.
201 Bonhoeffer, *DBWE* 3:124.
202 Bonhoeffer, *DBWE* 3:124–5.
203 Bonhoeffer, *DBWE* 3:124, n. [14].
204 Bonhoeffer, *DBWE* 3:124, n. [14].
205 Bonhoeffer, *DBWE* 14:733.
206 Bonhoeffer, *DBWE* 10:196–7.
207 Adolf Hitler was appointed Reich Chancellor on January 30, 1933. Two days after this, Bonhoeffer commented in a broadcast on the potential danger of Hitler's gaining power without naming him, saying, "If the leader tries to become the idol the led are looking for—something the led always hope from their leader—then the image of leader shifts to one of a misleader." Bonhoeffer, *DBWE* 12:280.

208 See Bonhoeffer, *DBWE* 10:356–7. Early in his stay in Barcelona, Bonhoeffer "emphatically rejected humanism along with mysticism and cultural Protestantism for their euphoria about human achievement and their confidence in the ability of men and women to reach God in their own strength." John W. de Gruchy, "Dietrich Bonhoeffer as Christian Humanist," in *Being Human, Becoming Human: Dietrich Bonhoeffer and Social Thought*, ed. Jens Zimmermann and Brian Gregor (Eugene, OR: Pickwick Publications, 2010), 7.

209 Bonhoeffer, *DBWE* 3:12. One example is the Lutheran theologian Paul Althaus, who understood the German race and nation as part of God's created order and law in his pamphlet entitled *Theologie der Ordnungen*. See Bonhoeffer, *DBWE* 3:12, n. [37]. Bonhoeffer rejects the doctrine of the "order of creation," which potentially contains a discriminatory concept of race. His rejection of the order of creation reflects his early experience of encountering diverse cultures beyond Germany. He traveled through many countries before writing *Creation and Fall*. However, as de Gruchy describes, Bonhoeffer clearly distinguishes himself from secular humanism. See de Gruchy, "Dietrich Bonhoeffer as Christian Humanist," 24.

210 See DeJonge, *Bonhoeffer's Reception of Luther*, 6–15.

211 See Christiane Tietz, *Theologian of Resistance: The Life and Thought of Dietrich Bonhoeffer*, trans. Victoria J. Barnett (Minneapolis: Fortress, 2016), 31.

212 Harasta, "Adam in Christ?" 62.

213 Bonhoeffer, *DBWE* 1:62.

214 de Gruchy, "Editor's Introduction to the English Edition," in Bonhoeffer, *DBWE* 3: 1–12.

Chapter 5

1 In recent decades, feminist theologians have claimed the insufficiencies of a one-sided account of sin. For example, Rosemary Radford Reuther suggests, "Sin has to be seen both in the capacity to set up prideful, antagonistic relations to others and in the passivity of men and women who acquiesce to the group ego." Rosemary Radford Reuther, *Sexism and God-Talk: Toward a Feminist Theology* (Boston: Beacon, 1983), 164.

2 Bonhoeffer uses the expression *Menschwerdung* (becoming human) rather than *Inkarnation* (incarnation) to emphasize God's becoming human.

3 In this regard, classical feminist thinkers such as Valerie Saiving and Daphne Hampson argue that traditional concepts such as "pride" or "egocentricity" do not represent the female's sinful experience. See Valerie Saiving, "The Human Situation: A Feminine View," in *Womanspirit Rising*, 2nd ed., ed. Carol P. Christ and Judith Plaskow (San Francisco: HarperCollins, 1992), 30–1. Then, Judith Plaskow published her dissertation entitled *Sex, Sin and Grace: Women's Experience and the Theologies of Reinhold Niebuhr and Paul Tillich* based on Saiving's essay published in 1980. In 1990, Daphne Hampson also criticized Reinhold Niebuhr's appropriation of the Lutheran concept of the sinful self in pride in relation to the distorted social structure represented by patriarchy in her *Theology and Feminism*. See Daphne Hampson, *Theology and Feminism* (Cambridge, MA: Basil Blackwell, 1990), 122. For a more detailed discussion of feminist theology and related issues, see Rachel Muers, "Feminism, Gender, and

Theology," in *The Modern Theologians: An Introduction to Christian Theology since 1918*, 3rd ed., ed. David F. Ford and Rachel Muers (Oxford: Blackwell Publishing, 2005), 431–50. See also Rachel Muers and Mike Higton, *Modern Theology: A Critical Introduction* (London: Routledge, 2012), 277–98.

4   The need to include the perspectives of all human beings in Christian theology is a foundational claim of feminist theologians. Among many theological loci, hamartiology is one of the main areas that feminist theologians have claimed for reflecting the perspectives of women as equal members of the human race. In this regard, Rachel Muers's comment is significant. Muers argues, "I refer to the claim that 'the Gospel is good news for women as well as men' (which is in Christian terms part of saying that 'women are human beings')." Rachel Muers, "Feminist Theology as Practice of the Future," *FemTh* 16, no. 1 (September 2007): 111. In a similar vein, mainstream liberation theology emerged in Latin America during the 1950s and 1960s within the Catholic church. The major concern of liberation theology is the "social injustice" and "poverty" caused by an inequal social structure. Liberation theology understands "God as manifest in the poor of history." Chopp and Regan, "Latin American Liberation Theology," 469. For a detailed discussion of liberation theology, see Chopp and Regan, "Latin American Liberation Theology," 469–84. See also Gustavo Gutierrez, *The Power of the Poor in History* (Maryknoll, NY: Orbis Books, 1983).

5   Bonhoeffer, *DBWE* 8:37–52.
6   Bonhoeffer, *DBWE* 1:107, 114.
7   Green, *Bonhoeffer*, 48–52.
8   Green, *Bonhoeffer*, 111.
9   Bonhoeffer, *DBWE* 1:77, 112 (SC-A).
10 Bonhoeffer, *DBWE* 1:107–8.
11 Bonhoeffer, *DBWE* 8:37.
12 Bonhoeffer, *DBWE* 8:37.
13 Bonhoeffer, *DBWE* 8:38.
14 Bonhoeffer, *DBWE* 8:38.
15 In Bonhoeffer's early works, such as *Sanctorum Communio* and *Act and Being*, the theme of Satan or the devil does not appear, but in his later period this theme is evident in association with the evil power of the state or Nazism. The editors of *DBWE* 4 argue that "Bonhoeffer's ire shaped the harsh rhetoric with which he described what he sensed was a lethal combat between the forces of Christ and those of Satan." Bonhoeffer clearly revived Luther's notion of Satan as a tempter or a deceiver in his present life situation along with Germany's political circumstances in his later career. Geffrey B. Kelly and John D. Godsey, "Editors' Introduction to the English Edition," in Bonhoeffer, *DBWE* 4:20. In his later works, Bonhoeffer's concern with the supra-individual or communal aspect of sin is associated with his use of terms such as "Satan," "the devil," and "evil." See Bonhoeffer, *DBWE* 8:24, 302; Bonhoeffer, *DBWE* 15:320, 388; Bonhoeffer, *DBWE* 16:207, 590, 605.
16 Bonhoeffer, *DBWE* 8:38–9.
17 Bonhoeffer, *DBWE* 8:38–9.
18 Bonhoeffer, *DBWE* 8:38–9.
19 Bonhoeffer, *DBWE* 3:109–10.
20 Bonhoeffer, *DBWE* 3:110.

21 Kathryn Greene-McCreight, "Gender, Sin and Grace: Feminist Theologies Meet Karl Barth's Hamartiology," *SJT* 50, no. 4 (1997): 419–20. In regard to the issue of passivity, Rachel Muers's creative reworking of the concept of "silence" (which can be treated as an expression of passivity) is noteworthy. Muers suggests that "silence" (as an act of listening or an ethics of communication) is one of essential characteristics of a Christian person. She argues that silences need to be understood "as occasions, not as condemnation or the defense of their author, but for listening to the texts in a way that takes them 'beyond' themselves." Rachel Muers, *Keeping God's Silence: Towards a Theological Ethics of Communication* (Oxford: Blackwell Publishing, 2004), 16.
22 Bonhoeffer, *DBWE* 3:110.
23 Bonhoeffer, *DBWE* 8:39–41.
24 In this respect, Lisa E. Dahill points out, the lack of attention paid to this passive side of the self is closely related to the danger of a naive application of Bonhoeffer's doctrine of self-sacrifice or self-giving by which those who are in the position of the powerless continue being submissive to those who are in power without recognizing the self's original dignity as the image of God. Lisa E. Dahill, *Reading from the Underside of the Self: Bonhoeffer and Spiritual Formation*, Princeton Theological Monograph Series, vol. 95 (Eugene, OR: Wipf & Stock, 2009), 5.
25 It may be controversial to claim that Bonhoeffer liberated himself from the frame of gender in his later period, but it does point to the more archetypal structure of Bonhoeffer's theological anthropology in his later understanding of the postlapsarian self's incurvature. For a more detailed discussion of this theme, see Chapter 6.
26 See Dahill, *Reading from the Underside of the Selfhood*, 5–6.
27 Bonhoeffer, *DBWE* 8:39–40.
28 Bonhoeffer, *DBWE* 8:39–40.
29 Bonhoeffer, *DBWE* 8:39.
30 Bonhoeffer, *DBWE* 8:39.
31 Bonhoeffer, *DBWE* 8:43.
32 Bonhoeffer, *DBWE* 8:51.
33 Bonhoeffer, *DBWE* 8:39.
34 Bonhoeffer, *DBWE* 8:39.
35 Bonhoeffer, *DBWE* 8:40.
36 Bonhoeffer, *DBWE* 8:39–40.
37 Bonhoeffer, *DBWE* 8:40.
38 Bonhoeffer, *DBWE* 8:40.
39 Bonhoeffer, *DBWE* 8:43.
40 On the one hand, in *Creation and Fall* Bonhoeffer denies marriage as a part of the order of creation. According to Ferenc Lehel's notes, Bonhoeffer says, "It is superficial reasoning to take this as a basis for speaking about marriage as an order of creation," *DBWE* 3:95, n. [5]. On the other hand, Bonhoeffer does not reject patriarchy but accepts it as "the normal order of things." See Karen V. Guth, "To See from below: Bonhoeffer's Mandates and Feminist Ethics," *Journal of the Society of Christian Ethics* 332, no. 2 (2013): 147.
41 Hannah Arendt, *Eichmann in Jerusalem: A Report on the Banality of Evil* (New York: Viking Press, 1963).
42 Arendt describes Eichmann's blind participation in Nazi evilness—"Eichmann came up with an approximately correct definition of the [Kantian] categorical imperative"—after observing the trial of Eichmann that took place in Jerusalem in 1961. Arendt, *Eichmann in Jerusalem*, 135.

43 Arendt, *Eichmann in Jerusalem*, 135, emphasis in original.
44 Bonhoeffer, *DBWE* 1:107. See DeJonge, *Bonhoeffer's Reception of Luther*, 246–8.
45 Bonhoeffer, *DBWE* 1:58–64. See DeJonge, *Bonhoeffer's Reception of Luther*, 246–8.
46 DeJonge, *Bonhoeffer's Reception of Luther*, 246–8.
47 Karl Barth describes the threefold nature of sin as pride, falsehood, and sloth and deals with the passive side of sin at length in volume 4 of *Church Dogmatics*, written between 1953 and 1959, but Bonhoeffer's essay "After Ten Years" was written in 1943. See Karl Barth, vol. 4., edited and translated by G. W. Bromiley and T. F. Torrance et al. (Edinburgh: T&T Clark, 1956–75).
48 On June 11, 1934, Lutherans Werner Elert and Paul Althaus signed the Ansbach Memorandum (*Ansbacher Ratschlag*) against the Barmen Declaration, composed May 31, 1934. The Ansbach Memorandum declares, "The Law, 'the unchangeable will of God'. ... obligates us to the natural orders to which we are subject, such as family, people [Volk], race. ...(cited in Kurt Dietrich Schmidt, *Die Bekenntnisse und grundsätzlichen Äußerungen zur Kirchenfrage*, 2:103)." Bonhoeffer, *DBWE* 6:56, n. [36].
49 In his lectures on Christology, Bonhoeffer begins to focus on the corporeality of Christ as a cross between divinity and humanity. Bonhoeffer understands the corporeality of the human as more than a mere addition to the ethical concept of the human being because it is inevitably or graciously related to Godself, who cannot be grasped or reached using a category or method of metaphysics but is known through the incarnation of Christ in the world. This theological significance of the corporeality of Christ is highlighted in his lectures on Christology in 1933. Bonhoeffer, "Lectures on Christology," in Bonhoeffer, *DBWE* 12:299–360.
50 In 1936, Bonhoeffer loses authorization to teach at the University of Berlin, and in 1938 he is banned from Berlin. In 1940, he is prohibited from public speaking, and in 1941, he is banned from writing for publication. See Bethge, *Dietrich Bonhoeffer*. See also Tietz, *Theologian of Resistance*.
51 See Green, *Bonhoeffer*, 234.
52 Bonhoeffer, *DBWE* 6:83.
53 See Bonhoeffer, "Christology Lectures," in Bonhoeffer, *DBWE* 12:207–304.
54 See Migliore, *Faith Seeking Understanding*, 170–1. See also Kelly, *Early Christian Doctrines*, 280–343.
55 Bonhoeffer, *DBWE* 6:83.
56 Bonhoeffer, *DBWE* 6:83.
57 The title in Bonhoeffer's *Ethics* in German is *Gestaltung* ("formation"). Bonhoeffer's use of the term *ethics* to mean formation (*Gestaltung*) is based on Rom. 12:2, "be transformed into a new form." See Bonhoeffer, *DBWE* 6:93, n. 72.
58 Bonhoeffer, *DBWE* 6:96.
59 Meconi argues that "deification of the human person is central to how St. Augustine presents a Christian's new life in terms of the Son of God's becoming human so humans can become God." David Vincent Meconi, *The One Christ: St. Augustine's Theology of Deification* (Washington, DC: Catholic University of America Press, 2013), xi.
60 Bonhoeffer argues that not even the Chalcedonian Christology addresses the full humanity of Christ. He states, "The presupposition for this doctrine is that the integrity of both natures must be preserved: the divine nature in its fundamental and unchangeable essence, and the human nature in its finitude and changeability. These two assertions are first made in isolation from each other—precisely

that which was forbidden by Chalcedon—and in such a way that the human nature, right from the start, no longer retained its completely human character." Bonhoeffer, *DBWE* 12:343. The Nicene theology affirmed Christ's full divinity, mainly led by the fourth-century theologian Athanasius against Arianism, which insisted Christ was not the eternal Son of God but an outstanding creature. Contrary to the Alexandrian school represented by Athanasius and Cyril of Alexandria, the Antiochian school represented by Theodore of Mopsuestia and Nestorius emphasized the full humanity of Christ. See Migliore, *Faith Seeking Understanding*, 170-1.

61 Migliore, *Faith Seeking Understanding*, 164.
62 See Bonhoeffer, *DBWE* 6:57.
63 Bonhoeffer, *DBWE* 6:87.
64 Bonhoeffer, *DBWE* 6:87.
65 In the original German, Bonhoeffer uses the expression *Menschwerdung* (becoming human) rather than *Inkarnation* (incarnation).
66 See Green, "Editor's Introduction to the English Edition," in Bonhoeffer, *DBWE* 6:6.
67 Green, "Editor's Introduction to the English Edition," in Bonhoeffer, *DBWE* 6:6.
68 Bonhoeffer, *DBWE* 6:88.
69 See Migliore, *Faith Seeking Understanding*, 164.
70 Bonhoeffer, *DBWE* 6:88, emphasis in original.
71 See Bonhoeffer, *DBWE* 4:259. Bonhoeffer argues that "both gifts belong to inseparably together. However, just because of this connection between them, they are not simply one and the same. While justification appropriates to Christians the deed God has already accomplished, sanctification promises them God's present and future action."
72 Karl Holl, *What Did Luther Understand by Religion?* ed. James L. Adams (Philadelphia: Fortress Press, 1977), 77, n. 49. Holl writes, "If one's faith is more than mere assent to historical propositions one also receives the assurance that the sin that yet accuses one can be conquered through the power of Christ."
73 Holl's interpretation of Luther's ethics is based on the lectures on Psalms in 1513-15 and the lectures on Romans in 1515/1516. See Karl Holl, *The Reconstruction of Morality*, ed. James Luther Adams and Walter F. Bense (Minneapolis: Augsburg Publishing House, 1979).
74 Holl, *The Reconstruction of Morality*, 49-50.
75 Luther's later soteriology, however, differed from his earlier works. In his sermon *Two Kinds of Righteousness* (1519), Luther's argument is intertwined with soteriological elements from his earlier and mature doctrines, and he begins to supply an interpretive framework composed of the two dimensions of righteousness, passive and active. Luther divides righteousness into two types—alien, passive, and perfect righteousness and proper, active, and progressing righteousness. Luther, *LW* 31:200.
76 Holl's communal interpretation of Luther's theology is noteworthy. Holl states that "Luther's doctrine of justification requires, indeed implies, a strong community concept. It is impossible to apprehend God without also feeling united with all the others belonging to him. The sense of God's presence does not extinguish but rather enhances our awareness of others. For ethics this means first of all a material approximation of the two commandments of love for God and one's neighbor. It is no longer a merely external formulation that connects the two commandments: the second is a direct consequence of the first." Holl, *The Reconstruction of Morality*, 51.
77 Bonhoeffer, *DBWE* 6:91, emphasis in original.

78 Bonhoeffer, *DBWE* 4:57. Luther's early approach, teaching lay Christians how to access Scripture themselves, had regressed, and Luther realized that qualified and trained Christians should help lay people to understand the Word of God. Luther finally found that the issue had two aspects: believers' reading of the Bible and qualified theologians' exposition of the Bible. After the Peasants' Revolt of 1525, Luther was convinced that it was not realistic to permit individual believers to interpret the Scripture. Luther and other early Reformers' exegetical optimism decreased considerably, and some Reformers suggested alternative approaches in the form of catechism, confession, and books.

79 See Holl, *The Reconstruction of Morality.*

80 It is controversial whether Bonhoeffer's attribution of Luther's theology is Luther's or Bonhoeffer's own interpretation of Luther through his contemporary Lutheran perspective. See DeJonge, *Bonhoeffer's Reception of Luther*, 23.

81 Bonhoeffer, *DBWE* 6:91. See Green, *Bonhoeffer*, 211–25. See the Christology lectures on the form of Christ. Bonhoeffer, *DBWE* 12:297–306.

82 See Bonhoeffer, *DBWE* 6:93, n. 72. Care must be taken in understanding Bonhoeffer's concept of ethics as formation in which the formation of the Christian person is not human-centered but Christ-centered. It is alien formation rather than active formation, in a similar way to Luther's alien and active righteousness. The editor comments that in Bonhoeffer's concept of formation, "An imitatio Christi, or 'imitation of Christ,' is rejected as an activity that starts from the human being." Bonhoeffer, *DBWE* 6:93, n. 73.

83 See also Bonhoeffer, "Basic Questions of a Christian Ethic," in Bonhoeffer, *DBWE* 6: 75.

84 Bonhoeffer, *DBWE* 12:299–360.

85 It is significant that Bonhoeffer distinguishes between Christ's presence in the church and in the world. In the world, Christ exists in a twofold form as church and state. In the church, Christ exists in a threefold form as Word, sacrament, and the Christian community. See "Lecture on Christology," in Bonhoeffer, *DBWE* 12:299–360. See Green, *Bonhoeffer*, 221, n. 115.

86 Bonhoeffer, *DBWE* 12:299–360.

87 Robert Dodaro, *Christ and the Just Society in the Thought of Augustine* (Cambridge: Cambridge University Press, 2008), 77. See Augustine, *City of God* 17.4.

88 Despite Augustine's argument that the church is the body of Christ, he does not equate the church community with Christ; he views it only as the body of Christ.

89 See Dodaro, *Christ and the Just Society*, 76–8.

90 Augustine, *Letters 1–99*, vol. II/1, *The Works of Saint Augustine: A Translation for the 21st Century*, trans. Roland Teske (Hyde Park, NY: New City Press, 2001), 87.7.

91 John H. Rist, "Augustine of Hippo," in *The Medieval Theologians*, ed. G. R. Evans (Cambridge: University of Cambridge, 1997), 19.

92 Dodaro explains that in Augustine's view, the Christian apostles in the New Testament and early martyrs corresponded to the model of heroic virtue. Dodaro, *Christ and the Just Society*, 213–14. See Augustine, *The City of God* 17.4.

93 See Bonhoeffer, *DBWE* 3:65.

94 Bayer, *Martin Luther's Theology*, 95.

95 See DeJonge, *Bonhoeffer's Reception of Luther*, 246.

96 Bonhoeffer, *DBWE* 6:76–102.

97 Bonhoeffer, *DBWE* 12:325–8. Bonhoeffer argues that "the church should be understood as the center of history that is made by the state. The church must be understood to be the center, the hidden center, of the state."
98 Bonhoeffer, *DBWE* 12:326. See Green, *Bonhoeffer*, 221, 221, n. 115. Green argues that "Christ's presence outside the church is a presence which is not revealed but is known in faith."
99 Bonhoeffer, *DBWE* 12:326, emphasis added. Bonhoeffer insists here that "Christ is the center of human existence, of history, and of nature—these are never abstract matters and are never to be distinguished from another."
100 Martin Rüter and Ilse Tödt, "Editors' Afterword to the German Edition," in Bonhoeffer, *DBWE* 6:417. According to the German editors' note, "Neo-Lutheran ethics—largely determined by *Volkstum*-theology and thus able to establish contact with the *völkisch* thinking of the National Socialists and the German Christians they controlled—proclaimed its so-called doctrine of two kingdoms [Zwei-Reiche-Lehre], a doctrine that until 1933 was by no means a prominent feature of the Lutheran confession." Bonhoeffer, *DBWE* 6:417.
101 Rüter and Tödt, "Editors' Afterword to the German Edition," in Bonhoeffer, *DBWE* 6:417. DeJonge distinguishes Luther's two kingdoms doctrine from the twentieth-century Lutherans' doctrine of two kingdoms. See DeJonge, *Bonhoeffer's Reception of Luther*, 77–101.
102 In his later theology, Bonhoeffer emphasized the individual person's participation in the state or the world in addition to the communal person's participation. See DeJonge, *Bonhoeffer's Reception of Luther*, 246. DeJonge states, "*Sanctorum Communio* may place more emphasis on the community and 'History and Good [2]' may place emphasis on the individual, but in both cases *Stellvertretung* is characteristic of both individuals and communities."
103 Bonhoeffer, *DBWE* 6:80, emphasis in original.
104 Augustine sees the source of ethical evil and sin as in a person's turning away from the ultimate good, God, toward an inferior or lesser good.
105 Bonhoeffer, *DBWE* 6:80.
106 "Readiness to take on guilt" is Green's preferred translation to emphasize the active aspect of taking on guilt. See Green, *Bonhoeffer*, 316.
107 Bonhoeffer, *DBWE* 6:272.
108 Bonhoeffer updates his previous concept of order (*Ordnung*), estate (*Stand*), and office (*Amt*) with the doctrine of the mandates as the basic forms of life. See Bonhoeffer, *DBWE* 6:389. See also DeJonge, *Bonhoeffer's Reception of Luther*, 130.
109 Bonhoeffer, *DBW* 1:127; Bonhoeffer, *DBWE* 1:157, 190.
110 As DeJonge points out, Bonhoeffer considered his non-Christian co-conspirators the subjects of responsible action, and thus such action seems not to be limited to Christian persons. DeJonge further explains, "That *Stellvertretung* can be characteristic of Christians and non-Christians (or the church as well as the rest of the world) follows naturally from Bonhoeffer's understanding of reality as a differentiated unity in Christ (put more traditionally, his two kingdoms thinking)." DeJonge, *Bonhoeffer's Reception of Luther*, 247.
111 Some major works that discuss this topic are as follows: Carl Schmitt, *Political Theology: Four Chapters on the Concept of Sovereignty*, trans. George Schwab (London: University of Chicago Press, 2005); Giorgio Agamben, *State of Exception*, trans. Kevin Attell (London: University of Chicago Press, 2005); Ted A. Smith,

Weird John Brown: Divine Violence and the Limits of Ethics (Stanford, CA: Stanford University Press, 2015); Paul Ramsey, "The Case of the Curious Exception," in *Norm and Context in Christian Ethics*, ed. Gene H. Outka and Paul Ramsey (London: SCM Press, 1973), 67–135.

112 Bonhoeffer, *DBWE* 1:189–90, n. 63 (*DBW* 1:127); Luther, *LW* 42:162.
113 This can be understood as the guilt of the other as well.
114 Luther explains: "I have never drawn a sword or desired revenge. I began neither conspiracy nor rebellion, but so far as I was able, I have helped the worldly rulers— even those who persecuted the gospel and me—to preserve their power and honor. I stopped with committing the matter to God and relying confidently at all times upon His hand." Luther, *LW* 46:31. There is tension between Luther's understanding of the church community's bearing the sin of others and the restraint function of the state. On the other hand, Bonhoeffer treats Luther's Reformation itself as an important social action. See Bonhoeffer, *Discipleship*, in Bonhoeffer, *DBWE* 4:111.
115 Mark U. Edwards Jr., *Luther and the False Brethren* (Stanford, CA: Stanford University Press, 1975), 70. Luther does not advocate that priests should punish injustices. Edwards explains: "His [Luther's] responsibility as a preacher was not to wield the word and punish injustices but to teach and wield the Word, which was his sword." Edwards, *Luther and the False Brethren*, 71.
116 "Fourteen Consolations," in Luther, *LW* 42:162.
117 Bonhoeffer, "Ethics as Formation," in Bonhoeffer, *DBWE* 6:272.
118 Bonhoeffer, *DBWE* 6:272.
119 Bonhoeffer, "Ethics as Formation," in Bonhoeffer, *DBWE* 6:76–7.
120 Matt. 7:18. See also Augustine, *Enchiridion* 4:17; Luther, "Freedom of a Christian," *LW* 31.
121 This turn reflects Bonhoeffer's personal context in that he was in an urgent situation due to his participation in a plot against Hitler on behalf of Germany. Bonhoeffer wrote only in code words due to the risk that his writings could get into the hands of the authorities. Sabine Dramm, *Dietrich Bonhoeffer and the Resistance*, trans. Margaret Kohl (Minneapolis: Fortress Press, 2009), 61.
122 DeJonge, *Bonhoeffer's Reception of Luther*, 233–9, 234, n. 118.
123 DeJonge, *Bonhoeffer's Reception of Luther*, 234, n. 118. Although DeJonge and Tietz compare Bonhoeffer's focus on God's active righteousness or punitive righteousness with Luther's emphasis on God's passive righteousness, precisely speaking, it is more appropriate to say that Bonhoeffer appropriated Luther's early theology rather than Luther's mature doctrine. Luther's equal emphasis on active and passive righteousness is one of the main characteristics of the theology of the young Luther, but this disappeared in Luther's mature theology. However, as DeJonge comments, Bonhoeffer still considered himself as a successor to Luther.
124 Bonhoeffer, *DBWE* 6:77.
125 Green, *Bonhoeffer*, 316.
126 See Luther, *LW* 25:260.
127 Bonhoeffer, "History and Good [2]," in *DBWE* 6:279.
128 DeJonge, *Bonhoeffer's Reception of Luther*, 235. See also Bonhoeffer, "Practical Exercises in Homiletics" (1936–7), in Bonhoeffer, *DBWE* 14:345.
129 Bonhoeffer, *DBWE* 6:288, emphasis added.
130 Bonhoeffer, *DBWE* 6:296–7.
131 See Bonhoeffer, "Ultimate and Penultimate Things," in Bonhoeffer, *DBWE* 6:146–70.
132 Bonhoeffer, *DBWE* 11:360. In contrast, DeJonge writes, "In 'World Alliance,' the chief difference Bonhoeffer draws between his position and the enthusiasts' is that

he understands peace as a concrete commandment while they understand it as law." Michael P. DeJonge, "Bonhoeffer's Non-Commitment to Nonviolence: A Response to Stanley Hauerwas," *JRE* 44, no. 2 (2016): 387.
133 Bonhoeffer, *DBWE* 6:151, emphasis in original.
134 Bonhoeffer, *DBWE* 6:296-7.
135 Bonhoeffer, *DBWE* 6: 297. See also Bonhoeffer, *DBWE* 8:37-38. Nancy J. Duff argues that "Bonhoeffer claims that responsible Christian action is defined by our relationship to Christ, not by following an absolute moral law." Nancy J. Duff, "Dietrich Bonhoeffer's Theological Ethic," *Princeton Seminary Bulletin* 15, no. 3 (1994): 266.
136 Duff, "Dietrich Bonhoeffer's Theological Ethic," 269.
137 Bonhoeffer, *DBWE* 6:279, emphasis added.
138 Bonhoeffer, *DBWE* 6:279.
139 Bonhoeffer, *DBWE* 6:279.
140 Bonhoeffer, *DBWE* 6:279.
141 Matt. 12:11-12: "He said to them, 'Suppose one of you has only one sheep and it falls into a pit on the sabbath; will you not lay hold of it and lift it out? How much more valuable is a human being than a sheep! So it is lawful to do good on the sabbath.'"
142 Bonhoeffer, *DBWE* 4:45.
143 Augustine, *Letters 1-99*, 87.7.
144 Augustine, *The City of God* 19.7. Augustine, *Letters 1-99*, 93.50. Augustine cites Prov. 13:22.
145 María Teresa Dávila, "Breaking from the Dominance of Power and Order in Augustine's Ethic of War," in *Augustine and Social Justice*, ed. Teresa Delgado, John Doody, and Kim Paffenroth (Lanham, MD: Lexington Books, 2015), 147, emphasis in original.
146 Augustine, *The City of God* 2.12, 2.21.
147 Augustine, *The City of God* 1.35, 20.9.
148 DeJonge, *Bonhoeffer's Reception of Luther*, 257; Bonhoeffer, *DBWE* 16:504.
149 Bonhoeffer, "The Church and the Jewish Question," in Bonhoeffer, *DBWE* 12:374.
150 Bonhoeffer, *DBWE* 6:279. Green suggests four dimensions of responsible action: vicarious representative action (*Stellvertretung*), correspondence to reality, freedom, and readiness to take on guilt (*Schuldübernahme*). See Green, *Bonhoeffer*, 316-21.
151 Bonhoeffer, *DBWE* 10:389.
152 Bonhoeffer, *DBWE* 6:279. Bonhoeffer also notes: "Wherever conscience and concrete responsibility clash, we must therefore freely decide in favor of Jesus Christ." Bonhoeffer, *DBWE* 6:282.
153 In his 1936 letter to Zinn, Bonhoeffer opposes Christians' involvement in violence in a war, saying that "for Christians any military service, except in the ambulance corps, and any preparation for a war, is forbidden." See Bonhoeffer, *DBWE* 12:260.
154 On the one hand, Nation, Siegrist, and Umbel follow Hauerwas's theory that Bonhoeffer was committed to nonviolence. See Mark Thiessen Nation, Anthony G. Siegrist, and Daniel P. Umbel, *Bonhoeffer the Assassin? Challenging the Myth, Recovering His Call to Peacemaking* (Grand Rapids, MI: Baker Academic, 2013). On the other hand, DeJonge rejects Hauerwas's claim that Bonhoeffer was committed to nonviolence by arguing that "Bonhoeffer's understanding of peace as 'concrete commandment' and 'order of preservation' relies on Lutheran concepts and is articulated with explicit contrast to an Anabaptist account of peace." DeJonge, "Bonhoeffer's Non-Commitment to Nonviolence," 378. See also Clifford J. Green, "Pacifism and Tyrannicide: Bonhoeffer's Christian Peace Ethic," *Studies in Christian Ethics* 18, no. 3 (2005): 31-47.

155 Bonhoeffer, *DBWE* 6:274–5.
156 Bonhoeffer, *DBWE* 6:274–5. In his prison writings on the first table of the Decalogue, Bonhoeffer distinguishes the first commandment from the rest. Ziegler explains that the first commandment "rightly controls the meaning of the rest, even as the other commandments elucidate and substantiate its force and significance." Philip G. Ziegler, "Graciously Commanded: Dietrich Bonhoeffer and Karl Barth on the Decalogue," *SJT* 71, no. 2 (2018): 130–1. It is clear that, for Bonhoeffer, in an extreme situation even the rest of the articles of the Decalogue should be redirected to serve the ultimate commandment. This is because the other commandments can function as absolute rules, ignoring the relation between the literal meaning and the intention of their giver. For Bonhoeffer's last commentary on the Decalogue, see Bonhoeffer, *DBWE* 15:633–44. For a detailed discussion of Bonhoeffer's later understanding of the Decalogue, see Ziegler, "Graciously Commanded."

Chapter 6

1 Bonhoeffer, *DBWE* 8:52.
2 Bonhoeffer, *DBWE* 1:107.
3 Bonhoeffer, *DBWE* 1:114–15; Bonhoeffer, *DBWE* 1:162–5. See also Berkouwer, *Studies in Dogmatics: Sin*, 424.
4 See Augustine, *Confessions* 2.4.9–2.10.18.
5 Oscar Romero, "Second Pastoral Letter" (1977), cited in José Ignacio González Faus, "Sin," in *Systematic Theology: Perspectives from Liberation Theology*, ed. Jon Sobrino and Ignacio Ellacuria (Maryknoll, NY: Orbis Books, 1996), 199.
6 See Gustavo Gutierrez, "The Limitations of Modern Theology: On a Letter of Dietrich Bonhoeffer," in *The Power of the Poor in History* (Maryknoll, NY: Orbis Books, 1983), 222–33. The concept of communal sin is closely related to structural sin. In this book, communal sin primarily refers to the sin of community, and structural sin indicates the sin of a group of people or a community or an individual who exercises evil power through improper social, cultural, or economic structures. The two notions are sometimes used interchangeably, depending on the context.
7 See John W. De Gruchy, "Bonhoeffer, Apartheid and beyond: The Reception of Bonhoeffer in South Africa," in *Bonhoeffer for a New Day: Theology in a Time of Transition*, ed. John W. de Gruchy (Grand Rapids, MI: Wm. B. Eerdmans), 353–65.
8 Bonhoeffer's notion of the "perspective from below" can be interpreted in various ways, such as "above to below" and "only from below." I appreciate the conversation of the German-American Bonhoeffer Network in 2018 on this point.
9 Bonhoeffer, *DBWE* 1:118.
10 González Faus, "Sin," 198.
11 González Faus, "Sin," 198.
12 Matt. 4:25, 9:36; Mk. 2:4, 2:13. Asian liberation theologians use different terms for the oppressed according to their contexts. For example, the oppressed are interpreted as *minjung* (the oppressed) in Korean theology, *Dalit* (the lowest caste) in Indian theology, and *Pyith-Dukkha* (mass-suffering) in Southeast Asian theology. See David Thang Moe, "What Had Dietrich Bonhoeffer to Do with Asian Theology?" *Asia Journal of Theology* 28, no. 2 (2014): 176–7.

13 However, in "After Ten Years" Bonhoeffer points out that people under evil structural power are not only oppressed but are also ignorant in their blind submission to duty.
14 Augustine, *Confessions* 7.7.11–13, 7.9.13, 9.4.7.
15 Augustine mainly used these biblical passages: Isa. 2:12, Prov. 16:18, 29:23.
16 Augustine, *Confessions* 7.7.11–13.
17 Bonhoeffer, *DBWE* 6:80.
18 Bonhoeffer, *DBWE* 6:80.
19 Migliore, *Faith Seeking Understanding*, 155.
20 Migliore, *Faith Seeking Understanding*, 156.
21 Bonhoeffer, *DBWE* 8:38–9.
22 See Bonhoeffer, *DBWE* 8:84–6.
23 Bonhoeffer, *DBWE* 8:84–6. See also Rachel Muers, "Anthropology," in *The Oxford Handbook of Dietrich Bonhoeffer*, ed. Michael Mawson and Philip G. Ziegler (Oxford: Oxford University Press, 2019), 196–209; Jennifer M. McBride, "Bonhoeffer and Feminist Theologies," in *The Oxford Handbook of Dietrich Bonhoeffer*, ed. Michael Mawson and Philip G. Ziegler (Oxford: Oxford University Press, 2019), 366; Hyun Kyung Chung, "Dear Dietrich Bonhoeffer: A Letter," in *Bonhoeffer for a New Day: Theology in a Time of Transition*, ed. John W. De Gruchy (Grand Rapids, MI: Wm. B. Eerdmans, 1997), 9–19; Karen V. Guth, "To See from Below: Bonhoeffer's Mandates and Feminist Ethics," *Journal of the Society of Christian Ethics* 332, no. 2 (2013): 131–50; Dahill, *Reading from the Underside of the Self*, 5, 210–29.
24 In this regard, Karen V. Guth contends that "Bonhoeffer regarded patriarchy as the divinely commanded order of relationship between men and women rather than the result of the Fall." Guth, "To See from Below," n. 11, 147. However, as I have discussed in Chapter 4, in *Creation and Fall* Bonhoeffer considers the male and female relationship primarily as an I and other relationship and secondarily as a husband and wife relationship.
25 Rachel Muers points out that Bonhoeffer understands "the equality of husband and wife" as "'modern and unbiblical.'" Muers, "Anthropology," 207.
26 See also Reggie L. Williams, "Bonhoeffer and Race," in *The Oxford Handbook of Dietrich Bonhoeffer*, ed. Michael Mawson and Philip G. Ziegler (Oxford: Oxford University Press, 2019), 383–96.
27 Bonhoeffer, *DBWE* 1:107.
28 Bonhoeffer, *DBWE* 1:178–92, 2:134.
29 Christine Schliesser, *Everyone Who Acts Responsibly Becomes Guilty: Bonhoeffer's Concept of Accepting Guilt* (Louisville, KY: Westminster John Knox Press, 2008), 111.
30 Bonhoeffer, *DBWE* 12:374.
31 For example, during the US presidential election of 2016, Bonhoeffer's resistance to the Nazi reign was used as an example against political or social evil by some political commentators. Commentators from both the Republican and the Democratic sides argued that the United States was on the way to a totalitarian or immoral society if it elected the other side's candidate. See Charles Blow, "Trump Isn't Hitler. But the Lying…," *New York Times* [Op-ed], October 19, 2017, https://www.nytimes.com/2017/10/19/opinion/trump-isnt-hitler-but-the-lying.html. See also Eric Metaxas, "Should Christians Vote for Trump?" *The Wall Street Journal* [Op-ed], October 12, 2016, https://www.wsj.com/articles/should-christians-vote-for-trump-1476294992. South Korean populist pastor Kwang-hoon Jun used Bonhoeffer's anti-Nazi expression "taking the wheel of the madman" to criticize the Korean governmental

policies of President Moon. Sang-Hun Choe, "The Populist Pastor Leading a Conservative Revival in South Korea," *New York Times*, November 11, 2019, https://www.nytimes.com/2019/11/08/world/asia/jun-kwang-hoon-pastor-.html?searchResultPosition=8. In regard to diverse interpretations of Bonhoeffer's theological legacy in the United States, see Stephen R. Haynes, *The Battle for Bonhoeffer: Debating Discipleship in the Age of Trump* (Grand Rapids, MI: Wm. B. Eerdmans, 2018).

32 Bonhoeffer, *DBW* 1:127; Bonhoeffer, *DBWE* 1:190.
33 See Schliesser, *Everyone Who Acts Responsibly Becomes Guilty*.
34 The final chapter of Calvin's *Institutes* contains a prototypal logic of civil resistance. See John Calvin, *Institutes of the Christian Religion*, ed. John T. McNeill, trans. Ford Lewis Battles, LCC (Louisville, KY: Westminster John Knox Press, 2011), 2.20.
35 Bonhoeffer, *DBWE* 6:146–70.
36 Bonhoeffer, *DBWE* 4:111.
37 Bonhoeffer, *DBWE* 1:178–92.
38 See Bonhoeffer, *DBWE* 1:190. This expression is also used as the title of an article by Tom Greggs. See Greggs, "Bearing Sin in the Church," 77–100.
39 Concerning Bonhoeffer's ethical and communal sense of guilt, see Bonhoeffer, *DBWE* 6:136.
40 Bonhoeffer, *DBW* 1:127; Bonhoeffer, *DBWE* 1:157, 190.
41 This is not to suggest that the two theologians, Augustine and Bonhoeffer, totally denied one of the two lives of a saint, but it does consider that both emphasized one life over the other life.

BIBLIOGRAPHY

Agamben, Giorgio. *State of Exception*. Translated by Kevin Attell. London: University of Chicago Press, 2005.

Althaus, Paul. *The Theology of Martin Luther*. Philadelphia: Fortress Press, 1996.

Aquinas, Thomas. *Basic Writings of Saint Thomas Aquinas*, vol. 1, edited by Anton Charles Pegis. Indianapolis: Hackett Publishing Company, 1997.

Arendt, Hannah. *Eichmann in Jerusalem: A Report on the Banality of Evil*. New York: Viking Press, 1963.

Augustine. *The City of God (De Civitate Dei) XI–XXII*. In *The Works of Saint Augustine: A Translation for the 21st Century*, vol. 7, translated by Maria Boulding. Brooklyn, NY: New City Press, 2013.

Augustine. *Confessions*. In *Augustine: Confessions and Enchiridion*, LCC, edited and translated by Albert Cook Outler, 31–336. Louisville, KY: Westminster John Knox Press, 2006.

Augustine. *Enchiridion*. In *Augustine: Confessions and Enchiridion*, LCC, edited and translated by Albert Cook Outler, 337–412. Louisville, KY: Westminster John Knox Press, 2006.

Augustine. *Expositions of the Psalms (Enarrationes in Psalmos) 121–50*. In *The Works of Saint Augustine: A Translation for the 21st Century*, vol. 6, translated by Maria Boulding. Hyde Park, NY: New City Press, 2004.

Augustine. *On Free Will (De Libero Arbitrio)*. In *Augustine: Earlier Writings*, LCC, edited and translated by J. H. S. Burleigh, 102–217. Louisville, KY: Westminster John Knox Press, 2006.

Augustine. *On the Holy Trinity (De Trinitate)*. In NPNF, vol. 3, edited by Philip Schaff, 1–228. Grand Rapids, MI: Wm. B. Eerdmans, 1978.

Augustine. *Homilies on the First Epistle of John (Tractatus in Epistolan Joannis ad Parthos)*. In *The Works of Saint Augustine: A Translation for the 21st Century*, translated by Maria Boulding. Hyde Park, NY: New City Press, 2008.

Augustine. *Homilies on the Gospel of John 1–40*. In *The Works of Saint Augustine: A Translation for the 21st Century*, vol. III/12, translated by Edmund Hill O.P. Hyde Park, NY: New City Press, 2009.

Augustine. *Letters 1–99*. In *The Works of Saint Augustine: A Translation for the 21st Century*, vol. II/1, translated by Roland Teske. Hyde Park, NY: New City Press, 2001.

Augustine. *The Literal Meaning of Genesis (De Genesi ad Litteram)*. In *Ancient Christian Writers*, translated by John Hammond Taylor, vol. 42. New York: Newman Press, 1982.

Augustine. *On Marriage and Concupiscence (De Nuptiis et Concupiscentia)*. In *St. Augustine: Anti-Pelagian Writings*, vol. 5, NPNF, edited by Philip Schaff, 257–308. Grand Rapids, MI: Wm. B. Eerdmans, 1978.

Augustine. *On the Merits and Remission of Sins, and on the Baptism of Infants (De Peccatorum Meritis et Remissione, et de Baptismo Parvulorum)*. In *St. Augustine: Anti-Pelagian Writings*, vol. 5, NPNF, edited by Philip Schaff, 11–78. Grand Rapids, MI: Wm. B. Eerdmans, 1978.

Augustine. *On Nature and Grace* (*De Natura et Gratia, contra Pelagium*). In *St. Augustine: Anti-Pelagian Writings*, vol. 5, NPNF, edited by Philip Schaff, 115–51. Grand Rapids, MI: Wm. B. Eerdmans, 1978.

Augustine. *The Nature of the Good* (*De Natura Boni*). In *Augustine: Earlier Writings*, LCC, edited and translated by J. H. S. Burleigh, 324–48. Louisville, KY: Westminster John Knox Press, 2006.

Augustine. *On Rebuke and Grace* (*De Correctione et Gratia*). In *St. Augustine: Anti-Pelagian Writings*, vol. 5, NPNF, edited by Philip Schaff, 468–91. Grand Rapids, MI: Wm. B. Eerdmans, 1978.

Augustine. *Revisions* (*Retractationes*). In *The Works of Saint Augustine: A Translation for the 21st Century*, vol. x, translated by Boniface Ramsey. Hyde Park, NY: New City Press, 2010.

Augustine. *Sancti Augustini, De Libero Arbitrio*. In *Opera*, CChr Latina, vol. 29, edited by W. M. Green. Turnhoult, Belgium: Brepols, 1970.

Augustine. *Teaching Christianity* (*De Doctrina Christiana*). In *The Works of Saint Augustine: A Translation for the 21st Century*, vol. 11, translated by Maria Boulding. Brooklyn, NY: New City Press, 1996.

Augustine. *Of True Religion* (*De Vera Religion*). In *Augustine: Earlier Writings*, LCC, edited and translated by J. H. S. Burleigh, 218–83. Louisville, KY: Westminster John Knox Press, 2006.

Ayres, Lewis. *Augustine and the Trinity*. Cambridge: Cambridge University Press, 2010.

Barth, Karl. *Church Dogmatics*, vol. 4. edited and translated by G. W. Bromiley and T. F. Torrance et al. Edinburgh: T&T Clark, 1956–75.

Barth, Karl. *The Epistle to the Romans*. Translated by Edwyn C. Hoskyns from the 6th ed. New York: Oxford University Press, 2015.

Batka, L'ubomir. "Luther's Teaching on Sin and Evil." In *The Oxford Handbook of Martin Luther's Theology*, edited by Robert Kolb, Irene Dingel, and L'ubomir Batka, 233–53. Oxford: Oxford University Press, 2016.

Bayer, Oswald. *Martin Luther's Theology: A Contemporary Interpretation*. Grand Rapids, MI: Wm. B. Eerdmans, 2008.

Beatrice, Pier Franco. *The Transmission of Sin: Augustine and the Pre-Augustinian Source*. New York: Oxford University Press, 2013.

Berkouwer, G. C. *Studies in Dogmatics: Sin*. Grand Rapids, MI: Wm. B. Eerdmans, 1971.

Bethge, Eberhard. *Dietrich Bonhoeffer: A Biography*. Edited by Victoria Barnet. Rev. ed. Minneapolis: Fortress Press, 2000.

Black, Clifton C. "Unity and Diversity in Luther's Biblical Exegesis: Psalm 51 as a Test-Case." *SJT* 38, no. 3 (August 1985): 325–45.

Bonhoeffer, Dietrich. *Dietrich Bonhoeffer Werke* [*DBW*]. 16 vols. Edited by Eberhard Bethge et al. Gütersloh, Germany: Chr. Kaiser Verlag/Gütersloher Verlagshaus, 1986–99.

Bonhoeffer, Dietrich. *Dietrich Bonhoeffer Works* [*DBWE*]. 17 vols. Edited by Wayne Whitson Floyd Jr. et al. Minneapolis: Fortress Press, 1996–2014.

Bonner, Gerald. *St Augustine of Hippo: Life and Controversies*. 3rd ed. Norwich, UK: Canterbury Press, 2002.

Brain, Michael. "Sexuality and Community in the Theology of Dietrich Bonhoeffer." *SJT* 71, no. 1 (2018): 67–84.

Brown, Peter. *Augustine of Hippo: A Biography*. Berkeley: University of California Press, 2000.

Calvin, John. *Institutes of the Christian Religion*. Edited by John T. McNeill. Translated by Ford Lewis Battles. LCC. Louisville, KY: Westminster John Knox Press, 2011.

Canning, Raymond. "uti/frui." In *Augustine through the Ages: An Encyclopedia*, edited by Allan D. Fitzgerald. Grand Rapids, MI: Wm. B. Eerdmans, 2009.
Carola, Joseph. *Augustine of Hippo: The Role of the Laity in Ecclesial Reconciliation*. Rome: Gregorian Biblical Book Shop, 2005.
Cary, Philip. *Augustine's Invention of the Inner Self: The Legacy of a Christian Platonist*. New York: Oxford University Press, 2000.
Cary, Philip. "Book Seven: Inner Vision as the Goal of Augustine's Life." In *A Reader's Companion to Augustine's Confessions*, edited by Kim Paffenroth and Robert P. Kennedy, 107–26. Louisville, KY: Westminster John Knox Press, 2003.
Cavadini, John C. *Visioning Augustine*. Hoboken, NJ: John Wiley & Sons, 2019.
Charry, Ellen T. "Book Review of 'Augustine's Invention of the Inner Self: The Legacy of a Christian Platonist.'" *TTod* 58, no. 2 (July 2001): 232–4.
Chopp, Rebecca S. and Ethna Regan. "Latin American Liberation Theology." In *The Modern Theologians: An Introduction to Christian Theology since 1918*, 3rd ed., edited by David F. Ford and Rachel Muers, 469–84. Oxford: Blackwell Publishing, 2005.
Chung, Hyun Kyung. "Dear Dietrich Bonhoeffer: A Letter." In *Bonhoeffer for a New Day: Theology in a Time of Transition*, edited by John W. De Gruchy, 9–19. Grand Rapids, MI: Wm. B. Eerdmans, 1997.
Class, Gottfried. *Der verzweifelte Zugriff auf das Leben: Dietrich Bonhoeffers Sündenverständnis in "Schöpfung und Fall."* [Desperate access to life: Bonhoeffer's understanding of sin in *Creation and Fall*]. Nguntegunterreukirchen, Germany: Neukirchen-Vluyn, 1994.
Conybeare, Catherine. "Review of *Creatio ex nihilo and the Theology of St. Augustine: The Anti-Manichaean Polemic and beyond* by N. Joseph Torchia." *CH* 70, no. 4 (2001): 777–8.
Dahill, Lisa E. *Reading from the Underside of Selfhood: Bonhoeffer and Spiritual Formation*. Princeton Theological Monograph Series, vol. 95. Eugene, OR: Pickwick Publications, 2009.
Dávila, María Teresa. "Breaking from the Dominance of Power and Order in Augustine's Ethic of War." In *Augustine and Social Justice*, edited by Teresa Delgado, John Doody, and Kim Paffenroth, 145–62. Lanham, MD: Lexington Books, 2015.
de Gruchy, John W. "Bonhoeffer, Apartheid and beyond: The Reception of Bonhoeffer in South Africa." In *Bonhoeffer for a New Day: Theology in a Time of Transition*, edited by John W. de Gruchy, 353–65. Grand Rapids, MI: Wm. B. Eerdmans, 1997.
de Gruchy, John W. "Dietrich Bonhoeffer as Christian Humanist." In *Being Human, Becoming Human: Dietrich Bonhoeffer and Social Thought*, edited by Jens Zimmermann and Brian Gregor, 3–24. Eugene, OR: Pickwick Publications, 2010.
de Gruchy, John W. "Editor's Introduction to the English Edition." In Dietrich Bonhoeffer, *DBWE* 3:1–23.
DeJonge, Michael P. "Bonhoeffer's Non-Commitment to Nonviolence: A Response to Stanley Hauerwas." *JRE* 44, no. 2 (2016): 387–94.
DeJonge, Michael P. *Bonhoeffer's Reception of Luther*. Oxford: Oxford University Press, 2017.
DeJonge, Michael P. *Bonhoeffer's Theological Formation: Berlin, Barth, and Protestant Theology*. Oxford: Oxford University Press, 2012.
Dodaro, Robert. *Christ and Just Society in the Thought of Augustine*. Cambridge: Cambridge University Press, 2004.
Dramm, Sabine. *Dietrich Bonhoeffer and the Resistance*. Translated by Margaret Kohl. Minneapolis: Fortress Press, 2009.

Duff, Nancy J. "Dietrich Bonhoeffer's Theological Ethic." *Princeton Seminary Bulletin* 15, no. 3 (1994): 263–73.

Edwards Jr., Mark U. *Luther and the False Brethren*. Stanford, CA: Stanford University Press, 1975.

Feil, Ernst. *The Theology of Dietrich Bonhoeffer*. Translated by Martin Rumscheidt. Minneapolis: Fortress Press, 1985.

Floyd, Wayne Whitson. "Dietrich Bonhoeffer." In *Modern Theologians: An Introduction to Christian Theology since 1918*, 3rd ed., edited by David F. Ford and Rachel Muers, 43–61. Oxford: Blackwell Publishing, 2005.

González Faus, José Ignacio. "Sin." In *Systematic Theology: Perspectives from Liberation Theology*, edited by Jon Sobrino and Ignacio Ellacuria, 194–204. Maryknoll, NY: Orbis Books, 1996.

Grabowski, Stanislaus J. *The Church: An Introduction to the Theology of St. Augustine*. St. Louis, MO: B. Herder Book Co., 1957.

Grabowski, Stanislaus J. "Sinners and the Mystical Body of Christ according to St. Augustine." *TS* 9, no. 1 (March 1948): 47–84.

Green, Clifford J. "Editor's Introduction to the English Edition." In Dietrich Bonhoeffer, *DBWE* 1:1–20.

Green, Clifford J. "Editor's Introduction to the English Edition." In Dietrich Bonhoeffer, *DBWE* 6:1–44.

Green, Clifford J. "Pacifism and Tyrannicide: Bonhoeffer's Christian Peace Ethic." *Studies in Christian Ethics* 18, no. 3 (2005): 31–47.

Green, Clifford J. *Bonhoeffer: A Theology of Sociality*. Rev. ed. Grand Rapids, MI: Wm. B. Eerdmans, 1999.

Greene-McCreight, Kathryn. "Gender, Sin and Grace: Feminist Theologies Meet Karl Barth's Hamartiology." *SJT* 50, no. 4 (1997): 415–32.

Greggs, Tom. "Bearing Sin in the Church: The Ecclesial Hamartiology of Bonhoeffer." In *Christ, Church, and World: New Studies in Bonhoeffer's Theology and Ethics*, edited by Michael Mawson and Philip G. Ziegler, 77–100. London: Bloomsbury T&T Clark, 2016.

Greggs, Tom. "Proportion and Topography in Ecclesiology: A Working Paper on the Dogmatic Location of the Doctrine of the Church." In *Theological Theology: Essays in Honour of John Webster*, edited by R. David Nelson, Daren Sarisky, and Justin Stratis, 89–106. London: T&T Clark Bloomsbury, 2016.

Greggs, Tom. *Theology against Religion: Constructive Dialogues with Bonhoeffer and Barth*. London: Bloomsbury Publishing, 2011.

Guth, Karen V. "To See from Below: Bonhoeffer's Mandates and Feminist Ethics." *Journal of the Society of Christian Ethics* 332, no. 2 (2013): 131–50.

Gutierrez, Gustavo. *The Power of the Poor in History*. Maryknoll, NY: Orbis Books, 1983.

Hampson, Margaret Daphne. *Theology and Feminism*. Cambridge, MA: Basil Blackwell, 1990.

Harasta, Eva. "Adam in Christ? The Place of Sin in Christ-Reality." In *Christ, Church, and World: New Studies in Bonhoeffer's Theology and Ethics*, 61–75. London: Bloomsbury T&T Clark, 2016.

Harnack, Adolf von. *History of Dogma*, vol. 5. Eugene, OR: Wipf & Stock Publishers, 1997.

Harvey, Barry. "Augustine and Thomas Aquinas in the Theology of Dietrich Bonhoeffer." In *Bonhoeffer's Intellectual Formation: Theology and Philosophy in His Thought*, edited by Peter Frick, 11–30. Tübingen, Germany: Mohr Siebeck, 2008.

Haynes, Stephen R. *The Battle for Bonhoeffer: Debating Discipleship in the Age of Trump*. Grand Rapids, MI: Wm. B. Eerdmans, 2018.

Hermanson, Amy K., "Saint Augustine and the Creation of a Distinctly Christian Rhetoric." In *The Rhetoric of St. Augustine of Hippo: De Doctrina Christiana and the Search for a Distinctly Christian Rhetoric*, edited by Richard Leo Enos and Roger C. Thompson et al., 1–9. Waco, TX: Baylor University Press, 2008.

Herrmann, Erik. "Luther's Absorption of Medieval Biblical Interpretation." In *The Oxford Handbook of Martin Luther's Theology*, edited by Robert Kolb, Irene Dingel, and L'ubomir Batka, 71–90. Oxford: Oxford University Press, 2016.

Hickson, Michael W. "A Brief History of the Problems of Evil." In *Blackwell Companion to the Problem of Evil*, edited by Justine P. McBrayer and Daniel Howard-Snyder, 3–18. Chichester, UK: John Wiley & Sons, 2013.

Holl, Karl. *The Reconstruction of Morality*. Edited by James Luther Adams and Walter F. Bense. Minneapolis: Augsburg Publishing House, 1979.

Holl, Karl. *What Did Luther Understand by Religion?* Edited by James L. Adams and Walter F. Bense. Philadelphia: Fortress Press, 1977.

Hume, David. "Dialogues Concerning Natural Religion." In *Principal Writings on Religion: Including Dialogues Concerning Natural Religion and the Natural History of Religion*, edited by J. C. A. Gaskin, 29–130. Oxford World's Classics. Oxford: Oxford University Press, 1998.

Hunsinger, George. "What Karl Barth Learned from Martin Luther." *LQ* 13, no. 2 (1999): 125–55.

Hunter, David G. "Augustine on the Body." In *A Companion to Augustine*, edited by Mark Vessey and Shelley Reid, Blackwell Companions to the Ancient World, 353–64. Chichester, UK: Wiley-Blackwell, 2012.

Irenaeus of Lyons. "Against Heresies (*Adversus Haereses*)." In *The Writings of the Fathers Down to A.D. 325: Volume I—The Apostolic Fathers with Justin Martyr and Irenaeus*, ANF, edited by Alexander Roberts, James Donaldson, and A. Cleveland Coxe. 309–567. Grand Rapids, MI: Wm. B. Eerdmans, 1989.

Jacobs, Charles M., and Robert C. Schultz. Introduction to *Admonition to Peace: A Reply to the Twelve Articles of the Peasants in Swabia*. In *LW* 46:5–16.

Jenson, Matt. *The Gravity of Sin: Augustine, Luther, and Barth on Homo Incurvatus in Se*. London: T&T Clark, 2006.

Jenson, Robert W. *Systematic Theology*, vol. 2. New York: Oxford University Press, 2001.

Katz, Sheri. "Person." In *Augustine through the Ages: An Encyclopedia*, edited by A. Fitzgerald. Grand Rapids, MI: Wm. B. Eerdmans, 2009.

Kelly, Geffrey B., and John D. Godsey. "Editors' Introduction to the English Edition." In *DBWE* 4:1–40.

Kelly, J. N. D. *Early Christian Doctrines*. Rev. ed. New York: HarperCollins, 1978.

Kelsey, David H. *Eccentric Existence: A Theological Anthropology*. Louisville, KY: John Knox Press, 2009.

Kolb, Robert. "The Lutheran Doctrine of Original Sin." In *Adam, the Fall, and Original Sin: Theological, Biblical, and Scientific Perspective*, edited by Hans Madueme and Michael Reeves, 109–28. Grand Rapids, MI: Baker Academic, 2014.

Krötke, Wolf. "Dietrich Bonhoeffer and Martin Luther." In *Bonhoeffer's Intellectual Formation: Theology and Philosophy in His Thought*, edited by Peter Frick, 53–82. Tübingen, Germany: Mohr Siebeck, 2008.

Livingston, James C. *Modern Christian Thought*. Upper Saddle River, NJ: Prentice Hall, 1988.

Lohse, Bernhard. *Martin Luther's Theology: Its Historical and Systematic Development*. Edited and translated by Roy A. Harrisville. Minneapolis: Fortress Press, 2011.

Luther, Martin. *Luther's Works*. [LW]. 55 vols. Edited and translated by Jaroslav Pelikan and Helmut Lehman et al. Minneapolis: Fortress Press, 1900–86.

Mann, William E. "Augustine on Evil and Original Sin." In *The Cambridge Companion to Augustine*, edited by Elenore Stump and Norman Cretzmann, 40–8. Cambridge: Cambridge University Press, 2001.

Marsh, Charles. *Reclaiming Dietrich Bonhoeffer: The Promise of His Theology*. New York: Oxford University Press, 1994.

Mawson, Michael. *Christ Existing as Community: Bonhoeffer's Ecclesiology*. Oxford: Oxford University Press, 2018.

McBride, Jennifer M. "Bonhoeffer and Feminist Theologies." In *The Oxford Handbook of Dietrich Bonhoeffer*, edited by Michael Mawson and Philip G. Ziegler, 365–82. Oxford: Oxford University Press, 2019.

McBride, Jennifer M. *The Church for the World: A Theology of Public Witness*. New York: Oxford University Press, 2012.

McBride Jennifer M., and Thomas Fabisiak. "Bonhoeffer's Critique of Morality: A Theological Resource for Dismantling Mass Incarceration." In *Dietrich Bonhoeffer, Theology, and Political Resistance*, edited by Lori Brandt Hale and W. David Hall, 89–109. Lanham: Lexington Books, 2020.

McCormack, Bruce L. "The Actuality of God: *Karl Barth in Conversation with Open Theism*." In *Engaging the Doctrine of God: Contemporary Protestant Perspectives*, edited by Bruce L. McCormack, 185–242. Grand Rapids, MI: Baker Academic, 2008.

McCormack, Bruce L. Introduction to *Mapping Modern Theology: A Thematic and Historical Introduction*, edited by Kelly M. Kapic and Bruce L. McCormack, 1–19. Grand Rapids, MI: Baker Academics, 2012.

McFarland, Ian A. *Difference and Identity: A Theological Anthropology*. Cleveland: Pilgrim Press, 2001.

McFarland, Ian A. *In Adam's Fall: A Meditation on the Christian Doctrine of Original Sin*. Challenges in Contemporary Theology. Chichester, UK: Wiley-Blackwell, 2010.

McGrath, Alister E. *Luther's Theology of the Cross: Martin Luther's Theological Breakthrough*. 2nd ed. Malden, MA: Wiley-Blackwell, 2011.

McSorley, Harry J. *Luther: Right or Wrong? An Ecumenical-Theological Study of Luther's Major Work, The Bondage of the Will, by a Roman Catholic Scholar*. Glen Rock, NJ: Newman Press, 1969.

Meconi, David Vincent. *The One Christ: St. Augustine's Theology of Deification*. Washington, DC: The Catholic University of America Press, 2013.

Migliore, Daniel L. *Faith Seeking Understanding*. Grand Rapids, MI: Wm. B. Eerdmans, 2004.

Moe, David Thang. "What Had Dietrich Bonhoeffer to Do with Asian Theology?" *The Asia Journal of Theology* 28, no. 2 (October 1, 2014): 175–202.

Muers, Rachel. "Anthropology." In *The Oxford Handbook of Dietrich Bonhoeffer*, edited by Michael Mawson and Philip G. Ziegler, 196–209. Oxford: Oxford University Press, 2019.

Muers, Rachel. "Feminism, Gender, and Theology." In *The Modern Theologians: An Introduction to Christian Theology Since 1918*, 3rd ed., edited by David F. Ford and Rachel Muers, 431–50. Oxford: Blackwell Publishing, 2005.

Muers, Rachel. "Feminist Theology as Practice of the Future." *FemTh* 16, no. 1 (September 2007): 110–27.

Muers, Rachel. *Keeping God's Silence: Towards a Theological Ethics of Communication*. Oxford: Blackwell Publishing, 2004.

Muers, Rachel and Mike Higton. *Modern Theology: A Critical Introduction*. London: Routledge, 2012.

Müller, Gerhard. "Luther's Transformation of Medieval Thought: Discontinuity and Continuity." In *The Oxford Handbook of Martin Luther's Theology*, edited by Robert Kolb, Irene Dingel, and L'ubomir Batka, 105–14. Oxford: Oxford University Press, 2016.

Nation, Mark Thiessen, Anthony G. Siegrist, and Daniel P. Umbel. *Bonhoeffer the Assassin? Challenging the Myth, Recovering His Call to Peacemaking*. Grand Rapids, MI: Baker Academic, 2013.

Nicoll, Jeff. *Augustine's Problem: Impotence and Grace*. Eugene, OR: Wipf and Stock, 2016.

Nielsen, Kirsten Busch. "Community Turned Inside Out: Dietrich Bonhoeffer's Concept of the Church and of Humanity Reconsidered." In *Being Human, Becoming Human: Dietrich Bonhoeffer and Social Thought*, edited by Jens Zimmermann and Brian Gregor, 91–101. Eugene, OR: Pickwick Publications, 2010.

Nielsen, Kirsten Busch. *Die Gebrochene Macht Der Sünde: Der Beitrag Dietrich Bonhoeffers Zur Hamartiologie* [The broken power of sin: Dietrich Bonhoeffer's contribution to hamartiology]. Arbeiten Zur Systematischen Theologie. Leipzig, Germany: Evangelische Verlagsanstalt, 2010.

Oberman, Heiko A. *Luther: Man between God and the Devil*. Translated by Eileen Walliser-Schwarzbart. New Haven, CT: Yale University Press, 2006.

O'Donovan, Oliver. *The Problem of Self-Love in St. Augustine*. Eugene, OR: Wipf & Stock, 2006.

O'Donovan, Oliver. "*Usus* and *Fruitio* in Augustine, *De Doctrina Christiana* I." *JTS* 33, no. 2 (1982): 361–97.

Osborn, Eric. *Irenaeus of Lyons*. Cambridge: Cambridge University Press, 2001.

Pangritz, Andreas. *Karl Barth in the Theology of Dietrich Bonhoeffer*. Grand Rapids, MI: Wm. B. Eerdmans, 2000.

Plaskow, Judith. *Sex, Sin and Grace: Women's Experience and the Theologies of Reinhold Niebuhr and Paul Tillich*. Washington, DC: University Press of America, 1980.

Plato. *Republic*. Edited and translated by Chris Emlyn-Jones and William Preddy. Cambridge, MA: Harvard University Press, 2013.

Plotinus. *The Six Enneads*. Abridged ed. Translated by Stephen Mackenna and John M. Dillon. London: Penguin, 1991.

Plumer, Eric. "Appendix 2 of Augustine." In *Augustine's Commentary on Galatians*. Oxford Early Christian Studies. Oxford: Oxford University Press, 2003.

Portalié, Eugène. "Augustinisme." In *Dictionaire Théologie Catholique*, 1:2485–561. Paris: Letouzey et Ané, 1931.

Prüller-Jagenteufel, Gunter M. *Ethik Im Theologischen Diskurs* [Ethics in theological discourse], *Vol. 7: Befreit Zur Verantwortung: Sünde Und Versöhnung in der Ethik Dietrich Bonhoeffers* [Released to responsibility: Sin and reconciliation in the ethics of Dietrich Bonhoeffer]. Münster, Germany: LIT, 2004.

Ramsey, Paul. "The Case of the Curious Exception." In *Norm and Context in Christian Ethics*, edited by Gene H. Outka and Paul Ramsey, 67–135. London: SCM Press, 1973.

Reuther, Rosemary Radford. *Sexism and God-Talk: Toward a Feminist Theology*. Boston: Beacon, 1983.

Rigby, Paul. *Original Sin in Augustine's Confessions*. Ottawa, ON: University of Ottawa Press, 1987.

Rigby, Paul. "Original Sin." In *Augustine through the Ages: An Encyclopedia*, edited by Allan D. Fitzgerald. Grand Rapids, MI: Wm. B. Eerdmans, 2009.

Rist, John M. *Augustine: Ancient Thought Baptized*. Cambridge: Cambridge University Press, 1997.
Rist, John M. "Augustine of Hippo." In *The Medieval Theologians*, edited by G. R. Evans, 3–23. Oxford: Blackwell Publishing, 2004.
Rumscheidt, Martin. "The Formation of Bonhoeffer's Theology." In *The Cambridge Companion to Dietrich Bonhoeffer*, edited by John W. de Gruchy, 50–70. New York: Cambridge University Press, 1999.
Rumscheidt, Martin. "Harnack, Seeberg and Bonhoeffer." In *Bonhoeffer's Intellectual Formation: Theology and Philosophy in His Thought*, edited by Peter Frick, 201–24. Tübingen, Germany: Mohr Siebeck, 2008.
Rüter, Martin, and Ilse Tödt. "Editor's Afterword to the German Edition." In *DBWE* 3:147–73.
Rüter, Martin, and Ilse Tödt. "Editor's Afterword to the German Edition." In *DBWE* 6: 409–49.
Saak, Eric Leland. *Creating Augustine: Interpreting Augustine and Augustinianism in the Later Middle Ages*. Oxford: Oxford University Press, 2017.
Saak, Eric Leland. *Luther and the Reformation of the Later Middle Ages*. Cambridge: Cambridge University Press, 2017.
Saiving, Valerie. "The Human Situation: A Feminine View." In *Womanspirit Rising*, 2nd ed., edited by Carol P. Christ and Judith Plaskow, 25–42. San Francisco: HarperCollins, 1992.
Schliesser, Christine. *Everyone Who Acts Responsibly Becomes Guilty: Bonhoeffer's Concept of Accepting Guilt*. Louisville, KY: Westminster John Knox Press, 2008.
Schmitt, Carl. *Political Theology: Four Chapters on the Concept of Sovereignty*. Translated by George Schwab. London: University of Chicago Press, 2005.
Seeberg, Reinhold. *The History of Doctrine*, vol. 1, translated by Charles E. Hay. Philadelphia: Lutheran Publication Society, 1997.
Slenczka, Notger. "Luther's Anthropology." In *The Oxford Handbook of Martin Luther's Theology*, edited by Robert Kolb, Irene Dingel, and L'ubomir Batka, 212–31. Oxford: Oxford University Press, 2016.
Smith, Ted A. *Weird John Brown: Divine Violence and the Limits of Ethics*. Stanford, CA: Stanford University Press, 2015.
Steenberg, Matthew Craig. *Irenaeus on Creation: The Cosmic Christ and the Saga of Redemption*. Leiden, the Netherlands: Brill, 2008.
TeSelle, Eugene. *Augustine the Theologian*. Eugene, OR: Wipf and Stock, 2002.
Teske, Roland. "Scriptural Index to *Answer to the Pelagians*." In *The Works of St. Augustine: A Translation for the 21st Century*, vol. 23, edited by John Rotelle, 543–59. New York: New City Press, 1997.
Tietz, Christiane. "Bonhoeffer on the Ontological Structure of the Church." In *Ontology and Ethics: Bonhoeffer and Contemporary Scholarship*, edited by Adam C. Clark and Michael Mawson, 32–46. Eugene, OR: Pickwick Publications, 2013.
Tietz, Christiane. "The Mystery of Knowledge, Sin, and Shame." In *Mysteries in the Theology of Dietrich Bonhoeffer: A Copenhagen Bonhoeffer Symposium*, edited by Kirsten Busch Nielsen, Ulrik Nissen, and Christiane Tietz, 27–48. Göttingen, Germany: Vandenhoeck & Ruprecht, 2007.
Tietz, Christiane. *Theologian of Resistance: The Life and Thought of Dietrich Bonhoeffer*. Translated by Victoria J. Barnett. Minneapolis: Fortress, 2016.
Trueman, Carl R. "Original Sin and Modern Theology." In *Adam, the Fall, and Original Sin: Theological, Biblical, and Scientific Perspectives*, edited by Hans Madueme and Michael Reeves, 167–88. Grand Rapids, MI: Baker Academic, 2014.

von Balthasar, Hans Urs. *The Theology of Karl Barth: Exposition and Interpretation*. Translated by Edward T. Oakes. San Francisco: Ignatius Press, 1993.

Webster, John. "'In the Society of God': Some Principles in Ecclesiology." In *Perspectives on Ecclesiology and Ethnography*, edited by Pete Ward, 200–22. Grand Rapids, MI: Wm. B. Eerdmans, 2011.

Whitford, David M. *Luther: A Guide for the Perplexed*. London: T&T Clark, 2011.

Wilkes, Nicola J. "Life and Health: Bonhoeffer's Normative and Divergent Accounts of Private Confession of Sin," *TTod* 71, no. 1 (April 2014): 58–68.

Williams, Stephen N. "The Sovereignty of God." In *Engaging the Doctrine of God: Contemporary Protestant Perspectives*, edited by Bruce L. McCormack, 169–84. Grand Rapids, MI: Baker Academic, 2008.

Wyrwa, Dietmar. "Augustine and Luther on Evil." In *The Problem of Evil and Its Symbols in Jewish and Christian Tradition*, edited by Henning Graf and Yair Hoffman, 124–46. London: T&T Clark International, 2004.

Ziegler, Philip G. "'Bound Over to Satan's Tyranny': Sin and Satan in Contemporary Reformed Hamartiology." *TTod* 75, no. 1 (2018): 89–100.

Ziegler, Philip G. "'Completely within God's Doing': Soteriology as Meta-Ethics in the Theology of Dietrich Bonhoeffer." In *Christ, Church, and World: New Studies in Bonhoeffer's Theology and Ethics*, 101–17. London: Bloomsbury T&T Clark, 2016.

Ziegler, Philip G. "Graciously Commanded: Dietrich Bonhoeffer and Karl Barth on the Decalogue." *SJT* 71, no. 2 (2018): 127–41.

Other Resources

Blow, Charles. "Trump Isn't Hitler. But the Lying…." *New York Times* [op-ed], October 19, 2017. https://www.nytimes.com/2017/10/19/opinion/trump-isnt-hitler-but-the-lying.html.

Choe, Sang-Hun, "The Populist Pastor Leading a Conservative Revival in South Korea." *New York Times*, November 11, 2019. https://www.nytimes.com/2019/11/08/world/asia/jun-kwang-hoon-pastor-.html?searchResultPosition=8.

Metaxas, Eric. "Should Christians Vote for Trump?" *The Wall Street Journal* [op-ed], October 12, 2016. https://www.wsj.com/articles/should-christians-vote-for-trump-1476294992.

INDEX

actus directus (direct consciousness) 80–1
actus reflexus (consciousness of reflection) 80–1
Adam and Eve 6, 26–9, 39, 42–3, 55–6, 62, 64, 66–70, 72–4, 78, 81, 89–90, 92, 95–102, 104–6, 111–13, 118–19, 139, 149, 179 n.88, 181 n.137, 184 n.187. *See also* sin
Althaus, Paul 37–8, 122, 185 n.209, 188 n.48
Ambrose 27, 55, 162 n.99
Ambrosiaster 27, 55, 162 n.89, 162 n.99
analogia entis (analogy of being) 24, 38–9, 92–3, 97, 128–9, 131
analogia relationis (analogy of relation) 51, 66, 92–5, 97, 100, 107, 129, 131
androcentrism 8, 111, 148
Ansbacher Ratschlag (The Ansbach Memorandum) 122, 188 n.48
anthropology 11, 13, 24, 29, 33–5, 37–8, 40–3, 47, 50, 60, 93–4, 97–8, 104, 109, 116, 122, 135, 140, 148–50, 153, 161 n.79
   anthropological transition 36, 41
   ethical 53, 58, 122
   holistic 4, 33, 35–8, 41, 148
   relational 4, 33, 40, 53, 58
   scholastic 35–6, 165 n.25
   soteriocentric 93
Aquinas, Thomas 164 n.5
   Summa Theologia, in *Basic Writings of Saint Thomas Aquinas* 157 n.14
Arendt, Hannah 120–1
   Eichmann in Jerusalem 187 n.42
Asian theologies 146, 149–50
association of authentic rule (*Herrschaftsverband*) 60–1
atonement 72, 74, 91, 112
Augustine of Hippo 1–2, 6–7, 9–12, 35, 40, 42, 45, 49, 55–6, 66, 69, 72, 76, 79, 87–9, 92–3, 95–6, 100–1, 104, 109, 111, 116, 124–5, 127–8, 131, 133, 138, 141, 147–8, 151, 154 n.3, 155 n.4, 156 n.3, 160 n.62, 182 n.161
   Ad Simplicianum 161 n.84, 161 n.86
   aversio ab (turning away from) 102
   on Christ 128–9
   Christianized Neoplatonic cosmology 3, 13–16, 20, 22, 25, 30
   Christian optimism 19, 57, 158 n.32
   The City of God 173 n.82
   civitas terrena (the earthly city) 48
   civitate Dei (the city of God) 3, 5, 48, 67, 73, 75
   Confessions 15, 22, 145, 147, 159 n.48, 160 n.72, 161 n.83
   corpus Christi (the body of Christ) 54, 62–3, 73
   creatio ex nihilo 17–20, 78, 88–9, 94–5, 158 n.23, 158 n.32
   definition of God 15
   doctrine of God to the doctrine of the church 2, 5, 13, 33, 53, 56, 75, 77, 86, 115
   earthly church 48–9, 62, 73
   Enchiridion 19, 159 n.40
   on evil 19, 158 n.30, 158 n.37
   Expositions of the Psalms 63, 164 n.9
   On Free Will 21, 157 n.12, 158 n.38, 159 n.41, 163 nn.109–10
   On the Holy Trinity 161 n.80
   homo incurvatus in se (man turned in upon himself) 40, 51, 69, 102, 116
   infant baptism theory 163 n.105
   and Manichaeism (dissatisfaction with) 13–17, 19–20, 24
   On Marriage and Concupiscence 162 n.100, 163 n.111
   The Nature of the Good 17
   and Nicene Trinity 24, 161 n.76
   order of creation (*see* order of creation)
   original sin (*see* original sin)

partly righteous and sinner 175 n.131
perfection 163 n.116
posse et non posse peccare 101
predestination 14, 30, 45, 57, 72, 97, 101
pride/egocentricity (notion of sin) 5, 7, 10 (*see also* pride)
Revisions 1.9.3; 1.9.4–5 163 n.107
and Simplicianus 25
Teaching Christianity 22
theodicy 14, 19–20, 30
totus Christus (the whole Christ) 11, 36, 53–5, 58, 61–3, 73–5, 164 n.10, 171 n.57
use of knowledge 157 n.14
Augustinianism 2, 34–5, 37–8, 44, 46, 50, 98, 152, 154–5 n.3, 164 n.5
Ayres, Lewis 15
Augustine and the Trinity 157 n.10

baptism/conversion 28, 36, 38, 41, 56, 68, 72, 165 n.13, 165 n.24, 166 n.49
infant baptism theory 163 n.105
Barth, Karl 65, 78–80, 83, 93, 172 n.76, 173 n.80, 177 n.27, 179–80 n.108
and Christocentrism 84–6
The Epistle to Romans 65, 79, 82, 86
and Scripture 79–80, 82
threefold nature of sin 188 n.47
The Word of God and Theology 79
Bartmann, Bernhard, *Dogmatik* 108
Batka, L'ubomir 38, 42, 166 n.49, 166 n.56
Bayer, Oswald 39, 48, 129, 164 n.1
Beatrice, Pier Franco 26, 55, 162 n.89
The Transmission of Sin 163 n.106
being (existence) 19, 25. *See also* created beings; human/human being
highest 35, 57
Berkouwer, G. C. 71
Bethge, Eberhard 65, 79, 82, 84–5, 172 n.76, 177 n.27
Dietrich Bonhoeffer 177 n.43
The Bible 79, 81, 85–6, 118, 122, 141, 146, 169 n.8, 178 n.65
body 17–18, 24, 26–7, 35–7, 49, 107, 111, 164 n.10, 170 n.38. *See also* soul
Bonhoeffer, Dietrich (1906–45) 1–2, 4, 7, 14, 23, 27, 30–1, 33, 40, 43, 50–1, 53, 64–5, 75, 162 n.97, 164 n.10

Act and Being (*Act und Zein*) 6, 54, 77–82, 84–5, 87, 100, 109–10, 117–18, 150, 176 n.22, 186 n.15
"After Ten Years" 1, 69, 117–21, 136, 147, 188 n.47
Christian personalism (*see* Christian/Christianity, personalism)
"Christology Lectures" 132
communal interpretation 6, 102
community *vs.* society 60
"Contemporizing New Testament Texts" 180 n.125
creatio continua 180 n.112
Creation and Fall (see *Creation and Fall* (Bonhoeffer))
crede ut intelligas (believe in order that you may understand) 78, 86–8
Discipleship 125–6, 137
dissertation 1, 5, 9–10, 53–4, 79–80, 104, 107, 124, 153, 155 n.11
and Elizabeth Zinn 193 n.153
on ethical relational person 60
ethics 7–8, 11, 50, 126, 190 n.82
Ethics 1, 10, 109, 128–9, 151, 188 n.57
"Ethics as Formation" 133
Habilitationsschrift 80
and Harnack 82, 109
historical criticism 78, 83, 85–7, 91, 93, 177 n.27
"History and Good (2)" 131–2, 138–9, 191 n.102
"Inaugural Lecture" 139
"Lectures on Christology" 129
lectures on Genesis 79, 82–4, 86, 95, 107
Letters and Papers from Prison 75, 145, 147
Menschwerdung (becoming human) 124, 185 n.2, 189 n.65
nihil negativum (absolute nothingness) 89, 92
nihil provativum (privative nothingness) 89
peccator pessimus (worst sinner) 70, 73
philosophical-transcendental epistemology 80
predestination 169 n.22
ratio in se ipsam incurve 80
revelation 172 n.76

Rüdiger Schleicher 176 n.18
sacrificium intellectus (surrender of thinking) 87
Sanctorum Communio: A Theological Study of the Sociology of the Church (*DBWE* 1) 9, 154 n.3, 155 n.6, 168 n.2, 169 n.8, 170 n.29, 171 n.44, 171 n.51, 173 n.82, 173 n.91, 174 n.106, 175 n.22
Sanctorum Communio (community of saints) 1, 3, 5–11, 53–6, 58–9, 61–3, 67–9, 71, 73–5, 77, 79–81, 84–6, 96, 99–104, 106, 108, 110, 112, 117–18, 121, 130, 132–3, 139, 145, 147, 150–1, 175 n.28, 186 n.15
Sanctorum Communio: Eine dogmatische Untersuchung 5, 9, 54
Sanctorum Communio: Eine dogmatische Untersuchung zur Soziologie der Kirche (*DBW* 1) 9, 171 n.49
scholarship 8–10, 53, 62, 151, 153, 171 n.57
and sin 67–71
assessment of original sin 54–8
as individual/supra-individual deed 59
Bonner, Gerald 16, 20, 27, 55, 158 n.32
Brain, Michael 106
Bultmann, Rudolf 180 n.125

cantus firmus 24, 40, 53
caro (flesh) 36–8, 49. See also *spiritus* (spirit)
Cary, Philip 22–3
Augustine's Invention of the Inner Self 160 n.68, 161 n.76
Catholic theology 93
Chalcedonian Christology 123, 188–9 n.60
Charry, Ellen T. 159 n.48, 160 n.68
Christ 1, 3, 5–6, 29–31, 33–5, 38, 53–4, 56–7, 60–2, 65, 68, 72–5, 81, 84–5, 88, 94–6, 99, 102, 107, 121, 123, 127, 129–31, 138, 141, 155 n.4, 186 n.15, 190 n.85

Augustine on 128–9
bound will and freedom in 43–50
in Christo (in Christ) 45
church of Christ 74, 84–5, 96
de Christo (away from Christ) 45
form (*Gestalt*) of 127
God's humanization in 7, 77, 109–10, 112, 116, 122–7, 138, 140–1
resurrection of 89, 125–7
righteousness of 36, 38, 41, 44, 132, 165 n.15
Spirit of Christ 45
Christian/Christianity 1, 14, 16, 19, 45, 47–9, 57–8, 121, 143, 152–3, 155 n.7, 157 n.14, 190 n.78. See also non-Christians
Christian freedom 2, 34, 50–1, 113, 116, 127–31, 134, 141, 148
Christianized Platonism 13, 30
civil rulers over 128, 137–8
ethics 2, 8, 24, 51, 92, 115–16, 121, 123, 126–7, 129, 131, 141
formation (*Gestaltung*) 126, 188 n.57
German 143, 148, 177 n.42, 191 n.100
personalism 54–5, 58–66, 75, 84, 95, 110, 122
characteristics 59
and ecclesiology 61–4
God and humanity 60
interpersonal concept 59
modernized 77
and sociology 58–61
pessimism 2, 30, 57, 162 n.92
responsibility 2–3, 6–8, 29, 71, 75, 92, 113, 115–16, 144, 148, 150, 152
Western 1–2, 30, 103, 141, 143
Christianized Platonic cosmology 4, 16, 35, 56
Christocentrism 2, 4–6, 8, 21, 33–8, 40–1, 43, 48, 53–6, 58, 65–6, 78, 83–6, 89, 91–2, 109, 111–12, 122, 127, 129, 132, 135, 141, 150, 173 n.80, 177–8 n.49
Christology 25, 33, 36, 63, 74, 115, 122–4, 127, 188 n.49
Christus als Gemeinde existierend (Christ existing as church-community) 5, 54

church community (*Gemeinde*) 1–3, 5–7, 49, 53–4, 56, 58, 60–8, 70–6, 80, 82, 84–7, 97, 99–100, 105, 109, 112, 121–4, 126–34, 137–8, 140, 144–5, 147–8, 150–1
class 1, 7, 10, 113, 116, 144, 149, 153. *See also* gender; race, human
Class, Gottfried, *Der verzweifelte Zugriff auf das Leben: Dietrich Bonhoeffers Sündenverständnis in "Schöpfung und Fall"* 9
classical theism 4–5, 24, 75
co-humanity 99. *See also* humanity
collective person 5, 54, 58, 60–1, 63, 66, 68–9, 73–5, 84–6, 95, 101–2, 128, 146. *See also* communal person; corporate person; individual person
communal person 5, 7, 11, 56, 58, 60, 66–8, 70, 75, 92, 129–30, 146, 182 n.144. *See also* collective person; corporate person; individual person
communitarian personalism 2, 5–6, 66, 78–9, 85–6, 95, 99–100, 103, 111, 169 n.16
community (*Gemeinschaft*) 60–1, 169 n.16
    community-focused personalism 75, 100–1
    community of love (*Liebesgemeinschaft*) 61
    vs. society 60
concupiscence (*concupiscentia*) 6, 28, 30, 38, 40–3, 51, 100, 103–7, 109–11, 115–16, 166 n.49, 184 n.190
    original sin as 25–7, 30, 38, 77
Constantinople Creeds 161 n.77
Conybeare, Catherine 19
co-responsibility (of first community) 102–3, 182 n.152
corporate person 54, 57, 63, 71–3, 120. *See also* collective person; communal person; individual person
corporeality 6, 26, 77, 101, 104–10, 112, 122, 126, 188 n.49
cosmology 13–16, 63

Christianized Platonic/Neoplatonic 4, 13–14, 16, 20, 56
    hierarchical 13, 15, 18–19, 31, 48
    monotheistic 156 n.2
    ontological 15
    Plotinus' 16, 157 n.16
cosmos 16
created beings 17–18, 20. *See also* human/human being
creatio ex nihilo (creation out of nothing) 17–20, 78, 88–9, 94–5, 158 n.23, 158 n.32
Creation and Fall (Bonhoeffer) 1, 6–7, 9, 54, 66, 77–8, 111–12, 115, 118, 122, 126, 132, 145–6, 149, 178 n.58, 185 n.209, 187 n.40
    barrier 170 n.43
    beginning (Gen. 1:1–2)
        analogia relationis (analogy of relation) 92–5, 97, 100, 107
        creatio ex nihilo (creation out of nothing) 88–9
        crede ut intelligas 78, 86–8
        tob and *ra* (good and evil)/trees of knowledge 89–92, 105, 179 n.90
    creation
        Eve (creation of the other) 97–100, 104, 118–19
        of humankind 95–7
    ecclesiocentric hermeneutics 84–6
    fall 100–1
        of community 101–3
        Luther/Lutherans 109–10
        and sexuality 103–9
    Green on 117
    knowing God 79–82
    Scripture 79–80, 83–4, 86
    theological exegesis 82–4
    word of God in 79–80, 83, 88
Creator 18, 25, 90, 96–7, 99–100, 105, 117. *See also* God
    creation of God 1, 6, 15–20, 24, 29, 38–9, 47–8, 99
culpability 3, 6–7, 27–31, 43, 51, 54–7, 66, 70–4, 110, 169 n.17. *See also* involuntary alien guilt
    of Adam 66, 72, 74, 104, 162 n.99
    alien 6–7, 29, 31, 51, 57, 71–3, 77, 110–12, 132, 140–1

biological imputation of 57
biological transmission of 28, 71, 108, 111–12
communal 56
personal 55–6, 66, 174 n.106

Dahill, Lisa E. 149
  Reading from the Underside of the Self: Bonhoeffer and Spiritual Formation 187 n.24
Dávila, María Teresa 137
Decalogue 128, 136, 194 n.156
de Gruchy, John W. 82–3, 112, 146, 185 n.209
DeJonge, Michael P. 49, 80, 110, 134–5
  Bonhoeffer's Reception of Luther 177 n.48, 181 n.130, 191 n.108, 192 n.123
Demiurge 157 n.20
desire (*Sucht*) 21, 39, 90–1, 104, 106, 159 n.62, 182 n.160, 183 n.170
divine/divinity 3, 24, 39, 47, 81, 87, 91, 123
  divine grace 100
  divine knowledge 81
  divine mandate 138
  divine other 91–2, 111, 117, 169 n.16
Dodaro, Robert 128
  Christ and the Just Society 19 n.92
dominion 94, 118
Donatism/Donatists 161 n.81, 161 n.86
Duff, Nancy J. 136
  "Dietrich Bonhoeffer's Theological Ethic" 193 n.135

ecclesiocentrism 2, 5, 50, 77–9, 84–6, 95–6, 100, 103, 110, 112, 127, 132, 141, 152–3
ecclesiology 5, 8, 10–11, 36, 49, 53–4, 56, 58, 71–4, 98, 109, 128, 150, 168 n.2
  communitarian 132
  and personalism 61–4
Eden garden 89, 179 n.82, 182 n.161. *See also* Adam and Eve
Edwards, Mark U., Jr. 133
  Luther and the False Brethren 192 n.115
egocentricity 5, 7, 10, 23, 40, 69, 78, 81, 91, 116–18, 121, 147–8, 185 n.3
Eichmann, Otto Adolf 121, 187 n.42

Elert, Wermer 122, 188 n.48
Epicurus, *Dialogues Concerning Natural Religion* 156 n.1
epistemology 21, 25, 34, 40, 49, 59, 78, 81–4, 87, 109
  philosophical-transcendental 80–1
  theological 78, 80, 84, 86, 109–10
Erasmus 44–6, 101
eschatology 19
eternity 3, 31, 65
ethics 7–8, 11, 19, 21, 94, 122, 125, 143–4, 153
  Bonhoeffer's 7–8, 11, 50, 126, 190 n.82
  Christian 2, 8, 24, 51, 92, 115–16, 121, 123, 126–7, 129, 131, 141
  ethical being 72
  ethical co-responsibility 71
  ethical evil 22, 130, 138, 140, 191 n.104
  ethical responsibility 7, 30, 45, 47, 57, 60, 74, 76
evil 1–4, 7–11, 13–14, 18–19, 27, 30–1, 33–4, 46, 53, 56–7, 76, 78, 88, 94, 96, 105, 112, 115, 119–21, 127, 130, 134, 140–1, 143–6. *See also* God; Satan
  ethical 22, 130, 138, 140, 191 n.104
  free will (source of evil) 20–5
  moral 20–2, 158 n.38
  problem of evil 14–17, 19–20, 88, 156 nn.1–2
exegesis, biblical 1, 6, 13–14, 26, 28–31, 34–6, 38, 43, 77–9, 82, 96, 98–101, 108, 110–11, 129, 182 n.152
existentialism 4
ex opere operato, sacrament as 38, 41, 165 n.24
external Church 48–9. *See also* internal Church

Fabisiak, Thomas 90
fallen angels 19, 158 n.37
fatalism 57, 75
Faus, José Ignacio González 146
first community 6, 66–7, 70, 78, 85–6, 89, 91, 94–103, 112, 146
  co-responsibility of 102–3, 182 n.152
Floyd, Wayne Whitson 59, 168 n.2

formation (*Gestaltung*) 126, 153, 188 n.57, 190 n.82
free will 27, 30, 43–50
  source of evil 20–5
frui (to enjoy) 22

gender 1, 7, 10, 99, 113, 116, 119, 144, 149, 153, 161 n.79, 187 n.25. *See also* class; race, human
Genesis 76, 78, 86–7
  Bonhoeffer's lectures on 79, 82–4, 86–7, 95, 107
  Luther's lecture on 38–9, 43, 47, 92, 94
Germany 8, 50–1, 61, 63, 67, 73, 82–3, 109, 111, 129, 131, 133–4, 138, 140, 150, 185 n.209, 186 n.15, 192 n.121
Geschlechtlichen 106, 184 n.181
Geschlechtlichkeit 104–6, 108, 181 n.142
God 1, 4, 14–17, 21–3, 25, 35, 39, 47–50, 53, 56, 60, 63–4, 69–70, 72, 80, 88, 90, 100, 151, 156 n.2. *See also* evil; Satan
  benevolent/omnipotent/non-omnipotence/omnibenevolent of 16–19, 28, 72, 88, 156 n.2
  community's rebellion against 66, 69, 90, 101
  creation of 1, 6, 15–20, 24, 29, 38–9, 47–8
    good/goodness 17–21, 23
  existence of 97, 107, 124, 156 n.2
  free action of 89, 122, 136–7
  freedom of 39, 89, 91–4, 96, 99, 129–30
  God in Christ 2–5, 7, 30, 33–5, 39, 45, 56, 65, 67, 71, 73, 75, 81, 129
  grace of 29, 31, 44, 46, 56–7
  guilty toward the world 123
  heavenly city of 3, 5–6, 24, 31, 49, 62, 73, 128, 158 n.33
  and humanity 16, 39, 42–3, 60, 65–6, 69, 77, 93, 96–7
  humanization in Christ (God's becoming human) 7, 77, 109–10, 112, 116, 122–7, 138, 140–1
  image of (*see imago Dei* (image of God))
  immanence 2, 23, 58, 92, 96
  knowledge of 25, 39, 80–1, 117
  like God (*sicut Deus*) 23, 90–1, 102, 116–17, 147
  monotheistic 13, 15
  relational image of 38–40, 42–4, 47, 50, 66, 68, 94, 98
  sovereignty of 16, 21, 28, 63, 72
  transcendence of 2, 31, 34, 56–8, 63, 172 n.74, 182 n.151
  Trinitarian God 20, 24, 30, 78, 92, 170 n.138
  triune God 24, 161 n.77
  word of God 79–80, 83, 88, 118–19, 136, 182 n.149, 190 n.78
  Yahweh God 180 n.116
gospels 40, 43, 129, 141, 146, 166 n.35, 172 n.74, 186 n.4, 192 n.114
Green, Clifford J. 65, 97, 103, 117, 134, 171 n.57, 174 n.110, 180 n.108, 183 n.166, 191 n.98
  responsible action, dimensions of 193 n.150
Greene-McCreight, Kathryn 119
Greggs, Tom 70, 102, 168 n.2, 172 n.80, 174 n.116
  "Bearing Sin in the Church: The Ecclesial Hamartiology of Bonhoeffer" 10
Grenze (limit) 6, 77, 89–90, 98–9, 107, 140, 179 n.83. *See also Mitte* (center)
Grobowski, Stanislaus J. 73
Guth, Karen V. 149, 195 n.24

hamartiology 7–8, 23, 50–1, 140, 186 n.4
  Augustinian 1–4, 6, 8–11, 13–14, 18, 20–2, 24–5, 28, 30–1, 40–1, 51, 54–6, 58, 61, 67, 69, 71, 74–5, 90, 101, 116, 121, 143–4, 148, 152–3, 154 n.3
  Bonhoeffer's 1–4, 6–7, 9–11, 13, 49–50, 53–4, 58, 63–4, 67, 72, 75–8, 86, 102, 104, 111, 115, 121, 141, 143, 148–9, 151–3, 154 n.3, 155 n.8, 168 n.1
  Lutheran 3–5, 13, 33, 40, 51, 55, 67, 94
  traditional 2–3, 71, 78, 117, 140, 152
  Western 2–3, 6, 10, 13, 34, 56, 58, 67, 78, 115–17, 143, 145–8, 153, 154 n.3, 163 n.109

Hampson, Daphne 185 n.3
Harasta, Eva 9, 104
   "Adam in Christ? The Place of Sin in Christ-Reality" 10
Harnack, Adolf von 57, 62, 82, 103–4, 107, 162 n.92, 177 n.27, 180 n.125, 183 n.170
   and Bonhoeffer 82, 109
   historical-critical methodology 78, 82–4
Harvey, Barry 62
   "Augustine and Aquinas" 182 n.153
Hegel, Georg Wilhelm Friedrich 171 n.57
Hermann, Erik 36
Hermanson, Amy K., "Saint Augustine and the Creation of a Distinctly Christian Rhetoric" 158 n.30
hermeneutics/hermeneutical method 16, 25, 34–6, 41–3, 55, 77–8, 81–3, 87, 100, 112, 115, 180 n.122, 180 n.125
   biblical 86
   ecclesiocentric 84–6
   theological 83
hierarchy 15, 56, 89, 149, 162 n.101
   of being 18
   Christianized Neoplatonic 22, 30
   hierarchical cosmology 13, 15, 18–19, 31, 48
historical-critical methodology 78, 82–4, 180 n.125
Hitler, Adolf 92, 122, 145, 151, 184 n.207, 192 n.121. *See also* Nazis/Nazism
holistic anthropology 4, 33, 35–8, 41, 148. *See also* relational anthropology
Holl, Karl 8, 51, 93, 125, 127, 139, 153, 172 n.74, 178 n.70
   communal interpretation 189 n.76
   The Reconstruction of Morality 125, 189 n.76
   What Did Luther Understand by Religion? 189 n.72
Holy Spirit 31, 37, 88, 168 n.92
human/human being 3, 7, 14, 18–19, 26, 28–30, 34–9, 41, 43, 50–1, 55, 63, 66, 71–2, 78, 80–1, 83, 87–8, 94, 96, 98, 100, 103, 107–8, 113, 122–3, 149. *See also* created beings

ability not to sin (*posse non peccare*) 101
ability to sin (*posse peccare*) 101
bodily existence of 105, 107, 123
corporeality 6, 26, 77, 101, 104–10, 112, 122, 126, 188 n.49
and free will (*see* free will)
God's becoming human 7, 77, 109–10, 112, 116, 122–7, 138, 140–1
good deeds of 130
human freedom 3, 43, 83, 91, 95, 97, 115, 122, 125, 127
humanization of 124–6
human other 91–2, 111, 121, 169 n.16
human solidarity 6, 58, 70–2, 75, 77, 110–11, 115
inability not to sin (*non posse non peccare*) 101
mutable will of 45–6
perfection 30, 38, 162 n.101, 163 n.116
powerlessness 3, 28, 121
relationality 39, 73, 97, 99, 104–6, 181 nn.141–2, 184 n.181
responsibility 2, 14, 28, 43, 47, 93, 121
superiority of first 29, 55, 173 n.82
true 107, 121, 123–5, 127
humanity 2, 4–8, 10, 14, 16–17, 19–22, 25, 28–9, 33–4, 39, 44, 53, 56–8, 60–1, 63–4, 68–70, 74–5, 77–8, 81, 90, 94, 96–7, 99, 102, 107, 111, 115, 117, 122–5, 145–6, 150. *See also* co-humanity
   aspects of 18
   fallen 4, 14, 34, 175 n.122
   fall of 103
   freedom of 90–1
   genuine 5, 29, 35
   and God 16, 39, 42–3, 60, 65–6, 69, 77, 93, 96–7
   primal state of 64–7
   true 6, 30
humankind (*Menschen*) 27, 31, 89–92, 94–100, 102–3, 107, 180 n.116, 182 n.152
Hume, David, inconsistent triad 156 n.1
Hunsinger, George 84–5
   "What Karl Barth Learned from Martin Luther" 177–8 n.49
Hyun Kyung Chung 149

I-centered perspective 148–9
idealism 59, 65, 80–1, 91, 93, 172 n.74
   concept of the person 59, 65
imago Dei (image of God) 4–5, 23–4, 33,
   42–3, 45–6, 48, 78, 92–6, 102,
   106, 119, 129, 148, 181 n.137
   image (*eikon*) 160 n.69
   likeness (*homoiosis*) of God 160 n.69
   relational 38–40, 42–4, 47, 50, 66, 68,
      94, 98
   imputation 36, 38, 41, 44–6, 50, 57, 72,
      131–2, 165 n.51
individual human being (*Mensch*) 95
individual person 5, 7, 11, 54, 57–8, 60,
   66–8, 70–1, 73, 75, 130. *See also*
   collective person; communal
   person; corporate person
inner split (*Zwiespalt*) 91
internal Church 48–9. *See also* external
   Church
involuntary alien guilt 3, 28, 71. *See also*
   culpability
inwardness 5, 23, 120, 160 n.68
Irenaeus of Lyons 17–18, 20, 23, 29, 158
   n.23, 158 n.32, 163 n.116
Israel 68, 146

Jenson, Matt 165 n.23
Jenson, Robert W. 93
justification (passive righteousness of
   God) 56–7, 80, 93–4, 123,
   125–6, 133–5, 138–9, 150–1.
   See also sanctification
justitia passiva (passive righteousness)
   93

Kapproth, Erich 83, 109, 182 n.149
Katz, Sheri, "Person" 170 n.38
Kelly, J. N. D. 26, 55, 162 n.89, 162 n.99
Kolb, Robert 66, 68
   "The Lutheran Doctrine of Original
      Sin" 173 n.90

Latin American liberation theology 146,
   150
Lehel, Ferenc 181 n.135, 187 n.40
liberal theology 79, 82–3
Lohse, Bernhard 49, 93
   Martin Luther's Theology 167 n.82

love 1, 3, 21, 49, 105
   love for/of God (*amor Dei*) 22–3,
      39–40, 48
   love of self/self-love (*amor sui*) 23–4,
      40, 48, 69, 147, 159–60 n.62
   for neighbor 1, 22–3, 29, 39–40, 136
   relationality of 69
Luther, Martin 2–4, 6–11, 14, 21, 23–4,
   28, 30–1, 34, 53, 56–7, 61, 63–4,
   66, 68–70, 72–6, 78–80, 84–5,
   88, 92, 101, 122, 125–6, 128–33,
   151–3, 160 n.75, 168 n.97, 182
   n.161
   on baptism 165 n.24
   The Bondage of the Will 37, 45–6
   coram Deo (before God) 36–7, 43, 61,
      153
   coram hominibus (before human
      beings) 36–7, 43, 61
   cor curvum in se (the heart curved in
      upon itself) 5–6, 69, 73, 77–8,
      81, 98–9, 102, 116–17, 120, 130,
      174 n.104
   creatio ad extra (creation toward the
      outside) 48
   "Disputation against Scholastic
      Theology" 35
   faith and obedience 43, 47, 126
   Fourteen Consolations 164 n.10
   free will 43–50
   holistic anthropology 35–8, 41
   imputation 36, 38, 41, 44, 46
   iustitia Christi (righteousness of
      Christ) 38–9, 41
   iustitia Dei (righteousness of God) 39,
      135
   iustitia passiva 93
   iustus et peccator (righteous and a
      sinner) 72
   on justified person 46–7
   Against Latomus 42
   lecture(s)
      on Genesis 38–9, 43, 47, 92, 94
      on Psalms 126, 166 n.43
      on Romans (*Lectures on Romans*)
         36, 40, 126, 134, 165 n.25
   morality 125–7
   peccatum radicale (radical sin) 42–3,
      50–1, 166 n.47

Reformation theology 35, 42, 49, 51, 80, 93, 126, 132, 138, 151, 192 n.114
relational *imago Dei* (image of God) 4–5, 38–40, 50–1, 66, 68
righteousness (passive and active) 166–7 n.60, 189 n.75
righteous relationality 39, 43
simul iustus et peccator (simultaneously righteous and a sinner) 36–8, 40–2, 44–6, 50–1, 61–2, 68, 73, 75, 112, 121, 132, 135
soteriocentric theology 51, 93–4, 97
Temporal Authority: To What Extent It Should Be Obeyed 49, 168 n.92
totus homo (the whole person) 4, 33, 35–8, 40–7, 50–1, 58, 61–2, 64, 68, 72–3, 104, 108, 111–12, 117, 164 n.10
trajectory of sin 40–3
   concupiscence 40–2, 51
   pride 40, 50–1
   unbelief 42–3, 51
Two Kinds of Righteousness 36, 38, 165 n.25, 189 n.75
two kingdoms 48–51, 129, 134, 138, 140, 167 n.82
will of an unjustified person 167 n.73

Manichaeism 13–17, 19–20, 24, 88, 156 n.2
manifestation 15, 19, 21, 49
   sinful 23–4, 29, 147–8, 161 n.79
Mann, William E. 159 n.46, 163 n.110
Marsh, Charles 65, 172 n.80
mass/massa pertionis (lump of perdition) 72
Matt. 7:18 159 n.40
Matt. 12:11–12 193 n.141
matter 16–18
McBride, Jennifer M. 90, 149
McCormack, Bruce L. 24–5, 154 n.2
McGrath, Alister 37
   Luther's Theology of the Cross 166 n.34
Meconi, David Vincent, *The One Christ: St. Augustine's Theology of Deification* 188 n.59
metaphysics 15, 17, 123, 188 n.49
Migliore, Daniel L. 23, 29, 124, 148, 161 n.77

Mitte (center) 89–90. *See also Grenze* (limit)
monergism 93–4
Muers, Rachel 149, 186 n.4, 195 n.25
   Keeping God's Silence: Towards a Theological Ethics of Communication 187 n.21
Müller, Gerhard 46

National Socialism. *See* Nazis/Nazism
Nazareth Jesus Christ 124. *See also* Christ; God
Nazi Germany 134, 140
Nazis/Nazism 1, 7–8, 50–1, 109–11, 122, 126, 131, 144, 146–8, 150, 181 n.137, 186 n.15, 195 n.31. *See also* Hitler, Adolf
Neoplatonism/Neoplatonists 13–18, 20, 24
new creations 89, 125–6, 155 n.7
New Testament 21, 84, 96, 137, 140–1, 180–1 n.125. *See also* Old Testament
Nicene Trinity 24, 123–4, 161 n.77, 189 n.60
Nicoll, Jeff 27
Nielsen, Kirsten Busch, *Die Gebrochene Macht Der Sünde: Der Beitrag Dietrich Bonhoeffers Zur Hamartiologie* 9
nihil (nothing) 17–19, 88–9, 92, 94
non-being 3, 15–20, 23, 156 n.2, 159 n.45. *See also* privation of good
non-Christians 14, 191 n.110. *See also* Christian/Christianity
non-entity 19–20
nothing/nothingness. *See nihil* (nothing)

Oberman, Heiko A., *Luther: Man between God and the Devil* 167 n.72
ochlos (crowd) 146
O'Donovan, Oliver 23, 160 n.62
Old Testament 21, 79, 84, 86–7, 111, 177 n.42. *See also* New Testament
One or the Good. *See* Supreme Being/ supreme God
ontological cosmology 15
order of creation 16, 18, 20, 24, 38, 98, 110–11, 126, 138, 149, 181 n.135, 181 n.137, 185 n.209, 187 n.40

original sin 1–6, 9–11, 13–14, 31, 33–4, 38, 40–3, 50–1, 53–4, 66, 70, 75, 77, 80, 95, 101–4, 107–9, 111–12, 115–17, 122, 128, 137, 143–4, 150, 155 n.4, 158 n.32, 161 n.86, 162 n.103, 169 n.8, 173 n.84
  vs. actual sin 55–8
  Bonhoeffer's assessment of 54–8
  as concupiscence 25–7, 30, 38, 77
  creatio ex nihilo (*see creatio ex nihilo* (creation out of nothing))
  free will (source of evil) 20–5
  ignorance and difficulty 29–30
  problem of evil 14–17
  reformulation of 71–4, 143
  sexual impurity 109
Osborn, Eric 163 n.116

pagan 16, 157 n.14, 158 n.30
Pangritz, Andreas 65
Pannenberg, Wolfhart 47
Pauline exegesis 4, 13, 25–6, 28–9, 36, 38, 128–9, 141, 161 n.82
Peasants' War 50, 133, 153, 190 n.78
Pelagius 71, 101
  Pelagians/Pelagianism 25, 28, 30–1, 45, 161 n.81, 161 n.86, 162 n.89
penultimate (*Vorletztes*) 136, 138–9. *See also* ultimate (*Letztes*)
Pfeiffer, Hilde 98
Plaskow, Judith, *Sex, Sin and Grace: Women's Experience and the Theologies of Reinhold Niebuhr and Paul Tillich* 185 n.3
Plato 157 n.20
Platonism 13, 30, 38, 63, 89, 147, 157 n.10, 157 n.22, 170 n.38
  concept of the person 59
  Platonic Augustinianism 65
Plotinus 17, 23, 25, 160 n.68, 161 n.83
  cosmology 16
  on cosmos 16
  emanation 16
  Enneads 15
Polanus 84
polemics 25, 45, 161 n.81
Portalié, Eugène 154 n.3
post-Enlightenment 2, 6, 53, 65

postlapsarian community 5, 7, 26, 29, 40, 42, 72, 76, 78, 90–1, 93, 105–6, 110, 115–18, 121, 152–3, 181 n.142, 187 n.25
power (*Macht*) 1, 19, 29–31, 35, 41, 73, 94, 103, 106, 109, 111, 116–19, 121, 125, 143–8, 166 n.45, 175 n.135, 182 n.60, 186 n.15, 194 n.6
prelapsarian community 6, 29, 55, 66, 89, 98, 100, 105, 108, 184 n.181
pride 5, 7, 10, 21, 23–7, 30, 40–1, 43, 47, 50–1, 69, 90, 99, 102, 116–21, 140, 147–50, 158 n.37, 161 n.79, 162 n.103, 163 n.109, 182 n.160, 185 n.3
primal community 67, 98–9, 107
primordial beings 15. *See also* evil; God
privation of good 3, 15–16, 18–19, 22, 89, 156 n.2, 157 n.12. *See also* non-being
procreation 27, 107–8
Protestants 64, 108, 181 n.137
protology 19–20
Prüller-Jagenteufel, Gunter M., *Befreit zur Verantwortung: Sünde und Versöhnung in der EthikDietrich Bonhoeffers* 9
Psalm 51 40, 166 n.43

race, human 1–3, 7, 10, 14, 54, 57–8, 66, 70–3, 90, 98–9, 109–12, 116–17, 122, 145, 149, 152–3, 175 n.22, 175 n.26, 180 n.118, 186 n.4
  co-responsibility of 103
  German 109–11, 185 n.209
  solidarity of 2–3, 27–30, 34, 70
rational beings 18–20, 24, 27, 128
readiness to take on guilt (*Schuldübernahme*) 131, 133, 191 n.106
reconciliation/reconciler 2–3, 5, 9, 30, 54, 56–7, 63, 65, 68, 72, 76, 112, 121–5, 127, 133, 140, 146, 150
Reformation theology 35, 42, 49, 51, 80, 93, 126, 132, 138, 151, 192 n.114
relational anthropology 4, 33, 40, 53, 58. *See also* holistic anthropology
relational human solidarity 71

relationality 5, 7–8, 26, 39–40, 43, 45–8, 59, 78, 94–5, 104–6
  between Christ and the church 62–3, 74, 86
  communal 97, 106
  between God and creation 88
  between God and human being 85, 92, 94
  of God and humanity 88, 94
  human 39, 73, 97, 99, 104–6, 181 nn.141–2, 184 n.181
  I and the other 6, 77, 98–9, 102, 105–6, 117, 121–2, 148, 169 n.16, 170 n.33, 181 n.141, 184 n.187
  of love 69
  between man and woman 94, 97–8, 105–6, 122, 149
  righteous 39, 43
  sinful 11, 66–9, 71, 105
  between state and the church 129–30, 138
  subject-object 59, 81
  voluntary 8, 47
Reuther, Rosemary Radford, *Sexism and God-Talk: Toward a Feminist Theology* 185 n.1
revelation of God in Christ 64–7, 80–8, 107, 111, 123, 180 n.125
Rigby, Paul, *Original Sin in Augustine's Confessions* 161 n.86, 162–3 n.103
Rist, John M. 128
Rom. 5:12 26–7, 55, 58, 162 n.89, 169 n.8
Rom. 13:1–7 128, 137–8, 141
Roman Catholic Church 8, 49
Romero, Oscar 146
Rumscheidt, Martin 70, 82–3, 172 n.74

Saak, Eric Leland 48, 164 n.5
  Luther and the Reformation of the Later Middle Ages 167 n.77, 168 n.88
Sabbath 136–7, 140, 151, 193 n.141
sacraments 38, 41, 80, 82, 127–8, 190 n.85
saints 6–7, 30–1, 48–9, 60–3, 67–8, 73, 84, 95, 126, 128–9, 131, 133–4, 136, 140, 145, 150, 153
Saiving, Valerie 185 n.3
salvation 45–6, 65, 167 n.73

sanctification (active righteousness of God) 56–7, 125–7, 132, 134–5, 139, 150–1, 189 n.71. *See also* justification
Satan 43, 46–7, 118, 158 n.37, 180 n.111, 182–3 n.161, 186 n.15. *See also* evil; God
Scheler, Max 60, 171 n.44
Schleiermacher 84, 177–8 n.49
scholasticism 35–8, 40–1, 49–50, 98
Scripture 2–3, 6, 13–14, 20–1, 30, 34–6, 42, 45, 64, 77–80, 82–4, 86–7, 100, 110–11, 152–3, 155 n.7, 161 n.83, 162 n.89, 177 n.42, 190 n.78
  and Barth 79–80, 82
  hermeneutics of 82
  meanings of flesh in (Luther) 37
Seeberg, Reinhold 51, 62, 69–70, 82, 84, 172 n.74
The self 6–7, 14, 22–3, 40, 47, 116–17, 120–2
  self-confusion 121
  self-deception 7, 115, 119, 121, 130, 144, 147
  self-denigration/self-denial 23, 102, 117, 119–20, 161 n.79
  self-love 23–4, 40, 48, 69, 147, 159–60 n.62
  self-obsession 24, 160 n.62
  sinful self 81, 117–20, 130, 185 n.3
Sermon on the Mount 49
servitude 44–7, 130
sexuality (*Sexualität*) 6, 77–8, 99–100, 110–12, 181 n.142
  creation of woman 98, 105
  and fall of humanity 103–9
  sexual impurity 109
sin 1–11, 13, 17, 20–1, 31, 33–4, 37, 41, 46, 51, 53–4, 56, 63, 66, 75–8, 81, 88, 93–5, 107, 111–12, 115–17, 121, 124, 127, 140–1, 143–4, 150, 152, 165 n.13
  active 7, 42, 116–18, 144, 147–8
  actual 26, 28, 42, 55–8, 165 n.25
  Adam's 26–9, 39, 42–3, 55–6, 69, 95, 110–11 (*see also* Adam and Eve)
  ancestral 27
  anterior/essential 146–7

bearing the sin of others 54, 71, 122, 132, 192 n.114
biological transmission of 3, 7, 27–9, 55, 58, 71, 75, 104, 110
chief 24, 28, 43, 109, 117, 147
communal 1, 8, 70, 143–7, 173 n.84, 194 n.6
corporate 68
dual structure of 54, 67–71, 116–22, 144, 147–50
first 26, 28–9, 39, 42–3, 66–7, 70, 90, 94, 101–4, 106, 108–12, 146, 182 n.161
forgiveness of 74, 125–6
free will's downward movement 21–5
as individual deed 59
inheritance of 26–8, 41, 70, 116
of Israel 146
Luther's doctrine of 40–3
original (*see* original sin)
passive 7, 11, 116–19, 121–2, 140–1, 143–4, 147–8, 153, 161 n.79, 163 n.109
as *peccata actualia* (sinful deeds) 41
peccatorum communio (community of sinners) 5, 61, 73
penalty for 26–8, 108
as pride/egocentricity 5, 7, 10, 23–5 (*see also* pride)
radical 42–3, 50–1, 166 n.47
and responsibility 150–1
sinful collective act (*Gesamtakt*) 69
sinful manifestations 23–4, 29, 147–8, 161 n.79
sinful relationality 11, 66–9, 71, 105
sinful solidarity 5–7, 14, 54, 78, 126, 183 n.168
social 145
as supra-individual deed 59
universality of 2–3, 7, 14, 27–8, 30–1, 34, 41–2, 55, 67, 70, 72, 110, 117
Slenczka, Notger 37
society (*Gesellschaft*) 60–1, 171 n.46
vs. community 60
socio-communal personalism 101
sociology 5, 8, 54, 58, 75
and personalism 58–61, 66
sola Scriptura (by Scripture alone) 35

soteriology 19, 24, 33, 36, 39, 41, 44–5, 47, 50, 72, 93–4, 126, 132, 189 n.75
soul 16–18, 24, 26–7, 31, 35–8, 92, 107, 111, 160 n.72, 165 n.16, 170 n.38. *See also* body
vestige of immanent Trinity 23–4
South African theology 146, 149–50
spiritus (spirit) 36–8, 43, 45, 107. *See also caro* (flesh)
Steenberg, Matthew Craig 18
Stellvertretung. *See* vicarious representative action (*Stellvertretung*)
Supreme Being/supreme God 13, 15–16, 23–4, 34, 38, 157 n.16
synergism 46

temporality 3, 59, 65, 67
TeSelle, Eugene 27
Augustine the Theologian 157–8 n.22
Teske, Roland, "Scriptural Index to *Answer to the Pelagians*" 162 n.89
theodicy 14, 19–20, 30, 87–8
theological determinism 31, 57
theological exegesis 78, 80, 82–4, 86, 88, 177 n.27, 178 n.52
theological hermeneutics 83
Tietz, Christiane 111, 134, 192 n.123
Tönnies, Ferdinand 60
Community and Society 171 n.44
transcendentalism 80–1
trees of knowledge and life (*tob* and *ra*) 89–92, 98–100, 105, 179 n.90
Trinitarian God 20, 30, 78, 92. *See also* God
Trueman, Carl R., "Original Sin and Modern Theology" 172 n.71

ultimate (*Letztes*) 136, 139. *See also* penultimate (*Vorletztes*)
The United States 150, 195–6 n.31
uti (to use) 22

vicarious representative action (*Stellvertretung*) 3, 7–8, 29, 54, 66, 71, 73–8, 109–10, 112, 115–16, 121–2, 127–9, 131–40, 144, 150–2
visible Church 3, 49, 153

voluntary representative action 74, 125–6
von Balthasar, Hans Urs 79
   The Theology of Karl Barth: Exposition and Interpretation 176 n.3

Webster, John 154 n.3, 170 n.31
Western Christianity 1–2, 30, 103, 141, 143. *See also* Christian/Christianity

Western church 10, 23, 25, 30, 74–5, 79, 88
Whitford, David M. 45
Williams, Stephen N. 21
Word/word of God 79–80, 83, 88, 118–19, 127–8, 136, 182 n.149, 190 n.78

Ziegler, Philip G. 179 n.82, 182 n.161, 194 n.156

www.ingramcontent.com/pod-product-compliance
Lightning Source LLC
Chambersburg PA
CBHW062220300426
44115CB00012BA/2144